T0368410

WAR
IN THE CASS CORRIDOR

BRETT D. LAWSON

iUniverse

WAR IN THE CASS CORRIDOR

iUniverse books may be ordered through booksellers or by contacting:

iUniverse
1663 Liberty Drive
Bloomington, IN 47403
www.iuniverse.com
1-800-Authors (1-800-288-4677)

ISBN: 978-1-5320-2442-9 (sc)
ISBN: 978-1-5320-2441-2 (e)

Library of Congress Control Number: 2017909705

Print information available on the last page.

iUniverse rev. date: 07/03/2017

CONTENTS

Chapter 1

IN THE BEGINNING

Her name was Louisa. The third of twelve children, she was born in the heart of the Depression in the mountainous coal-rich region of southeastern Kentucky, a rural area known as Bottom Fork, named such after the bottom fork of the Kentucky River. A breeding ground for innocence, virtue, and righteousness, it was not a town, but a hollow in the mountain, lying between the towns of Mayking and Jenkins, Kentucky.

The road through Bottom Fork, which wound its way between the mountains of Appalachia, was dotted with the families of both Louisa's father, Will, and her mother, Susie. Many of the homes lining the road were called "gentleman farms"; the houses themselves were not lavish but quaint. The farms, not large enough for commercial farming, were just big enough to support a family. Most had large gardens, free-running chickens for farm fresh eggs and fresh poultry, a cow for milk, usually a few pigs, and of course dogs. The farms were located in Letcher County, a dry county, meaning that there was no alcohol could be bought or sold. There was very little crime there, probably because most of the homes were virtual arsenals.

Louisa had been educated in the two-room schoolhouse just a few doors down from her parents' house. Her uncle Chester, her father's brother, was one of the schoolteachers. The school was both an elementary and middle school, thus the two rooms. The high school was located in the town of Whitesburg, about ten miles away. After graduating from high school, Louisa attended a college in the nearby Kentucky town of Morehead. After two years as a student there, she decided, mainly to gain experience, to take a teaching job in Colliers Creek near Pikeville, Kentucky. As part of her teaching agreement, she was provided room and board.

It was September 1951, Labor Day weekend. She and two of her sisters, Glenda and Carnel, had planned on going to a street dance held by the City of Whitesburg. The city blocked off the main street, and local musicians provided the music. Given that it was a big social event, people from all over the county attended. It was here that Louisa spotted him in the crowd. Wearing his air force uniform, he was a handsome man with wavy jet-black hair, blue eyes, and a medium frame. Looking at him, she could not help but be reminded of Tony Curtis, whom she loved. Having seen Curtis in the western movie *Winchester '73*, she had made a point to remember his name and had put him on her list of favorite movie stars. *This man could pass for his look-alike,* she thought. She followed the uniformed man through the crowd with her eyes, when suddenly he saw her eyeing him. He could not help but notice her pretty long brown hair. A petite woman with an hourglass figure, she was a cute little gal, he thought. He started toward her. As he got closer, he could see that, aside from a little lipstick, she was not wearing makeup, which he considered to be a positive. He walked up to her asked her name.

"My name is Lou," she responded.

"I'm Burt. Would you like to dance?" Normally a shy woman, she responded yes with much enthusiasm.

After a couple of dances in the unusually hot evening, Louisa and Burt decided to have sodas at the local fountain. It was crowded thanks to the dance, but they managed to find a seat at the counter.

"How long are you on leave, Burt?" she asked, hoping he would be in town for a little while longer.

"I had a thirty-day leave and it's about half gone, so I have a couple weeks left. My father is sick, so I'll be getting an early discharge when I get back to base. I'm sole support of my family right now."

"Where are you stationed?" she asked.

"Wyman Air Field, in San Francisco," he replied.

"My father is an independent coal miner. Who does your father work for?" Lou asked.

"Dad's a miner for Tri-State Coal. He's been there since nineteen twenty-seven. Who do you work for, Lou?"

"I am a schoolteacher at a small school near Pikeville."

Son of a coal miner, she thought. It was an almost immediate bond. Families of coal miners were tighter-knit because they never knew when, or if, they were going to lose their loved ones to the dangers of the mine. The miners themselves were as close as brothers. Each man knew when he entered the mine that his safety depended on every other man doing his job. Louisa knew from that point on that she and Burt would get along well. "The school where I teach is a little one-room schoolhouse. Where do you live when you are home, Burt?" she said, hoping he was a local man so she could see him again.

"I stay with my parents up on Millstone, but I grew up in Seco. I went to Seco High School, but I left school early to join the service because I wanted to see the world, or at least part of it. There's nothing here but coal mining or hauling coal. I wanted to get out of Letcher County."

She had often entertained the thought of leaving Letcher County, and even Kentucky. *This,* she thought, *could be just the man I could achieve that goal with.*

The night was going so fast that Louisa had forgotten all about her sisters. They had wandered off in the crowd to be with some of their friends. Scanning the crowd to find them, she saw them chatting with some school friends. She approached them with Burt alongside her, and introduced him to her sisters. With the evening drawing to a close, Burt asked, "Can I give you girls a lift home?"

Even though Louisa had enjoyed the evening and would have liked to leave with him, she did not want to come off as a cheap floozy.

"Reluctantly, I don't drive, and so I made arrangements for my oldest sister, Andora, to give us a ride back home, but I can give you my number and you can call me tomorrow evening." Having just opened the door for him to ask her for a date, she was desperately hoping he would pick up on the hint and say okay.

"Let me have your number. I'll be sure to call you tomorrow, then. Is about six okay?"

Relieved he had agreed to her offer, she said, "Six would be fine."

Soon after that, Andora arrived. She, Louisa, Glenda, and Carnel all headed back to Bottom Fork.

Chapter 2

THE COURTSHIP BEGINS

The next day would be a long one as Louisa anxiously anticipated the call from Burt. She hoped she had not angered him by putting him off until today. It was five until six. When the phone rang, it was Burt. Louisa, thinking to herself that he was prompt and glad that he had kept his promise, immediately felt an easiness come over her.

"How would you like to go down to the Annabelle? There's a triple feature tonight." Annabelle was the drive-in at Whitesburg, bought by a man named Doctor Craft, who was well-known throughout the region. He had purchased each one of his three children a drive-in, naming each one after the child he had bought it for.

Louisa gave Burt's question careful thought because going to the drive-in would probably entail some heavy petting. On the other hand, her going to the drive-in while living in the country was the equivalent of a New Yorker going to a Broadway play. And she only had one day left before returning to her job.

"Yes, that sounds like fun," she answered.

"Fine, give me directions to your house. I'll pick you up at seven thirty."

After hanging up the phone, she was elated that he had called. She began a mad rush to find something casual yet sexy to wear.

It was approaching seven thirty as Burt drove down the gravel road that led to Louisa's dad's home. He spotted the little bridge across the creek that then led to the driveway. Parking and making a move to get out of the car, he was first greeted with loud barking from three of Will's dogs, who were trained to alert the family that someone was on the property but not to bite. Burt was impressed by the size of the property, as it was a far cry from his old homestead in Seco. Seco was an old mining camp. The homes there had all been built in much the same way and had no acreage, just a small lot for each resident to eke out a meager existence.

Burt walked up to the front porch. Lou's father was there to greet him. "I'm Burt, Mister Holbrook," he said as he reached out to shake hands.

"Just call me Will," he responded.

"Nice-size place you got, Will. How much land do you have here?"

"Well, there is about ten acres of flatland, and then there is about another twenty acres of woods covering the hill behind the house. Yeah, I always liked fresh vegetables and a big garden. With twelve children, I needed a little help

7

from Mother Nature at times. Lou tells me you are in the air force. How long have you been in?"

"Four years, Will. I joined up when I was seventeen, and I'll be getting out between now and Thanksgiving. I noticed a smaller house behind the larger house. What do you use that for, Will?"

"I built that house when Suze and I first got married, but as the family grew, we could not expand it so we built the big house instead. Now we let the children live in it when they first get married. It helps them get a good start. When you come home and you are in need of a job, come see me. Four years of military service is good enough recommendation for me. Hang on; I'll go get Lou for you."

Lou walked out onto the porch with her mother, Susie, and saw Burt dressed in neatly pressed dress slacks and a yellow sport shirt that showed off his well-trimmed physique.

"Burt, this is my mom, Susie," Lou said.

"I am glad to meet you, young man. Now, I want you to watch over my daughter. She's a fine young woman, and she's been no trouble to us at all."

"I promise you, Susie, I'll keep her away from any harm. You ready, Lou?" Burt asked.

"Yeah I'm ready. Mom, I'll be home around midnight."

With that, Burt and Lou headed to the car. He was a real gentleman and opened the car door for her. After she got in and he closed the door, he walked around the car and noticed she had scooted to the middle of the seat. *A good sign,* he thought as he entered the car. He put the car in gear and headed down the road of Bottom Fork toward Whitesburg.

"Burt, you don't seem to be a man to quit school. I was just wondering, why you did quit?"

"Well, Lou, my dad is what I call an iron man. He can't read or write, and he just believes that for a man to get ahead in life, he has to have a strong back and will. Besides, I was tired of the lifestyle we were living. No running water, no indoor plumbing. About the only thing we had was a radio and electricity. Since Dad couldn't read, he never had any use for a car, so there was no way for me to get around or date. The quickest way for me to get a car was to join the service. I saved up a big portion of my pay and most of my winnings from the occasional poker game, and voilà! I got my car."

"So you like to gamble. Do you gamble a lot?" she asked.

"Well, I'm not a compulsive gambler, if that's what you mean. In the military, there's not much else to do down on the base but play cards. Most servicemen are kind of young, as I am, and not very good at cards or gambling in general, so they're easy pickings. I just seem to have a knack for anything to do with numbers, so I do okay. As I just mentioned, it's how I saved up enough money to buy my car. I also like to play the horses, but that's a little harder to win at."

9

"I'm not much of a gambler, but I love the beauty of a horse. I think I might like to go to a racetrack sometime," she replied.

"If you are serious, I'll make it a point to take you to one, then."

It was dusk as they approached the Annabelle; the shows would be starting soon. The older movies were always the first to be shown at the drive-ins. They would show the main attraction as the second movie to keep patrons from leaving after the first film. This way, the drive-in could sell more concessions. First up for the night was *Thirty Seconds Over Tokyo*, a movie Burt had already seen.

"Lou, I've already seen this movie. I like to watch war movies. I'm just fascinated with them. I am just amazed by how an airplane that weighs so much can even get off the ground. I guess that's part of the reason I joined the air force. I had hopes of someday learning how to fly, but it just didn't work out for me.

"There's a nice cool breeze blowing. How about we go sit on one of the benches by the concession stand and talk over there?"

The benches were apparently provided so the patrons could sit somewhere other than in their vehicles to eat their food and avoid making a mess in their cars. Patrons could also sit there and watch the movies in the cool night breeze, if so desired. Burt and Lou got out of the car and headed toward the benches. He took her hand as they walked. When they sat down, she put her arm around his waist and rested her head on his shoulder. At that point, he began to think about the last four years and the many women he had been with, some of whom had been looking for a good time, one night at a time. The man with the deepest pockets was the man of the night. Being in San Francisco, Burt had discovered that one-night dates were easy to find. He and his buddies called those women "good-time Sallies," which was a polite way of saying they were easily bedded. Having grown tired of all that, he began to think that maybe it was time for him to settle down and start a family. Was Lou to be the one he would marry? She was a pretty woman who came from a fine family and was educated. He was sure a woman like her would make a fine mother. With that thought in mind, he reached down, placed his hand under her chin, lifted it toward his lips, and kissed her softly. It was more of caress than a kiss, something to let her know he was willing to take his time with her.

She saw it as a sign that he was ready to take their short relationship to the next level. He was waiting for a response from her. Before she got caught up in a situation that compromised her virtue, she decided to let him know just how far she was willing to go.

"Burt, I've never been involved with a man sexually. And I just could never go home again if I got pregnant and had a child out of wedlock. It would break my father's heart. I just can't do that to my parents. I am saving myself for my husband. If that's all right by you, I would like to see more of you."

"Lou, I've been with plenty of women. I am just not interested in sex at this stage, so let's just have a good time and enjoy the movie. It's pretty good, from what I've been told. We'll take our time."

11

A feeling of calmness came over her, knowing he was not going to push her into doing something she didn't want to do. That's when she said, "Burt, let's go back to the car." She had made up her mind that she was going to do anything short of having sex to make him happy.

The movie was no longer her focus; it was just a series of intermittent glimpses to her as they kissed. *This is a good man,* she thought. While he wasn't educated, she could tell he was smart in other ways. Plus, he had served his country faithfully. She knew by the way he kissed her gently that he was experienced and was willing to take gradual steps in their relationship.

After some heavy necking, and with the feature movie ended, Burt and Lou decided to head back home. The return drive seemed to go much faster. Neither of them wanting the night to end, they soon approached her father's driveway. All the lights were out except the one on the porch. Burt asked, "What time do your folks usually get up?'"

"Let's put it this way: six in the morning means they slept in." Lou chuckled as they walked toward the front porch.

As they walked toward, the front porch it was then that he decided to tell her what his short-term plans were, and that he was going back early to the air base.

"Lou, your dad has offered me a job working in the mines with him. I'm going to take him up on his offer so I can see you more often."

"Oh, Burt, that sounds wonderful! You can come up to Pikeville and we can go on a date while you're here. I'm so excited." It was then that he held her tightly and kissed her—a long passionate kiss. With that, he headed back to his car and headed home. As he drove, he could not help but think that he had found the woman he wanted to start a family with.

Chapter 3

EXODUS

Burt had been true to his word. When he returned home from the service, he had gone to visit Lou at the school where she taught in Pikeville. He'd wanted to share the good news that he started working with her dad. Although he felt that the type of mining they were doing was dangerous, he'd had no better job offers at the time. He had made up his mind that he was going to start looking elsewhere while still working for Lou's father.

Having stuck it out in the mines long enough to buy an engagement ring, Burt had proposed to Lou at Christmas. She had, of course, said yes, and immediately began to consider the wedding date. She chose May. When school ended, they were married in Lynchburg, Virginia.

They honeymooned at Break's Interstate Park, a secluded area referred to as "the Grand Canyon of the South." Situated on the southeastern border of Kentucky and the southwestern border of Virginia, and administered by both states, it was a popular spot for visiting, even if not for honeymooning, especially in the spring when the plants and trees were in full bloom.

When the honeymoon was over, the newlyweds moved into a small log cabin about two miles down the road from Lou's mom and dad's place. She had gotten pregnant almost right away. It was almost nine months afterward, in February, when I was born. That's when Dad decided that working his life away in the mines was not a life he wanted. He'd figured that if he was going to make a career move, it would have to be before our family got too large.

His Uncle Andy's boy, James Lawson, had been talking about heading up to Detroit to look for work. Dad got in touch with James, and the two of them made an agreement to ride together. They would split the travel and living expenses while making a go of it in Detroit, until they each could make it on their own. Before leaving, Dad rented a shack of a house just down the road from Mom's parents' house for her to stay in.

It was March when my father and James got on the road to Detroit. The trip would take eighteen hours, starting from Letcher County, going through the hill country of Kentucky, and moving on to US 23, which was nicknamed the "Hillbilly Highway" on account of that fact that many families had left the rural states and headed north to Detroit to look for manufacturing work in the auto plants.

The first order of business when Dad and James reached Detroit was to find a place to live. They grabbed the local morning paper and started scouring it for places for let and places that would be hiring. They found an apartment on Detroit's southwest side, which was known as Mexican Town, located on the corner of Twenty-Fourth Street and Vernor Highway. The place was not luxurious, but the rent was cheap and it would not be far from any job within the city they could find.

Only a few days passed before they both had found jobs. My father landed a job working for General Motors at the Chevrolet Gear and Axle plant as a Hi-Lo driver. James had aspirations of becoming a chef, wishing someday to own his own restaurant, so he took a job at the Leland Hotel in the downtown section of Detroit. He had hoped to start out as a cook, but the owner started all would-be chefs as busboys so they would learn the business from the bottom up and this way test their tenacity. James, eager to learn and not afraid of hard work, accepted those conditions. The only problem he had was that he did not own a car. Being without a car was a minor inconvenience. Bus transportation was easily accessible within the city, which would have to do for now.

The two men would continue to share the apartment until late August.

James had received a promotion to salad chef. With that promotion, he was preparing to move out and get a place of his own. He got a different apartment in the same neighborhood in Mexican Town, just down the road a bit from the previous one, near the intersection of Springwells and Vernor. Dad's new job at GM kept him from going down south to see my mother and us kids.

Once James and my father had both gotten themselves established and were able to afford to be on their own, Dad headed down south to bring my mother up from Kentucky. It wasn't long after my mother joined my father in Detroit that she was pregnant again. Shortly after they learned that news, my dad drove my mother back down south so my grandmother could help my mother through the pregnancy. Not sure of when the baby would come, my father headed back to Detroit so as not to lose his job. It was June 1954 when my sister Veronica was born in Kentucky.

Soon after Veronica was born, Mother got pregnant a third time, with my sister Danessa. Given that the trip back to Kentucky took eighteen hours, she decided this time that she would stay in Michigan for the baby's birth.

With the family expanding rapidly, the time came for us to move into a bigger apartment. Dad found a really nice spacious three-bedroom house for rent just around the corner on Twenty-Fourth Street. We moved in a bit before Danessa was born. Mom could not be happier living in a house rather than in that dumpy apartment. She felt that she had three beautiful children, and a good-looking husband who was fortunate enough to be working. While she missed Kentucky and her teaching job, she was content being a housewife. She felt that God had smiled on her, so she made a point to thank him on a regular basis.

In 1957, I turned four. I was playing in the backyard when I was approached by a Detroit police officer. He said his name was Benny Garcia, and somehow he already knew my name. He called out to me and said he wanted to talk to me. My father then came outside to see what was going on. Benny had picked me up and was holding me in his arms.

17

Benny then asked my father, "Burt, why do you want to do this to your son?"

My father had no reply. I myself did not understand what Benny was talking about, so I asked him, "What did my dad do, Benny?"

"Brett, he is having an affair with my brother's wife."

"What does 'affair' mean, Benny?"

"It means he loves my brother's wife more than he loves you and your mother, Brett."

Tears welled up in my eyes. I could not bear the thought of my dad not loving my mother. I replied, "Benny, there must be some mistake. My dad loves my mother very much."

"No, Brett, there's no mistake. He doesn't love her anymore. I am going to be keeping an eye on you, Burt." With that, he put me down, got in his car, and drove off.

I dared not tell my mother about the incident, as it would surely break her heart if what Benny had said was true.

Through that whole ordeal, my father had not said anything. I suppose he was afraid of Benny, who had let my father know the rough road that lay ahead should he continue with the affair. My dad knew that if a cop like Benny had the guts to confront him, then the latter could be dangerous enough to hurt him or even the rest of the family.

Chapter 4

THE TERROR BEGINS

It was a cool, dry spring afternoon in May 1957, the kind of day one really appreciates after a long, hard winter. My mom always appreciated spring days like these more than many other people after she'd spent most of her life in the harsh winters of the Kentucky mountains. My father, Burt, was gone to work. He worked afternoons, a shift he liked. My mother was busy doing her household chores when there was a knock at the door.

"Brett, see who's at the door," my mother yelled. I walked to the front door, which was made with a heavy pane of glass. Through the glass, I could see it was a cop and another, much younger man, more like a teenager than a man. The cop looked a lot like Benny Garcia, except this one was completely bald. Thinking I did something wrong, I opened the door to find out what they had to say to me.

The teenager asked, "Where's your mother?"

I replied, "She's in my two sisters' bedroom. The one with the door open."

He then pushed me out of the way and darted toward the bedroom where my mother was, and took her into my parents' bedroom. The cop stayed outside on the front porch. After about ten minutes, the younger man emerged from the bedroom. He and the cop then left. Shortly afterward, my mother came out of my parents' bedroom sobbing, with tears running down her face.

She asked, "Why didn't you help me?"

"Mom, I didn't know that he was hurting you!"

With that, she walked over to the phone, called the police, and asked, "Can you send a police car to my home? I've just been raped." After hanging up, she walked into my sisters' room to make sure they were unharmed.

I didn't understand any of what had just happened. I mostly didn't understand the word *rape*. Something else I did not understand was why a cop would bring someone to my house to hurt my mother.

It was only a few minutes, but it seemed like an eternity to my mother, before the police arrived. They pulled her aside, taking notes and questioning her about the incident. One of the policemen came over to me and starting asking me questions.

"Brett, can you tell me what the man looked like?"

"Well, he wasn't a man; he was more like a teenager."

"Why did you let him in the house?" he asked.

"I didn't let him in. He barged in when I opened the door." With all the questions they were asking, I was beginning to feel like I was the criminal. "Why didn't the cop stop the teenager and help my mom?"

"Are you sure it was a cop, Brett?"

"Yes, I am sure. He looked a lot like Benny Garcia, except he was completely bald."

"Brett, you mean Benny Garcia was here?"

"Yes."

"Brett, we have a lady officer named Officer O'Malley coming. She is going to stay with you and your sisters till your dad gets here. Is that okay?"

"Where are you taking my mom?"

"We are going to take her to the hospital and have a doctor look at her. We want to make sure she's not hurt real bad."

It was about a half hour later when my father arrived. Officer O'Brian told him what had happened. My father immediately became frantic. I suppose he was worried that his whole life was about to become a shambles. Shortly after my dad had arrived, some detectives pulled up in front of the house. Another car pulled up. In the backseat was the bald-headed cop.

"Brett, is that the cop that was with the teenager?"

"Yes!"

"Brett that is Benny Garcia's brother. His name is Carlos Garcia." It was then that I realized that it was Carlos's wife my dad was seeing. Then the detectives brought the teenager up to me.

"Brett, is this the teenager that was with him?"

"Yes," I replied sheepishly, afraid that the young man would come back and hurt my mother again.

"Brett, that kid is Eurico Garcia. They call him Rico for short. Rico is Carlos's and Benny's nephew."

The detectives then had both Garcias taken away in a patrol car. Then they started asking my father questions. They told him where they had taken my mother, saying that they were going to have her brought home in a police car. Then one of them asked my dad in a low tone, "Mr. Lawson, are you having an affair with Officer Garcia's wife?"

He tried to deny it at first, but the officers convinced him it would be hard to protect his family against the wrath of a police officer if he did not tell them the truth. The cop would have many avenues of revenge if he wanted it bad enough to hurt the whole family. It was only then that Dad admitted what he done.

After a bit of time had passed, my mother arrived back home. The detectives spoke a few more words to my mother before they left. She waited until the police were gone before she read Dad the riot act.

"Burt, are you having an affair with a cop's wife?"

This time he admitted it more readily. "Yes."

"Burt, I saved myself especially for you!" The tears started streaming down her face. "How could you do this to us? What's the matter with you? Don't you love us anymore?"

Dad had no answers. He was speechless.

The way my mother had been brought up, divorce was not an option. "Burt, I'm going to forgive you this time, for the sake of my children. If it ever happens again, you are going to answer to Daddy," Mom said, referring to my grandpa Holbrook. While he was a country preacher, he was not a man you wanted to cross.

It was the "us" that got to me and set me to crying. My mother had made me realize that not only had Dad hurt her but also he had hurt me and my siblings by doing what he did. It would alter the way I felt about my father forever. My relationship with him would come to consist of what I termed a cautious love, never giving him my full love.

Throughout the events of this day, the one thing I could not figure out was why Garcia had brought someone to our house to hurt my mother. It should have been my father whom he should have hurt. It just seemed cowardly of Carlos Garcia. He had given us a message: he was a cop, and he was going to do whatever he wanted, even if it meant breaking the law. Like all the events that would drastically change my life, I would remember this one.

Chapter 5

THE MYSTERY

A few days after Mom had been raped, the phone rang. I answered it. It was a long distance call from my grandpa Holbrook in Kentucky. I held a brief conversation with him, telling him that I missed him and Grandma and that, most of all, I missed being in Kentucky. He told me he needed to talk to my father. I yelled for my father to pick up the phone. He picked up the extension in another room. As I was about to hang up, I heard Grandpa start talking to my father. I decided to listen in so I could talk to my grandpa once more after my father had finished speaking with him.

He told my father, "Burt, we have had a lot of men go missing lately. I'm calling to ask if you can get some information about what is going on and find out what happened to those men."

So as not to anger my father, I hung up the phone quietly. I could not help but wonder what was going on when Grandpa said, "We have had a lot of men go missing lately." What did he mean by "we"? I thought to myself,

He must mean men from Kentucky, but I decided I would ask my dad when he got off the phone.

When my father hung up the phone, I walked from the kitchen into the living room to ask him what Grandpa had meant.

"Dad, what did Grandpa mean when he said, 'We are losing a lot of men lately'?"

"He's talking about Masons, Brett."

"What's a Mason, Dad?"

"It's a member of a certain organization, Brett—kind of like a club."

"Who would want to hurt somebody just because they belong to a club, Dad?"

"They don't know. That's what we have to find out. Now we have to move to a different neighborhood, one closer to the Masonic Temple."

About a month passed before Dad found an apartment for us, one located in Detroit's lower east side, in the Cass Corridor. There were few affordable houses in the area, so it was back to apartment living for us. I was sure going to miss having a backyard to play in, and the afternoon picnics in Clark Park with Mom and my sisters.

Our new apartment was located directly on Cass Avenue at the intersection of Cass and Temple, the latter of which was where the Masonic Temple, which is why the street was named Temple. Besides Masonic business, the temple was used for concerts. Concert goers could easily remember the name of the street the venue was on. The front of the temple faced a park, one that was almost directly across from our apartment. I would be able to play in it. It wasn't Clark Park, but it was a park nonetheless. Not knowing its name, I just called it Masonic Park. It was while living in this apartment that I would meet one of the most powerful men in Detroit. His name was Vinny Maccabelli.

One day my mother and I were walking down Cass to the local A&P. She liked the fresh-ground A&P Eight O'clock coffee—and she had promised me an ice cream bar if I helped carry the groceries. When we arrived, there was a group of men marching in a circle and blocking the entrance to the store. Not understanding why they were doing what they were doing, I tried to go through the line. One of the men, who seemed to be in charge because he was not marching, yelled at the other men to tighten up the line. One of the marching men pushed me down as I attempted to go through. My mom picked me up and scolded me. She explained that those men had formed a picket line and that I was not to go through it.

Suddenly, another man, this one tall and lean, approached me and started talking to me. Apparently able to see that I did not understand what was going on, he asked me my name. I told him, "My name is Brett. What's yours?"

"I am called Vinny, Vinny Maccabelli," he answered politely. "I am very pleased to meet you, Brett. My friends call me Vinny Mac, but you can call me just plain Vinny."

He then started to explain that the store management was treating their employees very badly, saying that the workers were picketing in order to get a fair deal so they could earn enough money to feed their families. Striking up a deal with me, he said that if I went to the store across the street, he would buy me two ice creams. I took his money and went to the store across the street. I looked in the cooler but could not find the ice cream I wanted. Once I walked back across the street, I told Vinny that the other store did not have the type of ice cream I liked. We made another deal that I would buy only one ice cream from the A&P and then leave right away.

Vinny yelled, "Let the kid through."

I walked into the store, got the ice cream, walked back out, and showed Vinny that I had bought only one ice cream. Vinny then explained that he owned a barbershop just down the street on Cass. He invited me to come and visit him there. He then said goodbye and went on his way. My mother and I then made our way to Wrigley's, a store at the other end of Cass.

Chapter 6

THE EDUCATION

It was all over the news that the Russians had launched a satellite known as *Sputnik* that could orbit the earth. Washington was stirring with alarm. Soon after the launch of *Sputnik*, the United States, not wanting to be outdone, formed the National Aeronautics Space Administration or NASA for short. We were now in the Space Race. I often watched movies about space travel like *Buck Rogers* and frequently wondered if human beings would ever discover how to travel in space. Suddenly we in the USA had been launched into a magical and mystical time. I considered myself one of the many privileged children who were going to witness the events that were sure to come with the birth of the space age.

It was shortly after NASA was formed that I entered school.

In late summer when it came time for me to attend school, my mother took me to Burton Elementary School to enroll. Burton was a school for gifted children. Nestled among the tenements of Detroit's lower east side, it was located at the intersection of Cass Avenue and Peterboro. One of Detroit's most prestigious public schools, it was a place to which many parents longed to send their children. Few students, however, were accepted. Before any student could be accepted, the school would run a battery of tests. After my first try, the woman running the tests said that I did not qualify. That was fine with me, as it didn't matter to me what school I went to. But my mom was very persistent.

As I was getting up to go in for the second round of testing, my mom whipped out one of my baby pictures. She asked me about the shirt I was wearing in the photo.

I replied, "That was my ducky shirt." I called it that because it had little ducks in the pattern, but they were so small that you could not see them unless you were up close. From her bag, Mom pulled out the shirt and showed it to the woman conducting my interview, who was floored.

"That is remarkable I can't believe he can remember that?!" She then asked me questions about what else I could remember.

"Mrs. Lawson, I believe your son has a photographic memory. Because of this, we are going to admit him. The only problem is that we cannot admit him until January, as he won't be old enough until next year. Let me get your papers. We will see you in January." Mom, determined to see that I got a good education, was elated.

It was a couple of weeks later when dad told me that it was time for me to get a haircut. I suggested we go to Vinny's, and my dad agreed. When we walked into the barbershop, Vinny was sitting in one of the barber chairs reading the local paper.

I said, "Hello, Vinny."

He lowered the paper and said, "Oh, hello, Brett. Are you here for a cut or to visit?"

"I'm here for a haircut. I want to pay you back for the ice cream." I beamed.

"Okay, we'll let Stache cut your hair."

After a few minutes of cutting my hair, Stache put his hand on my head. It was at this point that I smelled alcohol on his breath. I soon felt a tugging on my right ear. I thought that maybe he had cut my ear. Then I felt a very sharp burning sensation on the back of my neck. After Stache finished, my dad paid him for the haircut. Then we headed back home.

When we returned home, my mother checked out my haircut. Inspecting my head, she said, "Burt, he cut a piece of Brett's ear off!" Then she noticed the cut on my neck.

That's when my dad took me by the hand and we headed back to Vinny's. When we arrived, my dad showed Vinny what the barber had done.

"Brett, did you smell alcohol on his breath?"

"Yeah, it did smell like alcohol." I knew that smell because my dad also drank alcohol.

Vinny then exploded, grabbed a razor, pushed Stache into one of the barber chairs, put the razor to Stache's throat, and said, "Look, you damn drunk. Look what you did to that kid. I'm going to cut your throat for that."

Stache pleaded, "Please, please don't, Vinny."

That's when I intervened and said, "Vinny, please don't hurt him. If you do, you'll be hurting his family too. Everybody can make a mistake once. Just make him apologize and promise not to drink anymore, especially on the job."

Vinny then let Stache go. Stache was crying a flood, having come within an inch of losing his life. He apologized and said, "Thank you, Brett. Thank you. I'll never forget what you did for me, Brett." Turning to my dad, he said, "Mister, you have a really fine son." He then headed for the door. But he turned around, looked back at Vinny, and said, "Screw you, Vinny. I've been waiting a long time for a chance to get even with you. Now I got you."

A few minutes later, Stache returned with a beat cop.

The cop asked me, "Did Vinny attack Stache? Don't lie, kid!"

Vinny had just put a razor to Stache's throat, but I had seen enough television to know that you don't talk to the cops. I told the cop that I did not have to talk to him. Then I said goodbye to Vinny. My dad and I once again headed back home. I didn't care what happened afterward. If Stache was stupid enough to involve the cops, that was his problem. I resented the fact that he had used me to try to hurt Vinny. The experience gave me insight into the type of man Vinny was. He was willing to kill a man over a minor incident such as this. I had learned a very important thing from this episode: don't ever, ever cross Vinny!

"Brett, those men are dangerous men so don't hang around the barbershop. You will only be getting in their way, and they will kill you if you do!"

Chapter 7

SOLDIERING

I was in my bedroom late in the evening when Dad called to me.

"C'mon, Brett, get ready to go. I'm going to take you to school." I didn't know that school started this late.

"Dad, they said I couldn't start until January. And isn't it kind of late?"

"No, Brett, I'm taking you to the movies so you can learn how to be a good soldier. There are a lot of things you can learn about by watching a movie. You'll be able to learn about the wars we had to fight, not only to gain our freedom but also to remain free."

"Is Mom going too, Dad?"

"No, just you and I are going."

While my dad's parenting skills were sometimes questionable, there was no question about his soldiering skills. I was hesitant to leave my mom by herself. My father was insistent, saying that since I couldn't read yet, there was no other way for me to learn. Whenever we went to the drive-in movies, we had to go into the suburbs, as there was no space in the crowded city for a drive-in.

This episode marked the beginning of a weekend ritual for my dad and me whenever war movies were showing. Often we would go twice in one weekend. The drive-ins would show a couple of war movies on Saturday, and then a different set on Sunday. Sometimes the movies were older, and sometimes they were recently released. I tried to absorb as much information from those films as I could. Somehow I knew it would be important for me to know these things, not only for my country but also for the world.

I liked going to the drive-in better than a movie theater because of the food. Dad, a smoker, liked the drive-in better because he could smoke there. The drive-in was his classroom where he could teach me well. He usually let me have my fill of either hot dogs or hamburgers while we were there.

Over the coming months, I would learn about the cities of famous battles, like Anzio, Tobruk, Iwo Jima, and Guadalcanal. At the same time, I would learn about weapons of war, things like bazookas, satchel charges, flamethrowers, and land mines. The things I found most interesting were the many types of aircrafts. Dad taught me what the letters at the beginning of the aircraft model stood for. Like in F-14, the *F* stands for "fighter," and in B-17 and B-29, the *B* stands for "bomber." I had decided early on in life that I wanted to become a pilot, if not for the military, then at least in the private sector. My dad taught me one thing about pilots that would stick with me all my life. He said that the Navy Blue Angels and the Air Force Thunderbirds were the best pilots in the world. One thing I wondered was why the former were called the Blue Angels. I understood why the latter were Thunderbirds— because the jets were very loud.

I asked, "Why are they called Blue Angels, Dad?"

"Brett, soldiers on the ground call pilots 'angels.' The reason for this is that when their asses are getting shot up on the ground and they see those planes coming, they say, 'Heaven must have sent them.' Since their particular planes are blue, they are called the Navy Blue Angels. Always remember, Brett that pilots fight for us in the air and we fight for them on the ground. Because they are little guys like you, we have to protect them while they're on the ground."

"I'll make sure I remember that, Dad."

While the movies my dad and I watched might not have been factual, some of them were based on true events. There were many heroes and many men who had won medals. A select few had won the Congressional Medal of Honor. One of these men was Audie Murphy. He was the most decorated soldier of World War II, yet he was a small man with not much weight to him. Murphy had been turned down by three other branches of the service for being underweight before landing in the army. Hollywood made a movie of his life story titled *To Hell and Back*, which showed him taking on German soldiers and German tanks that had him surrounded on three sides. Armed only with a fifty-caliber machine gun on a burning tank that could have blown up at any time, he continued to fight and call in coordinates for artillery rounds. He kept mowing down German infantry until they began to withdraw. Seeing that movie inspired me to become the best soldier I could be. Audie Murphy would forever be one of the men whom I admired most.

I treasured the time I spent with my father going to the drive-in. In the winter, the drive-in was closed, so instead we went to the walk-in theater called the Arc, which was located on Cass just down the street from our apartment and near my school. The admission for kids was fifteen cents; the admission for adults was only a quarter. The popcorn was a quarter also. It was quite an affordable night out—not as much fun as the drive-in, but it was cheap and nearby.

Going to school, going to the movies, and playing in Masonic Park filled my days. I was quite happy with the way things were. However, things were about to get very turbulent.

Chapter 8

FRIENDSHIP

I was in the second grade when I met Manuel. He told me that his surname which was Delafuente, but that was a long name. I had a hard time remembering it. So did everyone else in class. It was for this reason he insisted on being called Manuel D. Knowing that everyone would be able to remember his first name, he had mentioned his last name only once. One of the classes I had with Manuel was called Auditorium, a really fun class where the teachers, Mr. Simon and Mr. Barton, read stories to us. Oftentimes, the stories that were read to us were a prelude to a play that was put on by the older students in the school. One of those stories was about an emperor who needed a new suit of clothes. His tailor had told him that he would make his new clothes, very special clothes made just for him. Indeed, his clothes would be invisible. The emperor went along with the idea. I could not help but wonder *did the tailor hypnotize the emperor?* I had seen hypnotists on television pull tricks like that. For example, one hypnotist told a subject that his body parts would disappear and that he would not see his leg once the hypnotist woke him. I also thought, *If you can make a body part invisible, why not a whole person?*

As an immigrant from Puerto Rico, Manuel D's love for the United States and his patriotism could not be matched. And given Manuel's immigrant status, our teacher had him stand up in front of the class and explain where he had come from. He told the class that his family was very poor and it was very hard for them to get enough to eat. Good-paying jobs in Puerto Rico were very scarce. His father had decided to leave Puerto Rico and take advantage of all the opportunities in the United States. The jobs were far more plentiful here, and so was food, he said. He seemed happy just to have a decent place to live. Since moving here, Manuel D found that life was much easier. His family had been in the United States for only two years. He spoke both English and Spanish.

The teacher then asked Manuel D if he would like to start teaching the class the Spanish language. Looking honored to be offered the chance to contribute to the other students' education, he eagerly agreed to the task.

Manuel D made me realize how ignorant I had been about the great country I was living in. I looked at the Stars and Stripes in a whole different light after hearing his story. Deciding that I would try to be his friend and maybe make his life in this country a little easier, I approached him and asked if he would like to meet Timothy and me in Masonic Park. He declined, explaining that although he would like to join us, his mother, who worked also, needed him to help her with the household chores.

While playing tag on the playground during recess with Timothy (who had been my friend since the first grade) and a few other classmates, I noticed

Jesse, a colored boy I was also friendly with, standing around just watching us play. I walked over to talk to him.

"Jesse, you don't look like you're having any fun. Come play tag with us."

"Brett, I'm a nigger. I don't want to play."

I was stunned and couldn't believe that he had just said that about himself! "Jesse, that's a bad word, and besides, we all like you. We don't feel that way about you at all."

"Brett, I'm a nigger and that's never going to change." He then turned and walked off the playground.

I walked away from Jesse feeling down. I did not know if Jesse and I would remain friends or not. White people had hammered it into coloreds that they were no good and stupid. By Jesse calling himself a nigger he was indicating to me that he had accepted what white people thought of colored people and no longer wanted to associate with them. I simply did not understand why I was supposed to hate people because of their skin color and also why they were supposed to hate me. Into which category did Mexicans or people from the East Indies fall? Was this person too light to hate; was that one dark enough to hate? I didn't like to hate people and I didn't like being hateful to people. Why couldn't I just be kind to everyone? I didn't know who I was supposed to hate or why, or who I was supposed to be mean to. I promised myself that someday I would do something to change all that.

Later that afternoon, after classes were done, I walked down the school steps. Shortly afterward, I was greeted by two boys who were older than me, about twelve or thirteen years old, I guessed. One of them grabbed me aggressively and shouted in a rough tone of voice, "What you got against niggers, you honky?"

I responded, "I don't have anything against colored people."

That response only infuriated the teen. He cuffed me upside my head. Not stopping there, he began kicking me in my stomach and ribs. The other one joined in. Then he began to shout, "Do I look like an Uncle Tom, white boy? Huh? Do I?"

"Who's Uncle Tom?" I asked, not knowing what he was talking about.

He picked me up by the front of my shirt, stood me on my feet, and proceeded to tell me in a loud voice, "Uncle Tom is a nigger that kisses the white man's ass. Now do I look like a nigger that kisses the white man's ass? I and my friends are niggers! Just make sure you don't call us 'colored,' which means that you think we're Uncle Toms."

It was then that I saw Jesse walk up behind the two older boys. "Brett, I told you I'm a nigger."

It had taken me a while, but I finally was catching on. The boys were members of a gang called the Detroit Gangsters Alliance. The gang was local; its influence was in mostly colored communities. The DGA was an alliance of numerous gangs, forming one powerful unit. They were sending a message to white people that you could call their members "nigger," which to them meant that they were bad ass mothers. They were putting a positive spin on the word *nigger*, believing that by calling each other niggers, it would only serve to obtain respect for the word nigger. Never having encountered them before this point, I didn't know much about them except that they were involved in drugs. I wanted nothing to do with drugs.

Those two boys beat me up pretty good, but that episode made me realize that something more was beginning to take place. It had so far gone unnoticed, but it had begun with Rosa Parks and the Montgomery Bus Boycott. We had learned about Ms. Parks in class at school. The coloreds were tired of being oppressed, of not being afforded the same rights as white people, and of being treated like second-class citizens. They were looking for a true freedom. I agreed that they should have same rights as white people. Black soldiers had fought and died to keep us free also, so as far as I was concerned, black people had earned those rights.

As I was walking back home I began to wonder *what are they doing in this neighborhood? The city was segregated and this was a white majority neighborhood. They must be expanding their influence of drugs and violence into other neighborhoods,* I thought. I was very confused on how to address the coloreds. If I used the term nigger I would surely get beat up. The only option I thought I had was to call them by their first name if I knew it or call them sir, mister or lady. That way I would avoid a conflict but I would never ever call them colored again.

Chapter 9

THE SECRET WAR

It was bright sunny day in late spring in the Corridor. Something unusual was going on. I saw a large contingent of black men and teenagers gathered across the street from the park as I walked down Cass. This was unusual because the black people, for the most part, lived in a different part of Detroit. It was a short time later when I saw a portion of the larger group form a circle around a white man. They stayed stationary for a minute or two and then walked away, leaving him lying on the sidewalk. I walked over to where he was to see if he was all right, when I heard a man across the street yell out, "Don't touch that man, kid. The police are on the way."

When the police arrived, one of the detectives shouted, "Did anyone see what happened?"

I really did not know what had just taken place, but the detective saw me looking his way and started to approach me. "What's your name, son? I'm Detective Bozinski."

"My name is Brett."

"Did you see what happened, Brett?"

"I didn't see much, but I saw a bunch of black guys surround that man. When they formed a circle around him, I couldn't see what they were doing. A few minutes after that, they walked away, and then I saw the man they'd surrounded lying on the ground. Is he going to be all right?"

"Brett, he is dead."

I got a sinking, helpless feeling when the detective told me that. I had just witnessed a murder right before my eyes. The man was just taking a walk in the park and ended up dead. That could have been anybody, even my father or my mother. I wondered who that man was, and what he had done that led the group of black men to kill him. Most of all, I wanted to know how they had killed him. I hadn't heard a gunshot. Had they stabbed him? One thing was for sure, he had died without his family to comfort him in his last moments.

The Cass Corridor was becoming an increasingly hostile environment. What bothered me most about the murder was how brazen it was. It was committed in the middle of the afternoon with a lot of people around. The blacks involved had implicitly made a statement: "We can kill you even if there are people around watching us." I was just seven and a bit naïve, but I felt compelled to do something about it to try to keep them from doing something like this again.

Detective Bozinski's partner came up to us and asked if anybody had seen anything. Bozinski replied, "The kid saw the whole thing. Brett, if anybody asks your name, *do not tell them your name*, okay?"

Bozinski walked away to interview other witnesses, when a young black man approached me. Saying he was a policeman, he asked me my name. I didn't want to give him my name, but he said he was a cop, so I told him that my name was Brett. And that's all I told him.

Bozinski, seeing the black man, came back over to me and asked, "Brett, did you tell him your name?"

"Yeah, but he told me his was a cop and he needed my name."

The black man took off running. Bozinski gave chase. The speed of the suspect was far greater than the speed of Bozinski; the latter soon gave up the pursuit. Bozinski came back with his partner and told me, "Brett, they're going to kill you! They're not going to try; they are going to do it. Tell your mother that you have to move."

When the medical examiner and Bozinski left, I was approached by a black boy about my size and age. He said that the black men standing across the street wanted to talk to me. I had no idea what was in store for me, so I had my guard up. I walked up to the man who seemed to be in charge, stuck out my hand, and said, "Hi, nigger. My name is Brett. What's yours?" I heard laughter from the rest of the gang.

"I ain't a nigger. And my name is Darnell, little boy."

"Are you an Uncle Tom, then?" I asked because his answer had confused me.

One of the men shouted, "He's got you there, Darnell."

It even got a smile out of Darnell, who asked, "Who you been talking to, little boy?"

"Some guys that I go to school with."

"What's your last name, Brett?"

For some odd reason, I knew not to give him my real name. Heeding the advice of Detective Bozinski, I decided to give him a false last name. "Smith," I said. I picked Smith because when we were learning how to use the telephone in class, the teacher told us that Smith and Jones were the most common names in the phone book. I couldn't figure out why having my name could be so important to these men I was now speaking with.

"What did you tell the cops?"

"I just told them all that I saw some black guys walking down the street and then I saw a man lying on the sidewalk. I said that I thought he fell down."

"Brett, now we're going to tell you what happens when you talk to the cops: we cut your throat."

"I got it! Don't talk to the cops if you don't want to get your throat cut."

"Go home, little boy."

As I walked away, I realized I had narrowly escaped some serious harm. I was glad the gangsters had let me go, thanks to some quick thinking on my part. One thing about the confrontation was I realized that Darnell did not like me calling him a nigger. I was not a mind reader so I decided on calling them black which was a neutral word. I was not going to call them colored or nigger. I would give the blacks the respect they were looking for.

I walked in the opposite direction of our apartment in case DGA followed me, which took me a few blocks out of my way. I noticed someone tailing me, so I began running until I ditched him. That I was tailed was a sure sign that those men were not giving up and that there would be more to come. Exactly what was going to happen, I had no clue.

When I arrived back at the apartment, I immediately told my father what had happened in the park, saying that I had been a witness to the whole thing. I told him the cops had told me to tell my parents we had to move.

Dad already had plans of moving, so within a few days, we moved to a basement apartment at the corner of Cass and Selden. To me, that apartment was a death trap. It had only one way in and one way out, both through the same apartment entrance. If a fire broke out in the front room where the door was, we all would be trapped.

Chapter 10

THE GANG'S ALL HERE

A couple of DGA members cornered me at school and asked me, "Why do you want to ruin our game, white boy?" It was now obvious that the older men I'd had a run-in with before were both DGA and working together.

I responded to his question with, "Man, I told you before, I got nothing against Blacks. All I was doing was meeting with my friends in the park. I hate cops too, especially crooked cops," knowing that was what they wanted to hear. "I hate them because one of them, a Mexican cop, had his nephew hurt my mom. If anything, I'm going to do everything I can to send his ass to jail for doing that." The gang was really turning up the heat on me. I had to think of something quick, so I asked him, "What if I join up with you guys?" I figured that if I was going to die, of which the possibility was very high, I should at least give myself a chance to survive. Also, maybe I could figure out why that group had killed the man in the park.

"No, man, this is a niggers-only club."

"Man, you're no different from the white men you are fighting."

"Okay, say we do that for you. What are you going to do for us?"

"What can I do to help you?"

"Okay, you're in. My name is Robert, and this is Jameel. You already know Jesse. We'll let you know next time we need something. What name do you want to go by?"

"Will 'White Boy Brett' work?" My ruse of stalling for time so as to gain some insight into how the gang worked had succeeded. My membership in the DGA would be short-lived, but over the next few weeks, I would learn some, although not all, of their tactics.

The main goal of each gang member was to generate income for the gang. They did this by pulling armed robberies and muggings, and selling drugs. Ruthless, they would do anything for the almighty dollar. I learned that they had two divisions of members: ones who were under the age of twelve, and the much older members in their late teens, which were used more as enforcers. They used the underage gang members for most crimes. When the boys were caught, they were released to the custody of their parents because they were juveniles. There was only one problem with that: the young gangster would give the police a phony name, and the gang would send in phony parents to get him released. Thus the perpetrator and the parents would be untraceable, and the crime would go unpunished.

Trying not to participate in any crimes, I was never used as a drug courier, but I was used as a lookout. I didn't think the gang members fully trusted me, so they were testing my loyalty. One of those tests was given to me by Robert. He walked up to me and told me I had two days to get a new member or else they were going to kill me. This was how they recruited and how their gang had gotten to be so large. This was not a gang that had a few dozen members who had gotten together and formed the gang. It was a gang with thousands of members. At one point, I felt that the whole black community belonged to the DGA. Having no intentions of recruiting for them, I believed that the only choice I had was to formulate a new plan. While I had learned a lot about how the DGA worked, I had not learned everything there was to know. If I were to learn any more, it would have to be at great expense.

Once I realized that is when I came to the conclusion that the higher-ups in the gang were turning their lower-level members into junkies in order to control them, and also to keep them generating money. They were basically turning their lower ranks into slaves, something I wanted no part of. I am sure that many of the members were not happy with their role within the gang. They had been forced into a life of crime and drugs. I had only one option: to quit. I didn't know how the gang would punish me, but I was sure it would not be pleasant.

When word got around that I wanted to quit, Robert, Jameel, and a few of Robert's henchmen came to see me at the apartment. I had known that eventually they would find out where I lived.

Robert asked me, "Why do you want to quit our club?"

I replied, "You're turning your own people into slaves by putting them on drugs. I don't want to get involved in the drug scene."

"You can quit, but if you do, I'm gonna hurt you and your momma," said Robert.

I knew one thing for sure: that when Robert had made a threat to hurt someone, he would make good on it. I also knew from the short time I was with the gang that if it took four men to do a job, they would send a dozen to make sure it got done. So I concluded I was in for a hell of a fight—or I was going to die.

It was the next evening, as darkness was nearing, when Carlos Garcia came by the apartment and said, "Brett, I want you to go on patrol with me and meet some of my friends."

"Well, I don't want to go with you."

"If you don't go with me, I'll hurt your mom, Brett," he said.

I knew that he was capable of hurting my mother. Since he had already done so once, I had to take him at his word. I decided not to take any chances and to do as he asked. I didn't want my mom to be hurt again.

I said, "Okay. I'll go with you, Carlos."

I had no idea why he wanted me to go with him, but he had insisted that I do so. We walked up the stairs from the basement apartment onto Cass Avenue and headed toward Burton. We hadn't gone very far when we encountered three or four DGA members. Carlos said something to them in such a way that I couldn't overhear. One of DGA members called a black woman over to us. I could tell by the way she was dressed that she was a prostitute who was probably under the control of the DGA.

The DGA member who had called her over said to her, "I want you to take care of this little boy."

"I can't! I got a dose!" she said fearfully.

I did not want her to do anything to me.

The DGA member said in a stern voice, "I said do like I told you, bitch!"

She grabbed my hand, took me between some buildings, and lay down, pulling me on top of her. She then pulled up her dress and unzipped my fly. It took only a few minutes, and then she was done. I didn't understand anything of what was happening. I had not been educated about women's bodies or things of a sexual nature. We did not talk about those matters in our household. With that woman, I didn't feel anything except fear. After a few minutes, she got up and left. I was glad the experience was over. It left me feeling that Carlos was using the gang to teach me about sexual acts.

It was then that Carlos reappeared. He and I continued walking down Cass until we met another group of DGA members gathered near the school.

"Brett, these are some more friends of mine."

"Some of them are my friends too, Carlos." He seemed surprised to hear me say that, and it appeared to soften his attitude toward me a little, although I found it unusual that a police officer would be friends with gangsters whom he was supposed to be arresting. I held my tongue so as not to let anyone know how I felt. I couldn't help but wonder how Carlos's association with the DGA could possibly be beneficial to him.

I noticed that some members of the group we had been talking with began to encircle someone else. Remembering what I had seen the DGA do before when they had encircled the man in the park, I wondered if they were they going to use the same tactics to kill this person. But suddenly they began to disperse. I could see who it was they had surrounded. It was Manuel D.

He was babbling, saying, "I'm going to die! I'm going to die for my sister!" He kept saying it over and over. Once he recognized me in the group, he grabbed his sister's hand and led her over to me. Manuel D was seven years old, and his sister was at the most five. Why would the DGA want to hurt him or his sister?

He said, "Brett, you take care of my sister."

I realized that when the DGA had encircled him, their intention was to forcefully drug him. Or maybe they already had. Manuel was good student and a good person who loved the United States and everything it stood for. Why had they selected him?

It was at this point that Carlos walked over to Manuel and opened up his shirt, exposing the white of his T-shirt. It was almost as if he were making a target. Carlos then walked a few feet away from Manuel D and got down on one knee so that he was eye-to-eye with the boy. After chanting something in a foreign language, he shot Manuel D. The speed and the power of the bullet knocked my classmate instantly on his back.

I stood at the scene, stunned. I could not believe what I had just witnessed. I silently said a prayer, and I made a solemn promise to my friend Manuel D to bring his killer to justice. I was going to find out what gave Carlos the right to kill a seven-year-old boy. I was going to see that Carlos was brought to justice. In less than a week, I had witnessed two murders, both of them involving the DGA. I thought about going to the police to let them know what Carlos had done, but I was sure that when his superior confronted him, it would only tip him off as to who had informed him. With Carlos's connections to the DGA, it would be only a matter of time before I ended up like Manuel D. Besides, given all those factors, the other possibility was that the police would more than likely not believe me at all. I would have to get the evidence one piece at a time—and find something that Carlos would not be able to deny.

Chapter 11

THE PILOT'S SECRET

I asked my father while both of us were watching TV, "Dad, why do people call the area we live in the Cass Corridor?"

He explained, "Brett, a corridor is the gap between the missile batteries and/or antiaircraft guns. When planes go on a bombing run, the pilots fly between those guns and/or missiles. Since Selfridge Air Base is just down the road in Mount Clemens, a lot of pilots live in this area. The housing here is affordable for someone who has to live on military pay. It's the pilots who nicknamed it 'the Corridor.'"

The apartment building we lived in had four floors to it, and two basement apartments. The upper floors were structured with one main stairwell and a back porch so that each apartment could be accessed through the rear.

I had always been a shy child, and what I had experienced made it difficult for me to trust anyone who wasn't part of my family. I had only a few friends whom I felt were worthy of my trust. One of those friends was a girl named Justine Powers. She was petite with shoulder-length wavy black hair. She resembled Natalie Wood, being just as pretty as the actress. Her family lived on the fourth floor. My dad used to sit on the back porch with Justine's father, Virgil, on the first floor. Justine's mother and father were from Pound, Virginia, which was the first city you come to when you cross the Kentucky border into Virginia, not far from where Dad and Mom had grown up in Kentucky. One afternoon while my dad was chatting with Virgil on the first-floor back porch, Dad called me over to where the two of them were sitting. There, standing with the both of them, I noticed a young man who seemed to be in his twenties. He was thin, was not too tall, and had light brown hair cut in a military fashion. He was near to them and smiling, which instantly indicated to me that he was a friendly sort.

"Brett, this is Gary, Virgil's son and Justine's brother. He's a pilot for the United States military," Dad said.

"I'm pleased to meet you, Gary," I said, wowed by the fact that I had the opportunity to meet a real military pilot.

"Brett, your dad tells me you want to be a pilot, too."

"Yeah, I'd like to become a pilot someday."

"Well, come sit on my lap and I'll give you your first flying lesson." I complied and sat on his lap.

"Now your feet are your rudders, and your right hand is your stick hand. Brett, don't let anyone ever trash your stick hand because then you can't fly anymore. Now, you have to climb, so pull back on the stick so the nose of your plane goes up. Work your rudders with your feet now and level off. Okay, Brett, that concludes your first flying lesson. Now, what are feet used for?"

"Controlling the plane's rudders," I answered.

"What's your right hand called?" Gary asked.

"My stick hand," I answered.

"Now you got it! Right on both occasions, Brett," Gary said. "Brett, I have to go back to the base now, but I'll be sure to look you up when I get back in town."

It was not the last time I would see Gary, but I wouldn't see him as often as I would have liked. He left me feeling proud that I had a new friend who was also a pilot. I couldn't help but sense the pride that Gary and Justine's parents felt. They were a hardworking family, with a beautiful daughter, and a son who was a pilot in the United States military. While they appeared to be typical, something made me think otherwise. One reason I thought this was that Gary hadn't mentioned what type of plane he flew. I could hardly wait until the next day to tell the guys at school that I had met with a real military pilot.

Chapter 12

THE ASSAULT

I walked out of the school and was on my way on home when I ran into a kid named Diego who had been waiting for me. He attended not Burton, but Couzens Elementary. Known to be a troublemaker, he'd often tried to start a fight with me. What reason he had, I did not know. My dad had warned me not to get into any fights, as he didn't want me to get kicked out of school. I knew I was a much faster runner than Diego, so I found it easier and less trouble to run instead of fight. But he was a persistent sort. The next day, he started his bullshit again, only this time there was a teenager standing at one of the intersections. Diego yelled to him, "Rico, stop that kid."

As I got closer to the teen on the corner I stopped, knowing I could not outrun the much older teen, who was obviously stronger and faster than I was. When Rico got closer to me, I could see it was the same Rico who had raped my mom when we lived on Vernor and Twenty-Fourth. I decided I would have to stand my ground and fight Diego, hoping that it would be a fair fight without any interference from Rico. When Diego got close enough, I initiated the fight by grabbing him by the arm and swinging him around in a circle.

Only interested in making him leave me alone, I was not trying to hurt him. When I had enough momentum, I let him go. He landed on his face. Once he got up, he came at me again. I did the same thing with the same result, but this time I sat on his back, saying that I would stay there until he promised to leave me alone. He promised me, so I let him go.

When the fight was over, I asked, "Rico is Diego your friend?"

"No, kid, he is my brother. And he is a real sissy anyway."

Then a police officer walked up. He said to Rico, "How come you didn't help Diego?"

"The boy wasn't trying to hurt Diego. He just wanted him to leave him alone. He kicked Diego's ass twice already." Rico then walked off, which surprised me.

"What's your name, kid?" the officer asked.

"Brett Lawson," I told him.

"Brett, I'm Officer Isaac Simms. I would like it if you and Rico were to become friends and look out for each other. How does that sound to you?"

I was being forced into a decision to help someone who had hurt my mother, but the favor was being asked of me by a cop. Before I made a decision, I wanted a little more information to see how the policeman was associated to Rico. I asked him, "That sounds okay by me, Isaac, but how are you related to Rico?"

"He's my nephew. He's my brother's son, Brett," Simms said. That didn't make much sense to me because his brother's name should have been Simms also, unless they had different fathers. I remembered when we lived off Vernor that the cops told me that Rico was Carlos Garcia's nephew. That would have to mean that Simms and Carlos were somehow related. It was becoming clear to me that the officer was concealing information and that this was becoming a very complex puzzle. I needed yet more information before I could reach a conclusion.

I had agreed reluctantly to watch out for Rico with the intention of gaining more information through this association between him and Simms. Simms had been very sketchy about his family and his brother's name.

The next day, after the fight with Diego, I was on my way home from school when I saw Rico standing on the same corner he had been standing on the day before. As I approached the corner, he walked up to me and asked, "How far away do you live, Brett?"

"Just a few blocks away, at the corner of Cass and Selden," I replied.

"I'll walk you home so no one bothers you."

I was thankful to have someone who would help me should I run into some sort of trouble, but I was still uncertain about being friends with Rico.

I felt like I was betraying my mother. Still, he was much older and stronger than I and I was afraid he might hurt me too. Ultimately I was glad to have him escort me home. There was not much else I could do but accept his offer. Besides, not totally understanding how he was related to Simms, I wanted to pump him for more information.

As we arrived at my apartment, he asked, "Do any pretty girls live in your building, Brett?"

"Yeah, there's a couple. Justine is the prettiest, though. Juliet is nice too."

"Where does Justine live?"

"She lives on the fourth floor," I answered with hesitation, not knowing whether he had intentions of hurting Justine as he had hurt my mom or if he was being friendly. All I could do was hope he was not looking for trouble. I thanked him for walking me home, said goodbye, and went into my apartment.

The day after I'd met Officer Simms, Veronica and I were walking home from school together, as we did daily. Dad had insisted that I watch out for Veronica as we went back and forth to school. A blond-haired woman with long curls partially covering her face yelled to us, calling us by name, which puzzled me. She told us that her name was Maria Simms and that that she was Burt's girlfriend. I was puzzled by her name. It wasn't Garcia, so she couldn't be Garcia's wife. I wondered if she was Officer Simms's sister or his wife, or if the fact that her name was the same as his was just a coincidence. If she was related to him, then that would make a total of four police officers. There was Benny Garcia, Carlos Garcia, Isaac Simms, and now Maria Simms. I was beginning to feel like my family and I were being stalked by a group of cops. It made me wonder how many girlfriends my dad had. I was even more frazzled when Maria told us that she was pregnant. It was then I realized that she had to be Carlos's wife or ex-wife. *Either Simms is her maiden name or she is keeping her maiden name secret and is using an assumed name. Why?* I pondered. It was now spring of 1960, which would mean that my father and Maria had been carrying on with this affair for over two years and had not heeded the warnings of Benny and Carlos. Maria would probably give birth sometime in autumn of 1960. Why would a woman come up to another woman's two children and tell them she was pregnant by their father? I could see her scheme. She wanted my sister and me to go home and blab to our mother with this newly gathered information about her. I decided that I was not going home and telling my mother anything that would hurt her. She'd been hurt when Carlos had Rico Garcia rape her.

Sure enough, when Veronica got home, the first thing she did was start singing, "Daddy's got a girlfriend, Daddy's got a girlfriend."

That's when my mother asked my dad, "Burt, what is she talking about?"

He answered, "Oh, Lou, she doesn't know what she is talking about."

Mom wasn't buying it. She knew Veronica wasn't capable of making up a story like that. She could tell she wasn't going to get a truthful answer out of Dad, so she reminded him of his last affair and the consequences she had suffered because of it.

"Burt, if anything happens to me or my kids because you are having an affair, Daddy is going to kill you."

He had no reply. Angry that he had been caught, he grabbed his keys and left, claiming he was going for a short drive. I am sure he went to see Maria to have a discussion with her. Whether it was a positive or negative conversation, I could only guess.

In the early hours of the morning, when it was still dark, Dad came home. Mom had waited up for him to let him know that she still loved him. I never found out if he had told Mom that Maria was pregnant, but I knew that such was the case. While I loved my father, I couldn't stand what he was doing to my mother. She was still under age thirty and was still pretty. Why he was doing this to her? I couldn't understand. He was hurting her deeply and he didn't seem to care.

The one thing my mom could be sure of was the love and attention of her children. She had wanted Burt dead after his last affair, but she had forgiven him for his infidelity for the sake of her kids.

The next day, there was a knock at the door. I went to open the door to see who was there. As before, the callers pushed the door open and rushed in. It was Rico again. This time, Simms was right behind him.

"Rape that bitch!" Simms ordered Rico.

Helpless, I could only watch as Rico raped my mom again. I was stunned to see Simms standing behind Rico and instructing him to do that to my mom. My thoughts began to race. All I could think of was Maria. Somehow she was tied to this and was related to both Isaac Simms and Carlos Garcia. That made her related to Rico as well. She had to be the reason Simms was doing this, but was she his wife or his sister? Why were they keeping their relationships a secret? In either case, both Garcia and Simms had Rico rape my mother.

When Simms and Rico left, my mom went to the phone and called the police. When the police arrived, they contacted my father. Once my father was home, the police took my mom to get checked out, leaving my father to watch over me and my sisters. When Mom arrived back home, she called the one man whom she knew could always trust and confide in, her father. It would be two days before he would get to Detroit, taking one day to prepare and one to travel, but she knew he would be there for her. She was beginning to realize that her marriage was unraveling. And she could no longer trust her husband, who was surely to blame for these events.

Two days later, my grandfather arrived. Mom had anticipated his arrival. She needed his advice. She proceeded to tell him exactly what had happened. Being a powerful man, he used his connections to summon the police to find out what information they had on Rico and Simms. When the detectives arrived, Simms was with them. For the second time in my life, I had to explain to the cops that someone had hurt my mother. Simms was listening to every word.

When the detectives' backs were turned, Simms slapped me and said, "Say it wasn't me, Brett." It was then that two more detectives arrived at the apartment.

One of the newly arrived detectives asked me, "Brett, do you know a Justine Powers?"

"Yeah, she lives on the fourth floor of the building," I replied.

"Brett, Justine says you hurt her."

Shocked that Justine was hurt, I answered, "I would never hurt Justine. I like Justine and wouldn't do anything to hurt her. Besides, that's Gary's sister. He is a pilot. He is going to teach me how to fly someday."

My grandfather then shouted, "I am going to kill you if raped that girl, Brett."

I was overwhelmed! Only seven years old, I was being accused of the adult crime of hurting a female. On top of this, I felt bad for not protecting my mother; my dad was seeing another woman; my grandfather was now threatening to hurt me; and the threat from DGA was looming.

Finally I caught somewhat of a break. One of the detectives who had arrived first to talk to my grandfather checked inside my pants. He instantly noticed the greenish-yellow discharge coming from my penis. Not having had sex education, I had no idea what the detective had been looking for.

"Brett, how long ago did you notice the green stuff in your pants?" the cop asked.

"About three days ago. I have been having trouble peeing also," I answered.

That's when the detective said to my grandfather, "Will, it couldn't have been Brett. Brett's got the clap and he's just a little boy. It's totally impossible that he hurt Justine."

I felt relieved. I could tell these were good cops, ones who were going to help me and my mom. They were not going to take another person's word when determining what the situation was. Instead, they were going to check things out before reaching a conclusion.

"Brett, who did this to you?" my grandfather asked. "Has anybody been touching your private part?"

"Yes. Three members of the black gang called over a black lady who I guessed was a prostitute. They told her to lay me down. She pulled up her dress, and then she rubbed my penis between her legs."

Another detective asked, "Brett, did you see anybody talking to Justine in the last few days?"

"I didn't see anybody with her, but Rico walked me home the other day and asked if there were any pretty girls who lived in the building. I told him yes, Justine and Juliet."

"Which Rico are you talking about, Brett?"

"Rico Garcia, the one who hurt my mother the first time. And now he has done it again."

The cop who had checked my pants told my grandfather that they should get me to the hospital right away because I was in the advanced stages of gonorrhea. My grandfather and my mother took me to children's hospital, where I was checked by an urologist. The urologist told my mom the consequences of the disease and recommended that I be admitted right away. The cost of the operation was discussed. My family was unable to pay it. That's when my grandfather stepped in and said to my mom, "Lou, I want you and Burt to pack your belongings and meet me back at the house. We'll take Brett to Seco Hospital."

Chapter 13

MY SURGERY

Seco Hospital was one of many hospitals that the United Mine Workers had built and supported for coal miners and their families to utilize. It would mean another five-hundred-mile trip, but I had to go, as I was finding it harder and harder to urinate. I did not understand all of what was happening and I was a little afraid, but my mom reassured me that everything was going to be all right.

My mother, my father, and my grandfather all met at Seco Hospital. I was surprised and angry to see Maria there also. I could not understand what reason she had for being present. One other thing that was unusual was that a Kentucky State Police car with a Kentucky state trooper was parked outside the hospital entrance. My grandfather, telling me that the trooper was going to take me for a ride, said that I should go with him. I got in the car. The trooper asked me a few questions about who had done this to me. I told him as much as I understood at the time, saying that a couple of crooked Mexican cops named Garcia were involved and that a gang of blacks called DGA was to blame. I told him that they used a narcotic to disable people, and that after the intended victim was disabled, they inflicted hurt.

In our short drive, the trooper had figured out some of what was going on. He relayed the information to my grandfather, telling him, "They are using the kids to get to the adults, Will. None of this is Brett's fault." After the trooper had a brief conversation with my grandfather, he left.

My mother then picked me up and whispered in my ear so no one could hear, "Grandpa's going to kill your dad, Brett."

I whispered back to her, "Mom, that's dad's girlfriend, Maria! What's she doing here?"

She didn't reply, so I figured that Maria have been the reason that my grandfather was going to kill Dad.

My grandfather pulled out his gun, pointed it at my dad, and said, "Burt, I'm going to kill you for what you've done to my daughter and Brett. I can't for the life of me figure out why you would do this to Lou after she has given you such a fine family."

My father had no reply. With his silence, the tension began to build. My grandfather wasn't saying anything either. I felt that my grandfather was about to ruin not only his life but also my mother's and my father's, and most of all mine. I had to react before he shot my father. It was then that I thought about the little church on Third Street we often attended. I recalled being taught that Jesus had died for our sins, and that God had let us live because Jesus had done that for us. Maybe by offering my life in exchange for my father's, Grandpa wouldn't shoot at all.

That's when I blurted out, "Dad, I'll die for you."

My grandfather turned and walked toward me. He pressed the gun to my upper lip. Feeling the cold blue steel against my flesh, I remained silent, not wanting to influence his decision whether to kill me or not.

My grandfather and I stood like that for a few seconds, which seemed like an eternity. Then he put the gun down and began sobbing. He said, "I can't do it. I just can't do it. You should take Brett inside, Lou." My ploy had worked.

I then said, "Grandpa, none of this is our fault. Everybody hates hillbillies in Detroit, especially blacks. They blame us because they were slaves. If we have to die, can't we at least die fighting, Grandpa?"

Mom grabbed my hand and led me inside the hospital to check me in. This was the first time I'd had to go to a hospital for an operation. I was a bit frightened. The staff was all very friendly. They put me at ease and then led me to my room. It wasn't very long until a doctor came in and examined me. He told my mom what they were going to do, saying that I would be scheduled for surgery early the next morning.

He was not kidding. It was six in the morning when the nurses came into my room and started to prepare me for the surgery. My mom told me that the nurses were going to do something that would make me poop. After having me bend over the bed, one of the nurses gave me an enema. Then the nurse told me to hold the solution in and walk to the toilet. I took about two steps and told her that I couldn't hold it. I took two more steps toward the bathroom. The contents of the enema gushed out of me, creating a large puddle that spread all over the floor.

My mom then told me how disappointed she was in me. I couldn't believe that after I'd had what felt like a gallon of water shoved up my ass, she was mad at me because I hadn't made it to the toilet. I felt like a contestant in a twisted game show. "Let's fill his ass up with a solution and bet on whether or not he will make it to the toilet in time."

After that episode, another nurse came in and asked me if I wanted some soda. My mother was angry, and now the nurses wanted to give me a soda. I guessed that the nurse who was getting the soda was the one who had won the bet.

"Sure, I'll take a soda."

Coming back a minute or so later with a small glass with red liquid in it, the nurse told me, "This is a special soda. You have to drink it all at once."

I did as she said. It wasn't long after that I became groggy. I do not remember much of what happened after they wheeled me into the operating room, although I was awake enough to talk to the nurse who was strapping me down. She said, "Your mom told me you want to be a pilot."

71

"Yeah, I want to learn to fly someday."

"Well, we have a mask like the military pilots wear. I'm going to put it over your face. You have to take a deep breath." She put the mask over my face and told me to take a deep breath. I did not know what was in the mask but it stunk badly. It was an odor I'd never smelled before. She had me repeat the process, and had me count backward from one hundred. I began to count. I don't think I made it to ninety-five before I was knocked out.

When I awakened, more than twelve hours after my surgery, my mom was right by my side. She asked me, "Do you feel okay?"

"Yes," I replied, "but I feel sore below my waist."

"We have to get you up and you must walk to the bathroom to see if you can pee."

She helped me, as I was very weak and sore. I walked down the hall because there was no bathroom in the room we were in. I stood by the toilet. When I began to pee, it felt like I was pissing razor blades. It burned very bad. I hoped I would not have to pee again anytime soon.

The following morning, the doctor came in to examine me. He asked my mother if I had peed.

She replied, "Yes."

He explained to her that the surgery had been a success. They had inserted a tube to replace part of my urinary tract. In all likelihood, I would not be able to father children. Then the doctor gave my mom instructions in case anything should go wrong. I didn't understand how my being unable to pee had anything to do with children. The doctor said that they were going to keep me for another day, and would release me tomorrow.

When he left the room, I asked my mother, "What was that smell that coming from that mask when I was lying on the operating table?"

"Brett that smell coming from the mask was ether. They use it to make you sleep while they work on you."

For me, the next day could not come fast enough. I would not be returning to Detroit until after I finished recovering at Grandpa's house. I couldn't wait to get back to Grandma and Grandpa's house, where I knew I would get some of Grandma's home cooking, like homemade biscuits and fresh honey, along with sausage gravy—and plenty of it. There always plenty to eat at Grandma's house, as Grandpa had always been not just a good provider but an excellent provider. His children never had to go hungry.

The more I saw of my grandfather, the more I found out what a good man he really was. I recalled one incident when I was younger. I had been standing on the front porch when a man came walking up to my grandfather and I. He was a stranger to me, but in this part of the country there were no strangers, at least not to my grandparents. I found this out when the stranger said, "Brother Will," which instantly told me that whoever he was, he was a religious man. Most likely he was a Baptist, as the Baptist belief in the South was that we were all brothers and sisters.

"I've been on the road for four days now trying to make a living. I have not had a good meal since I set out. People tell me that if you're hungry, you can get a good hot meal at your house because people are welcome here."

My grandfather walked over to the front door without hesitating and shouted in to my grandmother, "Suze, set another plate for dinner."

This was just one example of my grandfather's kindness. His love for people, his love for his children, and his love of his country could not be exceeded.

The incident at the hospital showed me a side of my grandfather that I had never seen before. I was puzzled by his actions, which seemed very unlike my grandfather. What I learned was just how angry he was with my father for what he had done to my mother. I was slowly learning that, like Vinny was in Detroit my grandfather was a very powerful man in this region of Kentucky. I would be proud of the things that he would eventually teach me.

Chapter 14

THE DOG GENIUS

Eventually I would be surprised to discover that the things I would learn from my grandfather and my uncle Ronnie would affect world history, which in turn would make the world a safer place to live. I would also find out how talented they were when it came to training animals.

While I was recuperating, Uncle Ronnie taught me things that I would have to learn if I were living in the country, as my extended family did. He taught me things about dogs and hunting one afternoon while he was chopping wood, making certain to teach me about hunting with a dog.

"Brett, one thing you want to know for sure is never to let your hunting dog get on a raccoon near water."

"Why is that so, Uncle Ronnie?" I asked him.

"Well, Brett, if you're near water, a coon will try to get on the dog's neck and drown him."

"How do the dogs track them anyway, Uncle Ronnie?"

"They can smell them. You don't want to get your dog on a fox, either, because the fox will run your dog to death. Foxes are smart and fast. That's why they use them for fox hunts. That's also why people say, 'He's as sly as a fox.'"

"Thanks for the lesson, Uncle Ronnie. I didn't know those things. I knew from the movies that dogs could track humans, but I didn't know for sure how they tracked animals."

One afternoon after Uncle Ronnie had given me the lesson about dogs, my grandmother asked Veronica and I to go out to the garden and pick some potatoes and corn for the dinner she was cooking for my family who had arrived this afternoon. As we headed for the garden, Grandma yelled to us, saying we should let the dogs go first. The dogs, which Grandpa had trained to alert the family whenever someone pulled into the driveway, headed into the garden with us. They were going back and forth in a zigzag pattern in the garden, their noses to the ground all around us. When we got back to the house with the vegetables, Grandma asked us to go out to the "back forty," as we called it, to slop the hogs for Grandpa. Grandpa got the slop ready, and I, along with Veronica, headed for the hog house. As we walked, I noticed that the dogs ran to get in front of us. When we got back to the house after slopping the hogs, I was curious why the dogs had done those things.

I asked, "Grandpa, why do the dogs follow us every time we go into the gardens?"

"Brett, I have them trained them to let us know when there is a snake hiding in the tall growth."

"How do they know they're there, Grandpa?"

"We don't know how they know the snakes are there, but they know for sure when they are there."

"Do you think they can smell them?"

"Maybe they can, Brett, but I don't know for sure."

Suddenly I had an epiphany. It all seemed very simple. It had been almost two thousand years since Jesus walked the planet, and no one I knew personally or knew of had come up with the idea to teach dogs to sniff out drugs. Not even the Chinese, who'd had an opium epidemic during feudal times, had thought of it—and they were the ones who invented gunpowder. I decided to ask Grandpa to confirm what I thought to be true: that no one had yet trained dogs to sniff out drugs.

"Grandpa, drugs must give off a smell too. If dogs can smell coons and possums, then maybe they can smell drugs. If you can train them to smell drugs, I believe we can make a lot of money selling drug dogs for making drug busts, Grandpa. It would be a great help also in determining who is carrying narcotics and who is not, because it's the gangs who are mostly carrying the drugs. Do you think you can teach the dogs to do that?"

"Brett, I think you are on to something. No one I know of has taught dogs to smell out drugs. Maybe we can teach them to do that."

Leaving the matter at that, Grandpa and I went inside for dinner.

Over time, I finished healing from my surgery. My family and I packed up and headed back to Detroit.

Chapter 15

THE STABBING

I was standing in front of my apartment building waiting for my friends to join me in a game of bunting, in which we used a baseball bat and a ball like a baseball, but instead of taking a full swing at the ball, the batter had to bunt instead. I noticed a couple of men lying in the gutter a few blocks away on the opposite side of the street. A few minutes later, I noticed there was another group of three more. Then, there was four more, now lying on the sidewalk on my side of the street. I couldn't help but wonder who these men were and why they had become targets of the DGA. I knew from the murder that I had witnessed in the park to stay away from them and let the cops handle it.

Someone said the police are on their way. I did not know who called the police but soon after the police arrived, they began canvassing the neighborhood looking for witnesses. As usual, no one saw a thing. It was the gang's code and the street code, as everyone knew the punishment for being so inclined to talk to the cops.

During times when there were a high number of muggings and a high volume of drug activity, squads of cops would run sweeps through the Corridor looking for junkies who had needle tracks on their arms. For each needle mark, the addict would receive three days in the Detroit House of Correction. All the ex-cons who had spent time there called it "DeHoCo." The sweeps were an attempt to rid the area of any drug activity, which was the reason for most muggings.

During one of the sweeps, I was walking in front of my apartment when a DGA gangster walked up to me and ordered me to stick out my arm, which is what cops did to check your arms for needle marks. Then he poked me three times with an empty syringe. Isaac Simms, who was in charge of running the sweep on this day, shouted, "He's a junkie," and ordered one of his officers to take me to jail. I felt betrayed by Simms. He had asked me to watch out for Rico, and now he was having me taken to jail. I was held in a temporary cell, called a holding cell, where almost all of my cellmates were DGA members. I was beaten, urinated on, and ejaculated on, and had feces wiped on me. I was exhausted. And every time I sat down to get some rest, the beatings would continue. I soon became impervious to the pain being inflicted on me. A minor of seven years of age, I was being held illegally. And not one cop came to help me or take me home. I was denied sleep for most of the three days I was incarcerated. I must have passed out, because when I awoke on the third day, I found myself in my bedroom. My Uncle Ronnie had gotten me out. He had me take a shower because I stank.

"Brett, I'm going to be staying with you for a few days and seeing that you have no trouble getting back and forth to school. We don't want anybody to know who I am. Also, your dad is going to stay home with your mom to make sure nothing happens to her. I'll be watching you go back and forth to school."

"Thanks, Uncle Ronnie. I really miss being down South. I don't understand why everyone hates us so much here. I almost don't want to go to school, Uncle Ronnie, at least not here."

"You can't avoid your enemies, Brett. You have to fight them. You rest up a few days. As I said, I will watch you when you go to school."

My parents let me rest up for few days, but then I had to return to school. One day when I was on my way back home, my uncle Ronnie was walking on the other side of the street, watching me every step of the way. I had no fear. I didn't know why, although it was not because Ronnie was watching over me. It was something deep down, something more spiritual-like that made me unafraid. The DGA had threatened me, but deep down I knew I would do what was right.

As I was walking home, I saw two DGA members emerge from between two buildings. One held me around the neck while the other one injected me with some sort of drug. I saw a detective at the back of the building. He started toward the gang members and me. I waved him off, knowing that they were not working alone. Still, I didn't know how they were going to try to kill me. I continued walking down Cass while my uncle Ronnie watched over me from across street. My eyes began burning fiercely and watering. I was stumbling down the street. I saw a tall black man talking to another man. Suddenly he turned toward me. I could see he had something in his hand. As he came closer, I could see he was holding a knife. He then stabbed me with it in my chest, up near my throat. Because I'd been drugged, I failed to react. The impact of the knife was hard enough to knock me to the ground. Ronnie rushed from across the street. Taking out a white cloth, he put pressure on the wound.

"Brett, please don't die. Please don't die," Ronnie pleaded. "Dad will never forgive me for letting them stab you. Brett, hang on. An ambulance is on the way."

The detective who had been following me through the alley arrived on the scene. I was still conscious. He asked me, "Brett, which one did it?"

Surprisingly, the perpetrator was standing outside a store and I saw the perpetrator pass the knife to his accomplice. I raised my arm and pointed him out, and then I told my uncle Ronnie what the perpetrator had done with the knife. The detective turned around and pinned the perpetrator against the wall, after which the uniformed police officer took the latter away. I was closing my eyes intermittently and losing a lot of blood. I was trying very hard not to pass out, but my effort was futile.

I awoke the next morning in a hospital bed with a big patch near my neck, covering my wound. Maria and Isaac Simms were in the room with me. Once they saw I was awake, they brought Ronnie in. Ronnie, apparently curious as to why I had kept going, asked me, "Why did you keep walking after they drugged you?"

I replied, "I know how that gang operates. First they drug you, and then they shoot or stab you. After they drugged me, I knew there would another group with a gun or a knife waiting for me. If I was going to get stabbed or shot, I wanted it to be while you were watching over me. You said I have to fight them, and I can't fight them if I don't know who they are. It was the only way I knew to find out who was waiting for me."

"We're going to take you home now, Brett. Your grandpa is on his way up. He'll be here later on this evening."

"I can't wait, Uncle Ronnie. I need to go back to Kentucky for a while."

It was late evening when my grandfather arrived. He had come to assess the situation. Ronnie told him that it was a group of blacks who had stabbed me. Grandpa told Ronnie that he would be staying at his sister-in-law's, my mom's aunt Lydie's house.

It was early the next morning when my grandpa arrived at my apartment. After talking to the police in our precinct and finding out just what my family was up against, and discovering that we were taking on one of the most notorious gangs in Detroit, my grandfather had come to the conclusion that he would take my mother and us kids to Kentucky temporarily, while my father would stay in Detroit so he didn't lose his job. He said to me, "Brett, we are going to take you down south. We are going to teach you how to fight so you can protect your mother and the rest of your family."

I asked, "Grandpa, can't we just move out of Detroit?"

"No, Brett! You can't run from them. We're not going to let you run from those blacks. They will track you down no matter where you are, until either you kill them or they kill you. They are not going to stop until that day comes. So I am going to prepare you for that day."

I pondered what he had said, and wondered how he knew so much about fighting. He was a Southern Baptist preacher who should have been preaching peace and love, not fighting and violence. How he knew that the gang would not stop trying to kill my family was beyond me. I knew one thing, though: he was very wise man. I would follow his guidance.

We would take two separate cars back to Kentucky: Ronnie's car and Grandpa's car. It was a long trip back, but there was something about it. Every time we crossed the border between Ohio and Kentucky heading to grandpa's house, I just seemed to relax. It was as if someone had given me a powerful tranquilizer that calmed me. I felt as if a giant boulder had been lifted off my body. Crossing that border meant that I would soon be arriving in a place where I would be surrounded with love and kindness. There were no fights and no gunplay. I felt like southeastern Kentucky was my home and where I should be. Detroit was not.

Although he was raised in Illinois, Abraham Lincoln was born in Kentucky, as was I. He was one of our greatest presidents as far as I was concerned. He had kept the Union together and freed the slaves, and for that he was assassinated. His saying "A house divided cannot stand" was adopted by Kentucky as the state motto. These were things that made me proud to be born in Kentucky. I told myself I would try to emulate President Lincoln. It had been over one hundred years since civil unrest had led to the start of the Civil War. Now I was seven years old and caught up in the beginnings of a war—one that I did not want, but one that I would have to fight on the streets of Detroit in the Cass Corridor.

"Brett, we're going to rest for a day after the trip. Part of your family is going to be at Juanita's and the rest will be at Fannie's because we're going to teach you how to use a gun and we don't want any little children running around."

Chapter 16

GUN TRAINING

I was seven and half years old when my gun training began. It was six o'clock the morning after my arrival when Ronnie got me up for breakfast. Forty years of Grandpa working in the coal mines, the days always started early at Grandma and Grandpa's house with a large breakfast. Once at work, the breaks were far apart, so breakfast had to last until lunch. After breakfast, Ronnie and Grandpa took me out to the front yard and handed me the two .22-caliber revolvers that Grandpa had given to me on my seventh birthday. They were about the size of a derringer and had ivory handles. Very proud of them, I treasured them. Then Ronnie tacked a target up on the big oak tree standing next to the creek that ran beside of the house.

Next, Grandpa told me, "Brett, we want you to always fire three rounds." He had me stand about ten feet away from the tree. "Now try to hit the bull's-eye."

I fired three rounds. Grandpa examined the target and said, "Brett, you didn't even hit the outer ring. Try again."

I did as he said, and fired three more rounds. He again examined the target, finding the same result. That's when Ronnie intervened. I said, "Ronnie, I don't know if I'm aiming right because I can't see where the bullets are going into the target."

He retrieved a wooden pistol with no sight on it, brought it to me, and said, "Brett, the barrel on the gun has to be level." He then demonstrated on the wooden gun, also showing me how to hold it correctly. "Try it now, Brett," he said.

I fired three more rounds. This time Ronnie looked at the target. He said, "That is much better, Brett, but we still need some more work."

By this time, Grandpa was frustrated. He told Ronnie, "He just doesn't have the knack for using a gun. We're just going to have to figure something else out."

That's when Ronnie, an expert with a pistol, half scolded Grandpa by saying, "I've already got it figured out, Dad. He needs a gun with a longer barrel. The barrels on his guns are too short."

"Okay, Brett. That's enough for today. We are going to test you on some guns with longer barrels, and then we'll figure out which gun best fits you. We'll rest up for now, until tomorrow."

It was early the next day. The gun training was going to be much more intense. As the day started off, I noticed a person I had never seen before. As

I approached him, my grandfather said that this man was going to help with my training.

"Brett, this is my brother, your great-uncle Isthme. He's a shooting instructor for the Kentucky State Police."

What relief I felt when he told me that!

I was pleasantly surprised and honored to hear that I was going to be taught by someone who trained police officers. I was sure I was about to receive the best training in the country.

Uncle Isthme started out the training by saying, "Brett, we have to teach you about the different sights on guns. I brought a series of rifles and pistols so that you can find out how they work. Then we are going to see what caliber gun fits you best." There was an array of rifles with peep sights and the like, and some with other types of sights. I couldn't remember the names of all of them. Then he showed me a rifle that didn't have a sight; it had what is called a nipple instead, which is used to sight in the target. The weapon was a Kentucky long rifle. Isthme had me try to hold it up, but because the barrel was longer than that of a normal rifle, it made for a very heavy gun. I couldn't hold it up in a firing position.

My grandfather then told me some of the history behind that rifle, saying, "Brett, Kentucky is very proud of that rifle. It is named after the hunters who used it for game in this state. That rifle was used in two important battles. The first one was the War of 1812, at the Battle of New Orleans, where it helped to swing the tide of the war. After the Battle of New Orleans, someone wrote a song titled 'The Hunters of Kentucky,' which helped General Jackson become president. The second battle was the Battle of the Alamo. The men defending the Alamo lasted thirteen days. The Mexicans could not get close enough to them on account of the long range of the Kentucky long rifle, which has a longer barrel for much better accuracy and for shooting a longer distance. The battle for the Alamo ended when the Texans ran out of balls and powder, but they had done their job by stalling the Mexican army long enough so Sam Houston could muster up an army."

The reason my kinsfolk were teaching me about all those sights was so I would learn how to sight the gun. Uncle Isthme took the long rifle, placed it in both my hands, and told me look down the barrel and try to hit the bull's-eye. I did as he asked, putting the tip of the barrel level with the bull's-eye and pulling the trigger. It was a near miss, just an inch from dead center.

I told Uncle Isthme, "Looking down the barrel of that gun showed me how to sight the gun. I get it now, Uncle Isthme: level the barrel.

"Okay now, Brett, we're going to test you on different guns to see what fits you best. This is a .357. Remember to level the barrel."

About ten feet from the target, I did as he said and fired the gun one time. I hit the target, but the gun was hard for me to hold. Uncle Isthme continued the process until he settled on a long-barreled .22.

The day had been a long one, but the training would continue the next morning. It would continue with a different gun. They would also teach me exercises to do to strengthen my arms so I could hold the gun steady.

The next day started much like the others. The new gun would lead to an intense training session. Uncle Isthme started me a little farther from the target at a range of twenty feet or so. I fired three rounds into the target with Uncle Isthme standing to the right of me. After I had fired the gun, he grabbed my gun hand firmly and showed me how my hand must look when holding the gun properly. Then he said, "This time, I want you to fire until the gun is empty."

After I had fired twice, he began beating on my gun hand with a stick. It stung pretty badly. I then asked him, "Uncle Isthme, why do you keep beating on my hand with that stick?"

"Hold the gun right and I won't beat on your hand."

He showed once more how to hold the gun properly. "Now try it again—and hold the gun right."

I suddenly realized that holding the gun properly could mean the difference between whether you lived or died in a gunfight. I fired six more rounds, this time being much more aware of how I held the gun.

"That's much better, Brett. We are going to practice with a few more rounds and then break for lunch."

My training continued. After three days, with eight hours of intensive shooting each day, I began to notice something. Every time I pulled the trigger, the gun would move and the rear sight would block the bull's-eye.

I said, "Uncle Isthme, no matter what I do, when I pull the trigger, the gun goes offline of the target and the rear sight blocks the target."

He grabbed the gun, looked down the barrel, pointed the weapon at the target, fired once, and then said, "You are right, Brett. Now what do you think we should do about it?"

"Well, my hands and arms are in shape, so I have got good strength in them. It has to be the trigger pressure. As far as the sight goes, in the old days, gunfighters used to file the sights off so they could better see the target and so the gun sight didn't get hung up in the holster. Maybe that's what we should do."

"Okay, Brett, we're going to get another gun made for you. I knew something in your style wasn't right, so we'll rest for a day or two. That will give me time to get a new gun for you."

Two days later, Uncle Isthme handed me the gun he had bought for me. It was a .22 with an extended barrel, or as they say up north, a .22 Magnum. It was brand new and custom made, and came with a custom-made holster. I couldn't thank Uncle Isthme and my grandfather enough. It was a beautiful gun, almost too nice to fire.

"Go ahead, fire it, Brett," Uncle Isthme encouraged me.

"Are you sure, Uncle Isthme? I'd almost like not to fire it."

"Brett, it's a gun, not a trophy. It's meant for you to use it. Now, do like we've been teaching you. Fire three rounds with it."

I did as he told me, leveling the barrel and then firing three rounds from about thirty feet away. All three rounds were on target but not dead center. The cylinder rotation was beautifully smooth, and the trigger was set to go off with the slightest of pressure.

"What do you think of your gun, Brett?"

"Uncle Isthme, it's the finest gift I've ever received. I will treasure it always."

"What do you think of the way it fires?" my grandfather asked.

"I like everything about it. I like the smoothness of the action—it doesn't kick back powder in my face—and the ease with which the trigger pulls. It's a great gun, Grandpa."

My training would not end at this point. The next step was to teach me to shoot for a person's head, which was the reason for firing three rounds. Most people who are familiar with guns know that a .22 caliber does not have a lot of knockdown power, but three rounds to the head will do.

The next step consisted of first getting a silhouette of a human body made up. Uncle Isthme had one made. He had me stand about thirty feet away from it and fire three rounds, shooting only at the head. This routine continued until Uncle Isthme was satisfied that I was going to hit what I was shooting at and that my groupings landed in a pattern matching the size of a silver dollar.

There would be one more stage of training, which was for me to fire on the move. The idea came to me while we were resting on the front porch. All my training and having to resort to using guns made me think about the Old West when cowboys chased the bad guys and fired at them while on the run.

I asked Uncle Isthme, "Do you think those cowboys could hit anything while moving on horseback?"

He said to me, "I want you to fire and take a step, fire and take a step, fire and take a step, until you empty the gun." I continued to practice until I could fire and hit the target while running toward it.

Uncle Isthme stopped me at one point and asked, "Brett, how are you doing that well with no sight?"

"When I get ready to fire my gun, I zero in on the target. All I can see is the target, nothing else. If I am doing so well, Uncle Isthme, what is my ranking?"

"Brett," he said, "you are a sharpshooter, but you are very close to being an expert."

I was thankful for what my family had taught me. I now had confidence. While little in terms of size, I would not do well in a street fight, which requires a lot of physical strength. But when the guns come out, I would be superior in my abilities.

Chapter 17

LEARNING A NEW ROBBERY TECHNIQUE

It wasn't long after we returned to Detroit that the DGA started coming after me again. It had only been a couple of days. I was hoping that the DGA would just leave us alone. I heard a knock at the door. Since there was no peephole to see who was there, I opened it. Half a dozen DGA members pushed their way into the apartment. This was a tactic known to police as a push-in robbery, only they were not there for money or jewelry. They were there to hurt my mom and me. They grabbed her and began ripping her clothes off until all she had left on were her panties. She repeatedly begged them not to hurt her. All the while she was asking them why they were doing this to her family. I was forced to watch. One of the gang members held one of my arms and, with his other hand, held me by the hair of my head. The other gang members took turns raping my mom. When they finished, they left her in heap on the floor. Once they finally left, I walked over to her asked her what I should do. It was a white woman's worst nightmare to be raped and humiliated by a gang of blacks. They enjoyed humiliating white people in that manner.

Mom shouted, "Leave me alone! Don't touch me!" I'd never felt so useless. All the training I had gone through had been for naught.

It was about a half hour later when Ronnie and Grandpa arrived. By then, the cops had been called to the scene. I informed them of what had happened. Grandpa began quizzing me to learn what I had seen.

"Why weren't you carrying your gun when you answered the door, Brett?" Grandpa asked.

"Dad hid the gun so the other kids couldn't get to it. Even if I had my gun, they would have just taken it away. There were too many to fight at one time. Besides, there are hundreds of them, maybe even thousands of them. I'm going to need more than six rounds, Grandpa. I am going to have to fight the blacks outside, Grandpa, before the whole gang has a chance to get inside the apartment. Once they get through the door—and they have guns—we're not going be able to kill them fast enough. This apartment is a death trap, Grandpa. We're going to have to fight them in the open."

"I'm going to have to do some checking out of the situation, so stay by the apartment until I get back to you, Brett."

When my father brought my mother back from the hospital, he said she had gone catatonic. I did not know what that meant. He said she would not speak, or eat or drink anything. "Brett, see if you can get her to talk or eat something."

96

I did not know much about psychiatry, but I could see that my mother was in bad shape. I had to see what I could do. "Mom, it's Brett. I love you very much. All your kids love you, Mom. Can you at least say something to me, Mom?"

She wouldn't reply. I had Dad fix her some eggs, but she wouldn't eat them. All she would do is sit at the table with a blank stare on her face. Something came over me seeing my mother like this. It filled me with a terrible resolve. I had never been afraid of dying, although I was afraid of dying for the wrong cause. I had tried to handle things peacefully, but this had now become an all-out war. DGA was going to pay a heavy price for what they had done to my mother, even if I had to die trying.

A couple of days after Mom had been gang-raped, my dad and I were guarding her and my siblings. This time I was wearing my gun. At one point, Ronnie came to the apartment and told me to follow him, saying I should hurry. He told me to leave my gun with my dad. We headed toward Woodward Avenue in downtown Detroit, where all the people with money shopped. There were expensive women's stores and high-end menswear shops, and shops that sold furs and jewelry. King's Department Store was on Woodward. I'd always loved King's, Detroit's equivalent of Macy's. I had a fondness for it because I had walked to King's on Woodward just before Christmastime a couple of years back to get a Christmas present for my mother. After I walked in— King's was noted for its service—an elderly woman asked me, "Can I help you, young man?"

I shyly said, "Yes, ma'am. I want to buy my mom a Christmas present."

"Well, how much do you have to spend?"

I said, "A quarter."

"Oh no, you can't buy anything here for a quarter. Go up to the fourth floor. Maybe you will find something up there."

I headed for the elevators and went up to the fourth floor, where a beautiful young woman greeted me. I went through the same routine with her that I'd gone through with the woman on the first floor. This woman, however, seemed much more pleasant than the first one. As I browsed the knickknacks, I had to ask how much they were because I didn't know how to read yet.

I settled on a set of porcelain horses, a mare with two weanlings. They were very pretty. I asked the saleswoman, "How much are the horses?"

She replied, "Well, how much do you have?"

"I only have a quarter."

"Well, they are on sale. A quarter is just enough."

I proudly walked home with my mom's present, but I was disappointed when my mom thought I had stolen the horses. I explained to her that I had paid the saleslady what she told me to pay. Mom then understood. I did not understand my mother's objection until later, when I saw the price sticker on the figural. It said $5.99.

Following my uncle, I asked him, "Ronnie, why are we going to Woodward?"

"Just watch and learn, Brett." Ronnie and I stood on one side of Woodward next to a man who lit up a very large cigar, while my grandfather walked down the opposite side of the street. DGA was in a marauding mode, something the members often did, looking to mug or rob someone who appeared to be easy pickings. Some gang members were tailing my grandfather all the way, and must have figured that this hillbilly was ripe for picking. Then, suddenly, the DGA members whipped out their knives and guns. My grandfather quickly turned toward them and opened fire. A barrage of gunfire came at them from our side of the street. The shooter was the man I was standing next to, along with three other men. I didn't know what had made them choose my grandfather to rob, but it was obvious that Ronnie and Grandpa had done what the police had not done. They had done their own surveillance. A dozen or so DGA members now lay dead or severely wounded. At that moment, I understood why Ronnie had told me to leave my gun at home: so the cops could not blame me.

Shortly afterward, the cops arrived. This time they made it to the scene in record time, naturally. As usual, they started canvassing for witnesses. When they got around to asking me what I saw, I decided to play this game of life and death the same way the DGA did. So I told them the same thing the DGA members had taught me.

"I didn't see anything but cigar smoke, that's all." Having made my statement, I owed nothing more to anyone. Ronnie escorted me back to the apartment. Grandpa and Ronnie would stay with Aunt Lydie once again.

It was midafternoon the following day when Ronnie came and got me again. This time we walked down Cass past the Masonic Temple. When we arrived, my grandfather was waiting for me. Isaac Simms was there also. I knew that Simms's presence meant trouble. Some DGA members who were there headed toward Burton, but farther down the street. My grandfather began giving me instructions about what to do, and then he gave me a Ka-Bar, a military knife, to strap on.

"Brett, now don't be afraid. We will be backing you up all the way. You have to kill them. And kill as many as you can. Remember everything we taught you, and shoot for the head. We know you're good enough. You are as good as any man with a gun. We know you can get the job done. When you run out of ammo, use your knife and cut their throats." He then handed me a .22 semiautomatic pistol. "This has five rounds in the clip and one in the chamber, for six rounds total."

I was not looking forward to this fight, but I was not going to question my grandfather. I knew he was very wise in his ways. Plus, given the way I looked at things, this was a war. He was the general and I was a soldier, and I was going to be a good soldier. DGA hadn't gotten the message the previous day, and I knew they would never give in, so we were going to have to inflict heavy casualties on them. I had formulated a makeshift plan that entailed making sure they didn't get behind me. I knew from past experience that two or three would walk past you and grab you around the neck, while the remainder of the members would either stab you or inject you with a drug. I wouldn't let them inject me with a narcotic, so anyone in front of me was getting shot. And I wasn't letting anyone behind me because I couldn't take any chances with them.

I started across the street and readied myself for the fight. When the DGA members saw me, they accelerated their pace, walking toward me in single file. I fired my first round into the stomach of the first gang member, trying to be merciful by not shooting him in the head. He did not go down. The DGA continued their advance, so I fired my second shot in the first man's forehead. He went down. The others kept advancing. I fired the third shot at the next one coming, who didn't go down. It was if he were so heavily drugged that his brain did not recognize the fact he had been shot. Once I pushed him, he went down easily. Then I fired the fourth, and then the fifth, and then the sixth bullet. The assailants had all pulled knives on me, but I had not given them the chance to get close enough to use them. All my shots had hit their mark. I had felled five gang members.

I reached behind me for Simms to give me the second gun. Six more times I fired, only this time I was the one who was advancing toward the DGA. I was out of ammo, so I pulled out my knife and stabbed one of them in the chest. Because he was much taller than I, the knife wouldn't go in deep enough for him to fall. I had hit the bone in his chest, which would give him a severe wound but not be enough to kill him. The next one pulled out a pretty large gun. I figured I was a goner, but then Simms, who was still behind me, finally got into the fray and shot the man with a .357 Magnum. Suddenly, there was a break in the action. The DGA members left a large gap of about forty feet or so between us and them.

With my knife in my hand, dripping with their blood, I yelled, "You black assholes want to die?"

The one who was leading the gang yelled back, "What do you want?"

"I want you to stay off my turf or you're gonna die!"

"Where is your turf?" he yelled back.

"My turf is the north side of Burton and between Woodward and First Street. Just stay off those streets to make sure you stay off my turf. I have friends. You won't know who they are. They will be watching you, but you won't know where they are. So stay away from us! We're not looking for trouble. We won't hurt you." I got the feeling that I had earned some respect from the DGA by fighting them and not backing down. I was hoping that with the threat of someone watching them, they would be kept off guard and would at least stay on the south side of Burton and give me a path to get to school.

The fight was over. The DGA had retreated. I turned around. Simms grabbed a little black boy who couldn't have been more than six, and said to me, "Kill him, Brett."

"What for, Isaac? He didn't do anything to me."

"Brett, *I said kill him!*"

"No, Isaac, he's just a little boy. Plus, he hasn't done anything to me."

"Brett, if you don't kill him, I am going to kill you," he said, handing me his .357. This jackass had me put in jail for no reason. I had to take him at his word, knowing he was a damn crook. I put the gun under the little boy's chin and then pulled the trigger. The bullet ripped all the skin off his face so that all his facial muscles were exposed, but he didn't fall down.

Simms then said, "Look what you did to his face. Brett, you are going to have to learn how to kill without spilling blood."

I couldn't believe that jackass had just chewed me out for shooting a kid I did not even want to shoot! But I was curious what he meant about not spilling blood.

I crossed to the side of the street where Ronnie and my grandfather were standing. My grandfather told me to start walking back to the apartment, advising me to just walk away from the scene. I was learning to keep my mouth shut and let the cops clean up the mess. As far I was concerned, I did not have to answer to them anymore. I had done what I had done for peace, not for vengeance. All I wanted was to be able to go to school and make something of myself, but DGA was doing everything they could to stop me. We had given them every chance to leave us alone. While my grandfather may not have been proud of the violence, I was sure that he was proud I had learned to use my gun well. The cops weren't going to help us, so it was up to me and my mother's family to protect her. And violence was the only thing that the DGA understood.

Only one question remained: would the DGA stay off the turf I had declared as mine? One thing I knew for sure was that they would be relentless. Only time would tell.

There would be a peace, but it would be short-lived.

Benny Garcia came by the apartment after school on the day after my fight with DGA telling me he needed me to come with him, also telling me to grab my gun. I knew when he told me to get my gun that whatever he had planned was not going to be a good thing. Word must have had gotten around as to what had happened. I didn't want people other than my family to know it was I who had killed those DGA men.

While Benny and I were walking down Cass, an elderly black woman approached us and said, "Thank you, young man. It's about time someone taught those hoodlums a lesson. You did a fine job of doing that."

She made me realize something. Before she said that, I had felt that all black people stuck together, either through fear or out of loyalty to their race. That woman showed me that black people hated bad blacks, too. Just as I was about to respond to her, Benny pulled my gun from the holster and shot her with it. The only reason that I could come up with for why he shot her was simply that she had praised me for what I had done.

Benny then grabbed me and said, "Brett, let's walk to the school." We started walking toward Burton. He just left the woman lying in the street. When we got to Burton, we saw a group of DGA members gathered on the playground next to the school. Having kept the agreement, they were staying on the south side of Burton and off my turf. Looking toward the playground, I saw Cindy O'Connell, a friend of mine whose father was a police officer. She often waited on the playground for her father to pick her up after school. She was an average-built girl for a third grader with pretty blonde hair. She wore horn-rimmed glasses, which to me made her look even prettier. She had a crush on me. One day she was asked by the teacher to pick a partner and perform a ballet for our third grade class. I avoided looking her in the eye so she wouldn't pick me, but it was no use. She chose me anyway as her dance partner. While she was excited to be my partner, I felt silly. But I liked her nonetheless.

On this day, Cindy was playing with other girls from the school on the playground, when suddenly some DGA members grabbed her and started to form a circle around her. I could see her standing there in a drug-induced stupor. I had seen them do the same thing to Manuel D. How the DGA had found out that she was my friend, I didn't know. Some of them lined up in front of me, knowing I was wearing my gun, and others brought Cindy from the playground.

One of them said, "We got to get this boy some sex," and proceeded to pull her clothes off. All the while, Benny watched the event unfold and did nothing. The DGA men soon let Cindy put her clothes back on. It was just a few minutes later when her father, Officer O'Connell, pulled up to take her home, oblivious to what had happened. Before he left to go home, Benny walked up to him and said something to him.

Officer O'Connell then turned to me and said, "Brett, Benny says you are molesting my daughter. Is that true?"

"No, Officer O'Connell. I didn't even touch her."

"Brett, I believe you because your word is better than his word. We're moving to get away from the likes of him!"

Wow! I thought. *That is a massive insult to Benny!* And it was—one cop telling another cop his word wasn't worth a good healthy shit. It did wonders for my ego, which I believe is what Officer O'Connell had intended. I didn't know what Benny would do to get even, but I was sure that he would try something. That entire episode just served to show me how important it was to tell the truth, especially when a lying cop is making up false stories about you. Now all I had to do was convince the rest of the force that Benny and his brother were both liars and crooks. It would soon be a contest of who among the Detroit police would believe the Garcia brothers. At least I had one ally in Officer O'Connell.

"Go home, Brett."

I walked back to my apartment, although the walk seemed much longer than usual. I didn't know what had happened to the little old black lady that Benny shot with my gun. It was as if the Garcia brothers were trying to isolate me from my friends. Also, they hurt anyone who gave me a compliment. It had started with Manuel D. And now Cindy had been attacked. I didn't want to lose any more friends or see any of them get hurt, but how was I going to stop the DGA?

Soon after the incident with Cindy, the DGA started after me again. Who ordered them after me, I had no clue. It could have been Benny, or Carlos, or the head of the DGA. I really didn't know, but I soon would discover something that would help law enforcement. My gun was useless against the gang because there were so many members. Just barely eight years old, I was not yet ready to die, so I found another way to defend myself.

One day, the DGA, having set a trap for me, had me cornered not far from my apartment. They were yelling at me, saying that they were going to kill me. Once they started toward me, I yelled out in desperation, "You can't see me!" Then I took off running again.

As I was running away, I heard one of them say, "Where did he go? Man, he's the fastest white boy I ever saw."

It had worked! They had no idea which way I had gone. I don't know how it had worked. I had gotten the idea from watching old war movies in which the enemy would have a doctor administer sodium pentothal, also known as

107

truth serum, and then would interrogate the pilot or POWs while under this narcotic, sometimes coupling the drug with hypnosis. Most DGA members were under the influence of a narcotic, their preference usually being heroin, or a combination of cocaine and heroin known as a speedball. Telling the DGA that they couldn't see me was like making a hypnotic suggestion, even though I had not drugged them or put them under hypnosis.

However, I was not out of harm's way because another gang member, this one acting as backup, came running toward me with a gun pointed at me. I tried it again by saying, "You can't see me." It stopped him dead in his tracks. He had no clue where I was although I was standing less than five feet from him.

It was later on in the evening when Carlos came by the apartment. When I answered the door, I had my gun on me. I think that prior to seeing me at the door, he thought I was dead.

I told him what had happened earlier with the DGA, saying that all I had said was, "You can't see me." It may have not been the best idea to tell him that, but I thought I should, as officers in the future might have had to go up against DGA in a similar situation. The knowledge I had given them could save one of their lives. I was hopeful that Carlos would share this information with his fellow officers. I was going to have to trust him to use the knowledge I had given him to do good things, not evil. I hoped maybe it would turn him around so he would be a much better, honest cop. I felt very uncomfortable trusting him.

"You mean to tell me they couldn't see you?"

"No, they could not."

"All you said was, 'You can't see me'? You didn't do anything to them?"

"Yes, that's right, Carlos. It seems that there is a way to embed a hypnotic suggestion in their mind. If police were to use that posthypnotic suggestion and say that they are invisible, it could be a very powerful tool for law enforcement."

"Brett, I think you just made me a millionaire."

All I could think was that maybe I had won Carlos over to my side. At least I had my hopes that such was the case. If nothing else, perhaps he would at least leave me alone.

That weekend, with my father being off work, he sent me out to get some Eight O'clock coffee. All of a sudden, I heard a cry for help coming from a person somewhere out front. I looked down the block about one hundred yards or so and saw a stocky fifty-something man wobbling toward me. He was saying, "Help me, please. Somebody, please help me. I don't want to die."

I ran toward him. He had tears running down his face, and he couldn't see properly, a sure sign he had been drugged. While he couldn't see me, he could hear my voice. Instructing him to stay on his feet, I told him that I would get an ambulance for him. I looked farther down the block, where I saw three more men staggering toward me. I was confused as to what was happening, not knowing what to make of it, when I saw two men turn the corner where the Masonic Temple was. Running at full speed, I was pretty quick to make it to that corner in order to find out what was going on. I slowed to a walk once I turned the corner, where I saw a group of blacks tailing other men who had left the temple. I knew then what was going on. They were tailing them and drugging them, trying to kill them with a drug overdose. *Who are the men they are trying to kill?* I wondered. Just then, as if God had been listening to my thoughts, Carlos, who had his back to me, yelled out to the blacks, "Just the ones with the funny hats."

A clue, I thought. Slowly I was putting all these events together. I had seen enough to know that Carlos was collaborating with the DGA to murder the men in the funny hats. The DGA were not only selling drugs for profit and using them to get high but now they were also using drugs as a weapon to kill. The blacks were Carlos's army, I discerned, and he was the general directing his troops. It was enough evidence against him to put him away for a very long time.

I could have just walked away, but I wanted to try to stop the killings. I yelled out, "What are you doing, Carlos?!"

He turned to face me. Instead of trying to explain what he was doing, he said, "My cover is blown, my cover is blown." He then turned to the two DGA members who seemed to be heading this squad, and said to them,

"Turn him into a junkie! No, on second thought, turn his whole family into junkies!"

I did not understand what he meant when he said his cover had been blown. He could not be working undercover, I thought, since he was in full Detroit Police uniform, so what the hell was he talking about? Was he secretly working for another agency, like the FBI? I was now burdened with the task of finding out which agency, if any, he was working for. I knew that whatever was going to happen next, the DGA would make the first move.

The cops and ambulances started to arrive. Carlos and his army dispersed, and I went back up the street to make sure the old man was all right. When I got there, I found that he had already been loaded into the ambulance. The ambulance attendants would not tell me anything about his condition. There was nothing else I could do, so I headed to A&P for dad's coffee, and then I returned home. Not knowing what Garcia had meant by telling those DGA members to go after the men in the funny hats, I decided to find out what the funny hat was called. I was sure my father would know, so I asked him, "Dad, why do those men wear those funny hats?"

"They are Shriners, Brett. The hat is called a fez."

"What are Shriners, Dad?"

"They are high-ranking Freemasons, and they do a lot to help kids. Before a person can become a Shriner he must first become a Freemason. The Shriners put on a circus named after them, called the Shrine Circus. The Circus started in 1906 here in Detroit. That's why they are called Shriners. They also support hospitals all over the world where sick children can go. They don't charge any money for the services if the child is accepted for treatment."

"Well, if the Masons do all those good things, then why would anyone want to kill the Shriners?"

"I don't know why anyone would want to kill a Mason, Brett."

"Dad, I think I have figured out who has been killing all the Masons, but I don't know what their motive would be."

"What makes you say that?"

"I kept seeing a bunch of blacks at the corner of Cass and Temple on my way to and from school. I was suspicious of why they were hanging around in this part of town. I figured maybe they were selling dope to all the junkies, because I kept seeing all these men lying in the streets. I didn't know they were Masons. I don't know how many were actually dead. I had no idea they were Masons until I was on the way to get your coffee. I caught Garcia and the blacks from the DGA killing the Shriners."

"I am going to have to call your grandfather."

It was an afterthought, but I couldn't help but wonder, *is this happening to Masons across the nation, or is it just confined to Detroit?* For what reason did the blacks hate the Masons enough to kill them, and kill so many of them?

The only thing I knew about Masons was that there were no black people who belonged to the organization.

My grandfather made the trip from Kentucky to Detroit once more when he got the news about who was killing the Masons. While he was in Detroit, he, being a Mason himself, made a trip to the Masonic Temple. While he was there, he made arrangements for me to speak to a group of Masons and tell them what was going on, so as to make them aware that this was a dangerous area for Masons.

I did speak to the Masons, but I could not tell them was why the DGA had targeted them. When my presentation was over, they all applauded me for my actions.

After the meeting with the Masons, my grandfather informed me that we would be going back to Bottom Fork so I could practice and keep my shooting skills sharp. I took that to mean that there was another fight coming and he was going to get me ready for it. The morning after arriving in Bottom Fork, we were ready to start the lesson, when a Kentucky State Police car driven by a trooper appeared out front.

I was afraid I had done something wrong, but my grandfather soothed my fears by telling me, "Brett, the trooper is here to see how well you shoot."

We began the shooting lesson. Grandpa gave me instructions for something new to do. He said, "Before firing your gun, Brett, I want you to say, 'Kentucky State Trooper. Halt or I'll shoot.' In real life, if the person you're pursuing doesn't stop, then you can fire if you feel threatened." After a few more rounds of practice, my grandpa was satisfied with my session. We decided to knock off for the day.

"Brett, there is a reason I want you to say that before you fire," my grandfather said. Then the trooper then started toward me with a Kentucky state trooper jacket and hat. They had me put the items on; they fit perfectly. I remembered my grandpa taking measurements of arms and head, but given the way things were going at the time, I thought he had measured me to fit me for a coffin. I could tell that the jacket materials were of very high quality. The hat was of a fine material also.

My grandfather then had me raise my right hand and repeat after the trooper. I was so stunned that I could hardly remember what the trooper was saying, although when he said, "I do," I did say, "I do."

Just a few months past the age of eight, I was now being sworn in as a Kentucky state trooper. I believe that my grandfather and the trooper made me a state trooper so I would legally be able to carry my guns.

"Brett, I want you to always, always remember one thing. Liars are cowards—and they are the worst kind of cowards because they're even afraid of the truth—so don't ever be a coward."

Then they took my jacket away. I hadn't had the chance to notice if there a badge was attached to it or not. In any event, I wasn't going to question my grandfather's actions. I just knew to trust his judgment and to do as he instructed me.

Chapter 18

ASSAULT ON THE CIRCUS

It was dusk, soon to be night, when I went for a walk toward the temple. At the corner of Cass and Temple, I ran into a group of detectives examining a group of bodies lying in the street. I overheard one of the detectives say, "Why are we getting so many calls on dead junkies?"

I looked around to see if I could spot any DGA members before I said something, knowing the risk I'd run if I were caught talking to the cops.

"They're not junkies; they're Shriners," I replied.

"What's your name, kid?" one of the detectives asked.

"Brett," I responded.

"How old are you, Brett?"

"Eight," I answered.

"Are you sure they were Shriners, Brett?"

"Yes, I am sure. The blacks wait for the Shriners to come out of the temple, and then they surround them and inject them with a narcotic so they look like junkies. I suppose that they then get rid of the hats so nobody knows they're Shriners. For some reason, they have declared war on the Shriners. You can't let Carlos Garcia find out I told you; otherwise, he'll have the DGA after you and me. He's helping the DGA."

"I've been a detective for twenty-three years, and now I got a kid doing what a whole team of detectives couldn't do. Brett, how would you like to help us with another case?"

"Not with the Garcia brothers still on the force. They had me stabbed, and also hurt my mother."

"Brett, we need somebody to wear a wire so we can get the head of the DGA. We've been trying to get him for years, but we don't know who he is. We need to try to bust up this gang. We'll be watching over you the whole time. Please, Brett, help us. It's the right thing, and a brave thing, to do."

"Okay, I'll help," I said reluctantly. "What do I have to do?"

"Try to think of a way to get to the gang leader, okay?"

"Okay."

"Officer Powell will set everything up. Where do you live? We'll come by to get you and put a wire on you at the station. In the meantime, see if you can find out who the leader of the gang is."

A couple of days went by. I had an idea to do something that would keep me alive once I contacted the DGA. I would offer the gold watch that my grandpa Lawson gave to my dad, in the hopes that the DGA would take the watch in return for a favor. The favor I would ask for would be for them to kill Carlos Garcia. That would give the cops a motive and would hopefully be enough to arrest all involved.

Officer Powell came by to pick me up and drive me to the station house to set up the wire. I had worn a white shirt that was loose-fitting and kind of baggy as Powell had instructed me. There was a team of a half dozen detectives working on this case. Powell began to secure the wire on me with white medical tape. As he was strapping the wire on, he said, "Brett, you are going to die. Is there anything we can do for you?"

"Yeah, get my family out of here. Force them to move if you have to." I wanted to get revenge on the DGA so bad that I was willing to die to accomplish my objective.

The detectives drove me to a section of Detroit not far from where I lived, a place where DGA was operating. Almost immediately I spotted four DGA soldiers standing on a corner. I walked over and started talking to four or five of them whose job it was to generate income for the gang. That's why I chose them to set my plan in motion.

"I need your guys' help to kill a crooked cop." I emphasized *crooked*. It must have put the gang members at ease to know I wanted a cop dead.

The one who seemed to be in charge of the group said, "What can you give us in return?"

"I got a gold watch for trade."

"Wow, a real gold watch?"

"Yeah, a real solid gold watch."

"Who's the cop?" the leader asked.

"Carlos Garcia," I replied.

"Why do you want him dead?"

"He killed my friend."

"Okay, man. Let's see the watch." I pulled the watch from my pocket and showed it to them.

"Give me the watch," the leader said.

"No. I am not dealing with you. I want to deal with the man who is in charge of the DGA. I want to make sure you guys kill the cop."

"Well, give me the watch so I can show it to him."

"*No!* You get your leader so we can make the deal first. Then I will give him the watch."

The leader then said, "I'll return shortly." He turned and briskly walked away. I was nervous while I waited for him to return, but I calmed myself by thinking that I would find out shortly if my plan was going to work. When the leader returned, he had with him a short gang member who was much older than I.

"What cop do you want dead now?" the DGA leader asked.

"Carlos Garcia. He killed my friend Manuel D, so I want him dead. Can you handle that?"

Isaac Simms walked up while I was negotiating. I knew instantly that he was there not to help me but to screw up the whole operation. He just stood there for a moment before, for a reason I was unaware of, he ripped my shirt open and exposed the wire.

I had to think fast and let the detectives know what Simms had done, so I said loudly, "Isaac, why did you rip my shirt open?" I hoped the detectives I was working with would hear me and would get Simms out of there. Then Benny Garcia showed up, obviously to help Simms in screwing things up, and to protect the gang.

I quickly explained to the DGA chief, "The box on my chest drips medicine in the wound where your guys stabbed me."

I didn't know if he bought my story or not. I had to focus on getting the gang chief to commit to killing Carlos Garcia. I pulled out the watch again, and asked the DGA chief, "Do we have a deal?"

"We got a deal!"

That's when all hell broke loose, with squad cars all over the place, along with unmarked police cars. The gang chief was stunned. He had conspired to kill a cop for money. It didn't matter whether or not Garcia was corrupt; the gang chief had accepted the payment to kill a cop. One of the detectives picked me up and started kissing me. He said, "Brett, we're not going to let you die. We're definitely not going to let you die."

I asked for my gold watch back, but the detectives said they needed to keep it as evidence. It was another sacrifice that my family would have to make for the betterment of society. I just knew I would never see that watch again. I figured I would be satisfied with the fact that I had taken down one of the most notorious gang leaders in the state. While I did not feel the bust would end all gang activity in the city, and while I didn't know if the charges would even stick, I felt I had inflicted heavy casualties on the DGA. One thing I could be sure of was that the DGA would most certainly retaliate. There would be more death to come.

It was shortly after I'd helped bust the leader of the DGA that Benny Garcia introduced me to a man named John Popovich. He was in the backseat of black limousine. As I entered the limo, Popovich asked me, "What is your name, son?"

"My name is Brett, sir."

"Brett, my name is John Popovich, but all the kids call me Poppa John."

"I am pleased to meet you, sir."

I could not help but notice the luxurious black upholstery, the power windows, and the bar. John Popovich himself dressed in an expensive-looking gray suit and a cashmere overcoat. His hair was gray, short, and neatly trimmed. His short fingernails were neatly manicured. On each pinky finger, he wore a ring with a diamond in the center, surrounded by smaller diamonds. *Maybe a gambler,* I thought to myself. The habit dated from a long way back, but gamblers often wore diamonds. If they went broke, they could always sell their diamonds.

Everything about John Popovich smelled of money, and told me he had lots of it.

After introducing himself, he asked me, "Brett, how would you like to meet the president? I can arrange for you to meet him."

In late February of 1961, just shortly after my eighth birthday and shortly after my meeting with Poppa John, Benny Garcia drove me in a Detroit squad car from Detroit to Washington, DC, to see President Kennedy. Upon arrival,

Benny took me to a stage somewhere in Washington. I was standing on the stage with Benny standing behind me, and the president in front of me, a few feet away. The president was about to award me a medal for what I believed was my actions in the Cass Corridor.

Benny whispered in my ear so the president could not hear him. "If you accept that medal, I am going to kill you."

I didn't understand why he would drive me from Detroit to Washington to get a medal and then tell me not to accept it. Nor did I understand why he wouldn't honor the president's wishes.

I didn't know what to do, so I told the president Benny had threatened me.

The president then asked me, "Do you want the medal or not?" He seemed irritated, and unconcerned about Benny's threat.

I said, "Yes, sir, I do want the medal, sir." I didn't think Benny would really kill me over the medal, especially knowing that the president had issued it to me. Plus, the president was now aware of his threat. In response, Kennedy hung the medal around my neck.

I was then taken to an office somewhere in Washington and told to wait, as the president wanted to talk to me. Soon after that, the president entered the office and asked me, "What is your name, son?"

"My name is Brett, sir."

"Do you mind if I call you Brett?"

"No, sir, I don't mind."

"Brett, you seem kind of nervous. Is something bothering you?"

"Yes, sir, I am nervous. And there is something bothering me. You are the president, and that makes you the top cop in the country. When I get back to Detroit, if the local gang finds out I was talking to you, they are going to make me have sex with the whole gang as punishment."

He responded immediately by saying, "Brett, when you get back to Detroit, if the gang tries to make you perform oral sex, I want you to tell them that you don't have sex with men, and that you like women a whole lot better."

I smiled a big smile and said, "Okay, sir, I will certainly do that. I will consider it an order."

Just then Maria walked in. She was dressed in a uniform I had never seen before. She walked over to me and said, "Brett, it is okay to talk to the president. Nothing is going to happen to you for talking to him."

"Brett, I have a problem. And sometimes adults turn to their children for fresh ideas. We have a lot of foreigners entering the country illegally. Do you have any ideas that could help me stop that?"

"Can we mine the border, sir?"

"No, Brett. There are women and children crossing the border. We don't want to hurt anybody. We just want them to come through the border legally."

"Well, sir, the first thing I would do is put up a fence so the aliens know that they have entered the country. That way they would not have the excuse that they did not know they had crossed the border and did not know they had entered the United States. If a fence could be put up, it wouldn't be so much to stop the illegals. It would be more to stop vehicles from bringing in loads of illegals and driving across the border. Besides that, sir, the fence could be built to steer the illegals into the desert. That way, they would have to bring a lot of water to make it across the desert."

"Those are all good ideas, Brett. How did you think of those things?"

"I'll tell you, sir, if you promise not to make fun of me."

"Okay, Brett, that's a deal."

"I went there, and I came back. I don't know what the technical term for it is, sir, but I call it the fourth dimension, sir. They say I have a photographic memory. What happened when you asked me if I could help is that I pictured what the Southwest must look like. I was facing north when I saw the mountain ranges to the west, and north with a wagon train moving from east to west. What were the wagon trains crossing the desert and the cattle drivers constantly looking for? They were always concerned about water."

"Brett, that's all very interesting. The government is studying people like you who have been known to project themselves to places where they have never physically been before and then become able to describe what they saw in great detail. It is called astral projection. Brett, I believe you have some sort of gift similar to that. What do you think?"

"I am really not sure, sir, but if you ever need my opinion again, I will be sure to help with whatever I can, sir."

"Brett, I am going to call on you again, but for now, I have other, official business."

With that, he ended our conversation. Benny and I headed back to Detroit.

Chapter 19

EXPENDABLE OR NOT EXPENDABLE

It was a mild evening in the first week of March when my dad and I headed out to the suburbs for one of our weekend jaunts to the drive-in. This trip, however, turned out to be quite unusual. We went to grab some popcorn, hot dogs, and colas. Shortly after we finished our snacks, my dad stunned me with his next statement.

"Brett, they want you to assassinate the president."

"Who are they?" I quizzed.

My father refused to tell me who they were. Then I asked him, "Why me?"

"Because you are good with a gun, and you are expendable."

After all my grandfather and I had done for my father and our family, my father was now telling me that I was not worthy of continuing to live.

Maria must have had her baby, I surmised, *and he loves her and her baby more than he loves us.*

I probed further, asking my dad, "Why do they want the president dead?"

His response was, "The president's back is about to snap in half. He does not want to live as a cripple for the rest of his life."

He was my father and I loved him, but I could not believe he would get me involved in the killing of the president, even if Kennedy wanted to die, which I was not buying. I was not going to humiliate my mother and her family. I wanted no part in assassinating the president. As for being expendable, all I could think of was whether or not Maria gave birth to her baby. My father had started another family with her, all the while being incapable of supporting the family he already had with my mother. I had the suspicion that he didn't care about my mom and her kids, so I was going to stay alive and see that he didn't hurt my mother anymore. I was her oldest, and losing one of her kids would devastate her. She had almost lost it after the gang rape. I figured that if I had to die, I would do so while defending her, or least while trying to do some good with my life. Given the way Carlos and his team were ganging up on my family, there was a good chance I would not make it past the third grade.

A few days after that talk with my father, I woke up in the afternoon, around three o'clock. Trying to get up, I realized instantly that I had been heavily drugged. I assumed that the DGA had done it and that they had probably used heroin or morphine. I staggered through the apartment. Wobbly, I fell to my knees, barely able to stay conscious long enough to see that my father and mother were still sleeping. That was very unusual, as my father was usually up by nine in the morning. My parents should have been up hours ago, and my father should have been at work by now. I went to the girls' room and saw that the girls were also still sleeping. This had to be the work of DGA. They had followed Carlos's orders and had drugged my entire family. They were using the same tactic they'd used on the Masons. But how did they get in the house?

Dizzy and numb from the drug, I started toward the telephone. I could not make it to the phone standing up, so I crawled my way there. I knew enough to dial the operator, after which I waited. The operator answered, saying, "AT&T. Can I help you?"

I replied, "I need the police. The blacks are trying to kill my whole family."

In less than five minutes, three squad cars arrived at the apartment. Once I let the officers in, I told them I could not wake my parents, and believed they had been drugged. One detective named Schultz asked me my name. I told him it was Brett. The police checked my parents' pulses to make sure they were still alive, and then tried to wake them up. Then they went into my sisters' room to check on them. It was then that Officer Schultz reassured me that everyone was going to be all right, but he said he needed to know what had happened.

I told him, "Somehow the DGA, I believe, switched tactics, snuck into the apartment sometime during the night, and drugged my whole family on the order of Carlos Garcia. What I can't figure out is how they got in."

"Why would they pick you, Brett?"

"The reason is that I'm the one who took down their gang leader."

"Oh my God, Brett, I didn't know it was you. Every cop in this precinct, maybe the whole Detroit police force, knows what you did, but not everybody knows what you look like. I am sorry, Brett.

"We are going to take your family to the hospital to have a doctor check all of you out and make sure you are okay."

When we got to the hospital, the medical staff began to draw blood from all of us. The test results confirmed that indeed we had been drugged.

It wasn't twenty hours later when the same thing happened. My whole family was out cold again, only this time I was wakened by a group of men and women. I asked the group, "Who are you people, and what are you doing in my house?"

One woman who was part of the group answered, "Brett, we are the United States Secret Service."

I asked her, "Where is the president?"

Suddenly one of the men who were with her spoke up and said, "This kid's the real deal! Brett, how far back can you remember?"

"I can remember when I was a really little boy, but I don't know how old I was. I can remember when my mother was potty training me. She told some of the women in my family that she started potty training all of her kids at eighteen months. Because she didn't like changing diapers, she wanted to train us as early as she could. I can remember that."

"Brett, we are here to protect your family," the woman said. I'm going to have you take a pill that will help you sleep."

"Well, you are not doing a very good job protecting us," I quipped.

She had me take the pill without water. This pill dissolved, unlike any pill I had taken before. The drug knocked me out almost instantly. I didn't know how long I had been out, but it was at least twenty-four hours before I awoke.

Schultz was back, talking to my parents. After he finished with them, he came over to me and said, "Brett, we can't watch you around the clock, but we are going to be watching your apartment. Just remember one thing, Brett: if any DGA cross the threshold of your home, they are fair game."

"You mean I can shoot them once they enter my apartment?" I asked.

"Yes, Brett, you can. Remember, we are going to do everything we can for you." Then he said goodbye and departed.

I was left with a gloomy feeling. With the Garcia brothers on the loose, I was doomed for sure. I decided that I would stop them no matter what I had to do. And I was going to protect my mother no matter what. I figured the first thing I had to do was discover how DGA members were getting into the apartment. I decided I would stay awake all night and see if they showed up. This time I would be armed. Sure enough around three o'clock in the morning, the phone started ringing. The phone kept ringing, at least thirty or forty times. That's when my little brother Dwayne answered it. After having a brief conversation, he hung the phone up, walked to the door, and opened it. There was a group of four or five DGA members standing at the threshold. I pointed my gun and ordered them to leave. When they saw the gun, they scattered.

I had at least figured out how they were getting into the apartment, but I was still puzzled about what they might have said to Dwayne to get him to open the door. I didn't have to wait long to find my answer to that, because the next night the DGA rang the phone again in the wee hours of the morning. They were persistent. This time I answered the phone. The voice on the other end of the line told me to go see who was at the door. Half asleep when I hung up the phone, I started toward the door.

It was then that my father grabbed me and said, "Don't open the door, Brett." He had his snub-nose .38. Apparently he had also heard the phone ring. We waited to see if the phone was going to ring again, but it never did. We kept watch for an hour or so to make sure the DGA would not try again to get into the apartment.

I wondered where the Secret Service agents who had said they were there to help protect us were, as I had never seen the Secret Service during any of these occurrences.

Deciding that I would have to take matters into my own hands, I set out the next morning to find some members of the DGA. I ran across two of the younger members, and I gave them a warning.

"Whatever the gang does, tell them to leave me alone, and not to enter my apartment under any circumstances."

They did not heed my warning. All I'd accomplished was to piss them off. A group of older gang members caught me on the way home. I was just outside my apartment when they drugged me. While on the ground taking another beating, I saw a black police officer confront them. He made them stop beating me.

He reached down, helped me up, and asked me, "Where do you live, son?"

"I live in the basement apartment, right down there."

He walked up to the door and knocked. My mother answered. He told her, "Lady, they are trying to kill your son."

After thanking the police officer for getting the DGA members off me, I walked down the stairs and into the apartment.

It was about three in the afternoon when about thirty DGA members showed up, but this time Carlos showed up just after they did. I could not help but think that he was going to make me fight them all. That's when a strange twist took place. He said, "Brett, there will be four squad cars that are going to pull up in front of the apartment, and one on Selden. The one that pulls up on Selden will be a black cop. I want you to shoot that cop. So shoot the black cop. Got it?"

He then handed me a .22 revolver. Seeing as I didn't trust Carlos, I couldn't understand why all of a sudden he was helping me instead of trying to get me killed. I decided I would not hurt the officer. When the cop cars showed up, and when the officer on Selden got out of his patrol car, I aimed the gun at him and fired about ten feet over his head. I saw the bullet hit the wall of the church across the street and chalk up. The cop fell down on the street, pretending to be hit. Carlos then went with me inside my apartment.

"Now, Brett, we want you to shoot anybody that comes into the apartment," Carlos said. Then he left.

Benny was standing just inside the doorway with the door wide open. A white cop was standing near the bottom of the stairs leading down to the apartment. Isaac Simms was standing in the living room. I had no clue as to what was about to happen. It was shortly afterward that several DGA members starting coming down the stairs. They tried to come into the apartment three or four at a time, but the white cop on the stairs allowed only one at a time to enter. When each man came in, I aimed at his forehead to hit him in the brain. After I had shot a good number of the DGA members who'd come to attack me, Simms and I piled their bodies away from the door. The idiots kept coming at me even though their buddies had been shot. I continued shooting them as they entered the apartment, doing this until I was out of ammo. Simms then tossed me a .38 Special. I used it to shoot, until ten of them were dead.

The other black officer came down the stairs and saw what was going on. I noticed that it was Officer Gatewood, the black cop who'd stopped the DGA members from beating me the day before. Benny aimed his gun at Gatewood.

Gatewood looked at me, and without hesitation said, "Brett, I'm going to die for you. Now you can shoot me, Benny."

That's when the white cop who was on the stairs said, "Brett, if Benny shoots him, you have to shoot Benny."

Benny then shot the black cop in the chest. The white cop on the stairs took off running. Benny, taking off after him, fired at him.

Benny soon returned, running into the apartment. I said to Benny, "Okay, Benny, get down here so I can shoot you. They said I got to shoot you."

Benny yelled, "Give me that gun," and grabbed the .38 out of my hand.

Simms and Benny began the task of cleaning up the scene by removing the bodies. I did not know what this whole crime scene was about. All I knew was that the DGA had intended to hurt me and my family. They had entered my apartment with intentions of hurting us, and they paid for it. I still did not understand what their motive was.

Benny and Carlos had helped me with this situation. Had the Secret Service intervened and told Carlos and Benny to watch over my family? I especially did not understand why the DGA members had kept coming into the apartment when the cops were already on the scene. It had to have been that Benny and Carlos made a complete one-eighty, as previously they were hell-bent on killing me and my family. Did both Carlos and Benny have federal connections? How were they going to cover up this mess with a dead Detroit cop on their hands? I would be watching the newspaper to see how the incident was reported and how officials were going to cover it up. Officer Gatewood had saved me from a horrible beating by DGA, and now he had saved me from Benny, so I at least wanted to see that his family was taken care of.

Each day brought more and more questions. All I could do was keep track of the situation in my mind. The death toll was ten DGA and one dead police officer, all of those deaths totally unnecessary.

Chapter 20

THE SECRET SERVICE WANTS ME

It was a couple of weeks after the shootings at the apartment when Benny came and got me. I had seen no report of the incident in the newspaper. I could see that Benny was going to use the same technique as Carlos had, and that was to report the incident days after it had actually happened—and at a different location. Benny was taking me to meet Poppa John again. As we walked, I decided to ask him a few questions.

"Benny, just who is this Poppa John guy, anyway?"

He replied, "Brett, he's a crime boss."

"What's a crime boss?" I asked.

"Well, he is like the head of a gang who controls the gambling, such as the daily numbers racket, horses, football cards, and other vices."

"Why are you taking me to see him today?"

"He wants you to do him a favor."

We walked around the corner. Poppa John was pulling up as we arrived. Benny walked me to the car. I got into the car and said hello. Poppa John, not one to beat around the bush, immediately started to question me about my gun skills.

"They tell me you're pretty handy with a gun, kid. How good with a gun are you?"

"I really don't like to brag, but I am really good. That's because I was trained by the best."

"I need you to shoot somebody. Do you think you could do that?" he asked.

"Well, that all depends on who it is."

"I want you to shoot the president, kid. Do you think you can do that?"

Not really wanting to assassinate the president, I had to try to get to the Secret Service and warn them that Poppa John wanted the president dead. I would not have the opportunity to do that if today I told Poppa John no. This was the second person who had asked me to kill the president. Prior to Poppa John, my father had asked that I kill the president. I couldn't help but think that my father was somehow connected to Poppa John and his gang, probably because he liked to gamble.

Taking these things into consideration, I told Poppa John, "Sure, I could do that."

"Okay. I will make the arrangements, kid, and I will get in touch with Benny. Don't tell anyone you are going to see the president."

I didn't get why Poppa John didn't want me to tell anyone about going to see the president.

A couple of days later, my dad and Virgil Powers were on the back porch talking. They called me over to them. Mister Powers asked me to sit down next to him. Right away he asked me, "Brett, when you go to see the president, see if you can have him get my nephew Gary out of Russia. Please, Brett. I'll give you money. I'll even give you my car. We want him out of Russia real bad."

"I thought Gary was your son." I said.

Brett there are three men named Gary Powers. One is my son and one is my nephew and both are named after my brother.

I couldn't figure out how he knew I would be going to see the president, unless my dad had told him. I loved Gary and his sister, Justine, so I replied, "Mister Powers, I will try, but I don't think the president is the problem. No matter what I do, the Russians still have to be willing to letting him go."

"Brett, at least try to get him out of there."

"Mister Powers, if the president will cooperate, I will get him out."

"Thank you, Brett."

I left him with the knowledge that I was going to do everything possible to get Gary out of Russia.

It was early morning in April when Benny came to get me and take me to Washington. Before we left for DC, we stopped to pick up Isaac Simms, who was wearing a pair of my dad's safety glasses. He said to me, "I want you to tell the president I am your father."

"So you want me to lie to the president?"

"Just do as you are told," he said loudly.

The three of us--Benny, Isaac Simms, and I—traveled by police car Benny drove. We arrived in Washington. At the White House, Benny identified himself. We were taken immediately to a room adjoining the president's office. As Simms had instructed me, I introduced Isaac to the president as my father. The president then took Isaac into his office. Isaac emerged about ten minutes later and said, "I asked the president to get the nuclear missiles out of Turkey." I did not understand why a Detroit police officer would do such a thing.

It was after Simms was done talking to the president that I was taken into Kennedy's office. "Nice to see you again, Brett. Are there any favors I can do for you?"

"No, sir, there is nothing at the moment. But there is one I could do for you."

"What would that be, Brett?"

"Sir, I am going to be putting myself and my family in jeopardy by saying this, but there is a plan to assassinate you. The man whom I introduced to you as my father isn't my father. He is a Detroit police officer."

"Brett, I am going to put your mind at ease. The Secret Service is aware of that threat. I am sure they will protect me. As far as the cop, why would he do that?"

"Sir, I don't want to trust them, but they are cops and I have to listen to them."

"What does your father really do?"

"He works at General Motors, sir."

"What's his real name?"

"Burt," I answered.

"What is your middle name, Brett?"

"It's Donahue, sir. I am sure we have some Irish in our blood, sir, but my grandfather Holbrook says we are part Indian. My family comes from the mountains, and there are a lot of Irish, Scots, and Indians in the hills of Appalachia."

"You are part Indian, Brett?"

"That is what my grandfather has told me, sir."

"Brett, did you know that the Indians gave millions of dollars to the Irish during the Irish Potato Famine? The Indians are loved by the Irish people because the former kept millions of the latter from starving to death."

"No, sir, I had never heard that before."

"Do you know my middle name, Brett?"

"Yes I do, sir. It is Fitzgerald."

"Why do you think my parents named me that, Brett?"

"Well, sir, a lot of parents give their children a middle name of the surname of the mother I would be guessing by saying that Fitzgerald was probably your mother's maiden name."

"That is absolutely correct, Brett. Why do you think your mother named you Donahue?"

"It was not because her maiden name was Donahue, but because she just liked the name."

"What is your mother's maiden name?"

"It is Holbrook, sir."

"Now, Brett, why do you think I asked you all those questions?"

"Sir, I think you are being a little sly with me. What I hope is going to happen is that you are going to confront Officer Simms and ask him why he would lie to the president of the United States, which would bail me out and keep Simms off my back." He just smiled and asked me another question.

"What does your mother's father do for a living, Brett?"

"He is a coal miner, sir. As a matter of fact, both of my grandfather's work in the coal mines."

"Brett," he said, "where does your grandfather Holbrook live?"

"He lives in Kentucky, sir," I replied.

"I know who your grandfather is. Are you familiar with the Molly Maguires, Brett?"

"No, sir, are they a singing group, sir?"

He chuckled a little and then answered, "No, Brett. They were a secret society made up of Irish coal miners in Pennsylvania who stood up to the mining management for the injustices perpetrated against them."

The president was making it clear to me that he was definitely of Irish descent and that he was proud of the fact. When he told me that he knew my grandfather, he made me feel that I should be proud to be related to such a good man. He'd made it sound as if the two of them were old school buddies.

President Kennedy ordered someone to get my grandfather on the phone. A minute or two later, an aide announced that my grandfather was on the line. The president and my grandpa Holbrook held a conversation for about five minutes, and then Kennedy handed me the phone. My conversation took only a minute or so. During that time, my grandfather strictly ordered me not to accept any favors from the president.

After getting off the phone with my grandfather, I said to Kennedy, "Sir, my grandpa told me not to accept any favors from you, but I am going to skirt the issue because, in this case, I feel he has made a bad decision. He is not informed of all the facts. I am going to ask you for a favor, not for me, but for the Powers family. I would like you to get a friend of our family out of Russia. In exchange, I won't ask you do anything for me. Although I would like to, sir, I have to do what my grandfather told me to do."

There were a lot of things I would have liked to have asked the president to do. Feeling that my grandfather's demand was an offense to the president, I figured that my reply would soften the blow. I was slowly learning the ropes of interpersonal relationships and getting a worldly education. One of the things I had learned so far was that people usually make errant decisions based on piss-poor information. I felt that in the situation maybe I was right; maybe my grandfather didn't have all the facts.

"Who is the friend you want out, Brett?"

"It is Gary Powers, sir. He is the U2 pilot who was shot down over Russia."

"What would you suggest I do to get Gary out?"

"We have traded spies for spies before, sir. Maybe you could trade a spy for him, sir?"

"Brett, I can't promise you I can get Gary out, but I will look into the situation."

A few minutes later, a general came in and said to the president, "Sir, we are ready."

Putting his hand on my shoulder, Kennedy said to the general, "Have the Secret Service escort him down." I was escorted away from the president's office and then taken down a few flights of stairs that led into an underground bunker that was three levels below ground. The bunker was divided into very large rooms. There was nothing decorative on the walls. As far as I could tell, one room had a large amount of communications equipment. Still, I had no clue where I was.

Shortly after my arrival at the bunker, the president walked in. No one had given me any information about why we were there or where we were. It was obviously a secret. The president took a seat behind a desk. There was a large speaker to my right, hanging on a wall. Kennedy then called me over, telling me to sit across from him.

"Brett, do you remember when I asked you about the border with Mexico? You said you'd been to Mexico. Isn't that right?"

"Yes, sir, I remember."

"Tell me what you see now, Brett."

"I don't see much of anything right now."

"You see nothing at all, Brett?"

"Well, I am getting a little something. I am getting a picture of beach and water, and long grass about waist high. No houses or buildings around."

"It's Cuba, Brett. We are invading it."

"Did Cuba do something to us, sir?"

"No, Brett. The Communists have taken it over. We don't want a Communist country ninety miles off our coast. The Cuban rebels and the CIA want us to give them air support, but the invasion is supposed to be a secret."

146

"But, sir, won't we have to invade Cuban airspace? We have been through that once already, when Gary got shot down over Russia."

"That is exactly the point, Brett."

"Sir, does Cuba have attack aircraft?"

"No."

"Any air defense systems?"

"They have none, Brett."

"Sir, I don't want to do this anymore."

"What did you see? Brett, it is very important that you advise me, as doing so is in the best interests of your president and your country."

"Well, sir, I am sure of one thing: Cuba is not looking for a fight. Even though they are now Communists, they have been a peaceful nation. If you send air support, the whole world will be able to see any aircraft, and the invasion will no longer be a secret. Not only that, but if the rebels are not completely successful, they are going to be fighting in the streets. We will have no idea who is on our side and who is not. If we do send air support, Castro is not going to take this lying down. We are going to end up getting sucked into a war in our own hemisphere. The Soviets will be able to secure a military base and a foothold just off our coast. I don't want to put millions of people's lives at risk by giving you an erroneous opinion. Besides, we can't start a war with every little country that wants to go communist, sir, especially if they are not taking a militarily aggressive stand toward the United States."

He said, "The CIA is asking for the air support, Brett. What is your opinion?"

It was then that I realized the invasion had already begun, which gave me insight into why the president was consulting me. I believe he was testing me to see if I actually had visually just gone to the Cuba. I simply envisioned what Cuba would look like, as I had explained to the president before. He might not have known exactly how I could do such a thing, but he was sure that I was being truthful with him; that I was an all-American child with a vast knowledge of war, its strategies, the war machines, and the consequences of war; and that my loyalty to him and my country was unsurpassed. It was after these thoughts passed through my mind that I answered the president.

"How long will it take for Tuskegee to get to Cuba, Mr. President?" Realizing the invasion was already taking place, I believed that time was now a factor.

"If I decide to send Tuskegee, they are staged and ready to go. They can be there in ten minutes."

My response was immediate. "Send them, sir. We will have to face the consequences later."

The president then put the battle feed on the loudspeaker. The reply to the news that he was sending air support came back over that loudspeaker: "We don't want any niggers behind our asses."

I did not understand why the CIA responded as they had. I could now hear the small-arms fire. Then I heard a different voice say, "We got fried fish."

"Sir, if the CIA and the Cuban rebels are being overwhelmed, air support is not going to help them. I believe they have a spy among them. If an invading force such as the United States military gets beat by a ragtag force like the Cuban military, something is wrong, sir. I feel the Cubans had to be tipped off. Sir, they got to the invasion site way too fast and were able to concentrate their efforts on the invading forces. Sir, to save further bloodshed, I feel you should order them to surrender. This will save as many lives as is possible at this point."

We moved over to another desk. The president had one of the generals who had been in the communications room to come over to us and join the conversation.

For some odd reason, I had a knack for being able to predict what our enemies were going to do next. I did not know how I had this ability, but it was something that even the president recognized.

"What do you think Castro will do next, Brett?" Kennedy asked.

"Sir, he is probably going to ask one of his Communist buddies for military support."

"What kind of support?"

"He will probably ask for fighter aircraft, an anti-aircraft defense system, and in return, the Soviets will probably want him to let them set up nuclear missiles in Cuba."

"What kind of response to the actions taken by the Soviets do you think we should send, Brett?"

"Well, once we know for sure, and once we have proof the Soviets were bringing missiles to install in Cuba, can we surround the whole island with naval ships so no one gets in and no one gets out? That way, they can't export or import anything either."

"Brett, that's called a naval blockade. We will be able to do a blockade. Let me ask you: how did you acquire such a vast knowledge of military affairs asked the General?"

"General, sir, my father was in the air force. He was proud to have served his country. He was a good soldier. Wanting me to be good soldier also, he took me to see almost every war movie ever released. I learned quite a lot." It had become apparent that my father had done a good job.

"Brett, what makes you think Castro is going to ask the Soviets for help?" the general queried.

"Well, sir, I am a kid. I think like a kid. If you have ever been bullied and beaten up by a group of kids, then you know that what you do next is gather a bunch of your friends and beat up the kids who beat you up. Then what happens is that the bully's ringleader gets more of his friends, and you get more of your friends, and then you've got full-blown war. We tried to bully Castro on his playground, and now he is going to do everything he can to see that we don't do it again."

The general then said, "Brett, I have never met a kid quite like you. You are real asset to your country. All I can say is, thank God for war movies." He then walked off into the Situation Room and began chewing out his staff in a loud voice.

I heard him telling them, "There are some of the most brilliant military minds in the world in this room, but I have an eight-year-old kid who the president thinks is clairvoyant and who is telling me what Castro is going to do next. The whole problem is he is absolutely right. He has outthought all of us. The only thing I can say is that I am glad he is on our side."

The president had me escorted back to his office. He must have had more than one office, I thought, as I had no idea what building we were in. Soon after, he himself entered the office. Sitting down, he told me, "Brett, I am going to do something for you." He reached into his desk drawer, pulled out a wallet, positioned a badge in one of its slots, and handed the wallet to me. "Brett, I want you to work with the Secret Service. If you need to see me, you just show the Secret Service your badge."

I was standing outside the president's office when two officers walked by. I heard only part of their conversation. One of them said, "Now he's listening to a kid."

Shortly afterward, another officer walked by and said, "Brett, around here we call the president Jack, and *Jack* is short for 'jackass.'"

I felt something was drastically wrong when the president's men were calling their commander in chief a jackass. This man had humiliated the president right in front of him, not caring whether the president had heard him or not. I felt partly responsible, but then again, I had done only what the president had asked. Infuriated, I asked the president in a raised voice, "Sir, why do you let them talk to you like that? You are their boss, sir."

I could tell that Kennedy was extremely upset, because he took his pencil, slammed the eraser end on his desk, flipped the pencil over, and slammed the point on his desk. He kept repeating these actions over and over, not saying anything. He was really, really hot. Now I felt I was saddled with yet another task, namely, figuring out why the military men were treating him this way, why had they disrespected him in such a manner? I already had one lead, Benny Garcia. I didn't know how, but I knew that somewhere along the line, Benny had a hand in this.

Soon after my meeting with Kennedy, I was taken back to Detroit. Immediately upon my arrival there, Benny took me to see Poppa John once again. I knew I was going to get the third degree regarding why I hadn't killed the president, but I was prepared.

"Well, why isn't the president dead?" Poppa John asked.

"Sir, there are too many Secret Service around him, and I am sure there were cameras all over the place. I don't want to get shot just because you want the president dead."

"Well, the president was supposed to take back Cuba for us. I want him dead, and I want you to do it."

"Poppa John, the president tried to send the CIA, who were backed up by Cuban rebels, to invade Cuba. Somehow, someway, somebody tipped off the Cubans that we were coming. Kennedy did all he was able to do without starting a nuclear war with the Soviets. If that happens, there will not be a United States, let alone a Cuba. Now, why do you want me to do something I don't want to do, and something that is not good for you and not good for the country?"

"Kid, the president wants to die!" Poppa John then ordered me out of the car. As I got out of the car, I heard him tell Benny, "Kill him."

I started walking back to my apartment, knowing that yet another man wanted me dead. I was getting a little tired of men who had no respect for human life. Death seemed so simple to them, and it was. All that certain men had to say was, "Kill him," and the act would be done. It seemed to me that men like this solved all their problems with killing people who got in their way. Men like that reminded me of tyrants who ruled in medieval Europe, or of spoiled children who did not get their way. Instead of crying, they ordered someone's death. *They are not men,* I thought. *A real man would not only spare another's life but also would do everything he could to help his fellows stay alive.*

The way I saw it, everyone should do everything within their power to make as many friends as they possibly can because it is certain that we all make enough enemies without really trying—and there are more than enough enemies to go around. The only thing I could hope for was that Poppa John would have a change of heart; otherwise, I was a dead man. I did not know what the future had in store for me, but I was sure of my faith in God. I knew that he would watch over me.

Chapter 21

DETROIT GANGSTER ALLIANCE SEEKS REVENGE

As I was walking back from school one day, I noticed a line of DGA members on the same side of the street as my apartment. As I approached my apartment, they began razzing me. One of them asked, "Brett, are you talking to the cops?"

I did as the president suggested and said, "No, I am not, because I don't like sex with men. I like sex with women a whole better!" Amazingly, this reply left them speechless. It reassured me that the president was a very smart man who knew what he was talking about.

I was about to enter my apartment when Maria walked up to me and said she had someone she wanted me to meet. I walked with her over to where the man was standing, near where the DGA had been waiting for me. He was a tall man, about 6'2" or so, very lean and with dark hair. Obviously he was the type who kept himself in shape. He was wearing the same sort of uniform I had seen Maria wearing when I went to see the president. It resembled a navy uniform, with stripes on the sleeves like high-ranking naval officers wore.

Curious, I asked him, "Are you in the navy, sir?"

"No, I am the Secret Service. Where is your badge, Brett? I need you to go get it and come back here."

"Okay, I'll be right back." I rushed back to the apartment and then returned with my badge.

"Did you get it?"

"Yes."

"I need to show you something, so let me see your badge. Now I want you to take your badge, hold it like this so everybody can see it, and shout real loud, 'I'm the United States Secret Service.' And keep saying it while you walk down the street."

I did as he'd told me to do. I walked in front of the DGA members. After I'd taken a few steps, one of the DGA grabbed my badge and took off with it running. I was extremely pissed and disappointed as well. It showed me exactly why blacks were hated so much. They took whatever they wanted. Upon seeing something they wanted, they would just take it.

The man then pulled out another badge. He said, "Now, Brett, I want you to do the same thing with this badge."

I did as he had told me. This time no DGA member grabbed the badge. I did not understand why the man had me do the things he had me do. I was upset that my badge was gone. He told me to keep the badge that he had given me.

My reply was, "No, I want the badge President Kennedy gave me." I headed back to my apartment, dejected about the prospect of never seeing my badge again.

As I approached the man and Maria, I was stopped by an elderly man who asked, "Are you Brett?"

"Yes, I am."

He then started screaming at me, "I'm Gary Powers' uncle Gary. He was named after me. You leaked information that got Gary shot down." He then turned sideways and kicked me karate style in the face.

The man with Maria, who saw what was happening, told Gary's uncle, "Sir, I'm with the government. We leaked that information."

Gary's uncle, realizing he had been wrong about me, leaned over and said, "Brett, I'm going to die for you. I don't ever want you to ever forget the name Gary Powers. Gary was from Pound, Virginia. I am going to get the city to put up a sign that says, 'Pound, Virginia, was the home of Gary Powers,' so you don't ever forget the name Gary Powers. Brett, promise me you won't forget him."

"Sir, Gary is my friend. I am never going to forget him." I didn't mention to this man that I had already talked to the president about getting Gary out of Russia. If dying for me was his way of apologizing for kicking me in the face, then that was the way things were going to have to be. I did not want him dead, nor did I want anybody in Gary's family dead. Gary's uncle's death would be totally unnecessary.

I didn't understand any of what had just happened, from losing my badge, to the government leaking information, to a pilot getting shot down. It was information with which I would do what I did best, and that was remember, until I got enough information to figure out what it all meant.

I went back to my apartment to figure out how to get my badge back.

There was a knock at the door around 8:30 in the morning. As my dad answered it, I came up alongside him. It was Maria, who had a big smile on her face. She reached out and handed me my badge. I was so overjoyed that I hugged her, thanking her for getting my badge back. I had my dad put my badge away somewhere safe in the house, a location that he was the only one who would know about, so I would never lose it again. DGA's grabbing my badge taught me a valuable lesson. From now on, if I did anything at all for the Secret Service, I would do so without carrying my badge. That badge would not exist in my mind. I would do all my fighting without showing it to anyone else.

It was early May. The DGA had pretty much left me alone, probably, I thought, because of the Secret Service incident. I had made arrangements to meet my friend Timothy in the park. He and I were standing on the street when we saw that a group of DGA had gathered on the other side of the street outside the door of what I thought was a part of the Masonic Temple. I was curious as to what they were doing there. After crossing the street, I walked into that building. There stood a cop asking some boys questions and having them sign some papers. I did not fully understand what was going on. The cop asked me my name, and I told him my name. For whatever reason, he then asked me my grandfather's name and where he lived. I told him the information he requested, and then I mentioned to another officer that my grandfather was a charter member of the Masons.

Charter member, I pondered, *whatever that is. It must have some sort of ranking within the Masons, because my grandfather is a Mason.* The police must have been running some sort of sting. I wanted no part of it. I started back toward the door. As I was heading out, one of the cops told me not to go outside.

"I am not afraid of them." I then walked out the door. I was standing outside for about a minute when I saw Benny pulling up in a Dearborn squad car. Suddenly I was hit in the back of the head with what felt like a sledgehammer. I blacked out for a second or two and did not remember falling down, but I now was lying on the sidewalk with my tongue hanging out, and scraping grit off the sidewalk.

The cop who had been inside came up to me while I lay on the ground. He said, "Brett, you have been shot. Is there a message you want to get to anybody?"

When I heard the cop say that, I thought I was probably a goner.

"Tell the gang that I was trying to help them get their rights. Abraham Lincoln was born in Kentucky, and so was I."

Just then another gang member came running up with a gun. The cop told him not to shoot me on the ground. The gun was enough reason for the officer to shoot at the DGA, so he began shooting sporadically into the crowd, all the while shouting, and "Abraham Lincoln was born in Kentucky! Did any of you know that?!"

As I lay there, I felt the pain grow. It now felt like someone was drilling a hole into the front part of my head a few inches above my temple. This was accompanied by what felt like an electric shock, like the one I had gotten when I stuck my finger in a wall socket in my apartment. By this time, Benny was out of his squad car. I thought that it was Benny who had shot me. As I lay on the street near death, I thought, *Man that was a fast shot. From what I have seen of Benny's gun skills, he did not appear to be that fast.*

It was then that Benny picked me up and carried me to the waiting ambulance, while the other cop did something unusual. He yelled out, "Don't let him die, Carlos." This meant one thing to me: that Benny and Carlos kept the other cops confused as to which one was Carlos and which one was Benny. This way, they could keep any witness against them off balance, thereby leading any witness to misidentify them.

The attendants loaded me up. I was unconscious within a minute or two. I awoke in a hospital; I didn't know which. And I had no idea how long I had been unconscious. It would come to pass that throughout the whole time I was conscious, my parents would not come to see me. The only ones who were ever in my room were Simms and Maria. I suspected they were keeping the shooting a secret for some reason.

The doctors said that they were going to let me rest for a few weeks. One day as I lay in my hospital bed, a doctor came into my room, which was a private one. He first explained what was wrong with me, telling me that I had suffered brain trauma and that they were going to put something called a shunt in head to drain the fluid off my brain. Then he ordered me to stand up so he could check my motor skills. I tried walking, but I was unable to, as my body shook violently and I was very unsteady on my feet. It was as if I were an old man with Parkinson's disease. I thought, *Oh no, I am never going to walk properly again, or maybe not at all.* The doctor had me sit down, and examined my head wound again. About a week later I regained the ability to walk normally.

A few days after that, I was feeling more like myself. A detective from the Detroit Police Department came to see me about the shooting. He started questioning me.

"Brett, do you recall anything about the shooting?"

"All I remember is Benny Garcia was getting out of a police car. The next thing I knew, I was knocked down to the ground. I saw Benny reaching for his gun, but I don't think the shot came from the back."

"Brett, we want you to say it was Simms. That way, we can get rid of him."

"That would be telling a lie, which I won't do even though I don't like him. If you guys need to get rid of him, then fire him."

"We are getting rid of him, one way or another." The detective then walked out of the room.

After spending six weeks or so in the children's hospital recovering from the gunshot wound, I was released.

The detective who had visited me was true to his word. Simms came by the apartment and told me, "Brett, I lost my job because of you. I'm not a cop anymore. I need you to come with me. And bring your gun."

"You put me in jail for three days, and you did all that crap to my mother. Now you are blaming me because you got kicked off the force? I can tell you, Isaac, I didn't lie when they questioned me. I didn't lie."

I did not understand why he was blaming me. Knowing that he would find a way to hurt me if he really wanted to, I reluctantly went with him. When we got to his car, I saw that Rico was waiting for us.

Simms drove us to an area I was not familiar with. I asked him, "Where are we, Isaac?"

"We are in Royal Oak, Brett." He pulled up to an apartment that was similar to the one I lived in. Once we had walked up to the front door, he opened the screen door. The entrance door was already open. There did not seem to be anyone home.

"I need you to shoot through the screen," Simms ordered.

Doing as he said, I shot through the screen. He then told me to shoot at the telephone pole in front of the building, mentioning that I should aim low, about shoulder height. Again, I did as he said. Then he took me to a space between the building we had just been in and the building next door to it. All of sudden, I heard gunshots. Hearing one bullet ricochet off the building, I turned around to see Rico. It was Rico whom Simms had told to shoot at me. The shots I had heard were intended for me.

Simms yelled at Rico, "Your hand was shaking so bad, you couldn't even hit him from fifteen feet away. He's just a little boy, but he can shoot a lot better than you. You better get off that dope, Rico, or you're going to die."

I didn't know for sure, but unlike Simms, I didn't think Rico was trying to kill me. Given the shots he'd fired, I thought Rico had missed me on purpose.

Simms walked over to the telephone pole, the one that he had told me to put a couple of rounds into. He started digging my bullets out of the pole. They were not in very deep because I'd fired them from the low-power .22-caliber pistol I had with me, the gun that my grandfather had given me. I was thoroughly confused as to why Simms dug those slugs out.

Chapter 22

VIOLENT DEATH OF CINDY O'CONNELL

In June, about two weeks after I had been released from the hospital, Simms came to my apartment and told me he needed me to go with him. Knowing he was dangerous, and worried that he might do something to my mother, I agreed to go with him. We walked down Cass, where his car was parked. I asked, "What are you going to do for a job, Isaac?"

"I asked O'Connell for a job working for the Southgate police. He said no, so I killed his daughter."

"You mean you killed Cindy?"

"Yeah, I shot her. It was a good shot, too. I shot her right through the fence."

First they killed Manuel D, and now they had killed Cindy. I could not believe Simms had killed another cop's daughter. Even worse, he had gotten away with it!

As near as I could figure things, Simms, Garcia, and Benny were somehow working as a team together. But why had they targeted students from Burton? I was unsure at this stage what role Maria was playing in this operation.

As we got to his car, I asked, "Where are we going, Isaac?"

He replied, "I am taking you to Mexican Town," an area in Detroit off Bagley near where my aunt Lydie lived.

All night long, Simms had me sitting on a crate between the buildings, trying to make me perform oral sex on men and boys who walked by. When I refused, he slapped me upside the head. When he tried to get me to do something, I kept my mouth tightly closed. Why Simms was making me do this, I didn't know. I don't know why he hated hillbillies so much. Since I was a pretty fast runner, I thought about running away from him, but I didn't because I didn't know how to get back home. Another factor was my thought that the maniac might shoot me.

A stray cat had wandered by. I held her on my lap, just petting her. She began to purr loudly. It was as if she were telling me, "I've been looking for someone like you to love me. Please don't stop petting me." She sat there serenely, no scratching, no clawing, and no trying to get away. I kept petting her throughout the night. I knew in my heart that she was content just sitting there. It was as if she'd never had anyone to care about her before me and she knew that I felt I had no one at the moment that cared about me. It was as if Jesus had sent her to console and comfort me, as if she was there to let me know that Jesus loved me. I thought about my grandfather's abilities with animals and considered that maybe I had inherited a part of his ability. It was as if the cat was the only friend in the world who cared anything about me at that point in time. I named her Patches because she was a calico.

I did get some sleep sitting in that upright position, but not much. More times than not, I fell on the ground.

Then finally someone came by who knew me. It was Darrell from the old neighborhood in Mexican Town. Exactly where we were now was a mystery to me, but we had to be near Mexican Town. About an hour after Darrell found me, Maria came by. Although I disliked her, I could not have been happier to see her. She went around the corner of a building and returned with a police officer.

The officer asked, "Brett, what do you want us to do with Simms?"

I said, "Take him to jail." The police left with Simms in tow.

Maria approached me a few moments later and said, "Brett, your family is the Klan," which I didn't understand. Then once again she turned the corner of the building.

Suddenly, Simms turned the corner. He got on his knees, banging the sidewalk with his hand, sobbing, and begging me to forgive him. He begged me over and over to forgive him. He even began to cry, so I knew he was feeling remorseful. Not wanting to hear his pleas, I turned my back to him, telling him I did not even want to look at him.

Maria came back to get me. She took me to one of Detroit's many precincts. Which one, I didn't have a clue—and I did not care. I just wanted some rest. The cops had brought the cat with them, and another little boy, much younger than I. They had him hold my cat as they took a picture of him.

It was a week later, on June 23, 1961, when I saw a headlining story in *The Detroit Free Press* about two cops who had been shot in Royal Oak. When I looked at the pictures of the two officers, I saw that one of them was the police officer whom Benny had shot; the one had died for me at my apartment. One of the black officers was Officer Gatewood, so it was a positive identification. The other was the officer over whose head I'd fired so as to avoid hurting him. I was finding out little pieces of information at a time about how Team Garcia was operating. The story reported that the date of Gatewood's murder was June, but he had really been shot in March. The newspaper reported was that the crime scene was in Royal Oak, not Detroit. The next step was to blame a completely innocent black man named Biddleman. The paper reported that Biddleman had no recollection of the incident at all. It was obvious to me why he could not remember: because he had not committed the crime Benny shot Gatewood. I now understood why Simms had taken me to Royal Oak. He had set up the crime scene to make it look like I was the shooter of the two cops. I believe he took the bullets out of the pole so he could say that they had come from the shooter's gun. One thing that was becoming quite clear to me was that the Garcia team was willing to send an innocent man to jail in order to remain free. And they had no problem killing kids if they decided they needed to do so in order to stay out of jail.

It was almost the end of June when Simms came by the apartment and said, "Brett, you need to come with me. DGA is coming for you."

I did not trust him, but something in his voice, a sense of urgency and desperation, made me comply. He took me to another city, I don't know where, and then to a house there. He went in alone. Once he came back, he said, "Brett, I have to hide you out with this lady. She runs a home for unwed mothers. No one will look for you here." He then took me inside and introduced me to the woman who ran the home.

She introduced herself. "My name is Lucille, but everyone calls me Lucy. What is your name, young man?"

"My name is Brett."

"Now, Brett, you can't go outside now. We don't want anyone to know you're here," Simms said.

Three days after Simms took me to the home, Rico came by the home. I don't know how he knew where I was. He injected me with some kind of narcotic, coming back each day for about a week to do the same thing. Not only that, but he started the same routine he had used with Justine. He was raping women in the home, and, as with Justine, the women he raped blamed me. I could not figure out how he was getting them to blame me.

Since more than one woman had yelled rape, Lucy had Simms move me. This time he took me to another home, only this time he told me what city I was in, a city named Springwells Township, on a street named Holly.

"Brett, this house is your house. It was my father's house. My father and I want you to have it."

"Well, Isaac, I wouldn't want to take something from you without paying for it. I'm sure my father would buy the house from you."

"Brett, they are going to kill your family. They are going to spare you only because you know how to use a gun. Try not to stay outside for long periods of time."

Saddened, I turned and went into the house. It was a disaster area. There was no electricity, no television, and no food, and garbage was strewn throughout. The only thing that was working was the water. I was alone and separated from my family. I had no idea where Springwells Township was in relation to the Cass Corridor. It could have been twenty or thirty miles back to the Corridor for all I knew. How was I supposed to get back there? While I was at this house in Springwells Township, Benny and Maria took turns bringing me food. Usually the food consisted of a hamburger, fries, and a Coke, but sometimes it was Coney Island hot dogs.

Four days had gone by. I was trying to keep out of sight and maintain a low profile. I spent my days alone, with not one person to talk with. One day I decided to chance it and remedy this situation by venturing outside. I walked down the block, when I saw a teenager delivering newspapers. Spotting me, he came up to me and asked, "Hey, kid, what's your name?"

I replied, "My name is Brett." Then I asked, "What's yours?"

"I go by the name Zee."

"Is that your real name?" I asked.

"Don't worry about it, kid. Just call me Zee. Where do you live, kid?"

"Well, I'm not living here, but I am staying in the two-story pink and white house right over there."

"Well, here, take this paper and give it to your parents to read."

"My parents are not staying with me. And I can't pay you for the paper."

"Don't worry about it. I always get extras to give away. That way, if people like the paper, they start buying from me. I am the top paperboy in the country. I've won a few trips on account of signing a lot of new subscribers to the paper. I won a trip to Chicago, Washington, and New York. I've signed up quite a few people to take the paper. So, you are staying by yourself?"

"Well, yes, in a way. A group of cops brought me here, but don't say anything to anybody because they might hurt you and me both." After a pause, I added, "It was nice meeting you. I hope you win some more trips."

"Okay, kid, I'll check on you to make sure you are all right. And I will leave a paper for you every day to read. If the cops move your family in, tell them to get the paper from me."

When he told me that, I understood why he was the top in his field.

I walked to the stairs of the front porch and sat down to read the paper Zee had given me. As fate would have it, when I leafed through the paper I saw an article reporting that eight hundred and ninety-six Masons had died statewide. The article did not say how many had died suspiciously, but I thought that over eight hundred was an extremely high number. I could not help but think how many had been killed by DGA. Had the DGA branched out to other parts of the state?

It was just a few days later when I saw a headline that was just as shocking. It read, "Cop's gun goes off, kills' daughter across the street." Officer O'Connell's recollection was very sketchy at best. The story reported that all he could remember was that he was cleaning his gun. First off, a police officer would never, ever clean a gun while it was loaded. Second, a bullet traveling inside his house would definitely have hit one or more walls before hitting his daughter. Third, Simms had already confessed more than a month ago, when he'd set up that crime scene. Team Garcia was going to make Officer O'Connell go through his whole life thinking that he had killed his daughter, when in actuality it was Team Garcia. Cindy had been my friend and I respected her father, and now she was another victim of the Garcia brothers.

Chapter 23

DEATH OF JOHNNY DOE

The next day, Benny came by the Holly house with my food. As soon he left, some members of the DGA showed up. The locks on the front and back doors were not very secure. The DGA had forced their way through the front door. I was too little to stop them. It was then that I realized how good their surveillance was. They had tailed Benny, a person who was trained to recognize when he was being tailed and to foil anyone's attempt to follow him. This break-in also made me realize how badly the DGA wanted me dead. Now I was stuck. I had no way of getting away and no phone to use to call for help. The DGA members immediately grabbed me, injected me with a drug, and forced me into the bedroom. They left shortly after, knowing that either Maria or Benny would be coming. Also, this was a white neighborhood; their staying there would certainly raise suspicions. They had injected me with enough drugs to knock me out until the next day.

When Maria came to feed me the next day, I told her, "DGA comes by after you leave." I also told her that I thought they had tailed Benny.

After she left, some DGA members showed up. This time there was at least thirty of them. Some were across the street in the abandoned two-story pink house, and about a dozen or more were on the front porch of the house where I was staying. They were shooting drugs right out in the open. There must have been a hundred syringes laying on the ground in front of the porch.

Maria and Carlos turned the corner of the house. They had come the back way across the alley, showing up unexpectedly. Carlos looked around, saw what was going on, pulled out his gun, and asked me, "Have you been doing drugs, kid?"

"No. The blacks are the ones doing all the drugs. They hold me down and forcefully inject me with a drug."

Then one of the white kids I had been friendly with walked over to us. Carlos Garcia said to my friend, "This gun is a .44 Magnum. It will destroy your whole head." He put the gun up to the kid's face so the barrel was touching his cheek. Suddenly, for no reason, he pulled the trigger.

In horror, I looked at my friend's head. It was nothing more than a mass of blood, bone, and flesh. His skull must have been splintered into a thousand pieces. It was if someone had cut the back of his head open, removed the skull through the incision, and then dropped it so it would splatter all over the lawn. The boy's mouth, which normally was able to open three to four inches, was now open a foot or more. His features were distorted much like a reflection in

175

the mirrors of a carnival funhouse. It was as if he had screamed a silent scream one last time. Seeing his head gave me another reminder that there was a war going on. He was another innocent victim of this war.

Then it was my turn. Carlos put the gun up to my face and held it there for a long ten seconds. My legs were getting wobbly, but I kept telling myself to hang on and to be a man until the end.

That's when he broke the silence and said, "Kid, I don't know what it is about you." He holstered his gun. "This is a job for Simms." He then turned and walked away.

Not wanting to make a mistake when it came time to identify the cop who had just shot my friend, I asked Maria, "Which cop was that?"

"That cop was Carlos."

"Which Carlos was it?" I asked, not accepting anything less than a 100 percent positive identification and a full name.

"It was Carlos Garcia."

I now had a 100 percent positive identification.

The gang members had left the scene as soon as they heard the gunshot. A police car soon pulled up. As I walked to greet the cop, my legs were rubbery, but I had to hang on long enough to tell the cops what had happened.

As the cop was getting out of the car, I told him, "Garcia shot my friend with a .44."

The cop asked me my name, looked over the scene, and asked, "What is your friend's name, Brett?"

It then came to me that I was traumatized by what had happened and I couldn't hold up any longer. My legs giving out from under me, I blacked out. I awoke smelling an awful odor that smelled like ammonia. The cop said it was smelling salts. I don't remember much of what happened after that except that I went to bed to rest. I wasn't able to remember my friend's name, so I would refer to him from then on as "Johnny Doe."

It was the following day when Isaac Simms and Maria came by the house to gather information about the DGA's tactics and what they were doing to me. I told them that the gang members usually came by when I was sleeping. When I was awake, they would bang on the door until I answered it, and then force their way into the house.

"This time, Brett, we'll be prepared for them," said Simms.

"By the way, Brett, since you are living here, Dearborn decided it is going to annex Springwells Township, so now you are living in Dearborn," Maria said.

Somehow, I must have done something that Dearborn liked.

They both then left together. I did not know how they were going to protect me, and I figured I would just leave it to the cops, but I had an inkling that somehow I was going to be the bait.

I did not know how, but later on, Simms showed up through the back way of the house, so as not to be noticed. He said to me, "Brett, DGA is going to be here soon. Do not let them in the house. If they force their way in, then I can shoot them."

Sure enough, the DGA showed up. Three of them forced their way in. Simms was hiding, standing up against the wall of the front room. He shot all three. Then three more, apparently hearing the gunshots, entered the house. Simms shot them also. They just kept coming, and Simms kept shooting them. The DGA were acting just like they had when Officer Gatewood got shot. They just kept coming into the house. Unlike any normal person, who would run from gunshots, they just kept coming into the house.

A lot of DGA members had gathered around the abandoned house across the street as if they were waiting for me to go to sleep. This process went on for three days. On the third day, with DGA again gathering across the street, Isaac handed me a .44. He told me, "Tell them there ain't any blacks allowed in Dearborn. And if they don't leave, shoot a couple of them." I did as he said. The DGA members did not move, so I fired at them and dropped two of them. This seemed to be enough of a deterrent to stop them because those who remained started to scatter in different directions. "I questioned if DGA would stay away or would they come back for more? Would there be a peace? If so how long would the peace last?" was the question.

To my surprise, Maria brought my sister Veronica to the house. I was hoping she would bring the rest of my family. I had no idea what Maria and Isaac had told my parents. It worried me what Simms had said about the team's intention to kill my whole family. I did not know if the Garcias were going to kill the rest of my family or if they had plans to kill both Veronica and me. I had no idea of their plans. Veronica and I were completely at their mercy. Not only did I have to watch out for myself but also now I had to watch out for my sister. I had a feeling that the DGA would try one last time to kill me.

Sure enough, they showed up the day after Veronica arrived. I was overrun. Veronica screamed, "Brett, come and help me."

I ran to the upstairs porch. One of the gang members had his pants unzipped and was trying to force his penis down Veronica's throat. When he turned around and saw me, he ran toward the door. He ran through the porch door, out the entrance door, and down the stairs. I was giving chase. As I ran down the stairs, I noticed Patches lying there on the back porch, but I had no time to check on her. I ran out the downstairs front door in time to see one DGA member run to the left on Akron Street. Another ran to the right.

After I'd exited the house, I saw two cop cars pull up. One of the cops was Simms. He handed me a gun and said, "Don't let them get away, Brett. Kill them." Because I didn't know what caliber the gun was, and because I had to fire from a distance of seventy-five yards or so, and since the perpetrator was running, I tried to arch the shot. I fired two rounds and missed.

Then Simms yelled, "Brett, that's a .44." Knowing that, I leveled the gun and fired another shot at the head of the DGA member who had attempted to force Veronica into performing oral sex on him. I hit him where I had aimed. In the meantime, a Detroit cop car pulled up with a black officer in it. I assumed the Detroit police and Dearborn police were sharing the duty of patrolling Springwells Township, since it was recently annexed by Dearborn.

One of the DGA members came walking up. I kept the gun trained on him as he walked up to us whining, "You killed my brother."

I said to him, "Here's a tip for you, asshole. When you commit a crime, bad things happen, especially on my turf. So don't commit crimes. You think you can remember that, dirt bag?"

Then I saw Benny and another, unknown cop standing behind me.

The unknown cop started saying, "This ain't right, this ain't right."

I knew the unknown cop did not know all of the circumstances, so to shut him up; I put a scare into him. I told Benny, "The next time he opens his mouth, shoot him."

In the meantime, I was holding a DGA member at gunpoint, not knowing what else to do with him since he had surrendered of his own accord. I didn't want to shoot him. When I told Simms to take him to jail, his reply was, "We can't take him to jail, Brett. He has to die."

I was tired of Simms telling me that I had to kill someone simply because he wanted me to. I could tell by now that he was a cold-blooded killer. He seemed to like killing, whereas I was trying my best to keep from killing anyone. He made me feel that I was obliged to kill on his command, which was really pissing me off. His explanation was not satisfactory to me. The gang member was unarmed. Plus, the DGA could have killed me, but they chose not to. My decision about the member I was holding at gunpoint was either to let him go or send him to jail. And if the cops didn't like it, oh well.

"Well, you guys handle it. I don't want him dead, just punished. And if I am the one to judge him, then I say to let him go completely." I looked at the suspect and told him, "Go back to Detroit and tell your fellow gang members to stay off my turf. Stay in Detroit, man, because this is an all-white neighborhood. You can't hide in this city. I am not looking for a fight, so tell your buddies just to leave me alone." I heard the unknown cop say something. Benny shot him in the chest.

As the shooting of the cop occurred, the black cop yelled to me, "Brett, I am going to die for you, so you don't have to die. But Brett, I want you to do something for my people so that my death is not in vain." This would be the second black cop to die for me, and this one hadn't given me his name either. This cop told me that was willing to die so that that all black citizens of the United States would get their rights. He said that the DGA was willing to kill to get their rights. All groups of black people wanted equality, and they wanted it bad enough that they would die for it. I had tried once to honor such a request, but it had ended with me getting shot. How was I supposed do something for his people? I was young, but I knew enough to honor a man's last request. I'd already made a promise to myself to do just that. Why he had chosen me to help his people is something that I could not reason out. Maybe it was like Carlos had said that there was just something about me. Whatever it was, it was strengthening my belief in God.

I started back to the house to check on Patches, my cat. Entering through the back door, where I had last seen her lying, I picked her up. She was still warm, not yet stiff. One of the DGA must have wrung her neck, because there was no blood on her. I could not cry, but a solitary tear did manage to run down my face. To console myself, I told myself that God had recalled Patches to his side, as her job here on earth was finished. She had given me love and the strength to go on through one of the worst nights of my young life. All I could do now was bury her.

I looked around for something to dig her grave with. Finding a pop bottle, I broke it so as to give it a sharp edge. There was a patch of dirt right behind the house, so I dug the grave there. It was a shallow one, but it was deep enough to put Patches in. I covered her up and said a prayer, asking God to use her soul again to save another little boy's life.

A few minutes after I'd buried Patches, a Dearborn detective came into the house. He asked, "Brett, who made that shot?"

"I did," I responded.

"Which cop shot that black kid?"

"No cop shot him. I shot him."

"Where did the gun come from?"

"The cops gave me the gun."

"Which cop?"

"I don't know because I was keeping an eye on the target." It was not a complete lie. I thought it was Isaac Simms, who now was a Dearborn cop, but I was not 100 percent sure.

"Brett, I want you to see something." We walked over to Akron Street, where I had shot the DGA member. He was still lying in the road. His head looked like the head of my friend after Carlos had shot him.

"Look what you did to his head."

"Well, I was taught to shoot at the head, and that's what I did. I didn't tell the DGA to try and rape my sister. It's pretty simple, sir. Things like this wouldn't happen if they'd just leave us alone. Besides, I'm the good guy! Why are you coming down on me?"

Having no reply, he exited the house. I didn't know what the cops had done with the gang member, and frankly I did not care. I had told the cops that killing the gang member would not be beneficial to me. I felt that letting him go and telling the rest of DGA to leave us alone would serve a better purpose.

Chapter 24

THE MOVE TO DEARBORN

A few days after the shooting of the Dearborn cop, Simms came by the house and told me he was taking Veronica and me back to our parents. My mom did not seem upset about the fact that Veronica and I had been gone. I imagine that Maria and Simms explained that they had hidden us in Dearborn.

When the weekend came, I explained to my dad that Simms had told me that because the DGA intended to kill our whole family, we needed to move. I also told him that Veronica and I had been kept in Dearborn, a city with no blacks. That Saturday, he herded us all to the car and then set out for Dearborn. We began looking for houses in the northeast section, but houses for sale in that part of the city were either scarce or unaffordable. He drove in a southerly direction down to the neighborhood where I had stayed. My parents spotted a house right next to a school named Roulo. They contacted the real estate agent but were told that the sale of the house was pending. On Sunday, we went back to the same neighborhood and saw that the house Veronica and I had stayed in was now up for sale. Mom and Dad went through the house. It had been emptied and cleaned.

It was early August when Mom and Dad finalized the deal on the house and we moved in. I felt comfortable in this neighborhood. And now that I had my family living with me, I was fairly content.

One of the first things I did was scope out the neighborhood by finding out where I would be going to school. I walked the back way, going across the alley, between the neighbors' houses, and on to Franklin Street. I had seen the school before while we were driving around looking for houses, so I knew approximately where it was. I walked about half a block to the corner of Lowery and Franklin Streets. There it was: Franklin Junior High, where I was going to get my education and change the world for the better. Here I could attend classes and not have to fight my way to and from school.

On my way back home, I decided to take Holly Street, the street I now lived on. I saw two kids who looked to be about my age. One was a blond kid about my height and size, but he was a lot more muscular than I. The other one had a somewhat darker complexion, and was a couple inches shorter and pudgier. The two started walking toward me; I started toward them. The blond kid greeted me first, giving his name as Shawn Goodenrich. The other boy introduced himself as Duwad Abdul.

I then told them my name. Curious, I asked, "What nationality is your name, Duwad?"

"It's Arabic, Brett. By the way, everybody just calls me Duey."

"I'm just a plain Brett, guys. How about you, Shawn? What nationality are you?

"I'm Hungarian."

"Do you like sports, Brett?"

"I love baseball, basketball, and football. But I'm probably the best at football because I am pretty fast in a footrace. I think I would make a good running back," I said.

"Shawn is one of the fastest kids in our grade. How about you race him, Brett?"

"That's fine by me. Where do you want us to race to?"

Duey set the distance. Shawn and I were to race once he said go. Shawn and I lined up. We took off when Duey said go. I beat Shawn by two steps.

"I want you both to race again, only try this time, Shawn."

"I was trying, Duey."

We raced again, with the same result.

Duey asked, "Shawn, were you really trying?"

Yes I was trying Duey. He's pretty fast."

"Congratulations, Brett. You are looking at our starting backfield for Franklin's football team. You and Shawn will be the running backs, and I will be the quarterback."

"Brett, let me explain to you why Duey wants to assemble a really good team. This part of the city is predominately Arabic. People from other parts of the Dearborn area, which is predominantly white, look down on Arabs. Franklin is a small school compared to other schools. Franklin has not won the city championship since 1945, and people say it's because the Arabs can't play football well enough to win, adding that they will never win. We want to dispel that myth and put an end to some of the discrimination. What do you think, Brett? You want to help us win?"

"Guys, I learned from living in Detroit that whatever you do, color makes no difference to how well you do anything. I don't back down on a fight like this, so count me in."

I had previously noticed a large swimming pool in a nearly park, and also a baseball diamond at the intersection of Holly and Lasher Streets. Wanting to know more about the pool, I asked, "Who owns the pool in the park, Duey?"

"The city owns that pool."

"Can anybody swim in it?" I asked.

"Yes, anybody can swim in the pool, but you have to pay a quarter to get in, unless you live in the city. If you live in the city, then it's free if you have a tag sewn on your swimsuit, which you get from the recreation department."

I wanted to learn how to swim. Hopefully I would learn before the end of the summer.

I said, "I'll see you guys later."

There was much I had to learn about the city of Dearborn. Eventually I would find that it was a great place to live. I missed my friends who still lived in the Corridor—Skipper, Justine, and Timothy, to name just a few. The death of Manuel D was still fresh on my mind.

After meeting Shawn and Duey, I headed over to Lasher Park. There was a hill in the park that looked like it had been created for sledding and tobogganing. I walked up that hill. That is where I met Jake Barnett for the first time. It was a fad for the kids to take a large piece of cardboard and use it to slide down the hill, the cardboard acting like a sled. When Jake came back up the hill after having slid down it, he introduced himself, as did I. There was another kid who introduced himself as Michael Withers. I took a few runs down the hill and found it to be quite fun. Barnett took me over to his house to show me where he lived so I would be able to come see him whenever I wanted to. We ran into his older brother, Lucas. I introduced myself, and then Jake took me to the garage and showed me his dad's historical car. *How cool!* I thought. Barnett told me his dad drove it to work, except in winter. I thought to myself that if I owned a cool old car like that, I would only take it out on special holidays. I soon left for home, happy to have made so many friends in one day.

A couple of days went by. I returned to the Barnett house. Jake said to me, "My sister, Samantha, is taking us to the youth center. Do you want to go?"

"What's a youth center?"

"You can go roller-skating, play pool, and do a lot of other cool things. What do you think?"

"Man that sounds a lot of fun! Let me go home to get some money and change clothes."

"Hurry back," Jake said.

I came back dressed and ready to go. We headed to the youth center, which was located at Greenfield and Michigan Avenue.

We entered the building and headed for the roller rink, a nice-size rink with rails to hang on to. I went and got my rental skates, put them on, started skating, and immediately fell on my rear. Slowly but surely, after many spills, I got the hang of skating.

After I had conquered roller-skating, I took off the skates and headed downstairs to the billiards room. I walked in to find six immaculately groomed pool tables and two Ping-Pong tables. *What a wonderful place for kids this is,* I thought. The youth center was now my favorite place to go. I had not left, but already I wanted to come back. This place temporarily diverted my focus from the Garcias and what they had done.

It was past the dinner hour when Jake and I headed back home. Once we got back to the Barnett's' house, I said thank you to Samantha for taking us, and thank you to Jake for inviting me. Then I walked the short distance back home.

I told my mom what a great time I had, and what a really wonderful city this was. Then I said that I had learned to roller-skate in just one day, although I still was a novice. I told her my next conquest would be swimming, which I hoped to learn to do before the end of summer, seeing as the pool closed on Labor Day. I badly wanted to learn to swim so I could teach my father how to swim. I was not sure if he didn't know how swim, or if he could but had simply been traumatized by a bad experience he'd had when younger when a few of his friends held him under the water too long while horsing around. I wanted to learn to swim so I could help my father overcome his fear.

As if there was not enough for kids to do, on Saturday mornings the Dearborn Parks and recreation department held pickup baseball games at St. Bonaventure Field. The diamonds were directly across the street from the Goodenrich's house. The city supplied the bases and balls and some bats. Each kid has to bring his own glove. *This city is a kid's dream,* I thought. No wonder there was such a low crime rate; there was so much more for a kid to do other than get in to trouble.

The end of summer was near. I had set my goal to learn to swim, and I had accomplished that goal. The major stumbling block to my learning to swim was getting over the fear of sticking my head under water, and understanding I wouldn't drown if I did so. I was completely self-taught, having learned without any coaching at all.

It was now Labor Day, the day they drained the pool. And so that ended my summer of 1961. Of all the summers I could remember, this had been the most joyous one. With Labor Day here, that meant school the next day: my first day of school at Franklin. I had high hopes of turning a new page of my life.

Chapter 25

FRANKLIN JUNIOR HIGH

My mom had already registered us for school. I had one slight problem, and that was that Dearborn schools did not have half years like Detroit did, so my mom had me repeat half of my third grade year so I would not miss out on any schoolwork. Now, all I had to do was find the room for the teacher's class I had been assigned to. The teacher's name was Miss Runderson. When I found the class, I was surprised to see both Jake Barnett and Duey in the classroom, which was nearly full with an ethnic mix of students.

One of my classmates was a girl much taller than I, with striking good looks. She and I would become friends through the year. Her name was Corrine Hajeemy.

I had settled in quite nicely, and I made a few more friends. Everything was going smoothly, but as usual, Carlos wanted to see to it that my life was not so good. It was the weekend after my first week of school when he had me stand in front of my house with my gun on. Duey was walking down the sidewalk that led from his house to mine. Carlos was standing behind me, and Edwin Burns was watching me from across the street. Burns had moved into the pink house across the street from my house, the one that had previously been abandoned. Then Duey did something unusual. He yelled across the street to Edwin Burns, "Rape his mother, and then rape her again."

Carlos issued an order: "Kill him, Brett, or I will kill you."

I did not understand what was happening, but I didn't want to kill Duey, so I yelled to him to run. I had to do like Carlos ordered me to do, so instead of firing three rounds to the head as I had been taught, I fired two shots to the right side of Duey's rib cage and one to the left. I knew the bullets would follow the bone and not harm his vitals. He fell down face first and was knocked out on the third shot.

Just as Duey fell, a city car appeared. This vehicle was similar to a cop car, but it was used by the ordinance officer in making his rounds. I saw that it was Rahani, Duey's older brother. As he got out of the car, I pulled my gun and told him, "Rahani, please turn around. I do not want to shoot you; I just want to see if you have a gun on you." He did as I ordered, and then he went over to where Duey lay.

Edwin Burns checked Duey's wounds. Coming over to me, he asked, "Brett how many times did you fire your gun?"

"I shot three times, Edwin."

"Carlos, he hit Duey all three times." Turning to me, he asked, "Who taught you how to shoot like that, Brett?"

"My grandfather, mainly, but he had help from his brother and his son," I replied.

"Do you think you can shoot with my gun? It's a 7 mm. I'd like you to try to hit the tree in my yard. Do you think you can hit the tree from here?"

The tree was thirty to thirty-five yards away. I took the gun and fired three quick rounds, all three of which found their mark.

"Whew! Damn, Carlos! This kid's going to kill Rico!"

I walked inside the house and sat down on the sofa. I was thoroughly disgusted. Rahani soon came in and asked me, "Brett, why did you shoot Duey?"

I explained, "Rahani, if Carlos orders me to shoot someone, I have to shoot them. If I hadn't shot Duey, then Carlos would have killed me. I shot for Duey's ribs instead of his head. I'm not going to kill someone if I feel I don't have to. I didn't shoot to kill Duey, but I did fire three rounds. Now the Garcias may kill me anyway since I did not shoot for his head. Rahani, they have been killing my friends. They have killed three of my friends so far; at least those are the ones that I know of. The exact number of people they have killed is unknown to me. Now they are trying to make me kill my own friends."

It was not until Rahani said, "Brett, I am not going to press charges against you," that I relaxed. I was relieved to hear him say that. It seemed as if I had convinced him that I did not want to hurt anybody, especially Duey. I knew only a little about Rahani. Duey had said he was on the waiting to list to become a Dearborn cop. In the brief conversations I'd had with Rahani, he seemed to be sharp-minded and pretty straitlaced. I think at this point he already knew who the culprit was but was not letting on that he knew who it was. I believed his investigative instincts had kicked in and that he was going to do what he could to help me.

What reason would Carlos have to make me kill Duey? I pondered. I got the answer the next day, when my grandpa Holbrook showed up. He must have been at Aunt Lydia's house, because he arrived way too fast. He started reaming me a new one when he told me, "I told you and taught you to shoot for the head. That gun is not for shooting at the body."

"Grandpa, Duey was my friend. I didn't want to kill him."

"That man raped your mother. I want you to kill him!"

"Grandpa, Duey is just a little boy. He is just eight years old. It wasn't Duey that hurt mom; it was Rico. I only got it just now, Grandpa. Carlos told you it was my friend Duey who had hurt mom so that we would kill Duey instead of Rico. For some reason, Carlos does not want Rico dead.

196

It's obvious he is planning something else and he is going to use Rico to do it. You can't take those cops' word for anything. They are nothing but a bunch of lying thieves. Because they are cops, we automatically believe what they say. They're making us look like a stupid bunch of hillbillies. They feel they can tell us anything and, since we are just a bunch of country hicks, we will believe what they say. Grandpa, you're a man of your word! These cops are not men of honor. They are going to lie, cheat, and steal to get their way."

Grandpa had a look of confusion on his face. I think I had grandpa convinced of my argument once I told him that Duey was only eight years old.

It was almost two weeks later when I heard that Duey was home from the hospital. I was elated to hear he was all right and that my strategy had worked. I ran down the street. He was standing in front of his house. I asked him, "Duey, are you okay?"

"Yeah, Brett, I am okay. My wounds are almost healed."

"You don't hold a grudge against me, do you, Duey?"

I had done what I could for Duey. While he was hurt, he was alive. It was at this point that I told him I would guard him with my life. The best way for me to repay him was to catch the crooked-ass cops who caused him to get hurt, but I would need his and Rahani's help to do that.

"No, Brett. Rahani explained things to me. We'll just leave it at that."

Relieved to hear him say that, I hoped that what had happened wouldn't ruin our friendship. I was sure of one thing, though: it wouldn't make our friendship better.

As the days in southeast Dearborn passed, I accumulated more friendships. The neighborhood had a multitude of nationalities. There were Mexicans, Slavs, and Italians. Irish and Southerners were both considered hillbillies, but there were no black people. Dearborn was what the United States was about; it was a real melting pot of a city. It was an atypical Detroit suburb because of its high concentration of Arab Americans, as I learned from meeting more and more friends. The residents of this neighborhood called it the South End. Once I discovered that, I too used that name for southeast Dearborn.

Another one of my friends was Marius Gomez, he was one those guys who's every utterance is just plain funny. I had the feeling that if he had the right material, he could be a famous comedian.

Whenever I heard a good joke, I found it fun to tell it to Marius because he had such a good sense of humor. It was fun to hear him laugh. He, too, was a friend of Duey's, and lived a couple of doors down from Shawn Goodenrich.

We were nearing the end of third grade. To provide us with a little fun before moving on to fourth grade, Miss Runderson decided we should put on a talent show. She paired me with Duey a couple of days in advance. He and I got the goofy idea to do Jackie Gleason and Crazy Guggenheim. Duey was to be Gleason, as he slightly resembled him, and I was to do an impersonation of Crazy Guggenheim. On the day of the talent show, Duey brought a towel with him to class. He and I cleared Miss Runderson's desk to use it like a bar. He continuously wiped the bar just like Gleason did on television, and I told one of the jokes that Guggenheim told on *The Jackie Gleason Show* about the red ding-dong. When we were done, the whole class laughed and applauded at the same time. We were the hit of the talent show with that five-minute skit. From then on, whenever I wanted to ease tensions between Duey and me, I would say, "Duey, what is red and goes 'ding-dong'?"

He usually would smile and ask me, "Lawson, how do you remember all that crap?"

My grades were sufficient, so I was promoted to the fourth grade.

It was shortly after summer vacation of 1962 began that Carlos once more tried to keep Rico alive by fingering someone to take his place in death. At one point, Carlos had told me that when Rico came up the enclosed stairs at the back of the house that led to the upper flat, I was supposed to kill him. Since our family was so large we occupied both the upper and lower flat, and if someone crossed the threshold, I could shoot him. The only problem was that he then sent Diego to die instead of Rico. Needless to say, since it wasn't Rico, I didn't shoot. It had become obvious to me that Carlos wanted Rico alive, but what I didn't understand was why.

199

Carlos came back to the house later and asked me, "Why didn't you shoot Rico?"

"It wasn't Rico you sent, you sent Diego."

"Okay, Brett, follow me over to the back porch. I want you to shoot through the roof of the back porch."

I did as he said and fired through the roof.

A couple of days later my grandfather came by. The first thing he asked was, "Where were you standing at the time?"

We were in the upstairs flat. I showed where I had been standing in the front room.

"How did you miss from that distance?" my grandpa asked.

"Grandpa, I did not miss. There was nobody there when Carlos had me fire through the roof. Let me show you where he had me shoot through the roof."

I showed him where the bullet had gone through the roof. It was easy to tell because Carlos had hired carpenters to replace the board with a brand-new one.

He then asked, "How did you go through the roof from the living room?"

"I did not shoot from the front room, Grandpa. I shot from out here. And there was no one here but me and Carlos. Grandpa, you want Rico dead, but Carlos is protecting him because it's his nephew. Carlos is going to keep trying to get someone to die in Rico's place."

"Brett, I want you to kill that man." He wasn't asking; he was downright telling me to kill Rico.

Now I was feeling the pressure from my grandfather to kill Rico, along with the pressure from Carlos not to kill Rico. I was in a dilemma, not knowing what I was supposed to do at this point. I knew that Carlos was not going to set Rico up for me to shoot him. I felt like I was a hunter, a hunter who did not want to hunt, and a hunter who did not want to kill the game. But like all hunters, I would have to kill to survive. Rico was now the game. It was time for me to end his life for the purpose of protecting society.

I am not a proponent of executions, as I believe they are a sure sign that society has given up on the accused. I had exhausted all efforts to save Rico. Since Rico was part of Team Garcia, the other Garcias were doing everything they could to help him escape justice. I needed more information before I would take any action against Team Garcia. I did not feel at ease at all, but on edge; I was unable to sleep soundly.

Chapter 26

VINNY IS A TARGET

Three days the morning after Carlos had me shoot through the ceiling, I awoke not feeling like myself. My vision was a bit blurry as I was awaking. Once I rose from bed, I noticed that I was walking kind of wobbly. It was at that point I figured that I had once again been drugged sometime during the night. My first thoughts were that the DGA had not given up yet and were after me again. Through a window, I noticed that Maria, Benny and Carlos were outside the house on the front lawn. She was half smiling. Once I went out to see her, she asked, "How do you feel, Brett?"

She seemed almost glad to see me stumbling.

"I feel like I have been drugged, Maria."

"You were drugged, Brett. Rico gave you a speedball."

I knew that a speedball was a mixture of cocaine and heroin.

"How come I can't remember anything, Maria?"

"Carlos did that to you. He used a technique called drug-induced hypnosis."

I knew about drugs and hypnosis being used together, but I had not heard that term used before now. Another thing crossed my mind. If she knew that Carlos was going to have me drugged, why didn't she stop him? She had a gun, so she had no excuse to let Rico drug me. I could think of only one answer to solve the mystery of whether or not she was part of Team Garcia: she must have somehow helped Carlos get away with the murder of Johnny Doe. Carlos was still running around with his gun and his badge. I didn't know how he had gotten away with the murder of Johnny Doe unless Maria had helped him do it. Her testimony as an eyewitness should have put him away. Had she helped Carlos get away with the murder? Most importantly, why the hell had he drugged me? My guessing was that it was easier for him to control me that way. I now was beginning to see why he wanted to keep Rico alive. It was to use Rico to inject the target which was me or any other person Carlos had targeted—with a narcotic, so Carlos could then use hypnosis to control said target.

Benny said, "Here, Brett, put your gun on. I want you to go for a walk with me."

I thought, *Now I have been drugged and am going to have to shoot somebody.* We walked down Holly and turned right on Lasher, headed toward Roulo.

About halfway to Roulo Street, Benny told me, "We are going to be meeting a man. I want you to shoot him."

"Who is he, Benny?"

"He is considered a nobleman in the Italian community. He is highly honored."

Not good, I thought. All I knew about noblemen was that they were princes and lords. But it sounded like they were another gang. I did not need to piss them off also.

I noticed a man walking toward us from Roulo Street. As he got nearer, I could make out some of his features. He looked like Vinny. Once he was within a few yards, I could tell it was Vinny. He did not recognize me, which made sense, as it had been a couple of years since I had been to the barbershop he owned. I did not want Benny to know I knew Vinny. Moreover, I did not understand why Benny wanted Vinny dead. Vinny had not done anything to harm me, and I had no reason to kill him. I was not going to shoot him. I had to figure out how to get out of it.

Knowing I had a small-caliber gun, Benny asked me, "Brett, you want to use my gun?"

"No, I'll use my gun." I backed up about fifteen yards, enough so that I was out of pistol range and Vinny would not be harmed. I fired at Vinny. The bullet landed far short and to the right of him.

To cover myself, I said, "Benny, let me have your gun."

"No, Brett, you only get one shot."

I had just saved Vinny's life, but he lit into me, telling me he was going to kill me. He then turned around and headed back toward Roulo.

"Why didn't you kill him, Brett?" Benny asked.

Not wanting Benny to know what I knew or what my real intentions were, I replied, "Benny, you and your team have got to learn when someone can help you, how to take advantage of their knowledge, and how you can make use of it."

In those few moments I had devised a secret plan to become a friend to Vinny in the hopes that with his being a powerful man, someday he might be able to help me save someone else's life or even my own.

On the way back, as Benny and I neared my house, I saw Maria and Carlos on the sidewalk out front.

Benny and I got back to the house. Carlos told me he was a descendant of Santa Anna. He said that he and Benny wanted to take back Texas and California.

"Brett, I told you before that there's something very different about you. Maria said that even the president noticed it about you. You are very smart. You have the power to kill, yet you don't kill. I need someone like you to help me. You don't know how bad the Klan's treatment of my family and other Mexicans has been. That is why I grew up hating hillbillies and the Irish— because a lot of them were Klan members."

His statements allowed me to peer into his mind a little bit. I could tell he had a burning hatred inside him for racists and the Klan. His hatred had grown and festered over the years, until he could no longer cope with it without reacting violently. The tactics used by the Klan were bad enough that they had driven Carlos to kill. He was out to eliminate racism, and his way of doing this was to eradicate the Klan and anyone who supported them. Was that why he had gone after the Masons? Were they part of the Klan? While I did not like racists myself, I believed that killing them was another thing. The killing of Manuel D and Johnny Doe was inexcusable. I figured I should help Carlos come up with another way of eliminating racism other than killing off the Klan, and trying to overthrow the United States government so as to try to reclaim Texas and California.

"Carlos, I think you are looking at things in the wrong way. You know that the borders of the United States are not going to change. I don't know a whole lot about Mexico's history, but I do know that Spain took it over from the Aztecs and the Indians, who were there first. The Spanish stole all the gold when they controlled Mexico. In the present day, an acre of land in the United States is worth more than land in Mexico. So the best thing for someone from Mexico who wants to come to the United States to do is to buy some land. It does not matter where you buy the land. Maybe you want to buy the land in places like Washington, Florida, and even Michigan. And then it's yours. That way, Mexicans would just be buying the land back, one acre at a time. That is what the United States did. The government bought the land from the Indians and from France. Now, once someone from Mexico owns the land, then they can work on getting citizenship. That's a lot more peaceful way of getting land back. And I think that plan is workable."

He laughed a quiet sort of laugh and said, "Brett that is exactly what I mean about you. You always look for a reason not to use violence or your gun when you're trying to figure out a way to get things done."

I left him. Entering the house, I hoped I had convinced him to see things my way.

I didn't have to wait long before Vinny showed up with one of the neighbors, Louie, who lived just a few doors down. It was close to nightfall. I'd had no idea that Louie knew Vinny, and that was not a good thing for me.

All of sudden, Vinny started dishing out insults directed at me. He shouted out to me, "Hey, you little damn hillbilly, we are going to kill you!"

I thought, *Now that's real gratitude for you. I spared his life, and now the asshole wants to kill me.* While I was getting emotionally tired, I was beginning to realize that when Carlos told you to kill, if you did not do as he said, you were going to suffer the consequences. I could not give up on what I believed, but I just wished Carlos would pick smarter crooks to shoot.

"That's right, asshole, my name is Brett and I am a hillbilly. Can you even spell *hillbilly*, you dumb-ass wop? Besides that, don't you know hillbillies are from the mountains? Don't you have mountains in Italy?"

"Of course we got mountains in Italy," Vinny replied.

"Well, that means you're an Italian hillbilly, asshole. As far as you killing me, I can shoot a lot better than you. Anytime you want to fight me, fair and square, just let me know."

"You are a nigger kid," Vinny said.

"You are a nigger lover, Vinny."

It was then that Louie spoke up. "Vinny, he thinks you want to kill him because he keeps killing all the niggers." Then both of them turned and headed toward Louie's house.

For some reason, Maria showed up. I could hear Louie calling my name. Maria and I walked down the street toward Louie's house. Vinny and another man were standing by Louie, taunting him. Louie, a big barrel-chested man, was stuffed feet first halfway down a sewer. He started begging me, "Brett, please shoot me. They cut off my dick! Show me mercy, Brett. Please, please shoot me. Brett, I am going to die for you. They can't kill you if you shoot me."

I began to cry. I had enjoyed my talks with Louie, and could not believe Vinny had done this to him. I was about to lose yet another friend. Maria urged me to shoot Louie, so I shot him in the head. The light-duty .22-caliber bullet did not even knock him out. Knowing that he would bleed to death if I shot him in the neck, I aimed my gun at his neck and tried to hit his jugular. I fired the gun. Blood went everywhere, mingling with the gun smoke. Louie passed out right away. I was furious about losing Louie. I had spared a man whom I thought would be a valuable friend, and it cost me a friend, a friend who would rather die than hurt me. First, there was the incident with Vinny and Stache at the barbershop, and now there was this one with Louie. I would have to figure out how to return the favor to Louie and Stache.

Chapter 27

GARY POWERS COMES HOME

In February 1962, the president succeeded in getting Gary Powers released by releasing a Soviet named Vilyam Fisher in exchange. The swap was made across the bridge nicknamed the "Bridge of Spies," so called because many spy exchanges were made at this East-meets-West connection. Today it is called the Glienicke Bridge.

It was now June. My father and I were sitting on the front porch when Justine's father, Virgil, pulled up in front of the house. I was glad and surprised to see him. He walked up the walk leading to the porch and said his hellos. My father asked me to leave the two of them to talk. I went inside to make a sandwich while they conversed. It had just enough time to eat my lunch before Dad called me back out to join them. Mister Powers then asked me to go for a ride with him. It was while we were riding that he asked, "Brett, do you want to drive the car?"

I said, "Sure."

He pulled over to the side of the road and had me get behind the wheel. While I was driving, he surprised me by saying, "Brett, I am going to die. I want you to have my car in exchange for getting Gary out of Russia."

"Well, Mister Powers, what about Justine? Don't you think you should give her your car? I can't drive. Plus, it won't go to me. It will only go to my dad. And anyway, I don't need to receive payment for helping Gary."

"Brett, Justine is on drugs. The gangsters in the Corridor have turned her into a prostitute."

"No way, Mr. Powers, not Justine!" I said. I was floored. Justine was such a beautiful young woman. Now her life now would be ruined and miserable because of the drugs she was taking. Although she was four to five years older than me, I had a crush on her. This news just gave credence to the fact that the DGA were forcefully drugging many types of people.

With the knowledge I had on how they operated, maybe someday I could get revenge for Justine, but with Carlos and Benny helping the DGA, it would be a formidable task. Justine Powers had been my first real crush; she was very sweet, kind, and pretty. It was obvious that Rico having raped her had screwed her up psychologically. "Isn't there anything you could do to get Justine off drugs?" I asked.

"There is nothing more we can do, Brett."

I knew after Virgil said that there was nothing more his wife or he could do, they had given up on her. And I knew I would never see Justine again. When Mister Powers first showed up, I had expectations of seeing Justine and Gary soon. Instead, I had gotten nothing but bad news. Now I was about to lose not one but three friends: Gary, Justine, and Mister Powers. I was beginning to feel that my situation with my friends was expressed by the old proverb about a bird pecking on your window, that is indication that someone is about to die. Virgil then got in his car and left.

I dreaded every time one of my old friends showed up because that usually meant someone was going to die.

A few days later, Virgil showed up. He was standing across the street in front of Edwin Burn's house, when Isaac Simms drove up in his car and parked down the street from our house. What Simms was doing there I couldn't say. I did not know if it was Dad or Virgil who had lured him to the house. Seeing Isaac, Dad went inside, soon returning with my gun and holster.

Shortly after Simms arrived, Virgil said, "Brett, I am going to die for you."

I turned to try to walk away, when my father yelled to me, "Brett, you have to shoot him when he says that." I did not understand why Virgil wanted to die. His death would only hurt his family more, and I did not want to hurt Justine any more than she had been hurt already. I did not want Justine to hate me. I had already been through that when she got raped.

I did as my father told me, and fired on Mister Powers three times. He fell dead. I turned and walked away when I heard gunshots coming from elsewhere, followed by the sound of something hitting the ground like a thud. Then I saw something that looked like big black bugs in the air. Burns had come out to see what was going on. "Brett, Simms was shooting at you with your back turned!"

What a chicken shit cop, I thought, *shooting at a kid with his back turned to him.* I watched as the ambulance arrived and took Virgil away. Then I walked by to the front porch to sit with my father, who asked me, "What did you do that for?"

"You told me I had to shoot Virgil. Besides, he did not point to whom he wanted dead. He should have shot Simms himself in the first place." *Why in the hell does everyone count on me to kill someone? I just don't understand why all these people want somebody dead,* I thought. *They can kill those people themselves if they want them dead. I want no more of this. They're acting like I am some sort of hit man or an avenging angel.*

I was sick and tired of this group of policemen using me to get revenge on innocent people. I had made up my mind that the next time I was told that I had to kill someone; I was just going to walk away. I didn't care if the cops threatened to kill me if I didn't kill whom they wished me to kill. I was going to call the cops' bluff and walk away. If they wanted to shoot me, then they could shoot me.

While I had loved the Powers family, I did not want to be dragged into this fight. I was getting sick of all the death and killing. It was as if Team

Garcia intended to force me to kill my friends until I was dead, or until I quit carrying my gun so I would then be defenseless—or worse yet, until my gun was taken away.

I did not have to wait a full twenty-four hours before I spotted Carlos in the alleyway. Based on Team Garcia's previous antics, I knew another attack on me was forthcoming. He seemed to be checking out the Hameed's house, which faced Franklin Street, which ran parallel to Holly, and was kitty-corner to our house. The people who were coming from Burn's house were either drunks or junkies who would walk through the empty field that was next to our house and go between the Hameed's. It was shortcut to either the candy store or Desirae's bar. The candy store was where the drunks and junkies usually shot pool or played the pinball machines. The high scorer of the week on each of the pinball machines received a six-pack of soft drinks, winner's choice.

Carlos, who apparently had also seen the drunks and junkies, approached me and said, "Brett, I'm going to make you some money."

"What do I have to do to make money?"

"Well, when anyone comes through the field, I want you to tell them to stop and pay a toll."

"What do I do if they don't pay the toll?"

"Well, I want you to get your dad's shotgun. If they don't pay the toll, then I want you to shoot them."

The next morning, three teens cut through the field. I stopped them to pay my toll. All three paid me, but they threw the money on the ground. I saw Carlos hiding by the hedges belonging to the Abdallah's, who lived on the other side of the empty lot. I assumed he was watching over me, but that was not the case. It was just a few minutes later when another teen came out of Burn's house, only this one was staggering quite badly. He crossed the street and started through the field. I pointed the shotgun at him and said, "Stop and pay my toll of one dollar."

After throwing the dollar down on the ground, he pushed me down and grabbed the shotgun. Carlos continued watching by the hedges. The teen pointed the gun at me and tried to fire. That was going to be impossible because my father had not removed the trigger lock. I yelled to Carlos, "Aren't you going to shoot him?" It was quite obvious that Carlos had no intention of backing me up. I had it figured that the junkie was going to grab the gun from me and then shoot me with it, and that Carlos would then shoot the junkie. Carlos's story would stand up because both witnesses would be dead.

My father came outside. Carlos shouted to him in a loud voice, "I thought I told you to take that lock off that gun."

My father had no response. Carlos yelled, "I am going to kill your son, Burt." He then stormed off.

I knew that the Garcia brothers were corrupt, but I could not believe one of them would set up a nine-year-old kid in that manner. I was going to have to be more cautious in the future. Although Carlos tried to set me up for a shooting to get me killed, I remained optimistic that he would eventually get caught. I just had to keep dodging his setups until he was nabbed. In the meantime, I had to figure the best way to see that he was indeed caught. I hoped that Maria, if she had to choose a side to be on, would be on my side, since she was seeing my dad. I hoped that she did not want any more harm to come to my mom's family.

I did not have to wait long for the next round of battle of the wits with Team Garcia. Simms came by in his personal car and told me to come with him. He drove up Lasher, then turned on Franklin to Eagle Street, and then drove toward but stopped short of Roulo. There at the corner of Roulo and Eagle was the Italian American Club where a group of men who were playing bocce ball. One of them was Vinny. They invited me into their yard to join them. I had seen this game only once before and did not really know how to play, but they encouraged me, so I rolled a ball toward the object ball. My shot landed just a few inches from the object ball. Knowing very little about the game, I followed their instructions on what to do next. It had been less than a week since the incident with Louie, and now I was playing games with Vinny's men. After my turn was over, Vinny called me over to have a conversation with him. I felt uncomfortable to say the least, seeing that just a few days back, he'd wanted me dead. Why he wanted me dead I never found out. Maybe it was because of my taking a shot at him, even though I was not trying to kill him.

I did not know if these guys were going to kick the hell out of me or kill me, but I knew enough to show no fear. Still, for some reason, I felt safer with Vinny than I did with the Dearborn cops. Vinny and I squatted down. He talked in a voice just louder than a whisper, as if he did not want anybody to hear us. He then asked me a strange question about weather. "Brett, tell me, how does lightning work?"

It just so happened that I'd had a lesson in school about the types of clouds and what effect they had. It was the last lesson we'd had before summer break. Part of the lesson was also about lightning. I replied, "Vinny, when the air and clouds move, they create positive charges in the air and negative charges on the ground. And when the charges become too great, they discharge as a lightning bolt. The charges are just like any battery you have; red is positive and black is negative."

"See, the kid says it is about positive and negative charges. Tell me more, Brett," Vinny asked.

"Vinny, you ever hear the old saying that lightning never strikes the same place twice?"

"Yeah, Brett, I have heard that. Is it true?"

"No, Vinny it is not true. During a storm in a place like New York City, where the Empire State Building is, that building gets hit maybe a hundred times during one storm because it so high up in the sky."

"That makes a whole lot of sense to me. I never knew all that. Let me ask you, do you think someone could build some type of machine that could be used to hit another person and make it appear as if they had been hit by a lightning bolt?"

"I suppose that will be possible someday, but it would have to be something that could produce a very large charge of electricity. A lightning bolt has millions of volts in it, Vinny, and it travels at the speed of light. And when it hits you, it blows big holes in you."

"What does 'the speed of light' mean, Brett?"

"It's the time it takes light to travel from one place to another. Light travels at approximately 186,000 miles per second. That is why first you see the lightning and then, a few seconds later, you hear thunder—because sound travels much slower than light."

"Brett, I want you to stay in school, and I want you to study hard and do well. From time to time, I am going to call on you to have more talks with you. I enjoyed our talk today."

"Don't worry, Vinny. I already promised my mom and dad that I would finish school. But I need a little help from you. I need you to keep those damn Mexican cops off my ass because they are interrupting my schoolwork and making it impossible for me to concentrate on my studies.

On account of our short talk, I realized that Vinny did not have much formal education, but he was definitely not stupid. I knew he had gotten his education on the streets of Detroit and had risen to his position rapidly. I did not need to know what his business was, or anything about it. The less information I had, the fewer chances they were for me to get blamed for saying the wrong thing to the wrong person. There was just no way I was going to snoop into Vinny's business.

I walked away thinking and hoping that I had laid the groundwork for a fruitful friendship. The proof that I had accomplished what I had intended came when, a few days later, Benny and Maria stopped by my house to talk to me. Benny informed me that Maria had written a book titled *Telefon*, about how the Soviets had trained sleeper agents using the drug-induced hypnosis technique in which Team Garcia was well trained. Vinny had helped her get it published and then stiffed her once it came time to pay her share.

I asked, "How much did the book sell for, Benny?"

"It sold for two hundred fifty thousand dollars. Vinny was supposed to get half, but he kept it all."

Knowing they were irate and that they were not going to let Vinny get away with stiffing Maria for that amount of money, I told Benny to get the whole team together. I would get Maria her money.

The next morning, the team—Benny, Rico, Maria, Simms, Carlos, and I—gathered where Vinny was staying. When he came outside, we all were standing on the edge of pistol range. Maria yelled, "I want my money, Vinny."

"I don't owe you anything, bitch."

"You were supposed to keep half, not the whole amount," she retorted.

That is when I decided to intervene.

"Vinny, you are not a thief, but if you don't give the money to her, then that's what you are. Let me tell you what's going to happen to you, Vinny. If you don't give her money to her, they are going to kill you."

"Are you threatening me, kid?"

"No Vinny. I am not a cop. I am your friend, Vinny, and I am trying to save your life. They use .44 Magnums, Vinny. You're not going to get up ever again if you get hit with one of those guns. You will have the money, but you are going to be dead. Not only will they get away with it but also you will put your family at risk. If you want more money, Vinny, maybe you should go back to the publisher and tell him you want to get paid for the movie rights."

"You mean you get paid twice?"

Winging it, I said, "It depends on the deal you made. You get paid to print the book, and somebody gets paid for the movie."

"I'll see you get paid, Maria," said Vinny.

It was a couple of days later when I saw Maria again, at which point I asked her, "Did you get your money, Maria?"

"Yes, Brett, I got the money."

"All of it?" I asked.

"All of it."

I paused a few moments before I said, "You're welcome." I felt she was not even going to give me credit for getting the money for her. She eventually said thank you.

Chapter 28

SUCCESS WITH THE DRUG DOGS

It was an early morning in late spring when the telephone rang. My father answered it. "Brett, it's your grandpa. He wants to talk to you."

"Brett, what else do you think that dogs can smell?"

"Grandpa, I am really glad you called me, because I have heard a lot about plastic explosives. I think that you should train dogs to smell that stuff. It's real important that we find a way to detect that explosive because a criminal could take the explosive on a bus, a train, or even an airplane and go completely undetected. Another thing is to detect dead bodies when children are abducted or lost in the woods. Basically anything that has a smell to it. Did you find a way to detect the drugs, Grandpa?"

"We're still working on it, Brett. What kind of dogs would you want to use?"

"I gave that considerable thought, Grandpa. Whitesburg is the city nearest to you. A burg is a German city, and our last name is Lawson, which is a German but also an English name. Everything is pointing to using German shepherds. I think we should use German shepherds because the shepherd is better suited for protecting the officer, on account of its size and weight, should the drug dealer become violent. I don't know if those dogs originated in Germany or not, but I feel that by using shepherds, it would be Germany's way of apologizing for the atrocities the Germans committed in World War II. What do you think, Grandpa?"

"Brett, you know, I think you are right. You thought things out very well. I agree that shepherds would be the way for us to go. Your father will be coming down sometime in the next few days. I want you to ride along with him when he does."

"I'll be there, Grandpa."

After my grandfather hung the phone up, I asked my father, "Dad, can we take Shawn and Duey down south with us?"

He said, "Sure. If their parents will allow them to go, then they are welcome to tag along. So go ahead and ask their parents. Tell them we will be leaving Friday afternoon and coming back Monday night."

I ran down the street to Duey's house and got his father's permission. Then Duey and I went to see if Shawn wanted to go also. Shawn agreed to go too.

When Friday came, we headed down south. It was early Saturday morning when we arrived at Grandpa Holbrook's. Duey, Shawn, and I had slept for a large portion of the trip down. Dad dropped us off at Grandpa's and then headed over to Haymond, where his mom and dad lived, to have his mom fix him breakfast. He would get some sleep there. My grandma Holbrook fixed breakfast for us kids, but she was not aware that Duey could not eat pork because he was a Muslim. Seeing as pork was a big staple in my family's diet, she had no other meat ready. Even the gravy had pork in it. So it was eggs and biscuits with my grandfather's fresh honey for Duey.

After breakfast, I showed Shawn and Duey around the farm. After that, I asked my grandpa to set up a target and give me a gun to use for target practice. He did so. I let Shawn take his turn shooting first. Then Duey took a turn. Duey did not even hit the outer ring from ten feet away. Both my friends soon realized how difficult it was to hit the bull's-eye.

"We want to see how good you are, Brett," Shawn said.

I had my grandpa put up a silhouette, and then I told Shawn that I had been taught to shoot for the head, at which I would be aiming. I fired three rounds, all three of which hit the head. Shawn then said, "Do that again, Brett."

I racked off three more rounds, again hitting the target. Then I asked Shawn, "How's that?"

"I would not want to go up against you in a gunfight, that's for sure!"

"Now I am going to show you that I can do the same thing while running."

"There is no way! You can't do that!"

"Watch me," I said. I was about thirty feet away when I started running toward the silhouette. I emptied my gun into the head of the silhouette. There were no misses; all six rounds went into the head.

The shooting display was over. My grandmother made a spectacular meal for us, including some fresh chicken so Duey would be able to eat some meat. As we were eating, my grandma said, "You boys be sure you fill up on food because Burt will be here to start back home tonight. There are extra helpings for you, so eat as much as you want."

Evening came. Dad showed up and said, "Brett, we are going to leave around dark and travel all night because the traffic will be light. So be ready to go shortly."

Duey, Shawn, and I gathered our things and prepared to leave just before dark, just as Dad had said to do. We were about fifteen minutes away from Grandpa's farm on Kentucky Highway 15 when we came across about a dozen or so men who had stretched themselves across the highway so as to block the road and keep us from passing by them. They all were armed with guns and wearing holsters.

My father stopped. Part of the group came up to the car. One of them, who seemed to be the leader, stood on my side of the car and asked, "Y'all got any niggers in your car?"

I answered, "No, we don't have any niggers in the car."

"What you talking about, boy? There's one right behind you. Get out of the car, nigger," he said to Duey.

I got out of the car also, and said, "He isn't a nigger. He is Arabic."

"Well, little boy, he is a nigger to me! Do you know what we do to niggers around here?"

I didn't know if this was just a bunch of rednecks out having what they thought was fun, or if this was some kind of joke, or if they were serious, but mostly I did not know who the hell they were. It was quite evident they knew that we had been staying at my grandpa's house, as they knew to cut us off at the road. I had to do something, as I could not let anything happen to Duey. I had promised myself I would protect him even if I had to give up my own life after Carlos had made me shoot him. I was now going to have to put up my life in order to get Duey out of this jam. And I was going to humiliate these assholes in the process for calling my friend a nigger.

"Tell you what. I'll fight for his life. How about you pick somebody who you think is the best man you got with a gun, and we'll fight each other with our guns?"

The one who was leading the bunch said, "Does anyone want to fight this little boy?"

I heard a voice behind me say, "No way am I going to fight him, because I know who trained him."

Whoever had said that obviously knew my grandfather, and also who I was.

So now I was going to challenge the leader, who, after what he'd just heard about my grandfather, had to face me because he could not back down from a kid. I said, "How about you? I will take your word that you will let my friend go. Is it a deal?"

"You got a deal. He can go if you win."

I knew he would not back down, so I said, "When we are ready, someone say go."

I looked at him and said I was ready. He nodded, indicating that he was ready.

The object of a close-range gunfight is to try to get three shots off, one shot to the belly, one to the chest while moving the gun upward, and finally one to the head—all in less than three seconds. Someone said go. I used every ounce of speed I had in my hand to grab my gun so as to be the first to put a gun to the other's stomach.

227

I had my gun sticking in my opponent's belly before his had even cleared his holster. I had won.

The mob all began laughing. "We told you he was well trained."

Knowing I had won, there was no need to shoot. My opponent had lost by a wide margin. I told him, "Just put the gun back in the holster all the way. I won't shoot you."

He holstered his gun. I went back to the car, and my dad, my friends, and I continued on our way. I think Duey was a little shaken up. So was Shawn. But as the night went on, the three of us fell asleep, which is why I think my dad liked traveling at night.

It was almost noon when we got back to Dearborn. Duey headed back home. Shawn asked me to come with him to his house. When we got there, he told his father, Gordon Goodenrich Sr., "Dad, Duey lied to you. Brett did not miss Rico. I saw him shoot. Every shot went straight through the head. He did not miss even once—not even once."

"Are you really that good, Brett?"

"When it comes to firing a gun, Mister Goodenrich, I know what I am doing."

"I might ask you in the future to do something for me. I will let you know when the time comes."

"What is it you want me to do, Mister Goodenrich?"

"I don't know yet, Brett, but I will let you know once I decide. I might need a big favor from you."

"Well, if I can help, let me know." I then headed back home.

Chapter 29

A SOVIET IN THE WHITE HOUSE

Shortly after getting back from Kentucky, I was sitting on the steps of the front porch in the early afternoon when I kept hearing what I thought was thunder. It happened repeatedly, but there was not a cloud in the sky. I thought it was something called heat lightning and thunder. When my father came out of the house, I asked him, "Dad is there a storm blowing in? What's with all the thunder?"

"Brett, that's not thunder. It's our jets breaking the sound barrier. They are scrambling the jets because the US is getting ready to kick somebody's ass."

The crack of the jets breaking the sound barrier continued for long while. Normally I did not get shaken up easily, but for some reason on this day I was becoming a little scared. I could only hope it was not the Soviet Union we were about to go to war with, for that would mean total destruction of the planet.

Soon after the jets stopped with their thunder, Maria and Carlos came by. Maria told me, "Brett, we have to take you back to Washington."

"I am not going anywhere with you until I get an explanation of who you are and why you keep taking me to Washington. Who are you? You are not regular cops." I was going to stand my ground on this one, determined not to go with them until I got an answer.

"Okay, Brett, I am going to tell you, but you can't tell anyone else. We are the United States Secret Service."

Maria had just confirmed my suspicions about who she was. That explained the man from the Secret Service who had showed me his badge, and the one time I had seen Maria in uniform in the president's office. I still had the image of Johnny Doe's head in my mind, but I had gotten another piece of the puzzle. The next step was to find out who their boss was, and why he would authorize a couple of Secret Service agents to run around shooting kids.

"Okay, I'll go now. When do we leave?"

"Ten minutes ago, Brett. We have to go now."

"Let me put on a clean shirt and pants." I went into the house and gave myself what is called a "marine douche," which involves washing your armpits, wetting your hair, and putting on some deodorant. I grabbed my best shirt, the one with red and white stripes. Then I got into Maria's waiting car and we headed to Washington.

It was dark and late at night when we arrived. I was immediately escorted back to the bunker where the president and the joint chiefs had been when the Bay of Pigs invasion was taking place. I knew something big was happening; otherwise, we would not be back in the bunker. I did not see the president, so I told the Secret Service I was tired from the trip and needed some rest. They led me through a door behind which was a dormitory with about twenty to twenty-five beds, the same type of beds you would see soldiers sleeping on at a military base. Exhausted, I collapsed and fell asleep very quickly.

I was wakened in the morning and was told the president needed to see me. I walked in to a room where the president was. He greeted me cheerfully and asked, "Brett how would you like a cup of coffee?"

"No, sir, but I would like a glass of water." One of the aides brought me the water.

"Brett that is a really nice shirt, you look pretty dapper in it. I think I will get me one tailored just like it. As a matter of fact, I think I will get two or three of them."

Just about then, one of the joint chiefs approached me and said, "Good morning, Brett. Where are you going to today, Mars?"

"What do you mean Mars, General?" I asked.

"Well, we all think that you're a space cadet, so we figured you'd be taking a trip to outer space today."

"Why would anyone want to go Mars? There is no vegetation there because there is no water—and you need water to sustain life."

"Now how would you know all that about Mars when scientists don't even know?"

"I don't know."

The general walked off into the communications room. Soon afterward, another general came into the room and asked me, "Brett, we need to know: what do you think the Soviets are going to do next?"

I replied, "Sir, I don't even want to speculate on what might happen next. I got the joint chiefs making fun of me, calling me a space cadet. And then they are calling the president a jackass for listening to a kid. Also, I have been shot in the head. All this happened while I was trying to help my country. Now you want me to give you more fodder to make fun of the president, and of me?"

The general, seeming very upset, asked me, "Brett, who is it that said all those things to you?"

"Sir, I can't keep track of all of your staff. But if it is important for you to know, my suggestion is to pose that question to your staff. If the officer who said it is truly a good officer, he will admit that he said those things."

Storming off into the communications area which had no doors, the general said in a raised voice, "That kid described the beachhead at the Bay of Pigs invasion to a tee. He has never been to Cuba, nor has his family been there. He also knew what Castro was going to do even before Castro knew what he was going to do. Then someone called our commander in chief a jackass for listening to him. I want to know who it was."

The general who'd said that to me stood up and admitted it. What punishment he was given, I did not hear. The general whom I'd just been talking to then re-entered the room where I was. I had figured out who he was, the chairman of the joint chiefs, which meant that he was the Man. He asked me, "Brett, what do you think our options are?"

"Sir, if you keep things simple, we can launch a full-scale attack on Cuba, or we launch a nuclear strike on Russia, or do what I think is the best thing, which is the naval blockade. The whole objective would be to end the crisis peacefully. With a blockade, we'll be sending the Soviets a message that they can turn around and head back home, and no one gets hurt."

"What do think the Soviet response will be, Brett?"

"As long as we don't sink one of their ships, the conflict will end peacefully and there will be no need for an attack from Russia. I don't believe they will want to engage in a nuclear war and destroy the whole world, or even to start a land war in Cuba just so Cuba can have a nuclear arsenal. I just don't believe they want to fight us in Cuba. We will also need to prepare our nuclear missiles to be ready, just in case they launch a missile at us."

"Do you think they will launch a nuclear attack?"

"No sir. I think that would only happen if we attacked on Russian soil or invaded one of the Soviet Bloc countries in Europe. Ending the conflict peacefully is the best way to go."

The United States must have been under some sort of threat, because we remained in the bunker a few more hours. Whether we were preparing for a nuclear attack on the Soviets or another attack on Cuba, I did not know. The threat must have subsided, however, because we soon headed back to the White House.

There, I was taken to the room that had the red phone, which was a direct line to Moscow, for the president's use only. I was given a 9mm semiautomatic pistol and told to watch the red phone. A couple of hours went by. I had been alternating between pacing the floor and sitting down. I put my head down on the desk to rest, closing my eyes but remaining awake, when someone came into the room and picked up the phone. Pretending to be asleep, I heard him speaking Russian. That's when I jumped up to confront him. The perpetrator took off, running through the White House at an all-out sprint. I aimed at his back, but something inside me said not to shoot. I quickly ran to the door from which he had exited, and shouted to the Secret Service, "Who just ran out this door? Whoever it was, he was talking Russian on the red phone."

The Secret Service started scampering to gather all the agents. Since I had not gotten a good look at the man's face, they had me identify his voice.

There was only one of them who spoke Russian. When I heard him speak, I knew it was him, so I said, "That's him." They hustled him away.

One of the generals asked me, "Brett, why didn't you just shoot him?"

"Sir, I'm not familiar with a semiautomatic pistol. I did not want to miss inside the house and have a bullet go through a wall."

"How did you catch him?"

"Well, sir, I had been up for a while and was tired, so I put my head down to rest on the desk. I was awake, but I had my eyes closed. When he came into the room, it looked as though I was sleeping, but I could hear what he was doing. Then he picked up the red phone and started talking Russian. That's when I jumped up. He dropped the phone and started running for the door."

He chuckled and said, "Have no fear when Brett is here. Good job, Brett! We knew we had a leak somewhere. You just helped us find it."

The head of the Secret Service asked me, "Brett, what can do we do to prevent this from happening again?"

"You have to rotate the guards every two weeks so they don't get complacent."

After all was said and done, I concluded that the spy may have been the reason the Bay of Pigs invasion failed.

Chapter 30

VACATION IN HYANNIS

I did not know if the person speaking Russian was an aide or if he was working for the Secret Service. I could only guess. Had he been a Soviet mole, or had he turned on the United States for money? It would be something I would never know, but it was not my job to find out. I would just continue to follow orders. The problems inside the president's administration were mounting. I would convey, through my actions, that I would continue to support him to the best of my ability.

"Brett, I have a treat for you. I am going to show you how the other half lives. I am going to take you to where I live in Hyannis. You can spend some time on the beach with me and my family."

"When are we going, sir, and what will I do for clothes?"

"You can borrow some clothes from my nephews. And we are leaving now."

The president and I were back at the White House, walking down a hallway, when the general who had called me a space cadet approached us and said to the president in front of me, "We want you to die for us. We want you to die, sir."

The general then turned and walked away.

I was puzzled as to why the joint chiefs would wish the president dead. I felt like the joint chiefs had forced the president to choose between them and me. Firm in my belief regarding how the Soviets would react to our actions, I just hoped I was right to avoid bloodshed. The president, undaunted, continued down the hall with me close behind. We exited the White House and boarded Marine One. Suddenly I had to urinate.

The president asked, "Have you ever been on a helicopter before, Brett?"

"No, sir, this is the first time."

"You seem a bit uneasy, Brett. You aren't scared, are you?"

"No sir. Actually I feel more like privileged. It's just that I have to go pee." I asked him, "How long will I have to hold my water?"

"It's about an hour to Hyannis. Do you think you can hold it?"

"I don't know if I can hold it, sir. Maybe I better go to the bathroom because I wouldn't want to piss all over the seat, sir." He instructed the Secret Service to escort me to the bathroom and to have Benny drive me to the president's home in Hyannis.

When Benny and I arrived at the president's house, a beachfront home, we parked in what was the back, walked to the front of the house, which faced the beach and what I thought was the ocean, and then entered the house. The first thing I noticed, right away, was the bright white paint. It was meticulously kept, as if someone immediately wiped off any stains that might have soiled it. The entryway had the most beautiful emerald-green carpet, which looked as if it had just been put down. I was led upstairs and shown the office and the place where another red phone was. There was a bedroom at the top of the stairs on the same level as the president's office. Shown a room that had a double bed and a bathroom, I was told that this was where I would be sleeping. My job was to keep an eye on the phone.

The president, as with all military men, had been taught to keep his bunk neat. Afraid to mess up the bed and later not be able to straighten it up to Kennedy's satisfaction, I slept on the floor. The next morning, I decided to do a little exploring through the house. I headed down the stairs, wandered through the rooms, and found myself in the kitchen. Seated at the table were a bunch of girls having breakfast. The president was standing next to the stove with a woman, who was doing the cooking. He said, "Brett, these are my nieces. I like to have breakfast with them. Do you want some coffee and something to eat?"

I sat down at the table and said, "A couple of eggs with some toast and jam, sir. Why don't you sit down with us, sir?"

239

It was then that one of the girls, about five years old, said to me, "You are sitting in his chair. He sits at the head of the table."

All the girls got up from the table. Embarrassed that I had taken the president's spot at the table, I slammed down the juice the cook had served me and headed back upstairs without eating anything. The president followed, stopping me in the great room. "Brett, I want you to walk with me down the beach to another house where the men stay. Would you do that for me?"

"Certainly, sir, I would feel honored."

We walked a little ways down the beach, coming to the house where the boys and men stayed. It was beginning to seem like the Kennedys had everything set up like a college campus, with the houses set up like dormitories.

I asked the president, "Sir, how does your family afford all these houses and being near the beach? It must be terribly expensive."

"We all pool our money, Brett."

"That seems to be working, sir, with the majority of your family seeming to be college educated."

Once inside the house, the president introduced me to some of his nephews. We talked. They took me to an office and showed me the phone with a line connecting to the beach house. I sat in the office while the president's nephews came and went, asking me questions like where I was from, how old I was, and other personal stuff. One of his nephews, much older than the others, about seventeen years old or so, came into the office.

He said, "Brett, we like the Mexican cops."

That statement came as shock to me. He obviously was unaware of the crimes the Garcia brothers had committed. And what he'd just said came from out of the blue, as I had not said anything about any Mexican cops. What I could not figure out was how Benny and Carlos had passed all the security checks.

Kennedy and I had been at the boys' dorm for a couple of hours when we started back to the beach house. The president asked, "Brett, what are your plans after you get out of school?"

"Well, sir, the end of school is a little far in advance. In the Kennedy family, sir, you are good politicians, but in my family, we are good soldiers, so I will most likely end up joining the military. And hopefully I will be able to go to college after my tour of duty."

"What subjects do you like best?" the president asked.

"Sir, I have a couple of subjects I like. One is math. But the one I like best is history. I liked learning about the world wars and the Civil War, and especially inventions and who invented them. My favorite place to go in the whole wide world is a place that we have in Dearborn called Greenfield Village. There they have the Appomattox Courthouse, where Lee surrendered

241

to end the Civil War. They also have Edison's lab, and the Wright Brothers' cycle shop."

"They have all those of exhibits there?"

"Yes, sir, and there are a lot more historical exhibits. I'm just fascinated with the Edison exhibit. I want to someday learn how electricity works. I totally admire his creativity. Without him, the world would be a much darker place."

"What type of job do you have your eye on, Brett?"

"Well, sir, I can tell you one field I don't plan on going into."

"What's that, Brett?"

"That is politics, sir. I don't know how much they pay you, but it isn't enough."

"Brett, I'm dying. Knowing that, how do you think I should die?"

Not wanting the president to reveal information that he wanted to keep secret, I danced around the subject of what it was he was dying of.

"Sir, I don't think it is how you die, but how you have lived. You have to look back on your life, recall your accomplishments, and ask yourself, 'Can I do more before I go?' What do you think, sir? Can you do more?"

"I am not sure just how much time I have, Brett."

"You have served your country faithfully in war, and also in peace. Both your record and the record of your family speak for themselves. There is no doubt about your love for your country and your passion for freedom. The politicians and the public all realize that. They also recognize that with your family, it is not about money but about the good of the country. I don't know of any family more patriotic than yours. If you are comfortable with that, then there is nothing else left to accomplish for your family and your country, in which case you will not have any fear of death. Given these things, I think you should die a peaceful death, sir, at home with your family by your side."

"I think that is pretty sound advice, Brett. You are definitely wise beyond your years."

"Well, sir, you set me on the right path with your inaugural speech. I am sure that when anyone thinks about you, they will remember that speech."

We had arrived back at the beach house. Walking in, the president said, "Brett, the girls all think you are cute. Is there one you like better than the rest?"

"Well, sir, I think they are all very pretty, but then I don't recall seeing an unattractive female Kennedy, sir." Smiling, I said to him, "The men don't do too badly with the ladies, either, sir." I think he knew what I was implying.

"Brett, you are a pretty smooth character yourself." He smiled and then said, "You might be right about the men too, Brett."

The next day, I was upstairs in the president's office when I heard a couple of the girls yelling out, "Brett, where are you? We want to talk to you."

I walked down the stairs and to the door where they standing. I asked, "What do you girls want?"

"We want you to come and play with us, Brett. Please come and play with us." They took off down the beach.

I started out the door when a Secret Service agent stopped me and said, "You are not here to play, Brett. You are here to kill the president. We don't want anyone to know you are here, so you can't be seen out of the house. You are not in the same league as those girls, so stay away from them."

I was irate. All I could think of was that the Garcia brothers were behind this.

"I don't understand. I walked down the beach yesterday with the president, and now you tell me I can't talk to his nieces? I will stay inside the house if those are the president's wishes."

"Go ahead, Brett. Go talk to them," the agent said.

I held a short conversation with the girls about life around the compound, and then I headed back to the house. I was upstairs near the bedroom when one of the girls came into the house and said, "Mom, he smells like he pooped his pants. Can you check him out, please?"

The girl, whose name I didn't know, came upstairs. One of the Kennedy mothers followed her. The mother came over to me and said, "Brett, I'm one of the Kennedy mothers, one of the house moms. All the girls call me Etty. We need to check your clothes because you are starting to smell bad. We need your clothes so we can wash them. You need to freshen up."

I had no fear of Etty seeing me naked. She asked the president's niece to stand behind me. I began removing my clothing. As I was doing so, Etty said, "It's not his clothes. It's his breath."

I knew I had some bad teeth. I had not brushed for almost a week, and I couldn't brush now because I had no toothbrush. Feeling humiliated at this point, I asked, "Mrs. Kennedy, could I get a towel so I can take a shower? And can I have toothbrush also?"

"Brett, please, there are lots of Mrs. Kennedy's, so please call me Etty. There is a towel in the bathroom. When you are done, the housekeeper will bring you another one—and a toothbrush."

After I had gotten out of the shower, I heard Etty talking to someone in the great room. Catching only part of the conversation, I overheard her say, "That's a physical impossibility." Then she repeated herself, although this time even louder: "That's a physical impossibility. He does not even have pubic hair yet. I am a woman. I know these things." When Etty was finished talking, she came into the bedroom with fresh clothes. I got dressed and headed down the beach, where the girls were gathered.

As I walked up, the one who'd said I smelled bad said, "Nice butt, Brett. Gorgeous body too."

"Pretty face, Miss Kennedy," I replied. I had just learned a lesson about the female gender. All those sayings professing that women in general want to marry a man with a keen mind or a boatload of money might be true, but a nice butt and a good body is what really starts their motors. I headed back to the house to get something to eat.

It was later that evening when the president showed up. I was anxious on account of what the Secret Service had said earlier about why I was here. I said to Kennedy, "The Secret Service told me earlier that I was here to kill you, sir. I am not here to kill you. I'm here with you to save your life. Did one of those cops named Garcia tell you I wanted to kill you?"

"Brett, have you ever raped anyone?"

"No, sir, I've never raped anyone, but I have been falsely accused of raping a woman. Make that a couple of women."

"Who were the women, Brett?"

"One of the women was Gary Powers' sister, Justine. After she was raped, I was kidnapped and hidden in a home for unwed mothers. There, two women who were living in the home were raped, and they blamed me. All the time I was staying there, they were pumping me full of drugs."

"Who really raped them, Brett?"

"Rico Garcia, the Garcia brothers' nephew. Rico also raped my mother."

All of a sudden, from behind me, came a loud growling voice like the voice of a lioness who had just had one of her cubs attacked. It was Etty. She said, "*I knew it!* Your men lied to you, Jack. What are you going to do now, Jack? Brett is doing everything he can to keep you alive, and they want him to shoot you so they can shoot him. Brett does not fit the profile of a rapist. Women give their bodies willingly to men like Brett. Even your own nieces would be willing to give their bodies to Brett, but he is not quite ready yet." She was letting the president know she knew more about women, and was more educated in their wants and needs than he.

Boy that was a welcome relief! Finally I had someone in a position of authority believing in me—and who better than the wife of the attorney general of the United States? At that time, I loved just one person more than Etty, and that was my mother. Etty had things figured the same way I did. She knew, as I knew, that one of the president's men, whether it was Benny or not, had been filling the president's head full of bullshit. On account of this, Kennedy was making decisions based on untrue "facts" and erroneous information.

"Brett, tell me how the Garcias work? And how is it that they are getting away with what they're doing?" the president asked.

"Sir, somehow after Rico Garcia, Benny Garcia's nephew, rapes these women, Rico then terrorizes the victim and makes her say it was me, or some other man who is totally innocent. He continues to rape more women, and when he gets caught at it, his uncle Carlos or Benny gets him out of jail. They are using their nephew, Rico Garcia, to make trouble for me and other men in the city by falsely accusing us of committing rapes we did not commit. These are innocent men whom they have blamed for crimes they did not commit so they can harass them. Once Rico's victim says that I am to blame, Carlos has the victim's family come after me for revenge. Then Carlos spreads word throughout the whole city that I am a rapist, and every cop in the city wants me in jail. Sooner or later, the news even gets spread throughout the state, and they all want me in jail."

"Are you on drugs, Brett? Because they're telling me you are on drugs."

"Isn't one of our rights 'innocent until proven guilty'? Maybe you should have the men who said those bad things to you about me show you some proof that I did those things. In the meantime, I will explain what the Garcia men I told you about did to me. They used the same technique as the rape technique, only this time, I am a witness against the corrupt cop. Their goal now is to destroy the witness's credibility. First, the Garcias spread it around to other law enforcement officials that I'm a junkie, even though that is not true. They do this so I no longer have any credibility as a witness against them. Anyone connected with law enforcement no longer believes anything I have to say. No police officer is going to take the word of a junkie over that of another police officer. No one in law enforcement believes me, even though I'm not doing any drugs at all. Then, they either forcefully drug me, or have me injected with a narcotic by another party, such as a gang member, to make it appear the cops were telling the truth about my drug habit. All the while they are telling a complete lie. In fact, sir, they are telling you a completely fabricated story. Anybody in a position of any authority will automatically take the police officer's word, no matter what I say, whether it is true or not."

I continued, "I can honestly tell you that I am not interested in doing drugs or ruining my brain with drugs. My family is poor. I just plain don't have any money to buy drugs. I cannot believe the president of the United States would invite me into his home and try to force me to do something I don't want to do. As long as I am nearby, sir, I am going to protect you and your family to the best of my ability. I love it here, and would like to someday come back and enjoy the company of your nieces. I would not want to do anything to jeopardize my chances of coming back. Now, the choice you have is to believe either me and your sister-in-law and the physical evidence, or the men who told you those lies. If it were to be proven that they are lying to you, then you should severely punish them. If they lied to you, they will lie to you again. And every time they lie, they are insulting your intelligence, as if to say, 'The president will believe anything I tell him.' That's the whole problem. They are going to keep lying to you until you catch them in a lie and severely reprimand them. I thought that by my helping you, you would be able to help me, but I don't think that is going to happen, so I need to go home. I will just protect my mother back home in Michigan. I need to go home."

When I got up the next morning, I saw that my ride home had already arrived. The two Kennedy girls who had asked me earlier in the week to come play with them came into the house. One of them said to me, "Brett, please don't leave. We want you to stay with us, at least till the end of the summer."

I said to them, "Ladies, I would love to stay and have dinner and a movie together, but some of the president's men have said some bad things about me. And the president is not helping me protect my mother. I am going to have to do that myself. I have to go back home because I have to protect her. I'll tell you what. In about five or six years, why don't you have the Secret Service look me up?"

"Brett, my mom does not believe those men, and we don't either."

I heard a voice call out, "Brett, your ride is waiting. It is time to go."

"All I can say is to look me up in the future and contact me. That way, I'll know you want me to come back."

I left with the feeling that the president was indifferent to my situation. I could not believe that the man who held the highest office in the land felt that way. He had kept me in the dark. And it seemed that the joint chiefs wanted us both dead.

Chapter 31

A LASTING FRIENDSHIP

By the time I got back to Detroit, I had made up my mind that I was going to see if I could develop a better friendship with Vinny. If the president could not, or would not, help, for whatever reasons he had for not helping me, then I was going to turn to Vinny for help because I trusted him more than I trusted any cop I knew. I soon got the opportunity to enlist his assistance.

I was sitting on the front porch when a kid about my age approached me. It was Tony Savino, Vinny's nephew, whom I had first met at Lasher Park while playing a pickup game of football with Tony and a few other guys from the neighborhood. He said, "Brett, Vinny wants to have a talk with you. He is not going to hurt you; he just wants to talk to you."

"Let's go," I said.

We walked down Lasher Street and toward Roulo Street, continuing until we reached a house at the corner of Roulo and Lasher. There, sitting on the back stairs, was Vinny. He started asking me questions about my shooting skills and what caliber my gun was. Then he asked, "Now, Brett, are you sure you can hit what you're shooting at?"

"Yes, absolutely positive."

"How would you like to do me a favor?"

"Sure, Vinny. What do can I do for you?"

"A man owes me money. I need to collect it. Do you think you can help, Brett?"

"Sure. What do I have to do to help?"

"We have to go to Chicago. Do you think you can go there?"

"No problem."

"I will contact you when we are ready to go, okay, Brett?"

"That's fine, Vinny."

Two days passed. Vinny and his bodyguard, Tom Painslie, came by my house with Tom as the driver. The three of us headed to Chicago. The trip took about four and a half hours. We pulled up in a parking lot, entered into a building, and headed into a hallway that led to some sort of private club. There was a man whom Vinny seemed to be acquainted with, but not overly friendly with. Shortly after we had entered the club, which had a bar, a Chicago cop came in. I was standing behind the bar drinking a soda and watching over Vinny, like I thought I was supposed to. Then in came Carlos and Isaac Simms. With their arrival, the alarms in my head started going off. As soon as they arrived, I knew that things were going to take a turn for the worse. I turned my attention back to Vinny, and saw the man with whom Vinny had been friendly earlier lying in a heap on the floor. Tom was standing over him. I had not heard any gunshots, so I did not know if the man had been stabbed or hit in the head with something.

The cop turned to me and said, "Brett, I am going to die for you."

My first thought was, *Here we go again,* but then I thought about Louie, and how Vinny had wanted to kill me. I then got the funny feeling that the cop, like Louie, was trying to stop Vinny from killing me. I said, "If you are going to die, call your wife first." I could not believe it, but Carlos and Vinny let him call his wife.

After the man had called his wife, Carlos said, "Brett, he is a crooked cop. You have to shoot him."

I thought, as if *Carlos and Simms are honest cops. Maybe I should shoot them too.* I then pulled out my revolver and, as I had been taught, fired three rounds to his head.

That's when Vinny said, "Brett, you ride back home with Tom."

I didn't like the idea of riding back with Tom because I did not trust him, but that was Vinny's order. I had to do as Vinny told me to do. As Tom and I were headed for the door, it became apparent to me why Garcia and Simms were there. Carlos said, "Isaac, you help clean up. Then you can drive Vinny back to Detroit. I'll follow Tom."

Tom and I began the trip back home. A little more than halfway to our destination, I began to get sick from not eating and had Tom pull over to the side of the road so I could vomit. I spewed a bucket full.

To my surprise, Tom said, "Kid, I am going to have to kill you." He reached for his pistol. Just then, Carlos Garcia pulled up and got out of his car. I knew, for some reason, that I should not trust Tom.

"I'm not going to let you kill him alongside the road like a dog. He's better than that. He did what you asked; he did what he was supposed to do for you. Besides all that, the cop died for him," Carlos said to Tom.

All I could think of was how much it was going to cost me for Carlos to save my life, because I was definitely going to be indebted to Carlos for this. He must have known this was going to happen; that's why he said he'd follow us.

I was slowly becoming aware of how Vinny and his men worked. I had done something for Vinny, and then he had given the order for me to be killed. It could not have been because I was a witness to what had happened at the club, because Carlos and Simms were there too. It had to be because of trust. Vinny was not going to take any chances by leaving me alive. Whatever it was, I would have to find a way to earn Vinny's trust. In the meantime, I was going to enjoy the rest of the summer.

I headed the block and a half to Jake and Lucas Barnett's house to see if they might want to go to the Dearborn Youth Center to do some roller-skating.

When I arrived, Jake said, "No, we are going to go hustling the drunks shining shoes at the bars on Eagle Pass. Do you want to go?" It was really the intersection of Wyoming and Eagle Streets. The place was named Eagle Pass because it went through an underpass that led to Miller Road, which was where one of the major auto plants was located. Most of bar patrons were employed at that plant.

"I don't know that much about hustling, Jake," I said.

"Don't worry, we'll teach you. And we will give you some of the money."

"Okay, let's go."

They both had boxes full of brushes and shoe polish, which they grabbed before we headed toward the bars.

There were six bars, the usual "shot and a beer" joints. Since one of the auto plants was nearby, these bars had plenty of patrons. After Jake, Lucas, and I walked into one of the bars, Jake said to me, "Don't do anything or say anything, but watch me and Lucas."

I stood beside him as he and Lucas went from patron to patron asking, "Do you want a shine, mister? I only charge fifty cents...fifty cents."

When Jake found a man who wanted a shine, he got down on his knees and started cleaning his shoes. After they were cleaned, he began to polish them. When he got up, he collected the money, getting more than he'd asked for, a dollar bill instead of the fifty cents. This went on until every man in the bar had been approached. Then it was onto the next bar. Once we had made the rounds, Jake and Lucas had over twenty dollars between them. We then headed toward Dix Road to the local fish joint. When we got there, Lucas ordered a big platter of fries. The three of us shared it. My hustling lesson was complete. I went home with anticipation of getting my own shoeshine box with all the right colors of polish. I was grateful to Jake and Lucas. Times were tough; I could use the money.

Chapter 32

EDUCATING VINNY

A couple of days later, Vinny came by my house. He had Maria with him. My father and I were sitting on the front porch. Vinny said, "I want to show my appreciation for you helping me out, Brett. I have some money I want you to have."

"What did I do for this money, Vinny, and how much is it?" I asked.

Maria answered for him, saying, "It's a lot of money, Brett."

"Vinny, I can't accept your money because I did not work for it." I didn't know exactly what I had done to earn money from Vinny and felt it might not be legitimate.

"Brett, you are insulting me. You did me a favor. I want to pay you for it."

"Vinny, I did you a favor, right?"

"That's right, Brett," Vinny said.

"Okay, I got a proposal for you. My family likes to work for our money, so how about we trade favors and you get my father a job as a bookie? It does not have to be for you, Vinny, but maybe you know someone who needs help. My dad is real good at math and knows all about horses and numbers. I believe he can generate a lot of money for you."

He paused for a minute or two, and then said, "Okay, Brett, we will trade favors. But I want you to come by the house tomorrow just to talk."

The next day, I went to the place where I had met Vinny before. He was sitting on the stairs with a few men standing around. He stood up and said, "Brett, we are always looking for new ways of making money. I can tell by the way you thought of putting your father to work for us that you have kind of a creative mind."

"Vinny, how do you make your money?" I asked.

"I am into the rackets."

"That is all I need to know, Vinny, because the less I know about your business, the better off I am." "One thing that bothers me is that people hate Italians so much," Vinny said.

"Vinny, they don't hate Italians; they hate gangsters. There are Mexican gangs and nigger gangs, and even the Chinese have gangs. Nobody likes any of those gangsters, either."

"You really think so, Brett?"

"One thing I can tell you is that our system of government is based on the Roman system of government. They had a senate and an Emperor which made up their two branches of government. Our country's government is made up of three branches, the executive, which is the president, the legislature, and the judicial. The president also has a special power. It is called a veto."

"But that was Rome, Brett."

"Vinny, where is Rome? Isn't it in Italy? Do you think all those Romans just disappeared from the planet when the Roman Empire dissolved? Rome still exists, Vinny; just the empire dissolved. The people of the Roman Empire did not just disappear; they probably scattered throughout the countryside. So I am sure a lot of Italians have Roman blood in them."

"Is that true, Brett?"

"Vinny, yes it is true, although I don't know 100 percent for sure. Let me tell you about a great person who was Italian. Have you ever heard of a man named Marconi?"

"No. Who was he?"

"Marconi invented the long-range radio. Without him, the ships would not be able to communicate with other ships. All the musical stars owe their success to Marconi. Another great Italian was Galileo. Among people who study the planets and stars, he is considered the father of modern astronomy, and is held in the highest esteem by all educated men today. To tell you how stupid they were during Galileo's time, which was almost five hundred years ago, the Roman Catholic Church put him under house arrest for saying the planets revolve around the sun, something that is true. And I am sure you have heard of Leonardo da Vinci, the famous artist. He is credited with designing the first helicopter."

"Brett, how in the hell do you know all this?"

"I learned it in school, Vinny."

"You mean they teach you about Italians in school?"

"No, Vinny, they don't teach us about Italians. These people are not famous because they were Italian. They are famous for being smart and educated. The discoveries they made and their accomplishments are what they are famous for, Vinny. With your money and power, you have the opportunity to do some really great things for Italian people."

"What do you suggest I do, Brett?"

"Well, the very first thing you got to do is establish a reputation for running an honest game, so that everyone who likes to gamble wants to gamble with you. Nobody wants to gamble with you if you are noted for cheating people out of their money. They might not say anything if you cheat them, but they won't gamble with you ever again."

"How would you go about doing something like that?"

"Well, the first thing is to soften up a little bit on the gamblers. You need to get a bigger share of the gambling market. Remember—no one wants to gamble with you if they're afraid they're going to get their ass beat, Vinny. I like to play poker and gamble in other ways. I know the cops are going to look the other way because they have their hand in your pocket. I don't waste my money on playing the numbers because you never know whether the house is going to pay off or not. No one knows if the number comes out, if the house uses the Pontiac number, or the Detroit number, or whichever pays the least. You should pick one number and pay off on that number, and pay off the next day. And if the gamblers don't pay up quickly, then talk to them first. To me, Vinny, gambling is all right. If your organization does not control the gambling, that leaves other gangs to muscle in on you. The cops don't want to arrest you anyway, because they know that if they bust you, someone else is going to take over tomorrow, and then they've got to start all over.

"The other idea I have is that you should think about legitimate businesses. Instead of stealing from a business, you should buy the businesses, becoming sort of a silent partner. One business that I can think of right away is a pizzeria. Every kid I know just loves pizza. You should also consider helping other people start a business. You can be the owner until they make enough money to buy the business from you. Vinny, you have an opportunity to help struggling Italian families. Maybe someday you will be as famous as Galileo or Marconi."

"Brett, those are all good ideas, but I have got to go now. However, I want to talk to you some more, so I will send Tony to get you, okay?"

"Okay, Vinny. Good night."

I left Vinny feeling that my friendship with him was beginning to grow. While I did not think Vinny would protect me unconditionally, I got the feeling that I had gotten through to him. I felt he liked me because of the ideas I had given him. I also felt that he thought I was smart, and that I was loyal to him. That was the one thing I had learned in the short years I had lived: powerful men respected loyalty—and loyalty went a long way with Vinny.

I would have to wait for Vinny to call on me again to advance our friendship any further. I was not only turning Vinny into a friend but also I was recruiting for the war Carlos was waging, which would soon involve Vinny. I knew one thing for sure: if Vinny got in Carlos' way, Carlos would formulate a plan to attack him. That would be where my loyalty would come in. Even though Carlos was a cop, if he decided to wage war against Vinny, I would definitely side with Vinny. I was slowly preparing, just in case, for the day when Garcia would go after Vinny.

The summer was nearing a close. I would continue doing the best I could to build a case against Team Garcia but I would have to do it secretly.

The next afternoon, Benny came by the house and said he wanted to take me for a walk. We started to walk around the block. At one point he said, "Brett, I work for the CIA. I want you to give me your money."

I was astonished when he told me he worked for the cia—totally surprised. I had never met a CIA operative. "What money are you talking about, Benny?" I asked, thinking that maybe this had something to do with the money Vinny had tried to give me but that I had refused to accept. Vinny had told me that he ended up giving that money to his niece.

"You've got a lot of money now, Brett," he said, evading my question.

"You mean that I've got a lot of money and I have to give it to the CIA?"

"No, Brett, I want you to give it to me. Otherwise, I will put you and your whole family on drugs."

Not knowing how much money we were discussing or even what I had done to earn it, I was going to do everything I could to see that Benny did not get any money from me. I had seen my dad's pay stubs showing he earned about eighty dollars a week, so I figured that the most the amount in question could be was twenty or twenty-five thousand dollars.

"Okay, Benny, in that case, you can have the money." I was trying to stall until I figured out what to do, and ask my dad where the money had come from.

As we were returning to the house, I saw that Maria and Carlos were approaching us. As they neared Benny and me, Benny said to them, "I told Brett I work for the CIA, so he is going to give me the money."

"I want you to walk with me, Brett," Carlos said. Then he and I walked away from Benny and Maria. "Since you are giving up the money, I am going to teach you how we work. The first thing is that when one of our men is caught doing something illegal we find out who the lead investigator is. Once we find out who he is, we ask him what evidence they have against the man we want to go free. When we figure what the key piece of evidence is, we then remove it, making the case go down the drain. Then our man is released."

Jackpot! I had often thought about that technique from watching old westerns. It would have been hard to convict someone in the Old West with the flimsy evidence they gathered back then. *In the Old West,* I wondered, *what would have stopped a crooked sheriff or deputy from removing a major piece of evidence when there was very little evidence to begin with?* Now I understood how Team Garcia had gotten away with those eight-hundred-plus murders in the Cass Corridor. No one on the rest of the police force would even question police officers about the removal of evidence. It was the final clue I needed to try to stop the Garcias, but sadly, I would have to let them commit more murders, and I would have to memorize the perpetrators, and when, where, and how those murders were committed, before I even had a chance of stopping them.

The following day, Carlos came by with a large yellow envelope.

"Brett, I want to teach this to you." He pulled out quarter-inch-wide strips of paper with typing on them.

"This envelope contains my orders, Brett," Carlos said. He would not tell me who had given him the slips of paper or where they had come from. There were no markings on the envelope. At this point, all I could do was guess where they had come from. I presumed that since the Garcia brothers were either CIA or the Secret Service, their orders had arrived from Washington. After he read the slips, Carlos took a match and burned them. That let me know this was ultra-secret stuff. Still, I was a little confused. Washington would not have put a stamp of approval on mass murders, killing kids, and injecting kids with drugs—or would they?

I headed back to the house after my lesson with Carlos. I was met at the door by my father, who said, "Brett, don't mess with them. They're the CIA, and they are going to kill you."

"They don't want me dead, Dad. They want you dead."

I think that stunned him. He did not know that they had been teaching me the tricks of the trade. His statement had made me unsure whether they were really CIA or if they were the Secret Service. Maria had said they were Secret Service, and Benny had said he was CIA. If they were really federal officers, then they would be acting on orders from Washington. Otherwise, the team was working on its own agenda. I would have to remember the statement Benny made, and also the statement Maria made that her and Carlos were the Secret Service. Benny was CIA and Maria and Carlos were the Secret Service, and I would have to commit it to memory. Then I'd have to wait until they made a mistake and showed who they really were.

The first chance I got, I told my dad what had transpired between Benny and me. Then I confronted my father.

"Dad, Benny said I have a lot of money. Do you know anything about me having a lot of money?"

"I don't know anything about any money."

"Benny said if I did not give him the money, he was going to hurt the whole family."

"Well, I am not giving him any money because I don't have any money to give him."

One day the following week, I woke up to find that sometime during the night, I had been drugged. And my dad was staggering through the house like he had been drugged also. I staggered to the upstairs back window, looked out, and saw that Team Garcia assembled on the lawn. All the members were present: Maria, Rico, Isaac Simms, Benny, and Carlos.

Realizing that they were not there to wish us well, and seeing that I was outmanned and outgunned, I told my father, "Dad, they are going to kill us so they can take whatever money we have. I have a plan to put the money in Maria son's name, and my name, and yours, Dad. That way, Maria, along with you and I, can help protect the money." I figured that this way there

266

would be four of us protecting the money. If my dad and I were going to die protecting the money, then Maria and her son could die for the same reason.

It was then that Maria came into the house and said, "The team is after Brett's money. You can't keep the money."

I was puzzled by what Maria had said. Why could I not keep whatever money everybody was talking about? I told her what I had proposed to Dad about the money. No one had yet told me how much money it was. My dad was handling everything that was occurring. Throughout this whole situation, my mom was oblivious to any money.

I returned to bed with the thought that Dad and Maria would handle everything and do the right thing. Little did I know that my life was about to become even more tumultuous.

Chapter 33

FALSE ARREST

It was around noon when Isaac Simms came by my house and asked me, "Brett, do you to want to meet me at Little Maria's house and spend some time with me? Little Maria is going to be there. Maybe you can get to know her a little better."

Little Maria, who was my age, was Maria's niece. Their family was Mexican. Her family also went by the name Simms. I had met her and her brother, Darrin, who was a few years older than she, at the pool at Lasher Park. Darrin had a reputation as being a really tough kid, a reputation that was well deserved. I figured that maybe Isaac Simms's attitude toward me was softening up a little, as evidenced by his inviting me over to Little Maria's. I had no idea why he had invited me or what he planned. I agreed to meet him at her house in about an hour. I was being cautious because I didn't fully trust Simms and was suspicious at best, but I consoled myself with the thought that Little Maria would be there also, which would make me feel a little more at ease.

It was not very far from my house to Little Maria's. I walked down Holly Street and past Lowery Street. From there it was a short block to Welsh Street, which is where she lived. Soon arriving at her house, I walked up the back stairway to the door to the upper flat. Little Maria answered the door and welcomed me in. I was glad it was she who had let me in the house; I was glad to see her. Isaac Simms then came into the living room, where Maria and I were standing.

He said, "Brett, I am going to teach you about sex, so get naked."

Fearing I would get a disease like I had before, I replied, "Isaac, I'm not interested in learning about sex. I learned all that I need to know when I was assaulted in the Corridor. Besides, I am too young for sex."

"Would you like to have sex with Maria?"

"No, I wouldn't, Isaac."

Isaac Simms then told Little Maria to get naked.

I spoke up and told her, "No, Maria, don't take your clothes off. I don't feel comfortable with both of us being naked together. I or both of us could get in trouble. Maria, I like you because you're nice, not because I want sex from you."

With Justine's false allegation of rape in the back of mind, I had a sneaking suspicion that Maria Simms was setting me up to look like a sex criminal.

It was then that the older Maria walked in. She did not seem upset, but she was surprised. It was beginning to seem to me as if the whole Simms family was obsessed with sex. The elder Maria had another woman with her. She had a hairdo like Doris Day, so I nicknamed her "Blondie the Nymph." Nicknaming people was my way of avoiding knowing anybody's real name. Unless it was absolutely necessary that I know someone's name, I did not care to remember it. If someone wanted to know this woman's name, they were not going to get it from me.

This situation was now becoming a sex party with grownups and kids alike. I was an unwilling participant. I decided to leave, telling Isaac, "I want to go home."

Blondie the Nymph said, "Brett, you can't go home yet. I want to teach you how to have sex."

Blondie's statement did not comfort me. In fact, it only served to increase my desire to leave. I told the group that I was leaving, after which point I walked back home.

Their motive would become evident the next morning, when Benny took me to court and charged me with sexually molesting Little Maria, even though I had not touched her. I could not believe the team had done this to me, and that they had used Little Maria to achieve their ends. I didn't believe she was a willing participant in this scam. I had affection for her, and her feelings were reciprocal. She often was very friendly with me in class and when her parents were not around. Now her parents were doing this to me and my mother? They could not have hurt my mom any worse, having her son brought up on phony molestation charges. The team was trying to portray me as a sexual deviant, but why?

I never found out what the judge's verdict was. Whatever it was, I spent no time in jail.

When the elder Maria was in the courtroom, one thing puzzled me. She'd said to me, "I want you to stay away from my daughter."

Either she had lied earlier when she told me that Little Maria was her niece, or she had lied in the courtroom when she said she was her daughter. Whatever the case may be, she was supposed to be with the Secret Service. One way or another she was a liar. Her tally of lies was growing rapidly.

That was the advantage of having a memory like mine. I was building my case against Maria, one lie at a time.

Chapter 34

CUBAN MISSILES

The end of summer came. Entering the fourth grade, I was assigned to Mrs. Janzig's class. On our first day back, she jumped right in and assigned a writing assignment on our most memorable day of the past summer. I immediately began writing about the trip down to Bottom Fork to my Grandpa Holbrook's house we had taken over the summer. That was one of the most memorable and relaxing times of all my trips down south. My uncle Harrison took me fishing for catfish. I had looked forward to relaxing on the riverbank catching fish. I'd soon hooked a large fish. I could tell it was big from the way my rod bent. It was so big that I was unable to turn the reel. I asked my uncle Harrison to help me. Just as he started to set his reel down, his pole almost bent in two. He landed his own fish, a large catfish about eighteen inches long. My line broke, the fish getting away. When I had finished writing about that episode and turned in my paper, Mrs. Janzig commented to the class that I had written an interesting story and had good penmanship. She then took my paper and walked from desk to desk, showing it to each student. As she passed by my desk, she asked me, "Am I embarrassing you, Brett?"

"Well, *embarrassed* is not the word. I don't like to make the other students feel bad, Mrs. Janzig."

"Brett, you should not feel that way at all. You have set a goal for other students to aim for."

In the elementary grades, there were only three grades you could get: satisfactory, satisfactory plus, or unsatisfactory. I got a grade of satisfactory plus on my paper. Based on what my teacher had said, I knew I would do very well in her class.

There were rumblings of war in Cuba again. The school was showing films of what to do in case of a nuclear attack and making sure we students knew where the civil defense shelters were inside the school. One of the things we were instructed to do was to drink the water from the toilet tank. I had a discussion with a fellow classmate, Mohammed Haddad, who was Arabic but a devout Christian. He was an exceptional student and well versed in the facts of nuclear war. One of the situations we had talked about was nuclear winter, where there is so much dust and debris in the atmosphere that it blocks the sunlight and, as a result, everyone freezes to death. During such a crisis, there would be no food, no water, no Washington, and no financial institutions. Everything would be obliterated, and fallout would be everywhere. All living souls and all plant and animal life that survived the explosion would surely be gone shortly thereafter. No food and no water meant that there would be no way to live.

It was October and six weeks into the school year when Dad wanted me to go with him to an air show at Selfridge Air Base. The Blue Angels were going to be there. Since it was military stuff, which the other kids would not be interested in, my dad and I left my siblings at home with my mom and headed out to the air base. When we arrived at the base, we parked in a lot outside a fence that cordoned off a restricted area where some people could watch the air show. The blonde Doris Day look-alike—whom I'd named Blondie the Nymph—and the elder Maria were there, too. Not knowing why those two women were present, I couldn't help but wonder if Dad had brought me with him so he could see them.

Dad and I waited around for the show to begin, but it was canceled for some reason. We headed back home. I was seriously disappointed. I hoped they would soon reschedule the show. I did not have to wait long—the show was rescheduled for the next day.

Dad and I headed back to the air base. We went through the same procedures when we arrived. Not only were Maria the elder and Blondie the Nymph there, but also Rico Garcia was, standing along the fence.

Seeing Dad and me, he said something to me I did not understand. "Brett, whatever you do, don't go in the bunker. Only sissies go into the bunkers."

How did Rico know more about what was going on than I did? It was becoming obvious to me that there was not going to be an air show and that we were there for some other purpose. It was shortly after Rico had told me not to go in the bunker that Blondie the Nymph came over to me and asked me to follow her. I refused. She tried to force me to go by picking me up and carrying me, but I latched my hand onto the fence. There was no way I was going to be a sissy. Wild horses could not pull my hand from that fence. She continued to try to pull my hand free. She finally gave up and called out to my dad, who came over to help her pull me away. He knew I was too stubborn to let go, so he bent over and said loudly into my ear, ensuring that he could be heard over the noise, "Brett, they are going to launch the missiles. They want you to stop the launch."

I immediately let go of the fence and headed with Blondie the Nymph to what looked like a shack. There was a guard at the door. Blondie had what I called my ribbons, which were issued to me by President Kennedy. The guard let us in. I saw that the structure was a bunker like the one in Washington. There must have been a series of these bunkers spread throughout the country. We headed down the stairs and into the communications room. I was surprised to see women in there. I did know which branches of service were represented. One man of apparent high rank approached me and said, "Brett, you have to stop them. You are the world's only hope right now." There were people crying, and others turning away from me so I would not see them crying.

Blondie the Nymph sat down at the table and had me sit on her lap. A man dialed the telephone, spoke a code word, told me to stop the launch, handed me the phone, and said, "Brett, it's the president."

I spoke into the phone. "Mr. President, sir, I can't hear you. Are you there? Are you there?" I got no response. After a long pause, hearing nothing but silence, I looked at the man who had given me the phone and said, "He is not answering me, sir."

Then suddenly I heard the president say, "They told me you were dead, Brett."

"That is part of the problem, sir. You have too many people who are lying to you. They are, however, trying to kill me. The women and children don't want you to launch missiles on Cuba. Sooner or later, sir, we are going to have to come out of the bunkers, and when we do, there will be nothing left. Everything will be destroyed. We can drink toilet water for only so long, and the food will last only so long."

Suddenly I heard the countdown begin over a loudspeaker. It was at one minute. I was on a time limit, and knew it would not be long before we launched the missiles. The president had not responded. I resigned myself to the prospect that it would not be long before the world would end. Hopefully I would make it into heaven. I asked the president one last question: "Sir, do you think that when we get to heaven, I could play with John-John?"

That's when the president said, "Stop the launch!"

The countdown had stopped at seven seconds. From that day forward, I would always believe that seven was the luckiest number in the world. I had been given a monumental task, and I had come through for my country and the whole world. Some sort of peacefulness came over me. It was after stopping the launch that I realized what this crisis was all about. To me it was about men's egos, and the belief that the first country to back down is gutless and weak. It was an argument about the placement of missiles that had escalated to the point that each country was willing to blow up the whole world. They had forgotten about something, though: the women and children and their future. I believe that when I asked the president about John-John, it made him look at his son's future. That is why, I believe, he put a stop to the madness. This event made me feel as if I had been placed in front of a firing squad and had gotten a reprieve in the last few seconds, when in actuality it was the whole world that had gotten a reprieve. I would head back to school with no notoriety, which is the way I wanted things.

Chapter 35

MEETING COACH

The fourth grade brought on a new class that I could not wait to attend each Tuesday and Thursday: gym class. It was taught by a man whom all the boys loved. Well, I should not say all, because like all schools, Franklin had its share of delinquents. The man's name was Coach Csonka. He was tall and weighty but not fat. He made no bones about his large size. You did not step out of line in his class because if you did, you were sure to be severely punished. I had seen him punish other boys with the paddle. He had you first bend over and touch your toes, which tightened up your buttocks so the paddling would sting that much more. Then he would start slowly warming you (as he put it) with the paddle, until he let you have it full blast. The student then walked off rubbing his buttocks fiercely. I made it a point never to piss off Coach Csonka.

Coach Csonka was well-known throughout the whole state as the best coach for training ball-handling guards. He started teaching ball-handling skills with the very first class, setting up a couple of chairs at one end of the gym floor and having students form a line at one end of the court. His instructions were to dribble the ball down the court right-handed and then come back up the court left-handed. These basketball drills were part of almost every class. Once they were completed, Coach would announce free play, which meant we could play anything we wanted. A few of the more athletically inclined boys would split up and form three-on-three groups for pickup games. I discovered something else that I wanted to participate in: recreation. The gym was open to kids in the seventh grade and under from 4:00 p.m. until 7:00 p.m. From 7:00 p.m. until 10:00 p.m., older kids had control of the gym. There was also the upstairs rec room where you could play table tennis, checkers, and chess. I didn't know how to play chess, but I'd always wanted to learn. Also, the swimming pool was open for swimming.

It was springtime of 1963. Having just turned ten, I was about to shock my fourth grade class. Coach Csonka walked the class down to a field that was owned by St. Bonaventure Catholic Church. After observing a few moments, I could see a half-ass track of cinder and grass. Franklin did not have a track, so the school used St. Bonaventure's track. The coach marked off the distance of fifty yards. He then instructed us students to choose a partner to run with. I chose Goodenrich. When it was our turn to run, Coach raised his hand. We lined up in the starting blocks, the coach dropped his hand, and we were off and running. I beat Shawn by half a step and one-tenth of a second. I had the fastest time of the day. The coach grabbed me by the shoulder and shouted out my time. It soon got around that I had beaten Shawn. It was as if I had toppled a god, because Shawn was well respected among the Arab boys, and all the girls, including the Arab girls, who found him attractive as well. I soon received a little more respect among the Arab kids. I figured out that if I was to keep earning their respect, I was going to have to do it through competing on the athletic field, something I would have to do well.

I was doing well on the athletic field, and I was doing well in the classroom. Things were going fine for me all around—too well, I thought. Team Garcia had left me alone for a while, but in the back of my mind I knew they had not given up.

As I had figured he would, Rico Garcia came by the house and told me to come with him. I did as he said. We went toward Goodenrich's' house. Rico had me stand across the street from their house. Mrs. Goodenrich came out, at which point Rico did as he had done before: "Say it was Brett." Then he yelled it: "Say it was Brett."

I headed back to my house wondering why Rico had done what he had done to Mrs. Goodenrich. It was the next afternoon when the cops came by my house to question me. Refusing to sugarcoat anything, one of them asked me point-blank, "Brett, why did you rape Mrs. Goodenrich?"

Now I was beginning to understand why Rico had done what he had the day before. He had done the same thing to Justine. I replied, "I would not hurt Mrs. Goodenrich, who is Shawn's mother. Shawn is my friend. I would not hurt his mother. It was probably Rico Garcia who raped her."

"What makes you say that, Brett?" one of the cops asked.

I proceeded to tell him what Rico had done to Mrs. Goodenrich the previous day. Rico was well-known to the Dearborn Police Department. One of the cops said to me, "Thanks, Brett," because he knew that talking to the cops meant that I would be putting myself at risk. It had been a couple of months since the rape of Mrs. Goodenrich; Rico had neither been charged with nor arrested for it.

I was at school one day when Shawn came up to me and said, "Brett, my dad needs help. There are people trying to take his bar away. Brett, please help him. I am your friend. We really need your help."

"Why did you choose me, Shawn?"

"Because I know how well you shoot, Brett. So, will you help us?"

He was practically begging me, so I said, "Sounds really great to me. What day does he want me to go to work for him, Shawn?"

"Tonight at six o'clock. And bring your gun."

It was shortly before six when I headed to the bar, which was named Gooden's, a shortened version of "Goodenrich." Gordon, Shawn's father, had been a professional baseball player and had squirreled away enough money to buy his bar. It was obvious that Shawn had inherited his dad's athletic ability. The bar itself was a "shot and a beer" joint that was also known to have great burgers. It was constantly busy. Shawn was often there at night to help with the duties. The bar's main clientele were workers from the nearby auto plant.

I was there just a short time when Gordon came over and said to me, "Brett, we have a lot of riff-raff that came in. You are going to be my bouncer. Ask them to leave when I give you the signal to do so."

My reputation for being good with a gun had spread throughout the neighborhood. Gordon had placed his trust in me to help him maintain peace and order in his bar.

"Gordon, how much are you going to pay me?"

"We'll get you paid when the job is finished. Okay, Brett?"

"Okay, Gordon, I trust you. And I am sure you will be fair with me. Where do you want me to hang out?"

"You and Shawn stand at the end of the bar by the window."

Shawn and I were standing where we were told to stay, when Shawn asked me, "Brett, do you want something to drink?"

I replied, "I don't have any money."

"Your drinks are free when you are working."

"In that case, I will take a Coke." After Shawn brought me the Coke, I quickly slurped it down. Then I had another.

About an hour and half later, a certain patron walked in. He had a large frame and was quite husky. Gordon walked up to me and said, "Get rid of him, Brett."

I walked up to the man and said, "Sir, you have to leave."

"Why do I have to leave? I am not doing anything."

"Mr. Gooden does not want to serve you, so you have to leave."

I did not know why Gordon wanted the man out of the bar, but I was glad he left peacefully. Things were calm for the rest of the night. My cutoff time was twelve o'clock, at which point I headed back home.

I arrived at the same time the next day. The bar was very busy. Shawn and I were at the same place when Gordon gave me the order to throw someone out. It was not long afterward that a young woman in her middle twenties came in. She was walking around like a zombie and staggering through the bar. Gordon gave me the nod to ask her to leave. When I ordered her out, she tried to grab my gun. I wrestled with her for what seemed to be five minutes, although in reality it was no more than a minute. The only option I saw was to pull the trigger on her, so I racked off three rounds, after which she let go of the gun. The woman was knocked out. The cops soon arrived and called an ambulance for her. I explained that she had gone for my gun, so I had to shoot her. The bar began to get pretty busy. Some of the patrons coming in were acting a lot like the Masons down in the Corridor, like they had been heavily drugged. Who was doing the drugging and telling these junkies to go for my gun?

Later that night, Carlos came in for a drink and asked me to sit at a table with him. "Brett, I want to buy this bar, so I want you to ask Gordon how much he wants for it. So go ask him. Let me know what he says."

I walked over to Gordon and said, "That cop wants to know how much you want for the bar."

Very busy at the bar, Gordon responded, "Tell him the bar is not for sale."

I walked back to the table and said, "Carlos, Gordon said the bar is not for sale."

"Then ask him what figure he would definitely sell it for."

I repeated the question to Gordon, who got really upset and said, "Damn it, Brett, I told you! The bar is not for sale at any price."

"Carlos, he's not selling for any price!"

Carlos finished his drink and left. I went back to my position at the end of the bar. When I got a chance to talk to Gordon, I said to him, "I believe that cop is probably the reason you are getting so much riff-raff in the bar lately. I think all those people are being injected with a narcotic, either willingly or against their will. I have seen it done before when I lived in Detroit. That is why they are acting so strange. It could be that the cop and his people are trying to ruin your business so you will sell out."

"Brett, what I want you to do in that case, if you even think one of my patrons is high on drugs or too drunk on booze, is to get them the hell out of here. Got it?"

"You're the boss and it's your bar. But what if I make a mistake?"

"Don't worry. I will cover you, whichever call you make."

I could see things were going to get a little rough, so I would make sure I had some backup for when the time came.

Chapter 36

MEETING MY BEST FRIEND

The next evening, getting ready to head for the bar, I decided that I would take my dad's shotgun as additional backup. I started to head out to the bar when my dad, who had been laid off from the auto plant, saw me. He wanted to know why I was taking his shotgun.

"It's the weekend, Dad, and it gets pretty crowded in the bar."

"If you think you need a shotgun, I will go with you," he said.

It was crowded when we got there. My dad took up a position at the back wall to guard the back door. He had his snub-nose .38 in his pocket. The place was a bit crowded, so I put the shotgun at the end of the bar where I was stationed so as not to scare the regulars into thinking that the bar was too rough for them to enjoy themselves. Soon, in came the junkies. I decided to go outside and see for myself what was going on. It was just as I thought. Edwin Burns and a bunch of junkies had gathered outside.

I said, "Edwin, tell your friends to quit trying to take my gun away, or else I am going to continue to shoot them. If you don't stop, I am going to hold you responsible."

Soon afterward, Carlos came into the bar. Then, Burns came in. He walked over to me, stuck his 7 mm gun that he always carried in my face right next to my nose, and said, "Give me your gun, Brett."

I immediately slapped the gun away from my face. Then I stuck my gun in his belly and said, "Put your gun away, Edwin, because you are about to get gut shot. You definitely don't want that."

He put his gun away, looked over at Carlos, and said, "You're wrong, Carlos. This little shit isn't afraid of nobody."

My dad, standing in the shadows, was ready to react if something went wrong. "Who was that guy with the gun?"

I told my dad, "It is Edwin Burns, the guy who lives across the street in the pink house. I am not sure, but I think he is dealing drugs out of that house." I was glad that my dad was there to back me up. I didn't know for sure, but I began to think that Burns and Carlos were conspiring to disarm me by taking my gun away or having someone steal it.

The next few nights were uneventful. Dad was called back to work. Later in the week, a patron came in and sat down at the bar. An older man, thirtyish, he had seemed a little unsteady walking in. I decided I would keep an eye on him. An hour and half went by. Suddenly he shot the mirror behind the liquor bottles. I could tell he was about to shoot another round.

I quickly stuck my gun at the side of his throat and told him, "Please put the gun down." I asked him again, "Please put the gun down on the bar." He seemed to be in some sort of stupor, as if he was drugged. There weren't any empty seats at the bar; the patrons were almost shoulder to shoulder. I was surprised to see that the patron to my right did not move away from the bar. I looked to him for assistance, hoping he would grab the man's gun. He did not. I continued to ask the gunman to put the gun down, until he moved the gun in the direction of the patron to my right. Afraid he was going to shoot that patron, I had no choice but to shoot the gunman. It was a neck shot. I had spilled a lot of blood. I could not believe that no one had even lifted a finger to help me, or even moved away from the bar. When the police arrived, they jumped on Gordon. The patrons who had witnessed the shooting stated to the cops that I had done all that was possible to avoid shooting the gunman.

After things had settled down, I told Gordon that I needed Shawn so I could identify the people coming into the bar. Gordon agreed. Shawn and I stood together at the end of the bar that was closest to the front door. A lot of people who appeared high were asked to leave. Then one patron came in who appeared to be in a stupor, as had the gunman who shot the mirror. I asked Shawn, "Do you know this guy?"

"Holy shit, Brett, that is Travis Simmons!" he responded. "He's no junkie,

Brett. He is an absolute genius. He is not old enough to drink, though. I don't know what is wrong with him, but we have to help him."

We grabbed hold of him and sat him on the ledge by the window. While I was not brand new to the neighborhood, I was still a relative newcomer. Travis was definitely a person I wanted to be friends with. Based on the information that Shawn had given me, I looked up to him because I knew I could learn a lot from him. Plus, I basically enjoyed the company of intelligent people.

I left the bar early with Shawn and Travis in tow. We wanted make sure Travis got home safely.

A week after I had shot the gunman who shot the mirror, I headed to the bar with my dad's shotgun. After sitting in my regular spot for about two hours, I started to walk to the opposite side of the bar. Gordon had told me to leave the shotgun, which was not an unusual request, so I'd left it at my station at the end of the bar. I walked through the bar checking out the patrons. As I turned to walk back to my station, Gordon grabbed the shotgun and pointed it at me.

I was so shocked that I didn't know what to do. Before I could react, Gordon pulled the trigger and the gun went off. There was a lot of smoke and wind, but somehow I was still standing. The gun had been loaded with a blank. I did not understand why Gordon would try to kill me. That said, I was not about to stick around to find out why. I grabbed the shotgun and left.

That night I stayed up late to talk to my dad, as I was puzzled why he would put a blank in the shotgun. I asked him why he had.

"What the hell is wrong with you? I didn't put a blank in the shotgun! I did not buy any blanks." He went into the closet, opened the box of shells, and showed me there were no blanks in the box. "What makes you think there was a blank in it?"

I told him what had happened. He was furious.

"I don't want you going back to that bar. I can't believe Gordon would do that to you after all you've done for him!"

I was really puzzled about who had put that blank in the gun. If it wasn't Dad, then who the hell was it?

I was on my way to school one day when I started getting razzing from Marius and Duey. They were laughing about the fact that Gordon had made me work for free.

Shawn said, "That is right, Brett, we made you work and risk your life all for nothing. I was the one who planned it all, Brett."

"Well, Shawn, if that's a sign of your intelligence, you are not so smart. Your dad's bar is not going anywhere, which is a shame since that's how your dad makes his money. If you want to treat me like a Negro slave, I will blow that bar up or burn it down. I'm not looking for any trouble, but I am not going to let your father beat me out of anything I earned honestly. Do you get it? Why would you do that to me anyway, Shawn?"

"My dad did it because of what you did to my mother, Brett."

"What do you mean, what I did to your mother, Shawn?"

"You raped her, Brett."

"Shawn, I did not rape your mother. It was Rico Garcia."

"How do you know it was Rico Garcia?"

"Whenever Rico pulls a rape, he terrorizes the rape victim into saying it was someone completely innocent. In this case, he chose me."

"How do you know it was Rico?"

"He had me go down by your house with him, and he was yelling at your mother, 'Blame Brett.' He raped my mother too, Shawn."

"Brett, I am really sorry. Let me talk to my dad. You are sure it was Rico?"

"I have no doubt about it, Shawn."

I continued on my way to school, satisfied that my friend now knew who had really hurt his mother. Plus, I finally had the reason why Gordon had tried to kill me. It was a lesson in how men's and boy's innocence and destinies dangle on a string of truthfulness. I had nearly died based on a lie that was perpetrated against me. I would have counted on that shotgun to protect myself, but I would have only been shooting blanks. I had not counted on someone using the shotgun against me, but whoever had put that blank in that gun had inadvertently saved my life. The more of life I got to see, the more I believed that God was watching over me.

It was evening, almost nightfall, when Maria came by my house. "Brett, I want you to come with me to Gooden's bar."

"I can't, Maria. Dad told me not to set foot in that bar again."

"Why is that, Brett?"

"Gordon thought that it was me who raped his wife, when it was really Rico. He tried to kill me with my own shotgun. The only reason I am alive is that the shotgun was loaded with a blank."

"The gun had a blank in it?" Maria said.

"Yes, it was a blank, Maria. I asked Dad if it was him who loaded that blank, and he said no."

"Brett, I need you to come with me now. It is really important that we straighten this out right away."

I agreed. Maria and I headed to the bar. Once inside, she called Gordon over to talk to him while I stood near the front door. I was not taking any chances. After a brief conversation with Maria, Gordon called me over to the end of the bar where they were both standing. She then reached down to unzip my pants and showed Gordon my penis. He exclaimed loudly, "Oh my God, oh my God! It's impossible! He couldn't have raped her. He's just a little boy."

I was now going through the same thing that I had gone through with Justine Powers. Gordon had spoken the same words Etty had when she told the president at the beach house that I wasn't a rapist, the same words the Detroit cops had used. Why were the Dearborn cops so slow to catch on to Rico's tactics, I wondered? I was glad of one thing, and that was that Maria had taken my side and exposed Rico. I was learning that women were not going to tolerate sex crimes against themselves or other women, and that they wanted the right person prosecuted. They seemed to stick together when it came to crimes against women.

When we got back to the house, Maria told me, "Brett, put that shotgun in a safe place."

The next afternoon, Maria came to get me, instructing me to get my pistol. I returned with my gun and holster. She did not say anything except that I should follow her. We walked down Holly Street toward the Goodenrich house. Once we got there, we saw Rico, along with Shawn and Mrs. Goodenrich. Shawn and his mother came over to my side of the street and stood behind me, with Maria also standing behind me. Carlos was on the opposite side of the street and behind me.

I heard Shawn say, "Kill him for my mother, Brett."

I did not know how killing Rico was supposed to be my responsibility, but I was not taking any chances. I said, "Somebody give him a gun," thinking that if I had to shoot Rico, it would have to be in self-defense.

María handed Rico a .22 caliber revolver. I then ordered him to tuck the gun into the waistband of his pants.

"Rico, if you are quicker on the draw than me, and if you don't miss when you fire that gun, then you get to live. I am going to tell you right now, if you try to draw on me, you are going to die."

Rico started to cry. He called out to Carlos, "Dad, he is going to kill me!" which I thought was unusual because he had earlier called Isaac Simms "Dad."

Carlos said to Rico in a loud voice, "Rico, you are letting that stinking little hillbilly embarrass me. You either kill him or go to jail."

He then said, still crying, "I can't. He is better with a gun than me."

Then I heard Mrs. Goodenrich say, "Brett, please do not kill him."

That was fine by me because her rape was really none of my business, and I really did not want to kill Rico.

The one thing that bothered me the most was that Carlos had said to

Rico, "You are letting that little hillbilly embarrass me." It made me realize that while Carlos was being paid to protect me, he was telling his nephew to kill me. To me, he should have worked at defusing the situation. When he said that, it gave me some insight into his mentality, which led me to believe he had some sort of inferiority complex. He wanted to give all non-Mexicans the impression that all Mexicans were tougher and smarter than non-Mexicans. To me, he was psychologically unfit to wear that badge. Carlos's telling Rico that he had to go to jail had given me some hope of peace because that meant one less criminal on Team Garcia I would have to cope with.

Chapter 37

STORYTELLING TO VINNY

One evening after school, I was sitting on the steps of the front porch. Tony came to let me know that Vinny wanted to see me and wanted me to tell him another story. We walked together to Roulo Street, where we found Vinny sitting on the back stairs, his usual perch. He said to me, "Brett, let's go for a walk. I want you to tell me a story about the Romans."

"Vinny, I don't know a whole lot about the Romans, but I know things about Julius Caesar and the Roman army."

"Well, tell me something about Caesar." As we walked through the neighborhood, he started twirling a butterfly knife. I had never seen Vinny with a gun or a knife before. His twirling that knife made me a little nervous.

"Well, Vinny, the Romans had two branches of government. They had an emperor, which was like our president, and a senate, which made the laws. The Roman Empire stretched across Europe and even into North Africa. Caesar took a wife named Cleopatra, who was the queen of Egypt, and had a son with her. The Roman army at the time was the most feared army on the planet. No one messed with the Romans."

"Is that true, Brett?" Vinny asked with a smile on his face.

I took it as a sign that he was pleased to hear that. I continued telling what I knew.

"The Romans were so vicious that they used to throw the Christians in an arena called the Coliseum to fight lions, something that provided them with entertainment. I believe they did this when a person proclaimed himself a Christian. To the Romans, that meant the Christians were insulting the Roman gods. So the Romans tossed them to the lions. Naturally, the Christians lost."

"That was pretty cruel. But what is the Coliseum?"

Surprised he did not know much about modern-day Italy, I proceeded to answer his question.

"Think of it as a stadium where sporting events are held, because that is basically what it was Vinny."

"What do you think of religion, Brett? Are you religious?"

"When I was younger, I believed in the church and the Bible. Now, though, as I see all the violence and murders, I think that a person has to be tough in this city. I still believe that Jesus was a real person, and that basically the Bible tells you things you should do to be a good person. You go to church to learn how to be a good person, and you go to school to learn how to be smart person. One thing is for sure, Vinny: the Romans and the Roman Empire no longer exist, and now there are Christians all over the world."

"So what changed your view?"

"Now I have to do things that God can't do. I have been put in a situation where my family, my country, and I are in danger, and I must kill to protect them all. The Mexican cops continue to make war against me. One way to guard against them is to have a lot of friends, Vinny, like you, for instance."

We had walked the long way around the neighborhood, arriving at the Catholic school St. Bonaventure. Vinny told me, "Brett, I want you to guard over my niece and walk her to St. Bonaventure each morning. I want you here about eight thirty tomorrow. I will introduce you to her."

The next morning I arrived on time. From the house emerged a girl around the same age as I. She was a few inches shorter than I, with black hair down to the middle of her back. She was well-dressed in a dress that was layered, like she had petticoats under it. It was very bright white, and sparsely decorated with red and blue polka dots the size of a quarter. The dress was very well-made and looked to be very expensive. She looked very pretty in it. Vinny introduced us. "Brett, this is Laura. Brett, I want you to take good care of her."

"I will do my best, Vinny."

As Laura and I walked toward the school I was curious as to where her parents shopped for their clothes, so I asked, "Laura, where did you buy that dress?"

"Oh, Brett, I don't buy my clothes. My mother and I make them. I made this one."

"It's one of the prettiest dresses I have ever seen. It takes a lot of talent to make a dress like that. Are you an aspiring dress designer?"

"I am too young to know the answer to that yet. Tell me something, Brett: do you like me?"

"Yes, Laura, I think you are very pretty and talented. I would like us to very good friends."

"I like you too, Brett, because you have blond hair, and I like blonds."

Just about then, we arrived at the school. There were two guys in their late teens standing there as if they were waiting for us. One them, the larger of the two, said to me, "Hey you, hillbilly. I want you to stay away from my sister."

"Who are those two guys, Laura?" I asked.

"It's my older brother, Gianni, and his friend."

I told Gianni, "Vinny has asked me to watch over her."

"I'll watch over my sister," he replied.

I walked away feeling dejected, unable to figure out why Vinny had done that to me. He had set a trap, using Laura as the bait. If I did not walk her to school, Vinny would be mad, and if I did walk her to school, I was going to piss her brother off. I decided I did not need the bullshit. Plus, if I needed a girlfriend, I would get one on my own. While Laura was very pretty and I would have liked to establish a relationship with her, I just did not need the grief and the mind games that came with being friends with her.

I soon ran into Shawn Goodenrich. I approached him. He said to me, "Brett, my dad has got your money now. He wants you to come by my house and he will pay you. Brett, I want you to know that I want to be friends with you, and my dad feels the same way. I am sorry that we caused you all that trouble. I will never turn on you again."

"What time should I come by your house, Shawn?"

"He wants you to come by the house early Saturday or Sunday morning before he goes to the bar."

Saturday came. Anxious to get my money, I headed for the Goodenrich house. I knocked on the door. Gordon answered.

"How much do I owe you, Brett?" he asked.

"Five hundred sounds about right to me, Gordon."

"I haven't got that much. How does two hundred sound?"

"It is a little light, but I will take your word for it. Two hundred is fine."

"Brett, I would really like for you to come back to the bar. You did a really good job. The bar is much quieter now. I will pay you good money, Brett."

"Gordon, I would like to come back because I could use the money, and to me the work is easy. Once I have to pull my gun and the rowdy people see how fast I am, they don't want any part of me. The only thing is, Gordon, what do I do when someone else tells you a lie that you are willing to kill me for?"

"Brett, I am a good man. You are right. I am going to make it up to you somehow."

"Okay, Gordon. I have always felt that everybody deserves a second chance. Someone lied to you, and it almost cost me my life. I won't hold it against you this time, but if someone says something bad about me again, first consider where it's coming from."

"You are a good kid, Brett. I am going to make sure everyone I know is aware of it."

I headed home. While I didn't like being shot at, I knew deep down inside that Gordon was a good man. Plus, he had a good family. I found some solace in the fact that he was going to be praising me from now on. I was building an army of friends; now I could add Shawn and Gordon to my growing list.

My goal was to make as many friends as I could, to help me expose this group of jackasses somehow. Each lie they got caught in would make them more vulnerable.

It was a cool evening when Tony came to get me for another walk with Vinny. This time, though, I had questions. Once we began our walk, Vinny began twirling his butterfly knife. I said, "Vinny, I don't thoroughly understand it when someone says to me, 'Brett, I am going to die for you.' What does that mean?"

"Well, Brett, let's say you do something really bad and the cops want to kill you for what you did. Then, since I don't want you to die, I say, 'Brett, I am going to die for you,' which means that I am willing to give up my life so you can live. Then since I die in your place, the cops don't kill you. Do you understand?"

"I understand now, Vinny."

"It is time for another story, Brett. Do you have another one about the Romans?"

"I have a really good one about a slave who revolted. Want to hear about that?"

"Why was he a slave?"

"The Romans had lots of slaves, Vinny, but this slave was something special. He was a gladiator who fought in the Coliseum, as did other slaves.

The term *gladiator* comes from the name of the sword the Roman soldiers and gladiators used. It was called a *gladius*; thus the term *gladiator*. While enslaved, Spartacus and a few other slaves, about seventy of them, grabbed some kitchen utensils and fought their way to freedom. Spartacus and the other men who had been slaves recruited other slaves along their escape route. Their ranks eventually swelled to over seventy thousand, which included herdsmen and shepherds. The Romans, fighting two other wars, were startled when their troops were defeated by Spartacus. They chased the slaves north and south in what is now Italy. The slaves won many skirmishes but had been cut off from their supplies and were forced to make arrangements to leave Italy for Sicily. Spartacus made his arrangements to sail to Sicily by hiring a group of pirates. He paid them in advance. When the time to sail came, the pirates never showed, and Spartacus was defeated. How did you like that story, Vinny?"

"Wow, Brett, did that really happen?"

"Yes, Vinny. A slave took on the fiercest armies in the world and could have escaped the wrath of the Romans if only he had not trusted a pirate for his getaway. A man like that pirate is the type of man whom all men hate, a man who needed to die. Vinny, there is something for you to learn from that story."

"What's that I could learn, Brett?"

"Vinny, you are Rome. Your men are the slaves, and they could revolt unless, of course, you pay them well and take good care of them. Then they are soldiers."

"That sounds like solid advice. I've never doubted my men's loyalty—never gave it a second thought. Brett, I want you to be a one of my advisors. I am going to pay you to advise me."

"Vinny, I can't accept money to give you advice. You have done something for me, and besides, if you need advice, how do you know it will be good advice if I do it for money? Whenever you need advice on your car, Vinny, you get the best mechanic. You get sick, you get the best doctor. If somebody wants to go to war with you, Vinny, I'll fight alongside you with my gun. I will be by your side. Anything you want to know about war, those matters, you want to ask me. However, there is one thing you could do for me. You could get those Mexican cops off my ass."

"Brett, I want to pay you! Why won't you take my money?"

"It is not about the money. I told you before, it is about friendship. One thing you know, no matter what, is that Brett will tell you straight, and somebody else may lie to you."

"Okay, Brett. I understand."

We had arrived back to the house on Roulo. I said good night and headed back home. This walk had showed me the tender side of Vinny. He was willing to pay me just for giving him advice. He really liked the stories I told. I was satisfied that I had won another friend. My circle of friends was continuing to grow.

Chapter 38

VINNY'S LOSS

It was two in the morning when I was awakened by Isaac Simms. "Brett, I need you to come with me, and I need you to come with me now. I need you to back me up on a bust," he said.

"Why don't you just get another cop, Isaac?"

"The bad guys won't suspect anything if you are with me. Brett, please trust me. I really need your help."

I was getting bad vibes from this situation, but I elected to go with him, just in case he really did need my help. It was sounding more and more like there would be gunfire involved. I got dressed and grabbed my gun.

I walked downstairs and climbed into his car.

"I am going to sleep until we get there, so wake me up when we arrive, Isaac."

When I woke up, we were outside of what looked like a small warehouse. When we entered the building, I noticed a fairly good-sized room with a pay phone on the left wall. Next to that, there was a steel door that led to I don't know where, but it was probably connected to the main warehouse. Then in came two young men, who had a conversation with Simms. One of the men, who I had nicknamed Mouth because he spoke in a loud voice, said to me, "We need to know how good you shoot, kid. How big is your gun?"

"It's a .22," I said.

"Give him your gun, Simms. I want to see how he does with a man's gun."

Simms handed me a .357 Magnum that had been purchased for me by my grandfather while Simms, Carlos and I were in Kentucky. Simms was supposed to give that .357 to me when we returned to Michigan. However, he'd kept it for himself, never turning it over to me.

I took aim at a civil defense sign that was about twenty-five feet away. I fired three rounds, all of them hitting close to dead center.

The mouth got on the phone and said to the person on the other end, "Vinny, you have got to see this kid shoot! Get down here right away."

Then suddenly, gunfire erupted in the room. The two men who were in the room went down. About a minute later, two more men in blue suits entered the room from outside.

One of them said to me, "Brett, what are you doing? We wanted them alive." I knew then that Simms had set Mouth and his buddy up for a bust.

I did not know who the two men in the blue suits were, but I presumed they were detectives. Since Simms had the bigger gun, I pointed my gun at the men in suits, whom I had presumed were cops, and ordered them to the floor. They complied with my order. I was in the process of assessing the situation when Simms walked over to the men who were cops and shot each one with a round in the back while they lay on the ground. Simms had committed a major taboo by shooting the cops while they were on the ground. I did not know why that was so, but it was something Carlos had taught me.

It was about that time that my friend Vinny walked in. It must have been him whom the Mouth had called to come to the scene. Something was wrong—Vinny already knew how good I was with a gun. He got behind me and pulled my gun from its holster.

He pointed the gun at Simms. I whispered, "Vinny, that gun is not going to kill him, and besides, there has to be more cops on the way by now." He handed me my gun back.

Soon, Carlos arrived on the scene. I knew he had been called in for cleanup. Simms ordered me to the car. I didn't know what they were going to do with Vinny. It was four o'clock in the morning. I soon fell asleep. When Simms woke me, we were in front of my house. As I was getting out of the car, he warned me not to say anything to anyone about what he had done. I knew he was serious, so I took what he said as threat, not a warning.

I went by to see Vinny the next afternoon to find out what went on after I left.

I said, "Simms was setting you up to bust you, Vinny."

"How do know that, Brett"?

"Because those two men in suits were detectives and Simms shot them in the back while they were on the floor. As they entered the building, they said they wanted your men alive. What were the names of your men, Vinny?"

"One of them was Gianni, and the other was his friend Sal."

"You mean your nephew Gianni?"

"Yes. You mean you did not recognize him?"

"I only saw him one time before last night, Vinny. The question is just what do you want to do about it? He is a member of a team of corrupt cops, Vinny. If you kill him, the rest of the team is going to come after you. As your advisor, I suggest the first step is to get his badge taken away so he does not have the protection of the rest of the police force. Then, once he has been isolated, you can do anything you want to him."

"I'll consider what you say, Brett," said Vinny.

I went back home and pondered exactly what the options were, but I realized there was not much I could do.

A few days had passed since the murder of the two cops, Gianni and his friend. Maria came by the house. She said, "Brett, we need you at Lasher Park. Grab your gun." I got my gun. We walked together to the park. There was Vinny, Tony, and a few women lined up at one end of the park, and Maria, me, and Isaac Simms.

Maria said, "Brett, we want you to kill Isaac."

I looked around at all the people who were gathered at the park and figured that two of them must be Gianni's mother and father. They all must have really hated Isaac, and wanted me to execute him and give them what they felt was justice. I considered the situation. Isaac was going to die, knowing the last people he was going to see were people who hated him. I just couldn't shoot him. It would be different from shooting people like DGA members who were trying to kill me. Those times, I was only defending myself. I felt it was not my job to kill him.

I lowered my gun. As I did, Simms said, "He put the gun down."

That was new to me, but I think I figured out what it meant. It meant that I had lost my one chance to kill Simms.

That's when Vinny spoke up. He said to me, "Brett, I will die for you."

I surmised that Vinny wanted Simms dead so badly that he was willing to die to see him dead.

I replied to Vinny, "I am not going to kill you just so I can kill him, Vinny. Your life is much more valuable, and also more important, than his."

I turned to Maria and asked, "Why is everybody counting on me to shoot him?"

"You are now a hit man, Brett." Maria shocked me with that statement. I had no aspirations of killing anyone, especially for money. I could see how being a hit man was going to end for me: in an early death or, at best, prison. Most of all, whose idea had it been to make me a hit man? It certainly was not Vinny's thinking. Vinny had asked me to be his counselor, not a hit man. It had to be Maria. She was becoming more and more of a threat to my family. And she was especially focusing on my mother and me, which led me to the conclusion that she was trying to get rid of both of us. I believed that Maria was doing all that she could so my father would leave my mom, me, and my siblings. She came up with a new way of setting me up with each day that passed. I was afraid this was just the beginning of another one of her setups. Telling everybody I was a hit man was her way of telling everyone I was just another criminal. I was not going to go along with it.

Having made my decision about the situation, I said, "Isaac is a cop. This is a cop problem. Let the cops handle it. It is not my job to handle a cop problem." I then turned away and started walking back to my house.

Later that evening, Carlos came by while I was in the alley talking to some of my friends whom I played football and baseball with. He was dressed in full uniform, wearing his hat pulled down low and a pair of thick-framed black glasses so I could not identify him. But I knew it was him. The members of Team Garcia covered much of their faces so they weren't easily identifiable, but I had seen enough of Carlos to identify him. "Brett, I want you to give me your money," Carlos said.

"What money? What is the problem with your family, Carlos? Benny wants me to give him money too."

"I'm telling you, either you give it to me or I will take it!"

"If I have any money, my father must be in charge of it, so go bother him." I then went back to talking to my friends.

The next day Carlos came back, only this time he had brought Maria. He said in a stern, almost growling voice, "Brett, I want your money. If I can't have the money, then I will fix it so you can't have it either!"

Then Maria said, "I want support for my son."

She had said that as if it were my responsibility to support her son, which angered me. I told her, "I'm not the one screwing you. If you want support, you can take it up with my dad."

That's when Carlos pulled me aside and said, "Brett, I want you to kill all three of them, the kid, Maria, and your dad."

I thought, *First, he has tried to extort money I don't have, and now he wants me to kill a kid who can't be any older than four—and my father to boot.*

Quickly I said, knowing he was from Texas, "Carlos, you know, even Santa Anna let the women and children at the Alamo go free. This fight is between you and my dad."

"Well, then what kind of punishment do you think would be appropriate for your dad?"

"Well, the way I look at it, Maria wants support. He started two families. Let him work two jobs. He will be so busy working that he won't have time to spend with Maria and the kid."

Carlos smiled and said, "I like that one, Brett. How do you think of all that shit?"

"Carlos, it's all just logic."

"Now what do I do about the kid?"

"Well, the one good thing about you is that you know the law. I think you should start training him while he is young to be a good cop."

Secretly, I was laughing on the inside. I thought, *First off, he will be training the offspring of the man with whom his wife had an affair, and it will be a reminder every day of Carlos's life and what Burt and Maria have done to him. On the bright side, their son may grow up to be the cop that takes Carlos down. But on the other hand, he just might be one more crooked cop I will have to contend with.*

It wasn't long after I'd had that conversation with Carlos that my father got a second job at the Oaklawn Street Bakery. His shift started at 2:00 a.m. and ended at 10:00 a.m. Then he went to his job working for General Motors at 3:30 p.m. He was unable to get any more than four hours of sleep a day. Maintaining those hours through the week, he would catch up on his sleep on the weekends. He soon became very irritable and abusive toward me and my siblings. Dad did not know it, but it was Carlos's revenge, not mine.

I asked him, "Dad, why are you putting yourself through all this?"

"I am doing this for my son. I will do anything for him." It was becoming quite obvious that he loved Maria and her son more than he loved my mother and her children.

Chapter 39

THE SPORT OF KINGS

It was a late spring afternoon in 1963 when my father began taking me to the racetrack. Always a sports enthusiast, I instantly fell in love with the sport of horse racing. Although my dad was working two jobs, he managed to find time on Saturday afternoons for the both of us to go to the track. It had always been a passion of my father's, and I soon followed suit. I think my love for the sport is deep in my Kentucky roots. They raced from April until about mid-November at the Detroit Race Course. The thoroughbreds ran first at Hazel Park located on the east side of Detroit, and then switched tracks and raced at the Detroit Racecourse, which was located on the west side of Detroit. The first time I went to the track, it was to Hazel Park with my dad and my cousin James. Kids under twelve were not allowed into the area. Since I was only ten, we had to fib about my age to get me in.

I knew very little about horse racing, but the first thing Dad taught me was how to read the tote board. With some advice from me, watching the tote board and how the money was being bet, Dad hit five of nine winners, winning more than fifty dollars, which was almost half a week's pay. I did well at this game for the first time ever at a racetrack. Since my dad had won all that money, I asked if he would buy me a two pairs of pants and a couple of new shirts. He agreed, saying that I deserved some new clothes.

Going to the track with my dad would become a Saturday afternoon ritual. Sometimes when he had a day off during the week, he would even come to school and take me out of class so we could head to the track. I soon learned how to read the *Daily Racing Form*, which had the racing records of all the horses that were racing on the East Coast. In my spare time, I would shine shoes in the bars and mow lawns in order to earn cash to bet with. You had to be eighteen to bet, so I would give the money to my dad and he would bet it for me. I had a great deal of fun, even if I did not win. Going to the track together was something that made me feel like my father actually loved me, that is, until the bimbos started following us to the track.

The first one who followed us there was Blondie the Nymph, who had been at Selfridge Air Base. My father kept saying to her, "I'm with my son." He tried moving away from her, and she kept moving with him. Finally he caved in and left me alone. I couldn't even bet; I just had to sit in the stands. About an hour and a half later, he returned.

I was pissed, to say the least. I said to him, "Dad, we only have one day a week together. Do you think you can tell those bimbos to leave us alone while we are at the track?"

"Well, Brett, I'm going to leave your mother, but first I'm going to steal your money."

"What money, and how much is it, Dad?" I got no response. *Why won't anyone tell me how much money everyone wants to take from me?* I wondered. Even my dad wouldn't tell me.

I was turning a blind eye to what my father was doing, so as not to cause my mother any more hurt. But one morning when I was watching television in the upstairs living room, I noticed that my mom and dad were in the kitchen. When I went downstairs and peeked around the corner, I saw that my mom was crying, the tears streaming down her face like two small waterfalls. I had never seen her cry like that before. I knew something really bad was going on, so I asked her, "Mom, what is wrong?"

Sobbing heavily and struggling to get out the words, she said, "He's leaving us, Brett. He doesn't love us anymore."

She emphasized *us*. I could not believe that this egotistical prick that thought he was God's gift to women would leave my mother after all that had been done to her, being raped multiple times and also terrorized by Rico. I was both livid and heartbroken at the same time. My father did not care about her or us. Which one of the women he was leaving Mom for I did not know for sure, but he had a son with Maria, so I figured she was most likely to be the one. I assured myself that whichever girlfriend he was leaving my mom for, he would soon tire of her as well.

"You can go, Burt. We don't need you either. I am going to get a job so I can feed my children, and you are going to pay support to help raise them. I will even work two jobs if I have to, but I am going to take care of my children since you will not," my mother said to him. Mom had finally tired of Dad's ways and was letting him know it.

It was at this point that I could see Mom finally had enough of Dad's nonsense. She loved him dearly, but it was clear he was treating us like slaves. She had drawn the line in the sand and no longer cared what he did.

I spoke up, saying, "Mom, before Dad leaves, he has got a bunch of money that he put in his name and his son's name. It was supposed to go in my name, too."

"Oh, Brett, hush. I don't need to hear any horseshit right now," my mom said.

Before he left, dad told mom that the money was real. Team Garcia knew about the money. Everyone seemed to know about the money but mom. I knew only that some money existed, but I didn't know how much.

It was now summer. My sister Veronica and I had to pack to head down south. This time, though, it would be different; we would be traveling with Uncle Elmer.

When we arrived in Kentucky, Veronica was taken over to Aunt Fannie's house while I stayed at Grandpa Holbrook's house. Grandpa posted a target and tested my gun skills once again. I did well. Whenever Grandpa tested my skills, it was a sure thing that I was going to be involved in some sort of gunplay. I watched as Grandpa and Uncle Rollie had a conversation with each other in the front yard, which I was not privy to. It was three days later when Uncle Rollie came back to drive me to my Grandpa Lawson's house. I was visiting with my grandfather on the front porch when my dad pulled up. I had not seen him for over a month, but I was not excited to see him. Actually, I was resentful that he was even there. I did not have much to say to him, and he did not say anything to me.

Uncle Rollie went into the house while my dad sat on the front bumper. Grandpa Lawson remained seated on the porch. Uncle Rollie came back out and handed me a .22 Magnum. I was standing in front of my father. My uncle Rollie stood beside me.

"Brett, you have to kill your father," Uncle Rollie said.

"I have to kill my father, Uncle Rollie?"

My father seemed unafraid that I was pointing a gun at him and appeared to be quite content to die, but I did not understand why. The .22 Magnum was plenty enough gun to kill with. I was puzzled why he was not afraid.

"Yeah, Brett, you have to kill him. We all want him dead for what he did to his family."

I suspected that this was the topic of the conversation Uncle Rollie had with my grandpa Holbrook. Grandpa Holbrook wanted my father dead too, I supposed.

"Uncle Rollie, what has he done to me that I should kill him?"

"He stole your money, Brett."

"Uncle Rollie, those crooked cops are trying to kill me for my money, but I don't even know how much it is! I am getting pretty pissed off that even the cops know about the money and are trying to kill me for it when I don't even know how much it is! Can you at least tell me how much money it is?"

"It is seven and a half million dollars."

"I got seven and a half million dollars just for an idea?"

It seemed to me that everyone, including Team Garcia, wanted my dad dead, and that this was just a trick to get me to kill my father.

"No, Brett, the money was from your grandpa Holbrook. He figured out how to train the dogs so they could smell drugs. The state of Kentucky paid him for the rights to the drug dogs. They also paid him to train the dogs."

"Dad, how could you do that to Mom and me? You gave it to Maria's son, didn't you? I had no idea the amount of money was over seven million dollars. I want it back."

Then from out of the blue came Grandpa Lawson's voice. "Brett, just kill him for all he's done to hurt his family, and your mom's dad. He's not anything but a common thief, and he is of no good to anybody."

"Grandpa, you want me to kill your oldest son?"

I had no concept of exactly how good my grandfather Holbrook was with animals, or how hard he had worked to figure out the technique to have dogs sniff out drugs. It all made sense now, why Maria and the rest of Team Garcia first were trying to get the money out of me and then turned their efforts toward Burt. He had been stupid enough to turn the money over to Maria. It was now becoming clear that the money was also the reason they had tried to turn me into a criminal, so I would rot away in a jail cell somewhere. I knew that if I killed my father, I would never, ever get the money back. With that much money, Dad's son and his girlfriend Maria could disappear. I was going to keep him alive until I obtained every piece of information about his son that I could. He had even gone through the trouble of not telling me his son's name so no one in our family could track his son down. Tracking that kid down was the first thing I would have to do. That was it. I was going to get the money back that my grandfather had turned over to me. For that kind of money, I would even kill my own father, but not today. That my father had stolen that money just showed me what kind of man my father really was and how much he loved my half-brother. He had stolen money from my grandpa Holbrook, a preacher.

I turned to my uncle Rollie and said, "Uncle Rollie, I have never asked you for anything, but I am going to ask you for something now. I want you to look at my dad, and your dad, and remember this day forever. Someday, I will find out where my money went, and on that day I am going to need you to remember what my father did. I am not going to stoop as low as my dad and kill somebody over money. Someday, when I get enough information, I hope that all I have to do is to ask for it back."

I turned to face my dad and said, "Don't worry, Dad. I will somehow figure a way to earn more money." I walked away. I was crying on the inside, but I was not going to let my father see me cry on the outside. One thing was for sure: I would never trust my father again. I also would never love him like I had when I was younger, and I would permanently be suspicious of him.

Chapter 40

DEATH OF ERIC WITHERS

After a month in Kentucky, it was time for me to leave for home. I wanted to ride back with Uncle Rollie, but my father had driven back down and insisted that I ride home with him. I did not say much along the way. There was a lot of tension in the car. I was actually seething on the inside. When we arrived home, I went for a walk. I didn't want to hear anything he had to say, and I was not in any mood to take an ass-whipping. My father went into the house to talk to my mother. It was about an hour before he left. He left without giving her any money. I went through the cupboards looking for something to eat, but there was nothing in them—and no food in the fridge. A lone can of chicken broth was all I found. It had been very obvious that this situation had been going on for a while. Mom had tried to go to work, but she had no car and there were no jobs to be had in the neighborhood.

Mom came into the kitchen and asked me, "Brett, could you hustle a few dollars to buy a pound of hamburger meat, some beans, and some cornmeal so I can make some cornbread and beans?"

I was tired from the trip, but my brothers and sisters needed something to eat, so I said, "Okay, Mom."

I grabbed my shoeshine box and my little brother Dwayne, and headed to the bars. I polished shoes for about an hour and a half, and hustled over seven dollars. Then I headed to Franklin Market, a local butcher shop owned by a man named Martin that also sold liquor. Martin's clientele was mostly auto workers who came on their lunch breaks because of the market's proximity to the plant. They not only bought liquor but also lunch meat for sandwiches. Martin's was the only butcher shop and liquor store in the whole South End.

I had enough money for all Mom had asked for, and then some. I saw a couple of large cans of Spaghetti-O's, so I bought them for the kids. I got all that and a couple of slices of salami and cheese so that I could have fried salami with melted cheese for myself. Then I headed home.

I was outside when Carlos walked up from between the buildings on Franklin and said he wanted to talk to me. He thought he was being sneaky because he was not driving a police car. That way no one would notice he was there. "Brett, I am going to have to take the gun out of your hand because you are just too damn good."

I thought, *Great, just great. My father won't even feed us kids and now I've got Carlos trying to fix it so I can't carry my gun.* For some reason it didn't bother me. I knew I could carry a gun legally, and I also knew I was better with a gun than any member of Team Garcia.

It was a couple days after that incident with Carlos when I awoke from a deep sleep to see Rico with a huge needle and a syringe as big around as a fat cigar. He was sticking the needle in my arm. When I realized what he was doing, I jerked away from the syringe and felt a pain in my arm. I had broken the needle off in my arm, which was very dangerous. I believe he was trying to inject me with a hot shot, which was more than likely supposed to give me a drug overdose and kill me. The drug he usually used was a mixture of cocaine and heroin known by junkies as a speedball. It was soon after that I blacked out.

I woke up the next morning still heavily drugged and with severe pain in my arm. My mom had called my dad to come to the house to pick her and me up and take me to the Independent Medical Clinic, where the needle was removed. My arm was going to require a lot of time to heal, so for at least the next few months, I would not be able to use my gun properly. I assumed that this was what Carlos meant about taking the gun out of my hand.

The only way I had to protect myself was to get my grandfather to send me up a drug-sniffing dog so I could at least get some sleep at night. I had hopes that the dog would deter Team Garcia from entering my house. Within a couple of days, the dog arrived. It was Wolf, Uncle Ronnie's dog, a big fluffy friendly canine. Ronnie had named him Wolf because he was a mixture of wolf and collie. It did not seem that he was the type of dog for sniffing out drugs, but Ronnie had personally trained him, so I was sure Wolf would get the job done.

Two days later when I got up in the morning, I noticed Wolf by the upstairs back door. He was lying down like he had been in a silent alert position. It indicated to me that someone had tried to enter the house with narcotics. I went over to him, shook him, and tried to wake him, but he was not getting up. As I looked closer, I saw a bloody wound. Since there was no stab wound, I concluded that someone had shot him. I was extremely upset. Ronnie had trusted me with Wolf, and now he was dead. I presumed it was a member of Team Garcia who had killed him. The most likely culprit was Isaac Simms. This incident showed me just how desperate the team was to keep me drugged. I was going to have to come up with another solution to prevent Team Garcia from drugging me in my sleep. I would first have to come up with a way to protect a dog, as I did not know how many dogs of mine they were willing to kill to accomplish their goal.

A month went by before Grandpa sent another drug dog up from Kentucky. This time he sent a purebred German shepherd named Bear who was muscular and strong. Grandpa had trained the dog to alert me when someone was carrying drugs. When released, the dog was trained to paw at the area of the body where the drugs were. If the suspect resisted the dog's efforts, the dog would aggressively attack the suspect. All I was hoping to do was simply to have the dogs notify me once someone carrying narcotics entered the house.

I didn't have to wait long. I was sitting in the house watching TV when I heard someone coming up the back stairway. Bear immediately gave me an alert. I stood in the doorway waiting to see who was coming up the stairs. I could not believe it, but it was Carlos. When I saw him, I released Bear to find where the drugs were, and to keep Carlos out of the house. As I expected, Carlos resisted. Bear began attacking him viciously. Somehow during the melee, Carlos managed to pull out his gun and shoot Bear dead. I did not have a gun big enough to do combat with Carlos, so to go up against him in a gunfight would have been suicidal. This incident proved to me that the whole team, including Carlos, was out to turn me into a junkie. They came repeatedly because only one needle puncture would mean a deliberate overdose and that would raise the suspicions of the coroner and also the police. Multiple punctures would mean the victim was a regular user of narcotics. Continued drugging could mean only one thing: the next step was to give me an overdose that would kill me.

It was supposed to be a crime to shoot a police dog, or anybody's dog for that matter, but I knew that Carlos would be sure to cover up the fact that he had shot Bear. I could not believe Carlos had stooped so low as to shoot my dog. I was beginning to feel helpless. Team Garcia was hell-bent on being crooks. I was the only one who understood how they worked—and the only one who stood in their way. The crimes they were committing were mounting with each passing day. Every crime moved me closer to having them incarcerated. In the meantime, my grandpa had gone through the expense of buying a dog and the expense of training and then shipping it up from Kentucky. The shepherds he used were purebred and expensive.

I called my grandfather and said to him, "Grandpa, the crooked cop shot Bear."

"What did he shoot the dog for, Brett?"

"He was bringing narcotics in the house. Bear went after him. Carlos shot him."

"Brett, I can't keep buying dogs and training them. What do you want me to do?"

"No more dogs for right now, Grandpa. I will have to figure something else out."

I put a lot of thought into what I could do to stop the Garcia team from sneaking into my house at night and drugging me. The solution I came up with was to have my grandpa train a dog to lie across my body, a dog that would attack anyone who bothered me during the night.

My grandpa trained a dog to do just that. I named him King. At night when I was ready for bed, I would not have to say anything when I headed to my room. I would lie down in bed, and King would follow me and lie across my body.

I knew it worked because one night while I was in a deep sleep, King was growling ferociously. His growling had partially wakened me, but I was still not fully awake when I heard one of the police officers of Team Garcia whom I believe was Isaac Simms say, "That will work, Brett." I then heard him leave my bedroom.

I thought for a little while that I had beaten Team Garcia, but then I awoke one morning a few days later and found that King was not moving. I looked and saw that he had a butcher knife sticking between his shoulder blades, and dried blood all down his back. He'd not left my side, as he was still lying across my body when I awoke. He had been one of the most special dogs I had ever had. I was devastated at the loss of King.

It was a hard thing for me to accept, but Team Garcia was winning. Once more Team Garcia had found a way to beat me and the dogs. They were once again free to enter my house and do whatever they wanted—I had to sleep sometime. They were tag-teaming me and taking turns at harassing me in any manner they wished. I was not through fighting yet. Somehow, someway, I would figure a way to beat them.

The solution I came up with to stop Team Garcia from shooting my dogs was to train a lapdog to sniff out the narcotics. Team Garcia knew I was using shepherds, so I figured using a lapdog would essentially be like having a dog working undercover. That way, hopefully, Team Garcia would not realize the dog was a drug-sniffing dog.

Soon after I'd made this decision, my grandpa trained a small dog to do this job for me. I named her Daisy. She was working out fine. One afternoon Isaac Simms came into the upstairs apartment. Daisy came running from the bedroom, where she had been resting on the bed. She began barking relentlessly, which indicated that Simms was carrying drugs. Daisy's barking stopped Simms in his tracks, but she continued barking. Suddenly Simms pulled out his gun and shot her. The shooting of Daisy was low and cruel. She could not have physically harmed him in anyway. All she had done was bark.

Simms's shooting of Daisy showed me what a real chicken shit group Team Garcia was. As I looked down at her lifeless body, I got angrier and angrier until my blood was percolating. In a voice just below yelling, I asked Simms, "What's the matter, Isaac? Scared of little barking dogs? That dog could not have possibly hurt you! Someday, Isaac, I am going to kill you for shooting my dog."

It was now time for me to move into the fifth grade. Miss Picard, the fifth grade teacher, informed the class she was Finnish. Since we had a large student body consisting of Middle Easterners, she was going to have us concentrate on Middle Eastern culture.

One of the first things we learned about was exports from the Middle East; most of the countries' main export was oil. Curious, I asked Miss Picard a question: "How long will it take before the Arabs run out of oil?"

"Oh, Brett, that is not a very good question. The Middle East has plenty of oil. It will never run out. It is a virtual sea of oil."

I didn't agree, thinking that any sea of oil would eventually be depleted.

Purely coincidentally, I read an article in the newspaper about the fact that some Texas oil fields were drying up. That triggered my imagination.

I recalled a conversation I once had with my grandpa Lawson how he gets around to buying his groceries and supplies. He and my grandmother lived on a tight budget and did not have a car. He told me once, "We mooch a ride and give whoever drives us to the store some money for gas." It made me realize how important oil was to our economy. Without it we would have no cars and no jet travel, and many fewer jobs.

I was in my fifth grade gym class when Isaac Simms came into the locker room and asked me if I would like to see Manuel D later that evening. I was suspicious because I had seen Carlos gun him down. At first I thought, *Well, maybe Manuel D had survived the gunshot wound he suffered at the hands of Carlos.* Later on that evening, Simms picked me up at home. We headed from Dearborn to Detroit's lower east side, where the Corridor is located.

We pulled up near Burton and saw that a few DGA members were already gathered. Simms got out of the car and I followed close behind. I did not understand why, but Simms suddenly said, "Brett, I am going to die for you." Why did he wish to die, and why down here in the Corridor? Why had he dragged me down here? To get me killed? I could not let Simms die, though. There were many, many things I needed to learn from Isaac before I could let him die. I needed to know how he altered the ballistic reports. The other members of Team Garcia were getting away with all the murders they had committed. Simms was one link to all those murders. I could not let him die before I was finished learning what all they had done to get away with the murders.

When Jarrell, a DGA member, pointed his gun at Isaac, I quickly said, "Jarrell, do not shoot Isaac. Shoot me instead." Being shorter than Simms, Jarrell lowered the gun and aimed it at my head. Not knowing what caliber the gun was, I took my hand, grabbed the gun, and moved it so it was pointing at my chest. Jarrell moved the gun back to my head, and again I moved it to my chest. Finally he shot me. The impact knocked me back a few feet.

I could not figure out how, but I awoke in a hospital. I did not know which one. I had been placed in a private room. Soon after I awoke, Simms came in.

Really pissed off, he asked me, "How come you did not let Jarrell shoot you in the head?"

I told him, "Because I didn't want him to mess up my pretty face." I chuckled. He promptly pulled out a switchblade, carved up the left half my face, and then left the room. I had just saved his life and he cut up my face! A few seconds after Simms left, a nurse came in and saw that my face was bleeding. She ran to get a doctor. That's when I passed out again.

A few days later, Maria came to pick me up. I had two large cuts on my forehead that extended from my eyebrow well into my scalp. I had a four-inch wound next to my left eye where Simms had just missed cutting my eye out. Simms had also cut me high on the forehead. Part of my scalp was missing.

Basically, the whole upper left side of my face was scarred up. Simms had shown no remorse. He actually seemed proud of what he had done.

Then something happened that, at first, I did not understand. I found it curious that innocent men were willing to die for their loved ones. Rico had said to me, "Brett, I am going to get someone to die for you. I need you to pick out someone who looks like a sissy. In the jailhouse, males who are small and demure are turned into sex slaves by the tougher males."

I wasn't keen on having people die in my place. If I had ever done something I felt I should die for, then I would accept my fate. Rico tracked me down, insistent that I pick someone to die for me.

At one point he suggested Eric Withers. I did not understand what Rico was trying to do. I soon found out that Eric's younger brother, Michael, had done something really bad and was going to juvenile lockup. Most likely, Michael would become a sissy because he was young and small. What Michael had done, no one was saying. The plan was that Eric was going to take the blame for what Michael had done, and since Eric was over eighteen, he would take his younger brother's place in jail.

I was walking down Franklin Street with Eric's other brother, David, when we saw Eric. He called us over to talk to him. He told me had been let out for forty-eight hours, explaining that the cops give inmates that amount of time to get their affairs in order before they hang you. "If you don't show up at the jail, then they will find you and shoot you."

"Take the bullet, Eric," I said.

Then he whispered in my ear, so his brother could not hear him, "I am going to die for you, Brett." A single tear trickled out of his right eye. When I saw the tear, I knew deep down that he didn't really want to die. He was dying because he wanted his brother free, and the only way for that to happen was for Eric to take his place in jail. It was then that I realized that all of us, men, women, and children, are combatants on the battlefield of life. Eric was buying freedom for his little brother, paying for it with no coin but with his life. His act of kindness, love, and bravery struck home the meaning and the value of the word *freedom*. It is not a word, it's an emotion—and the feeling is priceless. Soldiers fight for and are motivated by the feeling of freedom. The bad part was that Eric was innocent of any wrongdoing.

After Eric walked away, presumably heading home, I put my head down to say a prayer that he wouldn't die. I had lost too many friends and was trying not to lose any more. I did not believe the cops would really hang him. I then asked his little brother David, "Do you really think the cops will hang him?"

"Yeah, Brett, they will hang him."

It was almost a week since I had seen Eric. When I saw his little brother Michael, I asked him, "How did Eric make out with the cops?"

"The cops hung Eric, Brett, with his T-shirt."

I did not want Michael to see me cry. I felt that Eric's death was my fault because I had gone along with Rico. How did Rico Garcia manipulate Eric Wither's brother Michael into doing whatever he had done? The bottom line was that Eric was dead. Rico Garcia had picked Eric to die, and his plan had succeeded. So Team Garcia had another victim. The cops had hung an innocent man. Picking an innocent man to die at the hands of the cops was nothing less than first-degree murder. I went into a depressed mood, crying off and on for about a week.

It was Edwin Burns who set me straight when he told me, "Brett, those men who are hanged want to die." He then explained, "Those men who are hanged in the jail would rather die than go to prison for a really long time. They would rather die than be forced to be a sex slave. They die so someone else gets to live."

The fact remained that Eric was innocent, and Rico Garcia had picked him to die. The cops had hung an innocent man. I was going to miss Eric. I was greatly upset, but no matter how I looked at it, the final decision was up to Eric to live or to die.

Chapter 41

RETURN TO HYANNIS

Benny, Carlos's brother, came by my house and made the comment, "Brett, I want to make you famous for killing the president."

"Benny, what does it take to get through to you? I want no part of an assassination plot. Until you and the rest of the team give me a complete explanation of what is going on, I will not get involved. I don't want to be famous, and I especially don't want to kill the president. If I am going to be famous at all, it will be for my drug dogs. If you need someone to kill the president, ask one of Vinny's men. You are going to need a rifle, and I am no good with a rifle. One of Vinny's men would be better suited for that job." I hoped I had convinced him. I think the rifle statement got through to him, as he began to understand that I was not the one for the job.

A few days later, Benny came by the house and said, "Brett, the president wants to see you again in Hyannis."

"Let me put on some clean clothes and grab my gun." I didn't know if this was a trick or if Benny was telling the truth, but I decided not to risk pissing the president off. Going to Hyannis was the only option I saw. I changed my clothes, first washing only my upper body, since time was of the essence. Once I had gotten ready, we were off to Hyannis in a police car

On arriving at the president's beach house, I was taken upstairs to his office. After I waited a short while, the president came in and said something very strange. "Brett, I am the real president. Do you know why you are here?"

"Benny said you wanted to see me, sir."

Benny then came into the president's office and said, "Brett, the president wants to die, and he wants you to shoot him." He then handed me a .22-caliber semi-automatic pistol.

I told him, "Benny, I have my own gun."

"I want you to use the gun I gave you, Brett," Benny said. He then exited the office.

I knew only one thing: Benny was trying his best to get me to assassinate the president. I would do so if things were explained to me properly, but I wasn't going to follow that order until I was told the consequences of my actions. That asshole was ordering me to shoot people and asking me to blindly trust him! That was not going to happen. God only knows what he had told the president. I was not going to hurt my mother and her father any more than what Burt had done already. I was about to make a decision that might get me in trouble with the president, but it was going to be a whole lot better than killing him. So I used the only option I had, and that was to fire a round into the floor. After I fired the shot into the floor, a man who resembled the president came streaking down the stairs and entered the presidents' office that I was in. The stairs led to the third floor, where the president's parents resided. Two Secret Service agents had rushed up the stairs to the office.

"What do you think now, Brett?" Benny asked, speaking of the two other men in the room.

"They both look so much alike. I can't tell which one is the real president."

One had auburn hair like the man I had seen on television, while the other had red, almost orange, hair. They both look very similar almost like twins. One thing I knew absolutely was that one was the president and one was an impostor. I could make no sense of what would be the advantage to the country or to the Kennedy family in having two men claiming to be president. Puzzled, I decided to ask a question to test them.

"What are you two doing to my country?" I asked aloud. Neither of them responded. I then figured out a way to test them both in my attempt to figure out which one was the real president.

"Which one of you is the real president?" I asked, expecting that the real president would be honorable enough to own up to what was going on. I was thinking out loud when I said to the auburn-haired one, "You are the one I see

336

on TV, and he [meaning the orange-haired one] is the one I have been talking to. Are you putting him on TV because he is more photogenic than you?"

One of the Secret Service agents said in a loud voice, "How the hell does a kid figure all that shit out? There is something that is very different about him."

Neither "president" spoke until the auburn-haired man said, "Shoot me, Brett."

I wasn't taking any chances, so I said, "Sir, I am trained to be a soldier, and I am a good one. If you order me to fire on you, I will fire on you, but until then I will not harm the commander in chief. I have a question for you. What was the name of the ship you commanded during World War II?"

The auburn-haired one answered in a bitter tone, "You already know the answer to that question, Brett."

The other one answered rather quickly, "It was PT-109, Brett."

I knew immediately that the orange-haired man was the real president. So I said to the auburn-haired man, "Sir, since you want to die, then maybe the best way for you to do so is in front of a camera. You can be killed by an unknown assailant while the cameras are rolling." I then looked at the orange-haired one and said, "Since you are not looking for any fame or glory, you will die with no fame, and quickly. And your counterpart will get all the glory."

I grabbed the president's arm and started to lead him to another part of the house downstairs. I wanted to figure things out. As we exited the president's office on the second level, I saw three men coming down the hallway toward the office. In case my Secret Service badge was no longer valid, I shouted out, "Kentucky state trooper. Halt or I will shoot!" The three men continued toward the president. I repeated my order, "Kentucky state trooper. Halt or I'll shoot!" but they did not stop. I quickly fired two rounds, wanting not to kill them but only to wound them. Two of the three men went down. The third one was reaching for his gun in a shoulder holster when I told him that if he did not pull his hand away from his gun, I was going to put a bullet right between his eyes. He complied with my order.

That is when one of the agents behind me said, "Hot damn, Brett! Where did you learn to shoot like that?"

"My grandpa Holbrook and my uncle Isthme trained me." Looking up at the third agent, I asked, "Why didn't you stop? All I wanted was to ID you."

I was standing down the hall while a trio of agents began looking for the bullet I'd shot in the president's office. One of them asked, "Where did you fire the bullet, Brett?"

"I fired to the right side of the president's desk."

The president then said, "Check the kitchen, too. The office is directly over the kitchen."

The Secret Service then escorted the president downstairs into the great room.

They kept me upstairs to aid in the search for the bullet that I was secretly hoping they would not find. If, in the future I needed to prove that I had been in the president's home, the bullet could be used as proof. The ballistics would prove that I was there.

I finally started down the stairs which ran from the great room up to the second floor. Benny followed close behind. While I was standing in the great room, I said to the president, "Don't let any more Mexican cops in your house, sir, because they are going to do harm to your family."

Benny, who was right behind me, said, "I am going to kill you, Brett, you damn little hillbilly."

Just then I heard one of the president's nephews tell the president, "I will die for you, sir."

I said, "I can't let your nephew die for you, sir. I will die for you."

I heard an agent on the stairwell say, "Brett, you can't die for the president. You are just a kid."

I went home realizing that I could do nothing to stop the president from dying. The only thing I could do was tell afterward what I knew of the circumstances of his death.

Chapter 42

HOLLYWOOD CALLS

When I arrived back in Dearborn, I went to visit Vinny right away. When I got to his house, he was sitting on the stoop. I sat down next to him. He began talking about a guy named Joe Valachi, an Italian man who had ratted out his buddies. Hollywood was going to make a movie about what he'd done, but the Italian communities did not want the film made because it would portray Italian people as mobsters and thieves.

"What's the problem with making a movie, Vinny?"

"We don't want any more bad press about Italians."

"Well, Vinny, the way I see it, Valachi squealed to the FBI, right? Wouldn't you want to tell the whole Italian community that he squealed? At the same time, you would be humiliating his whole family. Every Italian in your organization would curse the Valachi name."

Vinny chuckled heartily, and then said, "Brett, that's what I like most about you. You have the most unique way of looking at things. You see things from angles that no one else does! The funny part is that you are right—not all the time, but more often than not."

"Vinny, let me tell you how I think. There are two ways of looking at the situation. If you don't make the movie, no one makes any money. If you do make the movie, and make money from investing in the movie, then you get to make some money—and put out a positive image of the Italian people. You can invest in other movies and make even more movies, and all that would be legit. You can even put yourself and me in the movie. I think that would be cool, Vinny."

"Who would you get to help me get started?"

"Who else would you get but Maria, Vinny? She knows what you have to do, and she has all the connections in Hollywood."

I left Vinny that evening hoping that maybe, if he would help, I would be able to become an actor. He had ways of getting things handled. Maybe what I'd told him would be the push needed to get him involved in movies.

It was about a week later when Maria came by my house. I was talking to Lawrence Greenwood, one of my friends I played baseball with. She asked me, "Who is your favorite cowboy actor, Brett?"

"John Wayne. Isn't he everyone's favorite cowboy?"

"I need someone less well-known. Pick someone else."

"Oh, I know who would be good, the guy who plays Rowdy Yates on *Rawhide*. I don't know his name because they roll the credits too fast for me to catch it. What do you think about him?"

"What is it you like about him, Brett?"

"Well, Maria, he just looks like a cowboy in the time when the west was being developed. He is tall and lanky, and I don't think there were many fat cowboys at that time. And he has a movie star face."

After Maria left, I went with Lawrence. We gathered up a few others to go play a game of baseball at Lasher Park.

A short time after I'd gotten home from the park, Maria came by again. She was beaming when she asked me, "Brett, how did you know Clint Eastwood was right for the role in those Italian westerns?"

"Who is Clint Eastwood?"

"He plays Rowdy on *Rawhide*."

"I told you once already. Selecting him was pretty easy and logical. Whenever I watch a TV show or a movie, I look at the actor. Does he make me believe he is a real cowboy, or whatever character he may be trying to portray? If he does, then that actor has done his job. Eastwood does that. And other guys have said he is their favorite character on the show. It is just a small sampling of opinions, but I think it is pretty accurate." I didn't think it was any big deal, but I had given Maria my honest opinion.

It was a couple weeks later when Maria took me to a movie set. Vinny and I were to perform as bit players, but I had no clue as to which film we'd be in. I was glad to see Vinny on the set. It made me feel good that he had taken an interest in acting, even though it was a small part. He had one line: "Hit him, kid."

My part was a nonspeaking one. I was supposed to be sweeping the floor with a push broom. When it came time for Vinny to say, "Hit him, kid," I was to shoot the cop instead I hit him with the broomstick. Once I did this, the whole set erupted in laughter, including Vinny. I was confused, not knowing what was so funny. Then I realized I was supposed to *hit* the person, meaning "shoot him." So there was another take. This time, I was supposed to shoot a crooked cop, which was right up my alley. The director told me to keep the left side of my face, the part that Simms had carved up, away from camera. When the time came and Vinny said his line, I pulled the prop gun and said, "Drop the gun, cop." That was the end of our scene. Soon after, Vinny and I left the studio.

Chapter 43

SUMMIT WITH FIDEL CASTRO

In late September, Carlos came by the house. I did not remember doing so, but I nodded off. The next thing I knew, I was in Washington with Skinny Ray. Many members of Team Garcia did not want me to know their real names so I gave them nicknames. Skinny Ray was one of those that wished to remain anonymous. Team Garcia was now using drug induced hypnosis to knock their victims out by way of a posthypnotic suggestion so they could transport their victims without a struggle. They obviously did not care what physical or mental damage that could cause to the victim.

When Skinny Ray woke me out of the hypnotic state, I was in an office somewhere inside the White House. There were several men gathered around a large table, but I only recognized two of them, one of whom was the president. The other was Fidel Castro. Castro had an interpreter alongside him. It was then that I realized Skinny Ray, being so close to a group of world leaders and so close to the president, also had to be Secret Service.

The men at the table were speaking English, but I could only partially hear what they were saying. They seemed to be negotiating a peace agreement with Cuba and NATO. I had no idea why the president wanted me there, except maybe to get my opinion on dealing with Cuba.

From what I had been taught beforehand, I understood that men die to protect the women and children. Soldiers die to protect women and children. Castro had not attacked the United States. The United States had tried to attack him. It occurred to me what exactly Castro had done to cause the crisis: he had protected the women and children of Cuba. How could anyone really fault the Cuban leader for that? Then again, nuclear missiles were a major no-no. Facing Castro, I asked him, "Is Cuban pussy really that good?"

Suddenly Skinny Ray rather forcefully pulled me aside and said sternly, "Brett, you are embarrassing the president. Why did you say that?"

"Well, Skinny, I figure that men die to protect the women and children. I was just trying to figure why a man was willing to start a nuclear war to protect Cuban women. Cuban pussy has got to be damn good pussy."

He laughed a hearty laugh and then said, "I don't believe how you think, Brett. Hey, guys, you've got to hear the way this kid thinks." He then said, "Tell them the way you figured that, Brett."

I was trying to get out my answer to that question so as to try to figure how Castro's mind worked, to let him know we were all males, and to explain that while most of us liked women, not all did. It just seemed very simple to me. Castro had started the whole missile crisis out of his love for the women and children of Cuba. The Cuban people had suffered under an oppressive government that made them feel like whipped slaves. They were not going to suffer with a government again, and they were not going to let the United States dictate terms to their relatively young government. Castro was going to do anything he could to prevent that from happening. Communism was his answer.

I then repeated what I had told Skinny Ray to the men at the table. There was a pause of silence for about ten seconds, and then Castro burst into laughter. His laughter was a sign that he had realized the meaning of what I had said. I felt some relief knowing he had gotten the gist of it. I looked at the president. The expression on his face told me he was not amused. I simply was trying to find a way to understand how Castro's mind worked by probing Castro's mind with questions. We might reach a peace agreement today, but what about five or ten years down the road? Would Cuba start another missile crisis? Any agreement made today would have to link missiles in Cuba and would provoke an all-out attack from the United States. There would be no attack from the United States as long as there were no missiles in Cuba.

Skinny Ray took me to another room, away from where the summit was, so I did not hear any more of the proceedings. One thing I felt I had accomplished was that I'd amused Castro.

I was taken in a convertible limo to a warehouse somewhere in Washington. I was there about a half hour when the president arrived in another limo. The Secret Service began briefing me on what they wanted me to do. They told me that I was to crouch down on the floor of the convertible out of sight of the public. They put a wireless earpiece in my ear and handed me a .22 semiautomatic with which I was supposed to shoot the president. I then got into the president's limo and crouched down on the floor as instructed, with the president on the opposite side of the car. When I was in place, the driver exited the warehouse and began driving at a slow pace.

I heard a voice in my earpiece that said, "They can see the top of your head, Brett."

I crunched down a little more, hoping I wasn't being seen. We drove about another mile when I heard the voice in my earpiece tell me that they could still see me. I was still wondering who the hell *they* were. Getting pissed, I raised myself off the floor, knowing the .22 would not kill the president from this position and range. I moved right next to the president and I put the .22 up to his head. When I did that, he said, "Brett, I want you to get a message to my father. I want you to tell him from me, 'Dad, I skyed my shot.'"

"I don't know what that means, sir. Would you please tell me what you mean by that?" I asked.

The president, moving his arm and hand in an up-and-down motion, said, "I went straight up and straight down." It was a golf term used to describe a golf ball that goes really high up in the air but does not travel very far.

I put the gun down and said, "You are president of the United States! You are not a failure. You saved the planet from total destruction. I would like to believe that I helped you do that. I don't think that a total stranger should tell that to the man who made it possible. If I tell your father that message, both your mother and father are going to think they were failures. Your father, sir, is a good man and a good father. He provided you with money with which you were able to get your education. I think he deserves some acknowledgement from you. Just to be honest, I don't think I am going to be able to give any messages, because I think the CIA or Secret Service, whichever one is in charge of this operation, is going to present a scenario that pits me as a drug-crazed hillbilly kid who whacked the president."

He then replied, "Sky your shot, Brett."

Not understanding what he meant, I was hesitant. The president realized I didn't understand.

"Shoot at the sky, Brett. That's an order."

I then fired two shots in succession into the air.

He then grabbed my hand, patted it, and said, "Don't worry, Brett, I am going to take good care of you."

I took great comfort in what he said. There were only two men I trusted at this point: the president and my grandfather. The president had the driver pull over. I thought we were done. Suddenly, Skinny Ray came up to the limo, stood outside, and ordered me to fire on the president. Refusing, I fired a shot into the floor of the car. He repeated the order, and I again fired into the floor.

He then ordered me one last time. Figuring that this son of a bitch was going to keep this up all day, I shot a third time. The bullet hit the president in the foot, somewhere around his ankle.

When I exited the limo, Skinny Ray noticed the president was okay. He asked me, "Why didn't you shoot him?"

"Because he ordered me to shoot at the sky, and I did as he ordered me to."

Skinny Ray seemed pretty upset that the operation hadn't gone as planned. I left Washington knowing I had convinced the president to think about what his parents had done for him. And I had at least postponed his death. I was beginning to understand more about why he wanted to die, but I did not agree with his decision.

I went back to my fifth grade studies at Franklin and hoped the president had listened to what I'd said to him.

Chapter 44

MOM GOES TO WORK

After I watched the president's funeral on TV, and without being able to go to Washington to visit with him or having Team Garcia trying to get me to kill him, I found myself with a lot more time on my hands. My solution was to become much more involved in sports. One guy who was almost always willing to play sports was Travis Simmons. Another was Lawrence Greenwood. Travis was very good at almost any sport: baseball in spring and summer, and basketball and football in fall. What made him so good was that he was very quick afoot. I often had footraces with him to gauge how much faster I was getting. He usually was about a step faster than I, but I kept trying to be at least his equal. My friendship with Travis began to grow. My father liked him also because he never got anything less than an A on his report card. Dad always admired an educated person because he himself was not very educated. Travis had won every spelling bee that was held at Franklin during his tenure there. He never took books home to study because, as he told me, the teachers always gave a review of what they had taught in previous classes so as to prepare students for the questions on upcoming unit tests. Travis had a phenomenal memory. He soon became my best friend. I would not say I was off the mark to call him a genius. Many other people thought he was, too.

Winter was fast approaching, which meant turning to indoor sports for entertainment. One sport I stayed away from in the wintertime was swimming, because the pool was so damned cold. Basketball was my sport in winter. I enjoyed shooting baskets many evenings courtesy of the Dearborn Recreation Department.

My father expressed the desire to move back home. My mother had been deeply hurt by my father and set conditions for that to happen. The conditions were that he would buy her a car so she could get around and do some shopping and to get a job. She no longer had the desire to rely on him to give her money to feed us kids. Eventually my father moved back home and had purchased a used car for my mom, a 1956 Buick. Her desire to keep her family together was so strong she was going to do everything for her kids. She landed a job at a small nearby restaurant called Burke's, where she worked from five in the morning until two in the afternoon. While she did not show it, I was sure she was still very angry with my father. Whatever happened between them, she was determined he was going to take care of her kids and make sure we had plenty of food to eat.

It was spring 1964. With Mom now working, I wanted to go to the dentist. I knew my breath was horrendous, as one of the president's nieces had said I smelled like poop. This was reaffirmed when Kennedy's brother Ted told him my breath smelled like pig shit. So I figured it was about time that I get my teeth fixed. My mom made an appointment for me and I was off to see the dentist. Back then, we did not have regularly scheduled appointments with the hygienist or the dentist. The only time I or my siblings were taken to see the dentist was when we needed a tooth pulled.

When I got in the dentist chair, the dentist asked me, "What seems to be the problem with your teeth, Brett?"

"People keep telling me I have bad breath, Doc. I want to fix all the teeth that are making my mouth stink."

"Let me take a look at your teeth. Then I will tell how much it will cost to fix them, okay?"

He looked around in my mouth and told his assistant what he had to do to my teeth.

"Well, Brett, I can fix all but one, which we have to pull. The cost, though, will be five hundred dollars."

I looked at my dad, who was in the exam room with me, and asked, "Dad, do we have five hundred dollars?"

"I don't have five hundred dollars. Use the five hundred dollars you won at the track."

Thinking what a rotten bastard my dad was, I recalled that he had given away seven million dollars and now he was going make me pay for my own dental work. I thought *how am I to going pay for any future dental bills?* I told the dentist, "Doc, I do not have the money." I left the dentist's office with a deep bitterness toward my father; no, it was more like hatred. To treat my bad breath, I could only brush my teeth rigorously and chew lots of gum. I hoped the gum would not cause too much damage.

It was now summer 1964, Fourth of July. My cousin Alvin Webb was staying a few months with us. Mom had decided to buy sparklers for the little kids. Once she gave Alvin the money to buy the sparklers, he headed to the party store on Roulo. I had forgotten to tell Alvin to get the colored sparklers because the kids liked them better. He was a block away. I yelled at him to stop. Too far away, he could not hear me. I began to run at full-tilt boogie so as to catch him before he got the wrong sparklers. Hitting the ditch where in the wintertime the city carved out the ice rink, I skidded across Akron Street. I got up, took a look at my knee, and screamed. There was a four-inch gash in my knee. I could see a portion of the kneecap, which was all white, but there was no blood.

A girl whom I did not know walked me back to the house. My mom readied herself and then took me to the Independent Medical Center, where I received eight stitches to close the wound. Where a normal wound would take a month, this one would take ten weeks to heal. Later it got infected from all the debris on the road. I not only had to soak it twice a day but also take a heavy dose of penicillin. The most disappointing thing about the whole

353

incident was that I knew that with this type of injury, I was never going to be fast enough to make a pro football team.

However, the summer was not a total disaster. A new family had moved into the neighborhood, the Powers. Adel was short for the father's real name, which I did not know how to spell. His wife's name was Vonda, and their daughter's name was also Vonda. They had a son whose name was Ernie, and another daughter, Connie. Adel was Gary Powers's older brother. After they settled in, Adel looked me up and came to my house. He told me, "Brett, I am here to back you up. Anything you need, anything, you just let me know."

"I appreciate the help, Adel. I am outgunned and outmanned. You've really got to watch yourself because there are lots of crooked cops in this city. They practically do anything they want, and they know how to get away with it."

"Is that right, Brett?"

"One thing you can be sure of: I don't tell any tall tales. They are crooks."

"By the way, Brett, this is my son, Ernie."

"Hey, how are you doing, Ernie? Are you going to grow up and be a pilot like your uncle Gary?"

"No, I am going to be a doctor."

"You are going to be a doctor? Well, maybe you can be an army doctor."

"Well, maybe I can do that."

"Adel, maybe you should let the CIA know what is going on in this city. In the meantime, I will do everything I can to watch out for you and your family. But you should keep an eye on your back." My circle of friends was steadily growing. I felt secure in the fact that Adel would also be watching my back.

Chapter 45

THE DOMINO THEORY

It was now fall of 1964 and the beginning of the sixth grade. My teacher was Mr. Allgood, who had been a high-ranking officer in the military. He decided to teach the class about a place in Southeast Asia called Vietnam. He felt that it was not going to be long before some of the kids in his class would end up going there. Before we learned about the country, he taught us a military move called a "pincer," a formation of troops resembling the pincer of a crab. Two attacking forces form on each side of the claw, and then they attack the opposing force simultaneously to close the pincer. The reason South Vietnam was important to United States was that Vietnam formed such a pincer. The fear was that once South Vietnam fell to the Communists, the adjacent countries would also fall to communism. This type of occurrence was called the domino theory, which was something valuable to learn about. We had a world map above the chalkboard that could be pulled down to view Vietnam. Giving the lesson a little more thought, I began looking for other pincers on the world map. I saw a few more on the map. It began to make me think about how those places were also prone to attack.

One more thing Mr. Allgood did for me and for the whole class was teach us how to play chess. I liked all the strategy games, and chess was the king of them. He held his chess classes after school. In one of his lessons, he taught us to scan the board when our opponent made a move, asking ourselves why the opponent would move his piece to that particular square on the board.

Those lessons made me look at the whole globe as just another chessboard. I began to ask myself why the Communists would want control of Southeast Asia. It made me think of the saying about the Soviet military move, feint to the west, and attack to the east, which means to stage a phony assault in the direction opposite the one they really want to attack. As I thought about this, I realized that some other targets around the globe were much more valuable. This did not necessarily mean that only the Soviets wanted control of these potential hotspots. Maybe someone else did. I shared these thoughts with Maria in hopes I could learn more about military strategies. I thought maybe I might be of help someday to the United States military. Maria, it seemed, did not give much credence to my thoughts. She took my knowledge of military affairs lightly and did not realize my capabilities.

I had observed one more strategy on my own accord, and that was what seemed to be the object of both combating armies—to cut off the opposing army's supply routes, as was witnessed in North Africa when the Allied forces cut off the German supply lines that had supplied Erwin Rommel and his troops. Rommel, a fierce leader of those forces, was a brilliant tactician. The Allied forces finally beat him by breaking the German codes. Using the communications gleaned after the code was broken; the Allies knew where to wait for those supply ships to destroy them. The sinking of those supply ships made it much easier to defeat the Germans in North Africa. Lesson of the day: if you don't have any supplies, you can't fight. The actions of Allied code breakers saved millions of Allied lives.

The day after those lessons, Benny and Carlos came into our classroom. They were shoving Mr. Allgood around, seeming to be upset with him for some reason. They started going through all the desks and totally disrupting the class. I did not know why, but I thought they were doing this on account of a lesson Mr. Allgood had given about the domino theory. While dressed as Dearborn cops, they did anything they wanted. There was no one to get in their way. I had kept a journal about all the incidents Team Garcia were involved in. They may have been looking for my journal, but I was not sure. However, when I arrived home I was sure they had been looking for my journal because the whole house was a shambles. I relinquished the idea of keeping a journal. From that point on, I just kept the memories in my head.

I was keeping track of what Rico was doing. Rico; his father, known only to me as Mr. Garcia; his sister, Josita; and brother, Diego; set up shop at a place on Franklin Street called Desirae's bar. It was situated almost directly behind me on the opposite side of the street. "Setting up shop" meant that Rico and his family were suspected of dealing narcotics out of Desirae's bar. Also, he was trying to build a stable of prostitutes to earn his living. I stayed away from all that, as it was none of my business. Plus, I never knew if Carlos was protecting Rico since Rico was his nephew. Rico was out of jail. I did not know if Carlos had gotten Rico an early parole or if Carlos got the case against him dismissed. Or he may not have had anything to do with it at all, I did not know for sure.

The Saturday morning after the domino theory lesson, I was awakened by Carlos at around eight-thirty. He handed me my gun, which made me think immediately, *How did he know where my gun was?* We walked from the bedroom into the living room, where there were two more officers standing at my ten o'clock position. Carlos was at my four o'clock. Then I heard footsteps coming up the back stairs. The only person I knew it could possibly be was Simms. Carlos moved to hide behind the wall with his gun drawn. I panicked and thought *there is a high probability there is going to be a shootout. There are two innocent officers here who might get injured in a gunfight.* Not knowing what Carlos intended to do, my only choice was to shoot him with my .22, which I did. He was taken away in an ambulance. I assumed the other officers wanted him dead, but he survived.

It was a few days later when Carlos confronted me in front of the officers who had been in the house with him. He questioned me, asking, "Brett, why did you shoot me?"

"Look, Carlos, the only thing I know is that someone is constantly drugging me while I am sleeping. So if I catch that someone in my house, I am going to shoot him. You were in my house. I assumed you are one of the ones drugging me, so I shot your ass. By the way, did it feel good? Because it sure did not feel good to me when your family got me shot down in the Corridor! Another thing: stop wearing that stupid hat that you use as part of a disguise, because that way I will know it's you. And if I know it is you, I won't shoot you."

"You stupid little hillbilly, I am going to kick your ass for that!"

"Carlos!" one of the other officers said loudly. "Brett is telling you he only shot you because you were in his house. You didn't have a warrant either, Carlos, and there was a good possibility there was about to be a shootout. Brett feels you should have handled your business outside his house."

I knew one thing: this would not be the end of this episode.

A couple of days after that, Carlos and another member of Team Garcia I'd named Skinny Ray because he was so thin, were standing outside Franklin School after classes had ended. They called me over and started asking me questions about Vinny. I could tell by the way the conversation was going that they were going to try to kill Vinny. I was guessing it was Team Garcia, since they had set up shop at Desirae's bar. They were attempting to get control of gambling, drugs, prostitution, and the rackets. How much of that Vinny was involved in was unknown to me. I knew enough not to get involved in Italian business. As soon as Carlos and Skinny Ray finished questioning me, I walked calmly away. When I made it to the corner, I went full-tilt boogie to Vinny's house, being careful that Carlos and Skinny Ray did not see me break out into a run.

Once I got to Vinny's house, I saw Tony his nephew. I was gasping for breath when I asked, "Where's Vinny, Tony?"

"What do you need him for, Brett?"

"The Mexican cops are going to try and kill him."

"Okay, Brett, I'll tell him."

"No, Tony, I need to talk to him so I can tell him how they plan to do it."

Without further conversation, he went in the house, soon emerging with Vinny in tow.

"Brett, are you sure they are planning to kill me? What would be their reason for doing so?"

"Vinny, I am not sure, but I think they want to force you out of the city so they can take control and muscle in on your interests."

"How are they going to do it?"

"Exactly how I don't know. All I can tell you is basically how they work. They always attack in three waves. First, maybe two or three of them come up to you, so you have to keep your distance. Have two of your men get behind them. Next, the second wave of Mexicans will come up behind your men. Then the second wave of your men will come up behind the second wave of Mexicans. Just when you think they are done, they will send the third wave of Mexicans. Now, you will have your last and final stage of your men across the street, so the Mexicans are unaware that your men are there. Vinny, you are going to have to make sure your men across the street have big guns, like .44 Magnums and 9 millimeters, and that they are very good with those guns."

When the time came, Carlos and Skinny Ray came by my house in a patrol car. We headed over to Vinny's house. Armed with my .22 pistol, I knew I would not be any real harm to anybody. When we arrived at Vinny's, Carlos and Skinny Ray approached Vinny, who was standing on the porch with a couple of men alongside him. I was standing on Lasher, the street across from Vinny's house. Vinny's men soon took up position behind Skinny Ray and Carlos. I had no idea what was said by Carlos, Vinny, and the others. As I predicted, another patrol car approached down Roulo. It was Benny who got out of the car. Then I noticed Rico Garcia standing a few yards down the street from me. He was there to be the third wave.

After a few minutes of conversation, the Mexicans, outgunned and outmanned, backed down. I headed back to my house on foot, knowing that Vinny knew that my loyalty now lay with him and that I was going to do everything I could to protect him. I was certain I had cemented my friendship with him. This was evidenced the next day when he called me and asked me to come see him.

"Brett, I will forever be in your debt. You saved my life again. What can I do for you? You want some money?"

"No, Vinny, I don't want money, but you can do a small something for me. Vinny, if I am ever found dead, or my mother, or both of us, I want my father dead."

"Consider it done, Brett."

"Thanks, Vinny. I just want someone to back me up, too."

Chapter 46

A RIGHTEOUS COP ARRIVES TO HELP

In spring 1965, I entered the second half of sixth grade. I had just recently turned twelve. As usual, at Easter I was taken down south to my grandfather's farm. I'd had my fill of corrupt cops, shooting people I did not even know, and being ordered around by Team Garcia. It was at Grandpa's that I met Jordan Bowman for the first time. He was a police lieutenant for the Township of Taylor, Michigan. My grandfather introduced me to him.

"Brett, I want you to meet Jordan Bowman. He is going to give you some pointers on handling a gun." For some reason, Carlos was there too. I had no idea why.

I reached out and shook Jordan's hand. Judging by his strong, firm handshake, I could tell right away that he was good with a gun. I had no idea just how good he was until he showed me one of the tricks he used when putting on shooting exhibitions. He took a double-edged axe and stuck it in the tree in the front yard. Next, he took two balloons and stuck them to the tree, one on each side of the axe. The goal was to fire a single bullet and break both balloons with that one bullet. This was accomplished by hitting the axe with the dead center of the bullet, a very difficult task. Jordan took a shooting stance about thirty feet away, waited a few seconds to aim, and fired. His shot was right on; he broke both balloons.

He then attached two more balloons and told me give it a try. I broke one balloon and really thought that was good. Jordan had me try about a dozen more times, but I was unsuccessful at all attempts. Once I was finished trying, Carlos did something unusual; he snuck up behind Jordan like he was going to attack him. Carlos had a look on his face like that of a madman. I yelled to Jordan to make sure he saw him: "Look out, Jordan! Carlos is behind you!"

"I see him, Brett," Jordan said. I guess Jordan must have seen him in his peripheral vision.

I did not know why Jordan and Carlos were both at Grandpa's. From what I could tell, Jordan was an honest, no-nonsense cop, and Carlos was definitely a crook. It was like oil and water, which just don't mix together. It was beginning to look like my grandfather and Jordan had conspired to get rid of Carlos. They were both trustworthy with guns. Since Jordan was an honest cop, I was worried about his safety.

Once Jordan saw that I couldn't hit the balloons, he looked at my gun and said, "Brett, you need a sight on your gun. That is why you can't hit both balloons. You have to hit the axe precisely in the middle. You definitely need a sight for that. We will wait till tomorrow, and then we'll move to target shooting and see how you do at that."

The next morning around nine, which was a late start for Grandpa, who had gotten up early as he routinely did, I arose and saw that Grandpa had already put up a target. I noticed that Isaac Simms, along with Jordan and Carlos, was there. The fact that Simms was there made me very uneasy. I couldn't figure out why my grandpa had even let Simms on the property. Though I was a little fearful for Jordan's safety, I started practice shooting anyway at close range with my .22. I did excellently. Next we started from a farther distance away; Jordan let me try his 7 mm, a nice gun without a normal sight. It had what is called a dovetail sight. The gun was a compact gun. With the dovetail sight, it fit my shooting style really well. I did just okay because I did not have a lot of experience with the 7 mm semiautomatic. When I had emptied the 7 mm, I noticed that Simms walked over to the fence post and was doing something there where the target was. He had a knife in his hand, but I could not see what he was doing.

I asked Carlos, "What is Simms doing over by the fence post?"

"Isaac is the team's ballistic expert. He is digging out slugs to alter ballistic reports."

"You mean he wants to plant a bullet from my gun to convict me of a shooting I didn't do?"

"Well, not necessarily. We can go the other way also, and remove a guilty person's bullet from the evidence room. That is how Isaac gets paid, Brett. We can control who gets convicted and who doesn't."

My suspicions were confirmed. Some of the slugs Isaac was digging out of the fence post were from Jordan's gun.

Soon it was time for me to try the .357 with the four-inch barrel. I emptied the gun while running to the target, which I called charging the target. Making any movement and hitting a target while discharging a firearm is very difficult. I learned to run while shooting at a target so as to startle the person I was charging. Once again, I reassured my grandpa that I was able to hit my target.

I waited to talk to Jordan after Simms and Carlos had left, to tell him what they were doing. "Jordan, they were digging slugs out of the fence post to use them to alter ballistic reports. One or more of those slugs may have come from your seven millimeter."

"I will keep an eye out for that, Brett," Jordan said.

My father was supposed to come by later in the day, after I was finished with gun training. He and I were going to spend some time at Grandpa Lawson's. After my father picked me up, I was sitting in the car at Grandpa Lawson's house, listening to the radio. I saw my father and grandfather spot a black snake. They were trying to run it away from the house, but they did not kill it. My dad was deathly afraid of poisonous snakes, but black snakes are good because they devour mice and other vermin. They chased it, but it crawled up under the car and coiled around the spring. That's when my grandpa, the eternal huckster who once gave me red-hot pepper when I was just four years old and thought it was funny, came up with the brilliant idea of taking the car down to a local repair shop for an oil change. As we drove to the repair shop, my father warned me, "Brett, you better not say anything about that snake being in the car, or else I will kick the shit out of you, understand?"

"Yes."

Dad and Grandpa got out of the car while I stayed seated. The garage did not have a hoist; it had what was called a pit, where undercarriage repairs were made. The mechanic went down the stairs to the pit and began working on changing the oil. Not two minutes later he came screaming out of the pit. *"It's a snake! Snake! There's a snake down there! Oh Lord! I almost died!"*

That's when the manager came to the car window and asked me, "Son, did they know that snake was under the car?"

I thought about it. It boiled down to doing the right thing, saying yes and taking a brutal ass-whipping, or saying no and not getting involved. I chose the selfish option and said I knew nothing. I didn't know if the mechanic changed the oil or not, but the manager was really pissed and had a few choice words for my dad, who deserved it.

We dropped Grandpa off at his house and headed back to Detroit.

Chapter 47

TURNING INTO A MAN

It was a typical spring day in 1965, my very favorite time of year, with warm weather, the temperature around seventy. The wildflowers were blooming in the field next to our house and also in the field across the street. Baseball season was just starting. It was not going to be a typical day in any shape or form. I saw Maria going into the house of the next-door neighbors, the Abdallah's, who were of Arabic descent They had two daughters, Samara, who was the oldest and also the prettiest, and Neela, the younger one. Samara had a pretty shiny black hairdo. She wore no makeup, and was very pretty without it. The makeup may have been banned by her father, seeing as the father is king in a strict Arab household, or it may have just been her choice not to wear any. Some guys were not attracted to Arab girls and called them "eagle beaks." To me, it just showed how ignorant they were. Besides, at Franklin, there were some very attractive Arab girls.

It had been a little while since Maria had gone into the Abdallah's house. Upon exiting, she came up to where I was sitting on the front porch and said to me," Brett I need you to come with me."

By this time Carlos had showed up. Having no clue what was happening, I asked, "What is going on? I know it's serious because Carlos is here."

"Just come with me, okay?"

I followed Maria and Carlos next door. We entered the house. Maria said something to Samara. Samara's mother and father were sitting in the living room, as was her sister, Neela, and her brother, Mussein. Samara went into a bedroom, and came back out into the living room with two big cushions, like the ones you see in the movies during scenes where a sheik and the rest of his party sits in a circle on the floor watching dancing women. Going to the bedroom again, Samara reemerged with two more cushions and threw them down. One more time she left and came back with cushions, but this time she was naked. I instantly got aroused. Having just gone through puberty, I had never before seen such a pretty young naked girl with such a gorgeous body. Samara was a year older than I, thirteen-plus, as I had just turned twelve. Her whole family was in the living room, along with Carlos and Maria. Thinking that after all I had been through I didn't want any trouble, I was willing to have sex with Samara, although I did not want to do it in front of her whole family. I quickly turned around and tried to open the door. Maria stopped me and said, "Brett, it's all right. Her mom and dad want you to have sex with her. And Samara wants to have sex, too."

"Brett, Samara chose you because sometimes women need a man. Plus, she likes you and thinks you are cute. Think of it as you doing her a favor."

"Maria, if this is some sort of trick, I'll never do anything for you again."

I left the Abdallah's' that afternoon happy and fulfilled, feeling that I had finally become a full-grown man. My first true sexual experience had been everything I had hoped it would be. It felt absolutely marvelous, and it was with a beautiful girl whom I had satisfied as well. The experience was wonderful and had left me wanting Samara again almost immediately. I knew we were from different worlds. In the Arab world, I would have to cope with customs such as prearranged marriage, and sharia law as well. As far as I was concerned, there was just Samara and me, and that was all that I would care about. That, however, was not going to be.

Once we were outside the Abdallah home, Carlos said, "I can't believe you did that, Brett."

"What the hell do you mean, Carlos? You practically forced me to have sex with her, and now you tell me it was wrong? You are supposed to tell me not to do it before I have sex with her."

I had shut Carlos up, at least temporarily. What, if anything, he had planned in the future, I didn't know.

That was typical of Carlos and Maria. One told you to do something and punishes you if you didn't, and the other one punished you if you did.

Carlos had called the house and told me to carry my badge today. Ever since I had lost my badge in the Corridor, I made sure I left it hidden at home. Carlos telling me to take my badge to school was highly unusual. I had no idea why he would make such a request. I met up with both Maria and Carlos in the boys' locker room. I sensed they were going to play good cop, bad cop, where one does something bad to you while the other one does something good for you.

Carlos told me, "Brett, I need to see your badge."

I pulled out my badge. He grabbed it from me, saying, "You are fired, Brett. Now let's see you get your badge back!"

Maria spoke up and said, "He can't fire you, Brett. Only the president can fire you."

"Which one can fire me, Maria? Kennedy issued my badge, but he's dead. So what do I do now?"

I was really pissed at this point. Maria often lied, so I did not know if she was telling the truth or not. Now I was making decisions that could mean life or death for thousands of people based on the unreliable information that Carlos and Maria were giving me. I needed more facts and evidence if I were to have the whole team arrested. I believed Carlos had taken my badge because he figured out that I was the one who had tipped off Vinny, or simply he had put two and two together. He had referred to when I had caught Team Garcia killing the Masons, when I had told one of his bosses in Washington what the DGA had been doing in the Corridor. He lost his badge as a result. But not only did he get his badge back, the assholes made him field chief. I was present when they gave him the promotion.

The only way to get the information I needed was to continue to work for Team Garcia. I stated to Carlos, "Okay, Carlos, if that is the way you want to do me, then I will work without my badge to help you get the job done."

Chapter 48

MEETING OF AN ALL-STAR

My friendship with Shawn Goodenrich had healed. Once again we became pretty good friends. On a June afternoon, after my sexual encounter the previous spring with Samara, Shawn said his dad wanted to talk to me. So I headed to the bar to see what he wanted. The bar was packed. Gordon came over to me and said, "Brett, I want to make up for the way I treated you. How would you like to be the batboy at the All-Star Game next month? You will get a chance to meet the finest players in the game. What do you think?"

"You mean you can arrange for that to happen?"

"Yes, Brett. We players take good care of each other, even though some of us aren't in the game anymore."

"Gordon, I would be honored to go."

"I will make the arrangements."

When it came time for the All-Star Game, I was in a hypnotic sleep. I awoke to find that had my gun on, which usually meant I was going to have to shoot someone. Looking around me, I discerned that I was in a dugout with Simms at my side. I had no idea what stadium I was in, but I did know that I was not in Detroit. Obviously, Simms had made a major mistake in taking me across state lines, which made his action a kidnapping—a federal crime. I did not recognize any of the players. Still, I ran out to get the bats off the field and ran back to the dugout. All of sudden one of the players walked up to me. I recognized him because I had his baseball card. It was Joe Pepitone.

Simms was there too when Pepitone said, "Brett, I am Joe Pepitone. The players are tired of those crooks. My brother is a New York City policeman. I'm going to die for you."

I was extremely pissed. I knew my gun would not kill him, so it was useless to shoot Joe. When Joe said "those crooks," I surmised he meant gangsters. Joe had assumed Simms was one of the crooks. Knowing my gun would not kill either Pepitone or Simms, I replied, "Joe, I am not going to shoot you to kill someone else. I can keep you alive and kill them."

When I gave Pepitone my answer, Simms pulled out my gun and shot Pepitone right there in the dugout. With that over, Simms and I walked out of the dugout. I hoped that Pepitone would be all right. I knew that I had to kill Simms for shooting Pepitone, but first I was going to finish learning all of Simms's tricks of the trade. I had already formulated a plan to avenge the shooting of Joe Pepitone.

When Simms dropped me off, I told him, "Isaac, the next time you have to go on a hit, I want to go with you. I want to learn how to do what you do, okay?"

I never heard any more about the incident with Joe Pepitone, nor did I know if Joe survived. One thing for sure was that I would be gunning for Simms, but I was going to be very sneaky about it.

I was sitting on the front porch steps when Poppa John, acting like he had been drinking, pulled up in his limousine and asked me if I wanted to go for a ride. I had seen him before down in the Corridor, and at the Italian American Club, but I don't think he recognized me at those times. I don't know whom he knew in the Italian club, or if he owned the place. I declined his offer at first, but he practically begged me to go for a ride with him. He had his bodyguard in the car with him. I said, "Okay," and got in the car cautiously. It was just a few minutes into the ride when his bodyguard grabbed me by the hair of my head and stuck a weird gun in my mouth. It had a regular barrel, but at the end it had a piece of metal the size of a peach. My thought was that I was about to die. Then the bodyguard and Poppa John began laughing hysterically. They pulled up in front of my house. As they let me out, Poppa John asked me, "Hey, kid, where can I get a good blow job?"

I told him, "The bar behind my house called Desirae's. Ask for Josita."

About fifteen minutes later, Poppa John pulled up in front of the house again. I knew one thing: I was not getting in his car this time. Suddenly

Carlos came running through the field next to my house. He obviously had come from the bar. With his .44 Magnum in his hand, he said, "Brett, they stuck a gun in Josita's mouth. I have to kill them." He pressed the .44 into my hand and said, "Kill them both, Brett. Leave the driver alone."

Although Carlos had given me his .44, he still had his service revolver, a .357 Magnum. Not about to argue with him, I walked up to the limo and aimed the .44 at the window. Poppa John and the bodyguard began laughing again.

That's when Carlos said, "Shoot through the door, Brett. The windows are made of bulletproof glass."

I thought a .44 Magnum would go through anything, even bulletproof glass. In fact, I had been told that a bullet from a .44 would even go through an engine block. Carlos's instruction that I shoot through the door gave me an idea: if I shot through the door just right, the bullet would hit Poppa John. So that is what I did. I saw Poppa John wince, so I knew he had been hit. There was nothing else to do but finish him off.

I went around the car and shot through the driver's-side rear door. All this time Carlos was standing in front of the limo, keeping the driver from moving the vehicle. Suddenly, the driver unlocked the doors using the power locks. This indicated to me that the driver was in on the hit, which evidently was why Carlos had told me to leave the driver alone. I opened the door to which the bodyguard was sitting closest. I fired two shots at the bodyguard, and then turned to Poppa John, firing two more shots to his head.

Carlos walked around to reach into the car and grab the bodyguard's gun.

"Carlos, that gun was the same gun he stuck in my mouth. I have never seen a gun like that before. What kind is it?"

"It is a .38. It looks different because the thing on the end of the barrel is a silencer. It is a crummy setup because the silencer blocks the view of the target. This gun is meant for when you want to sneak up on someone, Brett," Carlos replied.

Carlos cleaned up the scene. After that, I left.

A couple of days later Vinny came by my house. I knew it must be important because Vinny had a couple of his men with him.

He asked me, "What happened with Poppa John?"

"Vinny, the bodyguard put his gun in both my and Josita's mouths. Carlos Garcia came through the field while they were in front of my house, telling me to kill Poppa John. While Carlos held the car up, I shot both of them. Vinny, I think they are killing your friends because I tipped you that they were going to kill you. And they are setting me up at the same time."

One of Vinny's men asked, "How did you get in the car?"

"The driver popped the power locks for me."

"Okay, Brett, I believe you. I'll take your word rather than the cops' for what happened."

"I did not want to hurt anybody, Vinny." Once again, my friendship with Vinny had saved my life.

And once again I had been forced to take someone's life at the request of the cops. I did not like it, and there was no way I was going to grow to like it. There was only one thing that I hated more than a corrupt cop: death. Not that I feared it, but I hated dealing with it. And maybe that was why I did everything I could to save a life—because I hated death so much. I hated the suffering that death brought, and all the grief that came along with that.

Chapter 49

A CITY CHAMPIONSHIP

September 1965 brought on the seventh grade at Franklin, and with that came a different class format. We students were assigned one homeroom teacher and six different teachers for six different subjects in six hours. School started at eight forty-five. Homeroom ended at nine o'clock, and classes ended at three thirty. This was all unfamiliar to me, having six different teachers. And, I had never experienced classes this way before. However, I soon became accustomed to the style of learning. I also became aware that we had some very good teachers at Franklin. One class that didn't change was gym. The routine remained the same. It was in this year that we were fortunate enough to get a new fellow student who was a real speedster named Kenton Roberts. We all got to meet him at the annual fall test of speed, where Coach Csonka tested our running ability by having us pair up, get in line, and run match races. Goodenrich drew Roberts's name. Once they raced, Roberts beat Goodenrich. When Shawn returned to the rear of the line, I asked him, "How fast is Roberts?"

"Brett, this guy is the fastest guy I've ever gone up against. He beat me by four or more steps."

I knew this guy was really fast if he beat Shawn that badly.

That year, health class became my favorite. Coach Csonka was the instructor for that class as well. I imagine he was chosen to teach it because he was the only teacher who was a constant with the boys. All the boys who had been enrolled at Franklin from the fourth grade, at the age of nine, had Coach Csonka for gym class, as they would until the time they left Franklin. Health class seemed a mystery until we started being taught about women's bodies and social diseases.

It hit us all that this wasn't just health class; it was sex education. Whether it was called health class because the board of education would otherwise not approve of the teachings or so as to prevent parents from raising a stink, I didn't know. It turned out to be a very informative and educational class. Not only did we learn about women's bodies but also we learned about our bodies as young men. The girls previously had their health class in the fourth grade as some of them were beginning to menstruate. Now it was the boys' turn to have sex education. I learned how men produce sperm in their bodies and that there are three ways by which semen comes out of the body: during sex, by way of a nocturnal emission, and through masturbation. Although I was not a doctor, I could see how this drive to ejaculate sperm could cause some men to commit heinous sex-related crimes. Despite this, I still believed that such crimes were inexcusable.

The most important lesson of this class was about drugs. I already had a familiarity with drugs, but I did not understand how and why people used them other than to control a victim. The one drug that stood out about to me was heroin, and the manner of its delivery, by needle and syringe. The needles made punctures in the selected body part, which eventually collapsed the vein. The body part with no circulation would soon have to be amputated to avoid blood poisoning. We were also taught that on account of the high number of wounded soldiers coming back from World War II, heroin was used to wean them off a much more powerfully addictive drug called morphine. They needed to be weaned because if they quit suddenly, it would send them into convulsions. If not treated properly, they could die.

The most humorous thing of the year occurred as the class was nearing a close. Coach was holding a question and answer session in preparation for the final exam. We were free to ask any question we wanted. The class clown, Mozada Ezee, whom everyone had nicknamed "Moz," decided to ask a question. True to form, he queried, "Coach, what if you go to have sex with a girl and you stick your penis in the wrong hole?"

Of course, Moz had asked this to embarrass the coach. Without any hesitation, Coach replied, "In that case, Mozada, my boy, you are going to have a brown penis."

The class erupted into uproarious laughter! It was so funny that half the class had tears in their eyes. Then the class was dismissed. It was time to study for the final. I chose Reza Sayon as my study partner. Studying each of the three days before the final, Reza and I covered every subject we had covered in class, because we'd never had to take any kind of final from Coach before. On the day of the final, the coach revealed that the test would consist of one question: "What is the difference between a dressing and a bandage?"

Reza and I groaned because we had not studied anything on first aid.

Reza and I had done well in the previous weeks, so we would pass the class, but not with the high grade we had hoped for.

With the new school year, Team Garcia intensified their efforts to get rid of me.

The first problem I had was that Carlos was setting me up for a gunfight with Rico Garcia. He had us face off against each other, just like in the western movies, and Rico was insured to win because Team Garcia had put three blanks in my gun along with three live rounds. They knew that I always fired three rounds in succession. Their plan was for me to fire three blanks while Rico would be shooting live rounds, and Rico would not be guilty of anything except defending himself. I spun the cylinder to where the live rounds were and that spoiled their plans, so Rico backed down. If I hadn't known what they'd set up in my gun, I would be dead.

The next thing I caught Team Garcia doing was taking my guns and also my dad's guns, using them to commit murders, and then putting the guns back in the place where we usually kept them. I figured that out in the following way: One day while sitting on the couch in the upper flat. Carlos came walking through the upper flat with my gun. He had a coat hanger down its barrel. I figured that this was his feeble attempt to try to score the inside of the barrel to alter my gun's ballistics. Whether doing that would really change the ballistics was something I didn't know.

The day after my gunfight with Rico, the Dearborn police came to our house. They were investigating a murder and wanted to check our guns. One of the officers was a sergeant. He asked me, "Do you have any guns in the house?" Then he grimaced and shook his head slightly, indicating that I should say no.

"No, all our guns are down south. We stopped keeping them here because people were trying to steal them."

Skinny Ray, who was standing behind the sergeant, said, "He's lying. He's got more than one gun himself."

"See what I mean, Sergeant? You might ask yourself how he knows so much about our guns."

"What do you mean by that, Brett?" the sergeant replied.

"Skinny Ray and the Garcia brothers keep trying to set us up by shooting people with our guns, and then putting them back where they belong. So, no, we don't keep our guns here any longer."

My father was now convinced we had to protect our guns, so he made arrangements to keep the guns at Uncle Rollie's house. When we felt we needed them, Dad would bring them back to the house.

There was one bright aspect to that fall: the recreation department sponsored a flag football league. Franklin had a team entered in that league, run mainly by three guys, Brooks Berhani, Shawn Goodenrich, and Duey. Brooks was a real character. He would sit in the student lounge and tell funny and sometimes stupid stories. After he told one of his stupid stories, he would walk away, giving the students who had been listening to him the feeling that he had deliberately told them a stupid story to make them look like a bunch of dumb asses. I would often help Brooks with his homework in the student lounge.

The other teams in the flag football league were from junior high schools around the city. The games lasted six weeks. We rolled over our opponents and ended up winning the city championship. When it came time for giving out the trophies, we learned that the city had given only Brooks fifteen trophies, whereas there were eighteen guys on the team. I was one of the guys who did not get a trophy. That hurt my feelings pretty badly, as I had made some significant contributions to that team. I just felt that the rest of the team looked at me as a second-class citizen.

It was my friendship with Travis that always made me feel better. When he was a wide receiver on the Franklin football team, he was one of the fastest guys. He was utilized sparingly.

When I lived in Detroit, I made the observation that the Mexicans were the majority, and thus in control in Mexican Town. They bullied people on their turf. When I lived in the Corridor, the blacks had their turf and were the majority, controlling activities and bullying any outsiders. Now, in southeast Dearborn, the Arabs were the majority and in control, and they bullied people on their turf. When white people are the majority, they bully other ethnic groups as well. The United States was being divided up into separate ethnic groups, with each having their own piece of the country.

It appeared to me that there were many nice people from all ethnic groups and of all skin colors. While nice people come in all colors, the problem is that so do assholes. The problem with American society was that we were not doing enough to get rid of the assholes, and we were bullying nice people. I had been going through life just trying to be a nice guy. Sometimes it was really tough to be nice.

It was becoming even harder for me to be nice because the Dearborn cops, along with Simms, had set Rico Garcia up to be shot. They stood him up in the lot across the street from where Edwin Burns had been living before he moved away. They told me I had to shoot him. Simms handed me his .44 Magnum. I could not believe Simms had turned on Rico, as he had been protecting him for quite a long time. But now that he wanted him dead, I was having a hard time believing it was my responsibility to kill Rico. Usually when Rico or I got into a situation where we did not want to shoot each other, we let whoever was the target run to get out of range of the gun. I did not believe Simms would let me go unpunished if I shot Rico. The cops were really pissing me off by making it my responsibility to punish Rico.

Having made my decision, I yelled to Rico, "Run for it, Rico." Knowing what to do, he turned around and started running. Waiting until he was out of range, I fired about two feet over his head. Then something extremely strange happened.

Simms said, "You ruined his head! You shot him in the head!"

"No, I did not, Isaac. I fired two feet over his head. Look, he is still standing."

"Brett, you shot him in the head."

I now understood what was going on. Carlos and someone else were using the type of hypnosis to make the subject hallucinate without the use of any drug. They were using anyone they could as a human guinea pig until they had this technique perfected, hoping to force a subject to hallucinate by way of posthypnotic suggestion. In Simms's case, fear was the trigger for the hallucination. This technique could be very dangerous should the subject be driving when an event such as this happened.

Chapter 50

SIMMS STRIKES AGAIN

In spring of 1966, Samara approached me and said, "Brett, I am pregnant. I need you to marry me."

Samara was totally unaware that I was sterile dating back to the time I caught a social disease in the corridor. I was not about to get hog-tied into a marriage I did not want, so I let Samara know exactly where she stood with me. "Samara it was almost a full year ago when we had sex. If you are pregnant, it is not by me. Besides that, I am unable to get you pregnant because I am sterile. Also, you were running around the house telling your family I raped you."

"Brett, please marry me. My father is going to send me to the old country if you don't marry me."

"Samara, I want to help you and I don't want anything to happen to you, but I am only thirteen years old. I can't get married without my parents' permission. They are not going to let me get married at my age."

Crying profusely, she said, "Brett, please, I did something for you, so please do something for me. If you don't marry me, my father will send me back to the old country and I could face beheading by my father's family."

Not familiar with Arab customs, I suddenly realized that Samara's father may not be able to send her back. I asked her, "Where were you born, Samara?"

"I was born in Detroit. Why did you want to know that?"

"Samara, you are an American citizen. Anyone born on United States soil is automatically a US citizen. You don't have to listen to your father. He can't make you go to the old country. So whatever you do, don't let him trick you into going. Stay here at all costs. If they try to make you go, you have to find some other place to live on your own, or with a relative."

She wiped her tears and said, "Thank you, Brett. I always knew you were smart. I liked sitting by you in class. I sat by you whenever I could."

At this point, I knew that any relationship I would have with her was unsustainable. She had started the conversation with a lie, falsely claiming that it was I who had gotten her pregnant, when our sexual encounter was over a year ago. One thing about liars is that if someone lies to you once, it is highly probable they will do it again.

I had been giving some thought to the situation with Team Garcia and had summed up the evidence I had against them. After the shooting of

Joe Pepitone, I needed to connect Simms with a murder, and I needed an eyewitness so it was indisputable evidence.

One afternoon in late June he came by our house and asked, "Brett, do you know of anyone who has any guns?"

"Yes, Vernoil does. He is mom's cousin. He has a nice hunting rifle."

"What kind is it?"

"It's a hunting rifle with a scope on it."

"That's just what I am looking for. Where does he live, Brett?"

"I don't know, Isaac."

"Who would know where he lives?"

"Dad would know."

"I'll find out where he lives from Burt then."

I couldn't have dreamed what would happen next. A bit later, Simms returned to the house. We drove to where Vernoil was living, somewhere in Detroit. At the door, Simms introduced himself. Vernoil, recognizing me, invited us in. Once inside, Simms asked to see his rifle. Vernoil brought out the case and took the rifle out of it.

Simms then said to Vernoil, "I want you to give me that gun."

Vernoil said, "I'm not giving you my gun. I paid three hundred dollars for this gun. That's a month's pay for me."

Simms said, "If you don't give me that gun, I am going to kill you and take the gun."

Vernoil was defiant once again and said, "I am not giving you my gun."

That's when I said, "Vernoil, give him the gun. He will kill you for it."

"You all get out of my house!"

We left without the rifle. I knew Simms would not give up until he got Vernoil's rifle.

I did not have to wait long before I was proven right. It was two days later when Simms picked me up to make another move against Vernoil. The date was July second. Simms did not say anything so as not to tip me off about where we were going. There was a second cop who rode along with us, one I did not know. When we arrived, I recognized the house right away. It was Uncle Frank's house. I knew it was his because he had two fences stacked on top of each other to make it hard for the dogs next door to jump the barrier. The house was located on Dragoon Street in Detroit.

Simms had me knock on the door. He wanted me to tell my uncle Bill that the cops wanted to talk to him. After knocking on the door, I was asked to enter the house. Uncle Bill, Uncle Frank, and their nephew Vernoil were sitting around having a beer. I told Uncle Bill that the cops wanted to talk to him. When Uncle Bill went outside, Simms's accomplice hit him in the head with his gun. Uncle Bill fought back. I watched in horror as Simms's accomplice shot Uncle Bill in the head, a portion of which—on the right side, about the size of a softball—fell to the ground. As the accomplice reached down to pick up the chunk of my uncle's head, a chunk from the left side of Bill's head fell to the ground. There was hardly anything left of his head. Having heard the gunshot, Vernoil came out to check on his uncle. A struggle ensued between Simms and Vernoil. Wondering what was with him, and because Vernoil was winning the struggle, Simms pulled out his gun and shot Vernoil in the head. A large amount of blood splattered against the side of the house. Vernoil spun around and then collapsed. Then a third person named Burley showed up. Simms and his partner forced me to shoot him. Uncle Frank had stayed in the house the whole time and never heard the gunshots. Simms may have even ordered him to stay in the house.

No cop cars had arrived. Simms drove me home. It was early the next morning when Simms and his accomplice drove all three bodies to Putnam Township in Livingston County, approximately seventy miles away from Dragoon Street in Detroit. This was done so they could stage a crime scene and not involve the Detroit police. Someone I did not know had driven Vernoil's car to the scene. Carlos was there to help with the cover-up.

The official report was that Burley, Uncle Bill, and Vernoil were heading out to go fishing. Vernoil, who was reported to be driving, was drunk. His vehicle left the road and hit a tree at a very high rate of speed. Typical of Team Garcia, they falsified the report so it stated not only an incorrect time of death had happened but also an incorrect location. The time the so-called accident happened was reported to be 5:30 in the evening of July 2, 1966.

What really happened was that they were all shot, and their bodies moved seventy miles away from the real crime scene. The crooked cops lied when they reported that Vernoil was drunk. They had jammed a stick against the accelerator pedal, causing Vernoil's car to crash, and making it look like the engine had come through the firewall and killed Uncle Bill.

My uncle Bill was a World War II veteran. He dodged bullets overseas so these assholes could wear those badges. Then he was killed while in his home country and by men who not only had sworn to protect him but also were paid well. The least they could have done for him was to protect him.

When word had gotten out Vernoil and Uncle Bill were dead, Simms came by the house and we were talking outside my house. I asked him, "Isaac, what did you do with Uncle Bill's head?"

"I stuffed it down in the seat to make it look like the motor crushed it."

"What did you want with Vernoil's rifle?"

"We were going to use it to blame you for the Kennedy assassination. We planted a Klan suit in Vernoil's house."

Maria walked up behind Simms and asked, "What did you do with the bullets, Isaac?"

It was Simms's practice to dig out the bullets from the body of someone he'd killed unless the bullets were unrecoverable, which usually happened when the bullet wound was what is called a "through and through," meaning it had gone completely through the victim. Simms refused to answer Maria's question.

"Brett, they found a Klan suit in Vernoil's house," Maria said.

"That's horseshit, Maria! Isaac just told me they planted that suit in his house. Let me get this straight. All you have to do to kill someone is turn that innocent person into a junkie, or plant a Klan suit in his house, and that's all right with you? Are you telling me all this is being approved by Washington?

I was attempting to get information from her to find out if Team Garcia was acting independent of Washington or if they were carrying out Washington's orders. Maria walked away without responding.

Maria had been staying in the flat above Aunt Lydie's apartment. The bottom line was that two more of my family members were now dead. I saw a pattern starting to develop. Maria's refusal to answer my questions made me realize she was just as guilty as the rest of Team Garcia. She approved of what they were doing. Otherwise, she would have given me the information I needed to convict them.

My grandma Holbrook came up from Kentucky to bury her brother and her nephew. For some reason, Dad would not let me go to the funeral home or to the graveside service. He never told me why. My grandma and grandpa Holbrook came by our house. While standing outside of the house, my grandma asked, "Brett, why is your friend doing this to our family? My brother was a veteran of World War II. He fought for our freedom."

"Grandma, let tell you straight. He is not my friend. He is a corrupt cop. And there is a bunch of them. They have ways of making me do stuff I don't want to do. Your family members are dead because Grandpa won't let us move till I kill the man who raped mom. While we live in this city, if they tell me to do something, I have to do it."

"Brett, we are not the Klan! So why is he doing this to us?"

"The best way to explain it is to say that there is a whole gang of cops who hate Irish and hillbillies. They are a bunch of nutcases. They are terrorizing us, and they are going to keep terrorizing us until they get the dog money."

My grandma, said to me as she was getting into the car, "I love you, Brett." I could tell she was heartbroken and upset on account of having lost her brother. She had raised twelve children and was a God-fearing, churchgoing woman. She'd grown up and lived in a part of the country where people were trustworthy. She and my grandfather were heading back to Kentucky, but they would soon, unbeknownst to them, have to deal with a problem they were not familiar with: killer cops. The problem I would have would be to convince them that it was the cops who were doing all the killing. Up to this point, they had trusted Team Garcia, which was pretty naive of the both of them. As long as Team Garcia was wearing those uniforms, no matter what I said about them, no one was going to believe me, because the badge was a sign of honesty. But they were not honest. That is how strong the power of that badge and uniform is.

I would continue to try to figure a way out of the situation. Right now the only plan I had was to kill Rico so we could move out of Dearborn. I could not kill Rico at this point because the rest of Team Garcia would kill me. First, I would try as hard as I could to win him over to my side. If I succeeded in doing that, then I could come up with an alternative to moving. With Rico on my side, I would be much more likely to come up with a better solution. I really did not want to have to kill Rico, but it was the condition my grandfather had placed on me before we could move. As much as I liked Dearborn, my brain was working overtime trying to figure a way out of Dearborn without hurting anyone. By moving out of Dearborn, I would no longer be in Team Garcia's jurisdiction. Then they would no longer be able to enter my house anytime they wanted to. Somehow I felt I was going to be able leave Dearborn without bloodshed. Getting out of Dearborn would mean true freedom for my family, and also for me. That day could not come soon enough. I looked forward to it with great expectations.

A few days later, something much unexpected happened. Maria came by with her son. She introduced him to me as Russell Thurston, Russ for short.

He looked to be around seven years old. Glad to finally meet him, I tried to make him feel at ease. "Welcome to the family, Russ," I said.

I thought I finally was beginning to make some headway with Maria, and that we were now a force of three: Dad, Maria, and me.

Then Carlos showed up and called me to the porch, where he was talking to Dad. I was sure they were not exchanging pleasantries.

"Brett, they stole your money and gave it to Russ."

"Carlos, I told Dad to put the money in Dad's name, Russ's name, and my name."

"Brett, they stole your money and they are not going to be giving it back. You have to kill his son. Otherwise, they are going to kill you for the money," Carlos said.

If I'd had any doubts whether the money was real, I no longer had any. Just exactly where Dad was keeping it, I didn't know.

"I am not willing to kill his son over that money, Carlos."

I looked back to see Maria crying profusely. I walked over to her and asked, "Maria, what is the matter?"

She responded, "You shot my son."

Oh no, I thought. *Now someone on the team is doing to Maria what they had done to Simms.*

I looked back to the porch, where Russ was standing. He was fine. I then whispered in her ear, so Carlos couldn't hear, "Maria, Carlos is doing something to make you hallucinate. I did not shoot your son. He is fine."

The three of them left, Maria, Carlos, and Russ.

I had avoided hurting her son. The incident showed me what type of person Carlos was. He wanted all three, my dad, Maria and Russel, dead at any cost. He wanted a war between me and Russ, and he wanted me to kill my half-brother. Eventually, I figured, he had a plan for me to kill Maria and my father.

Just as soon as I thought I was out of the woods, Maria, Carlos, and Russ returned. I was right back in the same situation. Although Russ was Maria's son, he was my half-brother, so I was trying my best not to hurt him. Carlos was really putting the heat on me. He had given me the signal that if I did not kill Russ, he would have Russ kill me. I was not carrying a big gun, just my .22. I figured the only way out of this mess was to wound but not kill Russ. Hopefully that would satisfy Carlos. So I wounded Russ by shooting him in the head, the bullet just grazing him. Carlos carried him off with Maria, who was crying even more now.

As I walked back onto the porch, my father said angrily, "I am going to kill you for that."

"Kill me for what? Saving your son's life? Dad, I don't think you comprehend what is going on. Those cops are a team, and they want you, your son, and Maria dead. I am doing everything I can to keep the three of you alive. If they end up going to see Rico Garcia, who uses a .38, your son is as good as dead. Instead of killing Carlos, the one who wants your son dead, you want to kill me?"

Obviously Dad did not believe that Team Garcia were the ones who wanted him, Maria, and Russ dead. All I could do was hope that he eventually caught on, but I had the suspicion that I would have to deal with not only the anger of Team Garcia but also my father's anger. The fight was beginning to be all about the money dad stole. I'd never wanted it to be about the money, I guess I had no hope of my father returning the dog money. I was being forced to do things to help someone else get revenge. The problem was that the revenge was for someone else's satisfaction, not mine.

Chapter 51

RAID ON BURTON

It was early March when Simms came into my house around one in the morning and woke me. He said, "Time to pay your debt, Brett."

Not asking, I assumed Simms was talking about the black officer who had died for me and asked me to do something for his people. Whether or not it was about that officer, I would do this job to pay my debt to Simms.

Dad had retrieved our guns from uncle Rollie's and we would move them around in the house so Team Garcia would not know where we kept them or if they were even in the house. I grabbed my father's shotgun, my pistol, and my holster. After I put on my down-filled vest, I told Simms, "Wake me up when we get there." Then I fell asleep.

When we arrived somewhere in southeast Detroit, Simms woke me. There were several plainclothes officers around us.

"They want you to develop a case, Brett," Simms said.

I asked what the job was. One officer spoke up, saying, "Brett, my name is Sergeant Hamilton. We are looking for narcotics in large quantities. Do you have any ideas we can work with, Brett?"

"Well, if you are going to go war, it is best that you fight in familiar territory and where you know the drugs are. So we will start at a place where I know the DGA will be operating, Burton Elementary. Let's go there. I will sleep the rest of the night. Wake me up in the morning, when classes are in session."

Simms woke me around nine o'clock. Hamilton was with him. We entered into the school and began assessing the situation. I went from classroom to classroom. In each one, there appeared to be a party going on. I went up the stairs to the second floor, where I found more of the same. Not only did half of the students look like zombies but also most of the teachers looked like they had been drugged.

The racial makeup of the school was 99 percent black. Now I always knew that, despite what a lot of people may say or think there are some very bright black people in the world. Still, this was meant to be a school for gifted children, but there no white students. I was proud to have attended this school. And I knew better than to think that educated people such as teachers did not go to college for four years and work their asses off just to become junkies. This was the doings of the DGA. They had taken over the school and were now running it. I could see that the first thing I had to do was to clean up Burton and get rid of the scum. Next we could concentrate on going after the drugs, which would hopefully lead us to a big stash of narcotics—or at least put a good-size dent in DGA's operations.

I discussed my strategy with the others, mentioning what we should do next. I told them we should first get a well-qualified principal and vice principal. We should also get someone to handle admissions that could identify potentially gifted students to attend the school. This would once again make it one of Detroit's top schools. Next we decided to scout through the school looking for possible drug dealings and dealers.

After a few days of implementing my plan, I thought it best that we throw everyone out and start admissions from scratch. I walked into the principal's office and grabbed the microphone for the PA system. The principal, an older woman, probably in her late sixties, tried to stop me from making an announcement, but she was so high that she almost fell over while doing so.

I said into the microphone, "My name is Brett Lawson. This is now my school. All you little niggers have got five minutes to get the hell off my land, starting now."

I walked out into the hallway to see there was a mad rush for the exits. A shapely black policewoman came up to me while I was waiting in the hallway and said in a flirtatious way, "You are a take-charge kind of guy, aren't you?"

I responded, "It's more like aggressive, miss. It is how you stay alive when you do what I do. So I don't have to keep calling you 'miss,' tell me what your name is, sweetheart," being flirtatious and giving her a big smile.

"My name is Clara. And what is yours again?"

"I'm Brett, Clara. I'm very pleased to meet you."

"Brett, what should we do about the girls? They have no other place to go. I can tell you right now, they feel much safer with you here."

"The girls can stay if they want, Clara." I based this decision on the fact that drug dealers forced young girls to take drugs and into a life of prostitution.

I walked through the school to check the classrooms. They were all empty. We had succeeded in creating a fresh start. We'd have no students until we got a social worker to work admissions.

The next day brought new frustrations. Some of the boys had returned. I tried to keep my cool once I saw a group of three black boys who looked like high school dropouts passing through the hallway. They were taunting me as they went by, saying, "We ain't afraid of you, white boy. We own this school, not you."

Fuming at that point, I said, "Look, you fucking Uncle Tom asshole. I'm going to make all you assholes my sissies. Then we'll see whose school this is."

"You can try, white boy, but it ain't going to do you no good."

I turned around to see Maria, who had been standing behind me listening to the whole conversation.

"Brett, let me show you something."

She took me into a conference room. They had Clara bring a little girl into the room.

Clara, after showing me the girl's arms, said, "Brett, this is what we are up against." The little girl must have had fifty needle punctures on each arm. She was no older than seven. Clara continued by saying, "Brett, most of the girls here in this school will most likely not even live to be eighteen. They have no life, no future. They will be forced into performing sexual favors for older men, and probably will die of an overdose from all the drugs being pumped into them. And this is not only happening here but all over the city. You are the only one who has the experience with drug dealers, and that knows how to help them."

At that point I lost it. The tears were streaming down my face; I could not control them. What kind of a man would drug a little girl so he could have sex with her? I knew Clara was right. "Who do you suspect did this to her?"

"We believe it was the father."

Just then a white Detroit police officer whom I did not know came into the conference room and said, "Brett, don't help them. All they raise is junkies and whores. If you help them, the department is not going to help you."

I could not believe he had said that in front of Clara. He had just disrespected every black officer on the force. This gave me more insight into why Team Garcia used drugs to punish people and turn them into junkies. If you are a junkie or a whore, no cop is going to help you, and if you are found dead, there will be no investigation into your death because the cops just plain don't care. As far as the cops are concerned, you just got what you deserved.

The unknown cop made my decision very easy. I did not need the help of the police. All I needed was Clara, for whom I was really doing what I was doing. I kissed the little girl on the forehead and said, "I don't know if I can help you or not, little girl, but I am sure going to try." Turning to Clara, I said, "Let's see how much she knows. Bring in a needle and a syringe."

Clara brought in the needle and syringe from a police first aid kit. I showed the little girl the needle and syringe and asked her, "Do you know what this is?"

"Yeah, it's a works."

Her calling the needle and syringe "a works" was enough for me to know she had been taught by hard-core addicts. Still, I decided to question her just a little more. "What do they do with the works?"

"They shoot the dope in you."

"Who are the ones that shoot the dope in you?"

The tears were now streaming down her face. She responded, "I don't know." Finding the man who was responsible for doing this to these young children was my highest priority.

Maria then came into the room and said, "Brett, you need to get your grandfather to send you a dog."

"No, I am not going to use dogs. That is supposed to be a secret, and we want to keep it that way."

Two black police officers came into the room and asked, "What do you want us to do about the little girl?"

"Let me tell you my plan. I want two black police officers outside the little girl's house, one on each side of the doorway and out of sight; one more officer across the street watching the door; one more inside the home; and a squad car nearby to pull the perpetrator's ass over. I don't care if it takes a month; I want you to catch him. It's obvious he has access to narcotics, so he is going to have them somewhere. When you catch him, check his car for drugs. Also check his house, the basement, and the attic. Check his momma's house and check his grandma's panties. Find out where the drugs are."

"Brett, why black police officers?" Maria asked.

"Oh, jeez, wouldn't it be kind of obvious if we used white police officers in a black neighborhood? Since we don't yet know where the dealer lives, we have to assume he is black and lives in a predominantly black neighborhood."

Simms took me back home, where I got some much needed rest. I was back at Burton the next morning and students were starting to trickle into the school. I started the morning off by observing the students. I saw the trio whom I had nicknamed Larry, Moe, and Curly, the three stooges. As usual, they were flaunting themselves like they still owned the place. I had to figure a way to have them arrested, but I could do nothing unless they were caught with narcotics. I couldn't have them searched them if I suspected them of carrying drugs. There had to be probable cause.

Maria came up to me and said, "Brett, we have to get a dog up here; otherwise, we are wasting everybody's time. It is time to call your grandfather."

I headed to the office with Maria beside me. We called my grandfather and briefed him on the situation. At first he refused to send a dog, but then he changed his mind.

"Brett, I am going to send Ronnie up with one dog. Whatever you do, don't tell anyone how we know the criminals are carrying the drugs."

"Okay, Grandpa, I will follow your orders." With that, I hung up.

At the minimum, it would take eighteen hours for Ronnie to arrive with the dog, given all the stops he would have to make for the dog to relieve himself.

Three days later, Ronnie arrived at Burton with the dog. He showed me how to tell if the dog detected narcotics, showing me the difference between a silent alert and an audible alert on the suspect. Because I had only one dog, I had school officials lock the front door so the dog had only one entrance at a time to watch. Hamilton had joined me with the dog, and Uncle Ronnie was backing me up. We posted the dog in the center of the hallway. The day began with a highlight when the three stooges walked in and the dog gave a silent alert.

I pulled out my gun and ordered the three boys to raise their hands. Two black police officers cuffed them and ordered them to the ground. The cops rifled through their clothes, finding on each boy what appeared to be approximately twenty packets of white powder.

I said to them, "Well, now, what do we have here? The three stooges bringing drugs into my school."

One of the three angrily asked, "How did you know we were carrying, man?"

"You assholes didn't you see that dog? That is my dog. We taught him to talk, but only cops can hear him talk. He told us you had drugs on you. You didn't hear him talking to us, did you?"

"Man, you are an asshole! Talking dogs! You are crazy!"

"I'm an asshole? You're the one going to prison for selling dope. I told you I was going to make you three my sissies!"

As the cops took them away, I looked over at Hamilton, who was laughing hysterically. He walked over to me, slapped me five, and said, "Brett, you are a work of art! I have never seen anyone like you, and I don't think I ever will again. Talking dogs! Now I have heard it all." He laughed loud and heartily.

"Well, if you think about it, it's true. It's kind of like sign language."

"Like I said, you are a work of art, Brett. I'd never looked at it quite that way," Hamilton said.

Just then, one of the black police officers walked in and said, "Brett, we got the guy who was hurting the little girl. How the hell did you know it wasn't her father?"

"Well, I didn't really. I just played a hunch. I did not think a father would do that to his daughter. Would you do that to your daughter?"

I went home that evening proud of the work I had done, knowing I had saved an innocent black man from life in prison.

Chapter 52

DISAPPEARING EVIDENCE

As I walked into Burton the next morning, I was greeted by a group of officers. One of them said, "Brett, all our evidence is gone."

I could not believe that the evidence hadn't been better guarded. It was obvious that the culprit was Carlos, and possibly Simms. I knew that sooner or later they were going to make me look like an asshole, and this was just the beginning. I was going to have to come up with a plan. The best way to keep Team Garcia from screwing up the case was to alert the rest of the Detroit police force to Carlos's tactics and outnumber him and Simms. I came up with a plan to create a phony case with some fake evidence, which was to be kept at the Thirteenth Precinct. The officer in charge there was a captain in the Detroit Police Department.

With the phony case in place, the cops took me down to the precinct's station house. I was told that Carlos was going to make a play to remove the evidence from there. It happened just as I'd said it would. When Simms, Carlos, and the captain walked into the office and asked the detective for the file, the detective could not find it. The captain began reading him the riot act. I was standing in the detective squad room where all the detectives had their desks when the captain was chewing the detective out who lost the file. The captain chewed him out so bad that even my ass hurt.

Three black officers had been watching as well. I asked, "Why didn't you arrest them?"

The black officers would not answer me, so I asked them again, "Why didn't you arrest those two? If you don't answer me, I cannot continue to help you."

"Brett, a black police officer cannot arrest a white person."

"*What, you* have to be shitting me! Besides, that son of a bitch is a Mexican. He's brown, not white. That is the most ridiculous thing I've ever heard in my life."

"No, Brett, it is true."

"I can't believe you men put up with that shit. I'm acting in an advisory position but I am going to get the city to change that policy right away. I need all of you to turn your badges in tomorrow. Not the next day—tomorrow. Not the day after that, but tomorrow! I want every black police officer in the city to turn their badges in at the mayor's office. Every last one! And if anyone doesn't turn in his badge, then the rest of you kick the shit out of him and take his badge."

411

The next day, the black officers took me to what I thought was the mayor's office. When we got there, I saw that the desk was piled about three feet high with all the badges. I saw a nameplate that read "Coleman Young." The man behind the desk said in angry voice, "Who in the hell do you think you are?"

I stood my shotgun on its butt end on his desk and replied, "My name is Brett Lawson. I am the baddest little mother you are ever going to meet."

"What do want?"

"I want these men to be able to arrest anyone who commits a crime in this city. They are not security guards; they are cops. The city is wasting money by restricting who they can arrest."

"Brett, I like your style, but I am not the mayor. I am a senator in the Michigan Legislature. I will see what I can do."

In the following days, the black officers gained the power to arrest white people or anyone else caught committing a crime in the city. Coleman Young, wanting to know more about the work the police and I were doing, came to the school to learn how we worked the dogs. Being a little sneaky, he sent some friends in carrying narcotics. We did not know who was carrying drugs; nor did we know which people were friends of Mr. Young. The dogs performed well with a 100 percent hit rate.

Mr. Young, obviously very impressed, asked, "Brett, how are they doing that? They caught every last one of the people with drugs."

"Mr. Young, I can't tell you how we do it, but I can say that my grandfather trained the dogs. We get paid to train them for police departments. If I tell you how he trains them, then all police departments will train the drug dogs themselves. If you ask me again, I am going to take the dog home—and we won't be back."

"Brett, how do they know the narcotics are there?"

I looked at my uncle Ronnie and said, "Take the dog. Let's go home."

Ronnie grabbed the dog and dropped me off at home in Dearborn and headed for aunt Lydia's.

A couple of days went by. Maria came by my house. I was relaxing in the easy chair. She practically begged me to return to Burton, saying, "Brett, they really need your help. They are not going to be able to figure how the dogs know the drugs are there."

Ronnie and I headed back to Burton the next day. When we arrived, Coleman Young had some German shepherds there, but they seemed to be just wandering aimlessly through the halls. It was absolutely pathetic, and a big waste of money and manpower. I knew it was going to cost me a lot of money if I revealed how the dogs were able to detect the drugs. I figured that since the others at Burton already knew about the dogs, I might as well tell them how the dogs know when a suspect is carrying. By telling them how the dogs could smell the drugs, if every police department in the country used the drug dogs, it would make a big dent in the pockets of the drug dealers. So I decided to tell them how the dogs knew the dealer was carrying.

I said to the senator, "Mr. Young, you have to teach them to smell the drugs."

"We already know that, Brett. We are just trying to work out the technique."

Detroit had worked on it for a couple of days. Their style was a little different from my grandfather's. The Detroit dogs would walk beside you if they detected drugs on you, remaining at your side until they walked you into a wall. If you tried to move, the dog would growl, and if you tried to get away, it would then bite you.

The school had pretty much been cleared of drug activity. As soon as the pushers saw the dogs, they immediately turned around and exited the building.

For some reason, Carlos and Isaac Simms showed up at the school one day.

Mr. Young came over to me and asked, "Why did cops from Dearborn show up? We don't need them here." He was concerned because black people perceived Dearborn as a racist city.

I told Mr. Young, "They are not Dearborn cops; they are Secret Service. And they are not here to help. They are here to screw the whole case up. You better listen to what I tell you; because they are going to make you and me both look like a couple of assholes. Just keep in mind that I am on your side."

Just when I thought we had control of the school, Maria came in and said, "Brett, go look down Cass Avenue."

I walked out and looked down Cass in both directions. Traffic was bumper-to-bumper for a couple of miles. The ones lucky enough to have found parking spaces were heading inside the school. The people were a mixture of races, some black, some white. I was especially pleased to see Asians showing up, because they seemed to be such good students. I did not understand why all these students were there. I walked back inside the school and asked Maria, "What is going on out there? Is there a fire somewhere and the streets are blocked?"

"You made the news, Brett. They are spreading it all over the city! Some kid is kicking drug dealers' asses. They are arranging a press conference today at three o'clock."

I was pissed to say the least. I knew this was another attempt at making me look like a real jackass. My fears were confirmed when the press started asking their questions.

One reporter said, "Brett, it is rumored that this is a Secret Service operation. Can you confirm that?"

I gave the standard response, which was, "Well, if I told you we were the Secret Service, and then it wouldn't be a secret anymore now, would it?"

"Brett, do you think Lee Harvey Oswald assassinated Kennedy?"

"No, he is completely innocent."

"What evidence do you have of that?"

"I can't get into that right now. I am focused on cleaning out Burton."

Then another question was fired at me: "Why did you choose Burton, Brett?"

"I went to Burton myself. It was one of Detroit's finest schools when I attended it."

Then a voice out of the crowd asked, "What did they teach you there, Brett, how to do drugs?"

It was obvious he was a Secret Service agent, planted in the crowd to back up Maria and Carlos. They had pulled that routine on me before while I was working at the White House. They would drug me and then make sure all of the Secret Service knew that I was high on drugs, believing I was high of my own accord.

"Only a jackass would ask a question like that!" I responded. Laughter erupted from the crowd.

Then the most important question popped up. "How do the dogs know about the drugs?"

My answer was, "That is a secret we don't want anyone to know."

As usual with all secrets, the press kept badgering me, wanting to find out what the secret was. My attitude was that if they were that persistent, then I would give them a line of bullshit. Not wanting to let my grandfather down, that is what I did: I fed them a line of bullshit.

The next morning I went back to Burton. Coleman Young had a concerned look on his face. Clara had helped establish a class just for the black girls. They had chosen to stay in the school. I had told Clara I would help all the girls who stayed at Burton to attend classes. Mr. Young was worried because now the school officials wanted to close that class down. He asked if I could do something to keep the black female students enrolled at the school. I waited in the class with Mr. Young. Soon the new principal showed up.

We had a heated discussion. I told him, "The only reason I am here is that I promised these girls that if they stayed, I would help them. Now you want to have them leave, after all they have been through. I say they stay. This will be an African Studies group."

He left, but was not satisfied.

After that incident, the teacher would occasionally have me talk to the girls in that class. I was free to teach them about events that were occurring in the civil rights movement. I also taught them a little about some of the famous people who were from state of Kentucky, and a bit about street smarts. The one thing I wanted them to remember most was the march from Selma to Montgomery, and who Martin Luther King, Jr. was. To make sure they remembered that event, I told them, "Selma is a girl's name, but this is a city, not a girl."

I continued to ask them where that girl Selma was. After finally getting it, they responded, "Selma is not a girl; it was a march."

The most famous person who was born in Kentucky was Abraham Lincoln. Another famous person who was born in Kentucky was Mohammed Ali. I felt the students should know that Lincoln freed the slaves, and also signed the Emancipation Proclamation, which set their freedom in motion.

I asked one day, "What is Kentucky most famous for?"

"The Kentucky Derby," they all said, just as I had taught them.

One day after I had taught the girls some of the facts I thought were important, Mr. Young wanted to see what I had taught them. Young and I took the girls out in the hall to show Young what they learned. So I started off by telling the girls, "You are not free."

"Oh yes we are," they responded in unison.

"Who says you are free?"

"Abraham Lincoln, who signed the Emancipation Proclamation, which says I am free."

"How did men in Africa hunt?"

"They hunted with a shield and a spear."

"Why did they hunt like that?"

"Because they were so darn good they didn't need a gun."

Suddenly Mr. Young spoke up with anger in his voice. "Are you making fun of me?"

"Making fun of you? If anything, I am complimenting you. There are tribes in Africa who form relays to tire out their game. When the game is tired, they just walk up and kill it. Besides that, Mr. Young, American Indians carried a spear, and some carried a bow and arrows. They are well respected by fighting men of all races for their fierceness and tenacity in battle. I am one of those men. Police officers carry a shield also; it's pinned to their chest. I can't believe you would be embarrassed about where you come from."

Young took the girls back to their classroom and did not apologize to me for getting upset with me.

One of the things I wanted to accomplish while I was at Burton was to establish a program that would afford the kids a snack during school hours. I remembered when my sister Veronica and I went to a little Baptist church in the neighborhood, where we would be served Kool-Aid and cookies. I thought that it would be a good idea to serve the kids a snack during the day. Clara headed up the program. It soon became the kids' favorite.

Chapter 53

THE CORRIDOR GIRLS

The morning after we started the snack program, I had my talk with the girls in the African Studies group. Getting a little irritable, I wanted to go back home. I was going to go to the bus stop; that's how bad I felt. Clara and Maria had a chat and determined I needed to have sex to take the edge off. Maria got me a small apartment four blocks down the street from Burton so I would not have to go all the way back home to rest. Since the school had pretty much been cleared of drug activity, the Detroit cops asked me to help them figure a way to make drug busts on the streets. I walked near the school and observed, but I did not see anything unusual, only a bunch of black cops who had rounded up a bunch of suspected teenage pushers. The kids, who had no drugs on them, were not about to give up any information or help in busting their superiors, which is who, the police were really after.

I told the sergeant in charge, "We need to catch them with the narcotics so we have something to negotiate with. Maybe then the pushers will be more willing to give up their contacts. It will all be legal then, since the dogs will give us probable cause to search them. Then we could also make undercover drug buys. We are going to have to run sweeps in high-trafficking areas with the dogs, but whatever we do, we've got to catch them with the drugs."

That handled, I went back to the apartment for some much needed rest. I slept until eleven o'clock the next morning, when I was awakened by Maria. She had me take a bath, as there was no shower. I started to get undressed when an absolutely gorgeous dark-haired girl entered the apartment. She started undressing without anyone telling her to do so. When she was completely nude, I was awestruck by her stunning good looks and body. I got the impression she was there for sex. In her having been methodical in getting naked, I felt she was telling me, "I am ready and I have no reservations." I felt lucky just to see her naked.

Nervous about what was happening, I looked at Maria and said, "Maria, this is not a trick? I am not going to have to fight a sex charge, am I?"

"No, Brett. I am going to be in the room the whole time so nothing bad happens."

I was a bit skeptical. I wanted to have sex with this beautiful young woman, so I was cautiously optimistic.

"What is your nationality, gorgeous?"

"I am Italian, Brett."

"So no one ever finds out from me that you were here, I am going to

422

name you Miss Italy. You are pretty enough to be a contestant in a beauty pageant. This way, not even wild horses could drag your name out of me. Is that okay with you?"

"Yes, Brett, that would be just fine."

It was not long before she was satisfied.

I thought that was the end of the relationship and that I would never see her again. All of a sudden a group of five girls entered the room. As Miss Italy was leaving, those five girls asked her how it felt to have sex with me.

"It feels absolutely great!" said Miss Italy.

I looked out the door to see how many women were standing in the hallway. There were about twenty young women. I say women because they were fully grown and mature enough to be responsible for their actions. The young women kept coming into the room, five at a time. I would give them each a nickname, such as Honey; Blondie with the Nice Ass; Missy; and Talk Dirty to Me. The party continued until the wee hours of the following morning, when my legs gave out and I collapsed on the bed. Maria grabbed my arm to check my pulse.

She said, "Brett, your pulse is way too high. You have Superman syndrome. I have to call a doctor for you."

When the doctor arrived, he told Maria that no man could have had sex with that many women in that span of time. Maria said, "I was in the room the whole time. I saw it. No woman left unsatisfied." Maria then said, "The doctor says he wants to give you a shot. Is that okay, Brett?"

I replied, "Okay." About fifteen minutes later I fell asleep.

Chapter 54

TELL A LIE AND SOMEONE WILL DIE

I slept for thirty hours before I'd finally had enough rest after the party with those women. It was time for me to head back to Burton to see what else I could do. Hamilton and another cop met me at the entrance to the school. Almost immediately they began asking me questions about the girls. I told them, "I am not supposed to talk about those girls."

"Oh, come on, Brett, which one did you like the best?"

"Well, I suppose I can tell you about that. That would be a toss-up between Blondie with the Nice Ass and Talk Dirty to Me."

"What kind of names are those?"

"I gave the girls nicknames so no one would know their real names and they could remain anonymous. If one of the fathers of the girls were to show up and want a piece of my hide, I could swear I do not know who his daughter is."

"Why did you name the one Talk Dirty to Me?"

"She liked me to talk dirty to her while I was having sex with her. I like talking dirty to girls during sex anyway."

"What did she do when you talked dirty to her?"

"Man, Hamilton, she put that body in high gear. It was only a couple minutes before she got off. It was just a few minutes more until she passed out."

Hamilton and the other cop gave me high fives and were laughing hilariously, almost in tears. Then Hamilton asked, "Did you really do them all, Brett?"

"Yeah, I really did them all—and some of them three of four times. I kept going until I couldn't stand up any longer. My legs gave out."

It was early in the morning when Coleman Young arrived. He said I was wanted at the courthouse. He asked me to sign some papers releasing the city from any responsibility should I get hurt. After I signed them, an officer drove me to the courthouse.

While in the courthouse, I was taken to juvenile court. There was no bailiff. I was standing near the prosecutor. The officer who had driven me there was at the back of the courtroom near the entrance door. No one informed me why I was there. I presumed I had been summoned to guard any witnesses who were going to testify against the DGA once they entered the courtroom.

One of the witnesses was one of the girls in the African Studies group. Two members of DGA were sitting at the defendants' table with their attorney. I was not informed of what charges, if any, they were facing, so I was winging it. Suddenly the little girl's eyes got as big as saucers. I could tell she was extremely distraught over someone who had entered the courtroom. I walked to the back of the courtroom and asked the officer, "Who just walked into the courtroom?"

He pointed to a little boy about eight years old. I walked over to the boy and stooped down in front of him. From out of nowhere, he pulled a .38 Special on me, sticking it up against my chest. At first, I said, "Not the right side of my chest. That's the one I got shot and stabbed in." I then asked him, "Do you want to die because if you shoot me, you are going to die? And the officer at the door is going to be the one who shoots you."

"No, I don't want die," he said in a soft voice.

"What is your name?"

"Damien."

"Did DGA send you, Damien?" I asked, with the gun still in my chest. He nodded his head.

"What happened? Did they turn you into a sissy?"

He again nodded yes, saying, "I don't want to be a sissy!"

"I'll make a deal with you. I won't let them use you as a sissy anymore if you give me the gun."

"Promise me."

"I promise."

He couldn't get the gun out of his hand fast enough.

I marched up in front of the judge and explained, "Your Honor, the boy over there has just surrendered his weapon. He said he was sent by the DGA. He has surrendered voluntarily. I promised that if he did so, we would protect him from the likes of DGA."

"Court is in recess. We will reconvene tomorrow morning at nine o'clock," said the judge.

My driver told me that he was going to stick around to handle Damien, so I decided to walk back to Burton. A young woman who looked a little older than twenty walked up to me, stated her name, and said that she was reporter for CBS.

She asked me, "Brett, is it true that a gang member stuck a gun in your chest in the courtroom?"

"How did you know my name and how did you hear about that so fast? It just happened!" I replied.

"A police officer told the press and word travels fast, Brett. Why didn't you just shoot him?"

"Well, for one thing, whereas everybody else saw a gang member, I saw a little boy of about eight years old who was being forced to do things he didn't want to do. If I had shot him, it would mean I had given up on him. Isn't that what we do to people on death row— society has given up on them?"

"Well, yes, Brett, but they have committed heinous crimes."

"Yes, but I am the type of guy who will do everything I can to see that you get a fair chance to live. After that, if you can't follow the straight and narrow, then I will give up on you. You only get one chance with me, though. Still think I should have shot him?"

"Have you ever been shot, Brett?"

"Yes, I have. The first time I got shot was in the back of the head. The second time was in the chest. I was also stabbed in the chest on another occasion. The one to the back of my head was the worst one. I was unable to walk and kept losing my balance when I tried to do so. I had uncontrollable tremors while I was being re-taught to walk."

"That sounds like a terrible ordeal. Anything else you would like to say, Brett?"

"Yeah, they hire really pretty reporters at CBS. You're pretty smart too."

"Brett, I bet you say that to all female reporters."

"No, I just say that to the pretty ones." I figured, *What the heck, why not give her compliment?* After all, she was a pretty good reporter. I wanted to show her that I could be mean but also sweet. Men should complement women more often.

"If I stuck a gun in your chest, would you shoot me, Brett?" the reporter asked.

"No. I would give you a chance for atonement first. But if I had to, with a beautiful woman like you, I'd try to sweet-talk the gun away from you. Besides, I don't think you're mean enough to shoot somebody," I said to her in a playful way.

"What do you mean by that?"

"Well, that is open for your interpretation, miss. You're smart. Figure it out. I might have to bang you around a little bit, though."

Figuring I had done enough for the day, I headed back to my room for some rest.

It was later in the evening when Honey and seven of her friends came to my room for another party. They left in the wee hours of the morning, as I just could not stay up any later than that this time.

A couple of days later, they returned. This time, as Honey and her friends were standing outside the door, Blondie the Nymph came up the stairs. She asked me if I would do a favor for an old woman.

Maria said, "Brett, she is my friend and she needs a favor bad. Do it as a favor for me, Brett."

"Okay, Maria. If it weren't for you I would never have met all those girls, so I'll do her a favor in return."

Maria walked out the door and told Honey and her friends that I was going to spend the day with her friend.

That is when I heard Honey yell, "You mean to tell me he would rather be with that old biddy than us?!"

Maria retorted, "Brett is a real man. You can't satisfy him because you are not woman enough to satisfy him."

The party went on for two days. Blondie the Nymph was satisfied with her visit, and she had left me satisfied. Honey did not understand that I was only returning a favor for Maria; without Maria, I never would have met Honey or the rest of the Corridor girls. I was very grateful to Maria. I felt the way Maria operated was like this: first, she did something nice for me, and then she shoved it up my ass, almost as if extracting payment for what she did for me. Only the payment is death, or life behind bars. I knew I was going to have to be on guard, not just on account of her tactics, but also against the rest of Team Garcia.

It was about two weeks after the party with Blondie the Nymph. I had been moved downstairs, where I was sleeping. There was a knock at the door. A girl whom I did not recall seeing was at the door. She said to me, "Brett, I am pregnant. You are the father."

Suspicious, I asked her a question: "Well, how many months pregnant are you?"

She answered quickly, "One month."

Knowing that I was sterile, I told her, "You are going to have to talk to Maria. She will know what to do."

She then turned around and exited the building. Returning a few days later, she had her father in tow. She stood there in the doorway and explained to me, "You are the only one I have been with. You have to be the father, you sex maniac. Dad, he made it with all of the girls, every one of them."

I was a bit taken aback to hear her talking so bluntly about her sex life in front of her father. It gave me the immediate impression that he was a fine father, as his daughter could discuss with him any type of problem she had.

Maria was in the room with me. I had briefed her on what the girl had said during the latter's last visit to my room.

Maria, pulling the father and his daughter aside, explained to them, "It is

432

impossible for Brett to get anyone pregnant since he was molested as a young boy and got a social disease

Her father was a first-class act. He said, "Young man, I think we have the wrong man. We are sorry."

"Well, sir, I did not appreciate her accusing me of getting her pregnant when I don't even know if I made love to her. Accusing someone of doing something they did not do is like sticking a knife in them. You can say you are sorry and pull the knife out, but the wound is still there and it still hurts."

"Brett, they say you gave some of the girls' nicknames. I would like you to give me a nickname. What nickname are you going to call me?" the girl asked.

"Well, I should be shitty and name you the Liar." It suddenly occurred to me that not only did all the girls like partying with me but also they liked that I had given them nicknames. My giving them a nickname seemed to have become a ritual with the girls. I guess that my giving them nicknames made them feel extra special.

"Brett, I am alone. I was looking for someone to be by my side, at least until I have my baby."

"I will accept that. I think I will call you Sweetheart because you are young and about to be a mother. Plus, I like that song 'Let Me Call You Sweetheart,'" I said.

"I like that, Brett. Sweetheart it is."

Her father then said that he was a writer. "I want to write a story about you, Brett. Would that be okay by you?"

I decided that for his protection I would address him only as Mr. Author, and I said, "Well, Mr. Author, I would like to someday write my biography. But I am sure you are a very good writer. You would probably do a much better job than I could, so if you need my permission, go ahead. Mr. Author, you have to be cautious in this neighborhood, though. The room I am staying in is just a temporary place for me here in the Corridor. I have to keep guns in my room. I would not want you to get hurt."

Sweetheart and Mr. Author then left the building.

It was a few days later when Maria found out from the rest of the girls that Sweetheart hadn't even been in the room the nights I'd had sex with all the girls. Three days later Mr. Author returned and asked me a few questions about how the DGA worked. I explained a few things to him, basically telling him how gangs functioned in this area. It was a short interview. I took him down to Burton and had Clara bring in the little girl with all the needle marks. When Clara brought the little girl in, I showed Mr. Author the many needle marks on her arms.

Mr. Author looked at the little girl's arms and said, "Brett, kick the shit out of them. Show them no mercy." He was referring to the drug dealers.

"Mr. Author, I am trying, and will continue to try." I didn't think there was an honest man alive who could look at that little girl and not feel anger.

A little while later, Sweetheart came to my room and said, "Brett, Josh, the father of my baby, does not want anything to do with me. He said that becoming a father is going to wreck his career, and that he won't be able to attend school."

"Is that why you blamed me? You loved him so much that you would blame someone totally innocent?"

"Brett, please do not think bad of me. I need someone like you to help me. My father says you are ten times the man Josh is."

"Okay, Sweetheart, come back tomorrow with your dad. We will go together to have a little talk with Josh and his parents. It is a real possibility that he won't marry you. If you try to force him to marry you, he will hate not only you but also your baby."

"Right now, all I want is for him to support me and my baby."

The next day came. Mr. Author drove me and Sweetheart up to Josh's parents' home. His mother answered the door. At first she refused to talk to me, except to say, "My son does not want to get trapped in a marriage." I knocked again after she closed the door in my face. This time when she opened the door, she began to listen to reason.

"Your son is going to have a baby. This should be a joyous occasion for you. You are going to have a grandchild. Basically, Sweetheart just wants Josh to support her and the baby. Legally, he has to support the child at least until it turns eighteen."

"Young man, you have a nice way of saying your words. I will discuss this with my son."

It took a few more visits before Josh accepted his responsibility to the child and Sweetheart. What exactly they worked out, I did not know. Nor was I interested in the details. The only thing I cared about was that she was satisfied and happy.

Sweetheart came by the room one last time to say goodbye and to thank me.

Mr. Author kept coming by my room, asking me questions to research his story about me. On one particular evening when Mr. Author was in my room. Simms and another, unidentified cop came by and asked me Mr. Author's name. I told them I didn't know. They camped outside the door inconspicuously and waited for him to come out. When he did, they grabbed him. I lied, telling them the man they had grabbed was not him.

They did not believe me, so they dragged him outside. Mr. Author yelled, "Brett, help me. Please help me."

I grabbed my shotgun, headed to the front porch, put the shotgun up to my shoulder, pretended like I was going to shoot, quickly swung the gun in Simms's direction, and fired. Nothing happened. Simms was still standing. It was now clear to me that the shell was a blank. I had been walking around with a blank in my gun. I thought, *Oh no, now Simms is going to try to kill me.* There was no clip in the gun, and the only shell in the chamber was a blank. I did not have another shell for the gun on me, so whatever Simms was going to do now, at least he couldn't shoot me with the shotgun.

Simms told me to stay on the porch while Maria, the mystery cop and I waited for about an hour for Simms to come back. Tired, I went and lay down on my bed. Soon afterward, Simms came in to my room and told me to grab my shotgun. He then ordered me to kill Mr. Author, who was standing on the porch along with Maria Simms and the mystery cop. I would have aimed at Simms, but I knew the gun was empty. Plus, my vision was blurred, which meant only one thing: I had been drugged. My vision was going from normal to blurry and briefly back to normal again. I was teary-eyed with only a split-second glimpse of what was in front me. I saw what looked like Mr. Author, with Simms behind him.

"Kill him, Brett," Simms said.

I had no idea what to do. I raised the shotgun with the intention of making it look like I was going to shoot, but I knew the gun was empty. I also had a small-caliber handgun that was not powerful enough to kill someone. I did not know how to help Mr. Author. Simms and the unknown cop were holding him up. As I was fumbling with the shotgun, it suddenly went off and Mr. Author went down. I was horrified. Where had that live round come from? I was getting weary from whatever I had been drugged with, so I lay down to rest.

About an hour later I was arrested by a black cop for first-degree murder. I was not held in a conventional cell. The narcotic made me sleep all night.

The next morning, I underwent intense questioning from Hamilton about what had happened. I told him my version of what happened—that I had tried to kill Simms but the shotgun was loaded with a blank. The second time, I had been drugged. I was trying to kill Simms, but the drugs made my vision blurry. As I tried to focus, the gun went off, and Mr. Author went down. The shell was a live round! It had to be Simms who loaded that gun! It was the same scenario as at Gooden's bar. Simms was the only one who had a machine for reloading ammunition.

I said to Hamilton, running a bluff, "The information I got is that Simms had driven all the way back to Dearborn to get another shell for that gun, which would mean he loaded the gun a second time. Second, Maria said I was the shooter, and the two cops held Mr. Author up. Why did she do nothing to help me? She is the Secret Service, but she did nothing to save Mr. Author's life."

Then it hit me! They had been holding him up. Why were they holding Mr. Author up? Isaac Simms and the unknown cop were the only two, outside of Maria, who were capable of drugging Mr. Author and me. We both had been drugged! The two things that I was 100 percent sure of were that (1) Mr. Author was not a junkie and (2) whomever had drugged me had also drugged him. Maria had given me a horseshit story saying that I had drugged myself. I wanted to see the toxicology report once it came out. I knew how these bastards worked. I was willing to bet my last dollar that Mr. Author had been drugged. *Who would want to kill Mr. Author?* I wondered. Then another revelation hit me. It was Maria! She wanted to stop Mr. Author from writing that book he was writing about me. And she was probably blaming me for shooting her son. She was doing everything to keep me broke and destitute or in prison. By setting me up to kill Mr. Author, they were going to kill two *assumed* junkies with one stone. It was now clear to me that it was she who had pressed the issue of bringing the drug dogs to Burton; she had arranged the press conference to expose the secret of the drug dogs. Maria had gotten the room for the Corridor girls, and she'd done nothing to help Mr. Author. She only watched as Simms and the mystery cop held Mr. Author up. It was now clear to me why she had done what she did, but she was claiming to have nothing to do with the shooting. Her main goal was to reveal the secret of the dogs' training so that my family could not make any money off Grandpa's dogs.

I just needed one more thing to prove I was right, and that could not come soon enough. I had been set up, and I wasn't going down without a fight. This setup had been perpetrated by three members of Team Garcia, Maria, Simms, and the unknown cop. I knew that with every setup they pulled, I had a good chance of getting out of the situation as long as I told the truth. I knew they were going to lie in order to make the charges stick, but I simply was not going to let that happen.

It was nine in the morning when I headed back to Burton to see Hamilton and find out about the toxicology report. On my way, I was met by five girls. One of them said, "Brett, we want to have sex with you." I could not tell if any of them had been at my place before. She said, "Brett, all the girls are ready to have sex with you."

"How many of you girls are there?"

"Every girl in our school is willing to have sex with you."

"You mean you told the whole school what we have been doing? I am very flattered, but I can't have sex with every girl in the school."

"Brett, please see us. Is there something wrong with us?"

"There is absolutely nothing wrong with you girls. It is just that I have to be somewhere right now. People are trying to send me to jail. I have to defend myself. Look me up when I get done with this job, which will be a year from now," I said, stalling for time.

As I finished talking to the girls, the CBS reporter approached me and said, "Brett, Coleman Young just held a press conference. He said you gave him exclusive rights to the drug dogs, and that you did it for free. Is that true?"

"First off, I can't give him the rights to those dogs."

"Why is that, Brett?"

"The reason is my grandfather, who is an absolute genius with animals, trained those dogs. He sold the rights to those dogs for a large amount of money to the state of Kentucky."

"Mr. Young said you already signed the papers that give him the rights, and you are supposed to do it all for free. How much is the city paying you?"

"I am doing this job for free because of a Detroit police officer named Clara. She told me that a group of little girls at Burton did not have a chance, and would probably die before they even reached the age of eighteen. She also told me I was the only one who could, and who knew how to, help them. How much do you think that's worth one million or maybe ten million? The City of Detroit doesn't have enough money to pay me what I deserve, so I have to do whatever I can to get the job done."

"What about the papers you signed with Mr. Young?"

"He lied. He said the papers I signed released the city from any responsibility for my actions. He also said he was going to give me the school building. What he doesn't know is that a person under the age of eighteen cannot enter into a contract. It is illegal even to ask a person under age of eighteen to enter into a contract."

"Well, how old are you, Brett?"

441

"I am under eighteen, miss," I responded.

"You mean you are risking your life, you are working for nothing, and Mr. Young tried to trick you into providing services to the city for nothing?"

"Appears that way, doesn't it?"

"Brett, you are a man every woman wants to meet. You are more of a man than men twice your age. Why did you sign the papers?"

"I knew it would be an unenforceable contract. I know one thing: today it is the Cass Corridor; tomorrow it is suburban America. Cities would rather try to solve the drug problems themselves than pay me, unless, of course, I will work for free. Now that I have a record of success, I can clean up any city, but there are people who don't want me to succeed." I told her that since I had a meeting, I had to end our conversation. Then I headed for Hamilton's office.

As I neared his office, Sweetheart met me in the hallway. She said, "Brett, they found morphine in my father's blood."

I entered Hamilton's office. He confirmed what I'd just been told. "He was drugged, Brett."

Pay dirt! Finally I found the evidence I needed.

"That means that with the live shell and the drugging, it is first-degree murder, right?"

"Right, Brett. We have to do a few more checks before we get a warrant for Maria and Simms. I did not know if Detroit police wanted a warrant for the mystery cop.

I walked out of Hamilton's office and started back to my apartment. As I was leaving I ran into Sweetheart.

Sweetheart asked, "Brett, how did you know my dad had been drugged?"

"Sweetheart, they've done this many times before. Unless Hamilton stops them, they are going to do this again, and then your father will have died for naught. If he doesn't stop them, I will be their next target."

"You mean they have done this before?" I could tell she didn't believe me.

"They used the same method in dozens of murders before this one. They use the same method of operation almost every time, namely, drugging their intended victims. That's why they will try to get rid of me—because I am the witness against them."

My job in the Corridor was nearing its end. I had to get with Hamilton and finish the case up later that afternoon.

Chapter 55

AIR FORCE SALUTES ME

I walked into Hamilton's office and asked him if he had gotten the warrants for Simms and Maria.

"Brett, we are going to charge you with manslaughter," Hamilton said.

"Well, I am not going to be so friendly now. You were supposed to be my partner, but you are letting those crooks set me up. Maria got the room I was staying in, and Simms put the live round in the shotgun. You are going to let them remain free? Well, I am just going to get an attorney and see if a couple of crooked cops can set up a minor so he lands in jail. I'm just fourteen, Hamilton."

"You mean to tell me you are still a minor, Brett? Just how old are you?"

"Again, I am fourteen. You are ready to charge me with a major crime but didn't know that I am a minor?"

I was frustrated at this point. I was going to set up Maria the next time

444

WAR IN THE CASS CORRIDOR ↰

I saw her at the school by making up a completely false story. I was going to set her up like she had done to me, and feed her lies, just like they had done to me. At this point I had nothing to lose.

When I saw Maria in the school later that day, I told her that a judge was issuing warrants for the arrest of her, Simms, and the other cop for conspiracy to commit murder. It was a bullshit story. The fact was that there were no warrants for her, Simms, or the mystery cop yet

After I talked with Maria, Mr. Young came into the building. I asked him "What's this garbage I hear about me signing over the rights to the drug dogs?"

"Well, you signed the papers. You should have read them."

"What is it I am supposed to do for you?"

"Brett, you are going to train the dogs and give them to the City of Detroit free of charge. And then the city will pay me."

"So you are going to make me do honky work for free, while you will be the only one collecting money off the dogs? We buy the dogs, train them, and bring them to you for free is that right?"

"That's right, Brett. You already signed the papers."

"Mr. Young, do you realize you broke the law? You could be not only sued but also put in jail. The reason for that is that a person under the age

445

of eighteen cannot enter into a contract. Plus, it is illegal even to ask a minor to sign a contract, unless you have the parents who are of legal age sign also—and I am only fourteen. Good luck enforcing your illegal contract! This operation is not about money, Mr. Young. One of your officers showed me a little girl whose arms are full of needle punctures. She was being forced to perform oral sex on grown men. That officer asked me to help all the girls at this school so that they might at least have a chance at a decent life. I was warned by the white officers not to help those girls, saying that they all turned out to be junkies and whores right in front of a fellow officer who happened to be black. That officer was Clara. And now here we are. Now what do you think of me?"

"Brett, I think I have misjudged you in the worst way. I am sorry."

It was the next afternoon when Maria and I walked to Burton and stood down the hall from Hamilton's office. Simms and the mystery cop, holding Hamilton by the elbows, were carrying him. They had him moving his feet as they assisted him to his office. It was obvious he had been drugged. There was not a chance in hell of getting a warrant to arrest the three of them. I had not expected them to drug Hamilton, but I had figured they would launch some kind of attack on him. My ploy had worked, though. I noticed that Maria was almost in tears. Team Garcia had now crossed the line in resorting to drugging a fellow officer, just one more thing I was witness to. Mr. Author, I, and now Hamilton all had been drugged during this operation. I was searching through my memory for a solution, a way to stop Team Garcia from drugging any more people, especially honest cops. It was definitely going to be a monumental task. I was sure I was going to have to make some sacrifices and take some risks to get the job done.

The next day I went to see Hamilton as I had planned. He said, "Brett, you are cleared of any wrongdoing, but leave the shotgun at home from now on."

"I will do as you ask, Hamilton," I replied.

I met up with Maria. I said, "Maria, I need to go back to the house. Can you get me a ride home?"

"Yes. I will take you home, Brett," she said.

My mom was sitting on the front porch having a cigarette. I went over to talk to her. Maria came with me. I had not noticed before, but once Maria showed me mom's arms, I saw they were full of needle punctures, about sixty of them, thirty on each arm. I didn't want to blame Maria, but it was as if Maria was saying to me, "See what happens when you do something good? We attack your mother." It had to be Rico, although the possibility did exist that it was my dad. There were two possible motives for the attack on my mom. First, Rico had done it trying to turn my mom into a prostitute to add to his stable of prostitutes and to fulfill his aspirations of being a top-notch pimp. The second possibility was that my dad, in trying to pump enough narcotics into Mom to kill her, or at best to turn her into a junkie, had the motive of getting custody of the younger kids. If she were a junkie, then she would be declared an unfit mother. It would then be up to me and Veronica to take care of her. Either way, the war was on. I was going to kill that wannabe pimp, and I was going to throw out the rule book. I would then have just one more variable to deal with: my dad. If nothing had happened to my mom, then I would have to assume it wasn't my dad who'd drugged her.

I was surprised the next day when Mr. Young showed up at my house. He told me, "Brett, the air force is going to do a flyover by your house."

"What is that supposed to mean? They aren't going to bomb us, are they?"

"No, Brett. It's a salute to you for helping the city out down in the Corridor. They are going to fly by at precisely four o'clock. Try to be outside so they can see you."

"I will be sure to be outside at that time," I said.

About an hour later, Benny came by the house and asked me, "Brett, what kind of bullets do they use with the guns on military aircraft?"

How did Benny find out that the air force was doing the flyover? I wondered. Knowing that the military used twenty-millimeter cannons and not pistol rounds, I feared this jackass would cause massive damage if he got a hold of a cannon or even maybe a missile. I told him, "Only .44 Magnums, Benny," because I figured he had a .44 Mag. I had no idea what he was about to do. If he was going to shoot down a military jet, he would need something more than a pistol round. I also knew there was nothing I could do to stop him from carrying out whatever it was he had planned to do. I could not kill him for what I thought he might do. I had to wait until he committed a crime.

"You sure that is what they use, Brett?"

"Pretty sure that is what they use, Benny."

The next day I walked out of the house and stood on the front lawn at 3:45 p.m. It was a couple of minutes later when I saw the planes off in the distance, making a wide approach. I looked down the road at Lasher Hill, where I saw either Carlos or Benny Garcia, I couldn't tell which. He had a little girl on the field with him, and was coaxing her, pushing her ahead from behind. She appeared to be no more than three years old, and was moving just past the hill. I had no clue as to what he was doing. The jets were approaching my house. Soon they roared right over my house. It was incredible, the loudness of the engines as they roared by. I never knew that jet engines were so loud.

The next day, the chief of police for Dearborn came by the house asked, "Brett, did you see anything when the jets flew by your house? A little girl was killed around here at that time."

"Yeah, I saw one of the Garcia brothers pushing a little girl from behind, near the hill."

A few hours later, the chief came back to the house, this time with Benny and Mr. Young.

"Brett, I want you to think carefully. Are you sure of what you saw?"

"Yes, positive. I saw the little girl being pushed along," I replied, being careful not to let Benny know that I couldn't see which Garcia it was behind the little girl.

"Brett, she was shot with a .44 Magnum. We believe one of the pilots fired on her and killed her."

"Well, chief, that's impossible. First, none of those pilots fired their guns. Second, they don't have .44 Magnums on those aircraft. They have twenty-millimeter cannons or Gatling guns. And while they always have missiles, they have no .44 Magnums. Benny, it costs a lot of money to train one of those pilots. They are a very valuable commodity, being well trained and highly skilled. They will kick your ass all the way back to Texas before they let you blame one of them pilots for what you did. Cops like you are a dime a dozen. Now you've done messed with the US military!"

Benny said, "You little bastard! You set me up! Die for me, Brett!" That statement from Benny was as good as a confession. He was admitting that he had committed a crime he would go to jail for, unless he got someone to die in his place.

"You shot an innocent little girl and I made you do it? Is that what you want us to believe?" I said to Benny. Not wanting to die for him, and not wanting him to go free, I said, "I can't believe you shot a three-year-old girl with a .44 Magnum and now you want me to die for it! There is no way I am dying for your crime. Be a man and say what you did!"

I was pretty hot. I knew when he asked me what type of bullets they use on those aircraft that he was going to hurt someone. This was just a senseless murder of a little girl. Team Garcia often committed senseless murders like this one. Then they did anything within their power to get away with the murders.

The chief left. I heard that later the Dearborn Police Department held a press conference. They went ahead and blamed the pilot anyway. It was an act of cowardice for the Dearborn police to blame the pilot, but it showed me just what lengths the city would go to avoid a lawsuit. Blaming someone who was innocent was Team Garcia's method also.

I was unprepared for what happened next. I was sleeping in my upstairs bedroom when I felt a prick in my arm. It woke me. I saw it was Rico poking me with the needle. Benny was helping him by holding me down. This was now the second time Rico had forcefully injected me. I struggled, trying to get up, but Benny, being a rather large man, put all his weight on me. I soon passed out.

The next thing I knew I was paraded before a judge. "Your Honor, this man is a drug addict. He is high on drugs right now," Benny said to the judge.

I tried to speak up and tell the judge that I had been forcefully drugged, but the judge was not listening to what I had to say.

The judge then asked, "Does anyone want to take responsibility for this man?"

I heard a voice from the back of the courtroom say, "I will."

I turned around to see my dad standing in the back of the court. I was released into my dad's custody. I spent the next few days at home thinking I had withstood an attack by Benny, but I soon found out differently. I was waking up in the morning high. It had to be Rico's doing. And whatever narcotic he was using, it was a powerful one—it almost crippled me. The attacks were coming with great frequency. I decided to sleep in Lasher Park, on the concrete slab under the picnic shelter. This kept me safe for a night, but then the attacks continued. Whatever Rico was using was screwing with my vision. I saw Rico, but I could not make out if it was Carlos or Benny with him. This was a new tactic Team Garcia was pulling on me. I was the witness who had seen Benny in the park with the little girl. Instead of killing the witness, like the mob would do, he was having me drugged so as to discredit any testimony I might give. He had also established that I was now a known addict, even though that was false. Now, if I was found dead of an overdose, no one would care what happened to me.

One night about eleven, the boy whom I considered to be my best friend, Travis Simmons, came and got me out of the park. His house was less than block away and saw some activity in the park and decided to find out what was going on I told him what was going on. He then called the cops from my home. The cops told me to stay in the house, saying they would keep tabs on me. One night soon after that, the Dearborn cops got me out of bed and took me outside. Then they put the house under surveillance. We, the stakeout team and I, waited for a few minutes. Two men entered the house. It was a very dark night. The stakeout team and I would wait outside for them to exit the house. Anybody inside the house would not get hurt should gunfire erupt. The cops rushed to the back door of the house to surround the two men, as they now were exiting my house. As we got closer, I could see it was Rico and Isaac Simms. I never found out what happened to Benny or what became of his status as police officer, but he never bothered me again after that night.

This was just one more example of how the members of Team Garcia actually enjoyed killing. They derived great pleasure from killing—and also from knowing they would get away with it. It had an effect similar to that of an addictive narcotic. It would have to be labeled "thrill kill." Maybe it was an adrenaline rush that gave them the high. In any event, it was very difficult to stop them from killing. The team members were constantly telling lies to get out of going to prison. They would do almost anything to avoid being incarcerated. Carlos once told me that the Soviets called US citizens "freedom junkies." He said that freedom junkies were anyone who killed to remain free. This was a case of Team Garcia being a whole gang of freedom junkies. Benny murdered the little girl in the park that he had led there. That was just one more murder a member of Team Garcia had committed and gotten away with. This time, though, I knew that I had enough evidence against Benny to convict him of murder even if Dearborn did not get rid of him. I also had Carlos for the deaths of Johnny Doe and Manuel D. I now had Isaac Simms for the murder of Sweetheart's father. Maria was not innocent either. She was an accessory to murder, as she had witnessed the murder of Johnny Doe and failed to report it to authorities. She also had information indicating that Simms had killed Vernoil and was also a part of Uncle Bill's murder.

While the evidence was mounting with each crime the team committed, I hoped I would be able to memorize all their crimes. I would continue to try to find a way to stop them. I knew they could only beat me for so long before I would be able to turn the tables on them, but first I had to stay alive to get a message to Washington.

Chapter 56

GRANDPA CALLS ME TO THE CARPET

Uncle Ronnie had come up to Dearborn to take me down south to see Grandpa Holbrook. I knew my grandfather was going to be pretty upset at me for revealing the secret about the drug dogs. When we arrived, that was the first subject he brought up.

"Brett, I can't for the life of me figure out why you would tell someone about the technique we used."

Ronnie, who had staunchly supported me through the Burton operation, did the same now when he told Grandpa, "Dad, Brett tried to lie. He told the press the dogs could hear the drugs on the drug dealers."

"He did what?!!" Grandpa replied. He was a bit tickled by that remark.

"Yes, Dad, Brett told the press that we taught them to hear the drugs, saying the dogs have supersensitive hearing. The press did not buy it and they pressed him for the truth. Then Brett told them the truth."

"Grandpa, I tried to lie, but when I was pressed, I thought about what you taught me about my word being no good if I was liar. Besides that, my father's girlfriend, Maria, knew about the dogs. She is the one who pushed me to get you to send the dog up to Michigan. A friend of mine, who is an Italian businessman, knew about the dogs, also. He was already asking me how a person could beat a dog so it could not smell drugs. I told him I did not know if the dog would lose the ability to detect drugs or if was possible to beat the dog at all. Maria knows this guy too. She must have told him about the dogs."

"Brett, you were a bit more creative than I would have been in coming up with an answer. It is going to cost us a lot of money, though."

Just then, Maria and Carlos pulled up. The five of us were on the front lawn. Grandpa was talking to Maria. I could tell he was a bit agitated. I asked, "Grandpa, what is wrong?"

"Brett, she has all the money and is refusing to give it back."

"How much money is it, Grandpa?"

"It is seven and a half million dollars."

I had no doubt about the money now because Grandpa's word was as good as gold.

"Grandpa, you told me that money would make me lazy. You never told me how much money, or even where I got it from. You also told me not to take any money from gangsters because they would kill me and take it back. So do what they do! Kill her and take it back."

I finally had enough information to start making sense of why everybody was trying to put me in jail or kill me. I guess I had been in denial. Everything was clicking into place. It had all started with my father saying he was going to leave my mom, but that first he was going to steal my money. My father had kept the money a secret from me and my mother in order to steal it before knew anything about it. That way, we would never even know it was gone.

Now I understood why Team Garcia kept putting me in dangerous situations. They wanted me gone so it would be easier for them to steal the money and keep it. The money was supposed to be in Russ's name, my name, and Dad's name. Carlos and the rest of Team Garcia, other than Maria, of course, all wanted my father, Maria, and Russ dead. The motive for the team was the money, which was the reason they wanted me to kill my father, Maria, and Russ. With those three dead and me in jail, the team would have control of the money. My father obviously could not comprehend that scenario.

A crowd was beginning to form in the front yard. I saw my friend Gary Powers. I grabbed him by the waist and hoisted him up, telling him that I was very glad to see him. My grandpa walked up and gave me my gun, and then he walked over to the fence and posted a silhouette on it.

He said, "Brett, they are here to see you shoot."

I drew my gun up and began marching toward the target, firing a round with each step. As I moved toward the target, out of the corner of my eye I saw Mr. Young watching it. I continued toward the target until my gun was empty. I walked over to Mr. Young and asked, "What are you doing here?"

"That was mighty fine shooting, Brett, straight through the head every time. Brett, we had a gentlemen's agreement. I want to get some of your drug dogs for the city."

"No, Mr. Young. We did *not* have a gentlemen's agreement. You told me I was signing one agreement, but you had me sign a totally different one. You lied about the paperwork, saying it was to protect the city from any liability. The sad thing is that I trusted you. I would have lived up to any agreement I signed if it was legit. When you make a gentlemen's agreement, you *say* what you are going to do. Then you put down in writing what you are going to do, and then you shake on it. That's a gentlemen's agreement. Now, we told you to keep the dogs a secret, but you didn't. You called a press conference and blabbed it to the entire country. If you had kept quiet, we all could have made some money. Soon, the dogs won't be working only in this country, but all over the world. And other countries will be training their own dogs."

"Which one of these men is your Grandpa, Brett? I want to see if he will teach us to train dogs."

"Come on. I will introduce him to you." I walked over to where my grandpa was standing, with Mr. Young by my side. I said, "Mr. Young, this is my grandfather, Will Holbrook. Grandpa, he wants you to train drug dogs free of charge," I said sarcastically. I did not know if they had reached an agreement, but I did know that Grandpa was not about to work for free.

Early the next morning, Grandma fixed a very large breakfast. My grandpa told me to eat a lot, saying I was going to need the energy. After breakfast, I was taken to an abandoned coal mine and was escorted in by Uncle Isthme, Ronnie, and Grandpa. We walked deep into the mine until there was no light except the light from the flashlights they were carrying.

Ronnie said, "Brett, we have to do this to you. The way we punish you is by leaving you in the mine. If you find your way out, you get to live. If not, then you die here. You'll just rot away. No one will ever find your body." They all hugged me and then began to walk away.

I yelled, "Don't I get a flashlight?"

"No light at all," Ronnie said.

After they were gone, it was completely dark. I could not see anything. The only thing I could think of that I did wrong was that I had revealed the secret about the dogs.

There were no walls, no exit, nothing. I was in the mine a good forty-five minutes before my eyes adjusted to the dark. I could see a glimmer of light about the size of a pinhead. I gradually walked to the light, which grew bigger and bigger until I had found my way out. Ronnie asked me, "Brett, how did you ever find the way out?"

"I saw the light, Uncle Ronnie."

Ronnie said, smiling, "Dad, he saw the light."

Then Grandpa repeated what I had said. "He saw the light!"

This was some sort of hillbilly fun fest. I did not see the humor in what they had done. They believed they had taught me a lesson of some sort, but I did not get what it was. After thinking about it more seriously, I could only surmise that it had something to do with the Bible.

It was the middle of the afternoon when I got back to Detroit. I was about to enter the house when I saw a crowd gathered in a circle in the alleyway. I went over to see what the commotion was. Ernie, Adel's son, and Dwayne, my brother, were fighting. I did not understand why these two boys were fighting. Ernie, Dwayne, and Ronin Tierney were the best of friends. Now, two of them were at each other's throat trying to kill each other. The fight continued. I was pissed that they were fighting. Dwayne wore Coke-bottle glasses, was cross-eyed, and had poor vision. I finally called the fight off and told Ernie he had won.

I said to Adel, "They were the best of friends. They are supposed to fight *for* each other, not fight *against* each other, Adel. Dwayne has terrible vision.

460

Ernie was fighting a person who is half blind. I am not happy that you did not break the fight up, Adel."

Two days later, as I was standing near the back door of my house; Isaac Simms was quizzing me about the operation at Burton. Adel came by and said, "Brett, I am going to die for you."

All I could think of was that he was willing to die because of that stupid fight between Dwayne and Ernie. I could not let him do that. Knowing I did not have a gun that had a big enough caliber, I yelled back "No, Adel. I don't want you to die."

"Brett, I am going to die for you," he repeated.

Then Simms asked me, "Who is that, Brett?"

"It's Adel Powers," I said. I didn't want to tell him, but if he caught me lying, he would punish me for sure.

"Where does he live?" Simms asked.

"He lives three doors down on the right, next to the house that sits toward the back, near the alley."

It was two days later in the early morning when I saw the cops and an ambulance in front of the Powers's home. The paramedics brought somebody out on a gurney covered with a sheet. They said it was Adel, claiming that he had shot himself with a shotgun.

After the cops and the ambulance left, Simms came by the house and said to me, "Anybody says that to you again, let me know."

When Simms said that, I knew that Adel had not committed suicide. It was Simms who had shot him. I was going to make a point of getting Simms for killing Adel, but I was going to be very sneaky about it. I was going to wait until all the information from the coroner and the cops was finalized. Let the cops tell all the lies they want, but this time, somebody died for me.

About three days after the shooting, I asked Simms, knowing he would be caught off guard, "Isaac, they said Adel lined up the pictures of his wife and kids. Is that true?"

"Yeah, he sat them on the coffee table."

"Was he dressed up to say goodbye?" I asked.

"Yeah, he was dressed up real nice for his family. He had his shoes on, too."

"Were they tennis shoes or dress shoes?"

"He had on regular dress shoes."

I immediately went upstairs to my dad's closet to get a pair of his dress shoes. While there, I grabbed the shotgun my dad kept in the closet. I slipped the right shoe on and tried to pull the trigger. It was impossible to pull the trigger with my toe with those shoes on because the trigger guard was in the way. Adel could not have possibly pulled the trigger with his finger because his arms were too short. Score another one for Team Garcia. I would have to keep this information under my hat so the evidence didn't magically disappear. The evidence was beginning to pile up. There was no statute of limitations on murder. The next step was to figure out whom I should turn to for help. The Dearborn police were out of the question.

Chapter 57

RIOTING IN DETROIT

In July 1967, riots broke out in the city of Detroit. They were sparked by a police raid on an illegal after-hours nightclub known as a Blind Pig located at Twelfth Street and Clairmount. The rioting began in the early hours of Sunday, July 23. Business in the city had come to a halt. A curfew was put in place. Black-owned businesses marked their businesses with "Soul Brother" signs so they would go unscathed.

Once again, a few days into the riot, Uncle Ronnie told me, "Brett, the Detroit police need your help in Detroit."

"Ronnie, they are sniping at white people with rifles down there."

"They want you to go. They need your help."

"Ronnie, I am not going to risk my life and not get paid for it."

"What do I need to offer to get you to go?" Ronnie said.

"Ronnie, I am not going to help those cops, because they are trying to get me killed!! The only way I would go into the city down there is if I was in a tank."

"Brett, I've got to take you down there. The rioters killed a cop and a fireman. They need you there."

The next evening around dusk, Ronnie took me to a place in Detroit I was not familiar with. He pulled up alongside a tank and said, "Okay, I got you a tank, Brett. Let me help you get inside." He then boosted me up on the tank. I climbed inside, where there was a platform to stand on. Then the tank driver showed me how to operate the machine gun.

Ronnie, who had climbed inside with me, said, "Brett, they killed a cop. The cops are no longer going to mess with these rioting fools, so shoot at anything that moves."

We had been patrolling the streets for about an hour when the driver suddenly stopped. I couldn't figure out what was going on. Carlos had driven a Dearborn police car to the scene which was somewhere in Detroit. I was standing on a platform on the tank behind the machine gun which is located outside the hatch. Carlos was taking kids who had been caught on the street after curfew and lining them up against a building. They were a mixture of sizes and ages, the oldest looking no more than thirteen. When he had finished lining them up, Carlos ordered, "Kill them all, Brett."

There was a curfew in place throughout the city, as I've mentioned. I figured the kids had broken curfew, as mentioned before. Was it worth killing them, especially with such a wicked weapon as a machine gun? I decided that I would miss and let them go, so I yelled to the kids, "I am going to count to three. When I get to three, take off running." Once I counted to three, they all took off. I fired three or four feet above their heads to make sure I didn't hit them.

To my surprise, Carlos began lining up another batch of kids against the wall. All the boys looked similar to those in the first batch. I knew that if I missed this time, I would be the one getting shot.

Carlos finished lining up the kids. My plan was to shoot as few as possible. I yelled to them to run, and then I saw two or three go down. I told Carlos to drive his police car to Mexican Town while the tank followed, but a Detroit armored vehicle blocked our way and refused to move. I asked the gunner how the turret worked. He showed me that the turret was on some type of balanced hydraulic system, saying that you could only shoot when the turret was level and not moving. I immediately thought the turret had to be redesigned and gear driven. Somehow I knew that those changes would be crucial to future armored battles.

When we arrived in Mexican Town, I told Carlos to line up a bunch of Mexican kids so I could gun them down like he had me do those kids in Detroit. He rounded up a kid I recognized, my childhood friend Darrell. That is when I realized that if I gunned these kids down, I would become what

Team Garcia had become. Abandoning the idea of gunning them down, I asked my driver to take the tank to Dearborn. When we arrived there, I had Carlos walk in front of the tank as it moved down Akron Street. I aimed the machine gun at him. He frantically begged me not to shoot him.

He said, "Brett, please don't shoot me. Your dad is having an affair with my wife."

"Carlos, that's ancient history. I am not going to shoot, but I want you to stop drugging me. Is that a deal?"

He wouldn't answer me, so I asked again, "Is it a deal, Carlos? If you don't answer, I am going to shoot you."

"Okay, Brett. It's a deal."

I had the driver drive by my house. When we were about one hundred and fifty yards away from Lasher Park, I had him fire a shell so I could see the explosive power of the gun. He did as I asked. The explosion was not a large one. *The gun needs changing, too,* I thought.

The riots ended a few days later. I was never again asked to go into Detroit.

Chapter 58

A GIFT FOR COACH

In early August 1967, football season was approaching and schools were holding training. I had written off playing because of my knee injury. Duey came by the house and asked me to join the team, saying they were short of players. He guaranteed I would be a starter. Even with his assurance that I would be a starter, I was not confident.

Despite my reservations, I went down to St. Bonaventure Field the next day, where the team held their practices. I knew that one of Duey's goals was to win the city championship, not only for himself and the Arab community but also—and mainly—for Coach Csonka. Franklin had not won the championship since 1945, mainly because it had a small student population.

Wanting to check out the practice sessions, I sat down and watched the team practicing. My archrival, Coach Wyacek, showed up. Students had nicknamed him Jughead because his head was almost as big as a beach ball. Plus, he had a large ego. He was a big beefy man with a frame of about six feet three inches.

As he approached me, he said, "Brett! We have a new girl in school today," implying that I was a sissy because I had not joined the football team.

That was typical of him. He was always a smart-ass. And because he had an education, he thought he could bully others with his smarts. He tried to manipulate people's thoughts and make them do what he wanted them to do.

I responded, "If you let me play without a doctor's physical, I will play right now."

"No, Brett that is the one thing you have to get first. We have to know for sure you are well enough to play."

I had shut him up temporarily. Later, I got my physical and then went to practice. I talked to Goodenrich because he and Duey knew everything about football. That was one of the reasons they were so good. Not only did they know all the rules but also they were talented. I asked Goodenrich, "What position are you playing, Shawn?"

"I am going to be playing flanker."

I was a little timid about what position I would play. Not having a lot of experience with organized football, I said, "I will play behind you, Shawn, until I learn more about how to play the different positions."

I was sent to practice with the scrubs and played in the flanker position. Gradually, I learned how to play not only flanker but also halfback and

BRETT D. LAWSON

fullback. Coach Csonka made it clear that the way for us to win the championship was to have a tenacious defense. He said that we would be using a 5-3-3 defensive strategy. I watched Coach Csonka drill the defensive line, getting into the smallest details.

Finally it came, the first game of the season. Woodworth was our first opponent. It was a crummy day. The temperature was in the low thirties and there were extremely high winds, which meant we would not have much of a passing attack. Because of this, we would have to rely on the ground game.

All throughout the game, both defensive sides were stubborn, neither giving up much ground. In the fourth quarter, the game was still scoreless. The wind had shifted; Woodworth now had the wind at their back. Implementing a passing attack, they had reached their own forty-five-yard line when the officials issued the two-minute warning. Woodworth lined up in a passing formation. They centered the ball. The quarterback dropped back to pass and then let the pass go. One of our defensive backs stepped in front of the intended receiver and made a mad dash to score as the time ran out. The game had ended. We had a narrow victory of six to nothing, but a win was a win.

The next day, Friday, the office staff announced that the school's football team was still undefeated and had no tied games. I learned why Duey had put together the flag football team. It was not so much because he was seeking the trophy. It was so he could scout the other teams, looking for any advantage he could get. From my conversations with Goodenrich, I learned that the two

470

most important games of the season were against Lowery and Stout. Shawn said I was going to play in the Lowery game for sure.

The Lowery game came much too soon. Winning the season was on the line. Lowery had a running back that was notorious for being the fastest kid in the city of Dearborn. His name was Rickenbacher. His speed had kept Lowery undefeated. The game was scoreless in the first quarter. Coach Csonka had developed a special play earlier in the season, one that gave us an opportunity to score quickly when we needed to. I was sent into the game. My plays were the two-twenty and the one-twenty smash, depending on the formation. Duey gave me the instructions to go through the hole I normally went through twice in a row.

We were on our own forty-five-yard line. Then, Duey gave me the instructions for the special play. He said, "Run for Coach, Brett, and watch Marius throw your block. Run at the biggest guy on the field." Duey got the ball and handed it off to me. The hole was wide open when I went through the line. I saw Marius throw the block that would spring me into the secondary. I turned and ran at Rickenbacker, but seeing that I would make it to the end zone, I headed for the corner of the end zone, with Rickenbacker in hot pursuit. I don't think I'd ever run that fast in my life. I began to cramp up. Soon it felt like someone had stuck two daggers in my thighs, so I stepped out of bounds at the two-yard line.

Jughead came up to me when I was at the sideline. He said, "Brett, do you know how far that play went?"

"No, I don't, Coach."

"The play went for over fifty yards. How did you ever outrun that guy?"

We and Lowery were trading touchdowns. The score was fourteen to seven in our favor when I was sent in to relieve Goodenrich as defensive back. The opposing team saw that I was now in the game and immediately got after me. They pulled a shift. Rickenbacher cut in front of the linebackers. Given my lack of knowledge and experience, I lost track of him, but then I saw him running down the wide side of the field. I had the angle on him, but he turned on the afterburners, pulling away from me with every step.

I returned to the sideline. Jughead immediately started reaming me out. "Do you know how far that play went? It went eighty yards, and you let them score it."

"I don't understand why you would have me guard the fastest guy in the city when you know I couldn't possibly keep up with him! I don't understand, with my knee injury, why you would have me guarding somebody that fast! That sounds like a bonehead play to me, Coach. So why would you do that?"

I was dejected. Lowery had scored. Now the score of the game was fourteen to thirteen, as Lowery had missed the extra point. If they scored again, they would have a six-point lead, which meant that we would have to score a touchdown and an extra point to win.

I spotted something unusual. Every time Duey rolled out on play action, the defensive back stopped guarding our wide receiver. So the next time Duey came to the sideline for a conference with Coach Csonka, I told him what I had noticed.

He came back later. I told him again, "Duey, the safety is going to stop."

"He keeps stopping because the play is stopped," he snarled.

"Not if you roll out, Duey, because he thinks you are going to run the ball. He is getting fooled on the play action," I snarled back. He went back to the huddle and called for a play action pass. Then he rolled out to the left. Sure enough, the safety stopped. Duey threw a pass to our wide receiver, which was left all alone in the end zone. Our receiver caught the ball for a forty-yard reception and a touchdown!

The score was twenty to thirteen when Lowery got the ball back. If Lowery scored a touchdown, the game would possibly be tied and our undefeated and untied season record would be gone. Lowery, unstoppable on the ground, relied heavily on Rickenbacher to gain yardage, which was grinding out yardage without the benefit of a sustained passing attack. Our opponent had reached our thirty-yard line after the two-minute warning. The next series of downs stalled their drive. Suddenly the whistle blew, ending the game. The final score was twenty to thirteen.

By defeating the next two opponents, Maples and Fairlane, which were weak teams, we continued our winning streak. We deliberately held the score down instead of running the score up in the games against these two teams.

We did this so as not to tip Stout, our final opponent of the season. We did not want Stout to know how powerful our team really was.

The last game of the season came. We were playing Stout for the championship. Both teams were undefeated at five and zero. We had the home-field advantage. Coach Csonka had the team in the gym for last-minute preparations. He asked me, "Where were you for practice yesterday, Lawson?"

"I was at the track, Coach."

"How many times a day are you not eating now?" he asked.

"I do pretty well at the track, Coach."

The Stout team showed up with a noisemaker of their own, a big bass drum. The game was a real defensive struggle, drive after drive on both sides. Neither team had scored. It looked like this game was going to end up in a tie, and thus we would end up as co-champions. Duey came to the sideline and, in a frantic voice, said, "Brett, we need to score badly! Have you spotted anything?"

"No, Duey, but I will come up with something." I could not believe he was asking for my help when after the Lowery game, he wanted to kick me off the team.

Goodenrich came over to the sideline with time close to running out. He had a broken chin strap, so he asked Coach to put me in.

"Take Lawson's chin strap. He will be the last person to go in."

"Coach, we could lose the game!" Shawn said.

"Then we will lose without him. He is not going in."

I could not believe that Coach would not put me in because I had missed one practice. My dad had pulled me out of school to go to the racetrack. This did not seem like Coach. He was very pissed off. I handed my chin strap over to Shawn, who then went back into the game.

Duey then came back and said, "What do you have, Brett?"

"They are guarding the ends, Duey, but the middle of their defensive line is wide open," I answered, being the forgiving person I was. I could not bear the thought of losing this game, despite my having been chewed out by Coach.

"What play should I run, Brett?" Duey asked.

"Throw a jump pass in the middle to Brooks out of the backfield."

With less than two minutes left in the game, Duey ran the ball and was inside the ten-yard line. Then he ran the play, throwing the jump pass to Brooks. Brooks caught the pass but was a yard and half short of scoring. Seeing he was short, he fell into the end zone for the score right as the time expired.

After the game, I went to Coach's office. Jughead was in there too.

I said to him, "Coach, the game is over. There is nothing I can do about the fact I did not play. I would never cut practice the day before a momentous game as this. I looked at winning this championship as a going-away gift from this class. I wanted to be a part of that. I feel you took my absence as an insult to yourself and Coach Wyacek. There is something you should know, and that is that I am pretty good at betting the ponies. I help keep my father from losing a lot of money. So when he tells me he wants me to go to the track with him and forget football, he is not asking me to go. He was a military man; he gives me orders. There is no arguing about it."

I think I left him with a good impression of how I felt. All I wanted him to know was that I would have rather been at practice.

That would not be the last time I would have Coach Csonka as a coach. Basketball season was soon approaching. I wasn't a very good basketball player, although I was a decent guard and handled the ball well. I did not shoot the ball as well as I would have liked, so I would forgo basketball for track and field in the spring.

Spring rolled around. It was time for track season. I had always watched with great enjoyment the track events in the Olympics. When I was little, I had aspirations of participating in the Olympics and winning a gold medal, but I soon realized what great athletes and great performances it took to win the gold. I concentrated on three events. The first one I really liked was low hurdles and low hurdle relays. The next one was the long jump. Last was the triple jump. While I did not earn a lot of points, I had a lot of fun. I don't think Franklin even won one meet, but I never paid attention to the scoring.

Track-and-field season ended. Shortly thereafter, the school year was over.

Chapter 59

HEADING IRAQ OFF
AT THE PASS

Once the football season was over, I got an outright notice from the team that my breath was unbearable. Even Mohammed Haddad said it was time to get my teeth fixed. The team had told two of us (Bill Roark also had bad teeth) to breathe through our noses because our breath was very bad. I found that to be very embarrassing.

I asked my mom, "Mom, do we have the money for me to go to the dentist?"

Her reply was, "No, we don't have the money, but you can go to the city dentist, which only costs residents a dollar."

I told her to make an appointment for me to go. She made appointments for the whole family to go to the dentist because we all had bad teeth. The kids at school used to call Veronica "Booga-Wooga with the green teeth." Veronica was very pretty except for her teeth. I could not figure out why my father, who'd previously had control of millions of dollars, had not saved any money to help my mother and her kids. There were times when I thought, *Maybe he is just saving it for me for when I become of legal age.* He could not have been that stupid to let Maria have all that money.

The day of the dental appointment came for the boys.

I was first to go in to see the hygienist. She cleaned my teeth. She then called the dentist in to examine me. He stated, "Some of your cavities are too large for me to fix. You are going to need some crown work. You will have to go a private dentist."

"No way to fix them, eh?"

"You need extensive dental work, son, dental work that I can't do on your teeth. The shape your teeth are in is the result of years and years of neglect." I walked out of his office extremely disappointed.

He told Veronica the same thing, that she needed extensive work on her teeth. The rest of the kids' teeth were not in as bad a shape as ours. If I was going to get any dental work done, I was going to need a couple of thousand dollars, which was more than the original estimate a few years ago. And I would need to go to Dr. Peyton.

After track-and-field season ended, the next major event in my life was driver training, which I awaited it with great anticipation. A driver's license meant more to me than anything because of the freedom it would give me. I had suffered through the oppression of Team Garcia for nearly ten years. Now, with a driver's license, I could go where I wanted, anytime I wanted. I could get a job anywhere I wanted, doing anything I wanted. A license would also allow me to get the hell out of Garcia's jurisdiction if I so desired. I was finally about to enjoy some of the freedom that I had been thirsting for.

Another blow to the Kennedy family happened in early June. Bobby was assassinated in California on the fifth of the month. I felt somewhat close to Bobby's family because of the kindness the president's nieces had shown me, but most of all the kindness of Etty had made me feel that way. I could not help but wonder if the Garcia brothers had been involved. I knew that for some reason they hated the Irish. Did the team hate them enough to hurt the top Irishmen and their families? It was beginning to look as if such was the case. And if so, they were two for two. I was the only nonmember of Team Garcia who knew how they operated.

The day finally arrived. I began driver's training in late June. Dearborn had its own training course, with some of the most rigid standards. It was ranked among the top ten in the country. The course would last two months and include road testing. Dad had given me a little help with my driving by letting me drive around the neighborhood.

When all was said and done, I passed the local driving test, but not nearly as easily as I had anticipated. In addition, the instructor said that I was overconfident, behaving cockily on the road. When I got my training certificate, I went down to the police department, where new licenses were handled, and got my learner's permit. While I was able to drive, I had to have an adult in the car with me. The learner's permit gave me some freedom. I soon earned my full driver's license.

It was after I had gotten my license that Maria came by the house with a CIA photograph of a Soviet T-series tank. She raised a general by the name of Schwartzberg on the telephone.

The general said, "Brett, I am General Schwartzberg. I need to know your thoughts about that tank."

"Well, sir, it has a long gun, but it looks like it has a relatively small bore to it."

"We can retrofit our tanks with a bigger gun."

"General, sir, I think we should get a new tank because that gun will rip us open like a can of sardines. If all it takes is one round from the Soviet tanks, they will obliterate our armored divisions."

"Do you have any thoughts or ideas on how we can make improvements to the situation, Brett?"

Once again, Hollywood would play a major role in sparking my imagination. I searched through my mind to find the movie scenes featuring tank battles. I thought about the line from the movie *The Battle of the Bulge*. During one of the tank battle scenes, the Germans are destroying our Sherman tanks. Telly Savalas' character radios in that the German tanks have bigger guns. The Sherman tanks' guns can't penetrate the German tanks. He says, "It's like we are throwing tennis balls at them." The German tanks of the World War II era had thicker armor and a bigger gun than our tank, the Sherman. Although the Sherman was very reliable, it did not have enough knockout power to penetrate German armor.

"Well, sir, I think we should design a new tank with thicker armor and a bigger gun. Sir, I was inside one of our tanks. The turret was bouncing around after moving the gun. I think that the gun and turret should be gear-driven. I also think we should use a new type of steel for the tank, something that cannot be penetrated by a small, inexpensive missile."

"Do you know how much that is going to cost, Brett?"

"General, sir, I don't know how many men it will take to man a tank like that, but do you think the mothers of the men in that tank care what it costs if it will save their lives? Not only that, but if the taxpayers know it will save the lives of those men, they won't mind either."

Iraq had nationalized its oil fields; the state now owned all the oil. I got a call from an executive with an oil company. He told me his name, which was not necessary, as I was going to keep it a secret. He wanted to know if I had any ideas about the oil situation in Iraq.

"Well, sir," I told him, "I can tell you what. I would say something like this to them, sir: 'This land is your land, and blood has been shed so that the Iraqi people could have that land. The oil is your oil—it is on your land that your ancestors fought for. But what is atop the soil, the American people paid for with money from the US Treasury. Now, do you want to tangle with the United States military, or do you want to resolve the matter peacefully?'"

He thanked me and hung up.

He called back the next day and asked me, "*How* did you know that what you told me would work?"

"Well, it was kind of like a chess move, sir. The government of Iraq attacked the oil industry in Iraq by nationalizing it, so now we knew we had to counterattack. The Arabs respect boldness and are fearful of it at the same time. The other reason is that I live in a predominantly Arab neighborhood."

"How much do we owe you, Brett?" the executive asked.

"How about twenty million dollars, how does that sound to you?" I replied, knowing I would never see the money.

The oil exec hung up with no reply. I did not hear from him again.

Within a few days of my conversation with General Schwartzberg, he called me back. "Brett, I am in charge of obtaining the oil for the security of the United States. We want to seize the oil operations in Iraq. What is your opinion on that?"

"Sir, my opinion is that doing so would be a very serious mistake. To just take their oil would turn every Arab nation in the Middle East against us, and possibly start a new conflict. We should be avoiding war at all costs, at least until all negotiations have failed. Also, sir, we are Americans, not bandits. If we rob Iraq of their oil, who do we rob next when Iraq is out of oil? The American public should pay for the oil they use."

"Brett, Iraq is gouging us for the oil. They want to swap arms for oil. What do you think of the issue of selling the Iraqis the armored vehicles? And how can we resolve it?"

"I am going to have to think on that one for a couple of days, sir. I will have my dad call you back."

It was a couple of days later when I called the general back. When I had him on the phone, I said to him, "General, sir, I think I have a solution to the problem with Iraq. I think we should sell the armored vehicles to Iraq in return for selling us the oil, if they hold the prices down. We should also make Iraq one of our loyal allies. Things will go much smoother when you try to make a friend out of a potential enemy."

"Brett, I am going to suggest that to the Defense Department. Then I will get back to you."

Three more days went by. The general called and said, "That won't work, they said, Brett."

I responded, "I don't want to be insubordinate, but I believe it will work."

"Okay, Brett, run your plan by me."

"Sir, our staunchest ally in Europe is England. Our best ally in the Middle East is Israel, and Israel must be protected at all costs. We have to protect and keep both England and Israel as allies. We do not want to jeopardize our alliances with either one should we sell the armored vehicles to Iraq. So we let Israel, England, and Saudi Arabia know that we are going to sell the armored vehicles to Iraq. This will only work if we have a tank superior to the one we sell to Iraq. Notifying the Saudis' that will bring the Arab contingent to our side. Iraq could only want those armored vehicles for two reasons. One, they want to protect themselves. Two, they want to go on the offensive. Because they are running out of oil, they want to take over peaceful Arab countries like Hitler did during the Blitz."

"Who do you think Iraq will attack first, Brett?"

"Sir, I don't know how many oil reserves Iraq has, or how long before they will need to replenish their cash by capturing more oil, but if I had to guess, it would be Saudi Arabia. They have the largest landmass, so they probably have the largest oil reserves. Now the reason for selling the tanks is that someone is going to sell Iraq some armor, so it might as well be us. The country we don't want selling Iraq any armor is the USSR or China, as we don't want either of them gaining a foothold in the Middle East. Not only that, but armor gets old. New parts and men will be needed to repair the armor. That is going to cost extra. Then, at some point in time, the armor will be obsolete, or even irreparable."

"What do we do if Iraq is attacked?"

"That is the whole point of making Iraq our ally. We will help Iraq defend its country by providing military advisers, sir."

"Brett, how did you ever come up with this plan?"

"Sir, I don't know exactly how I do it, but somehow I feel that God gave me the talent I have so I could protect the United States at all costs. I think I was put here to help men like you."

"Brett, you are an absolute genius. This plan is absolutely brilliant. I want to talk to my boss about this. I will definitely be calling you back about the details."

"Yes, sir I will be looking forward to it, sir."

Chapter 60

I AM GOING TO SEE THE USA IN MY CHEVROLET

It was 1968 and the peak of summer when Dad and Mom went shopping for a new car, taking me with them. They currently owned a 1963 Ford and a 1956 Buick. Both those vehicles had seen better days. It was time to replace the Buick. Mom liked the Ford best because of its smaller size and maneuverability, so she would be driving it after the purchase of the new car. We went to two Chevy dealerships in Dearborn, and then ended up at a third dealership in Wayne, Michigan. None of the three dealerships had the car dad wanted in stock, but since at the Dearborn dealership the salesman's wife worked with my mom, my parents decided he was trustworthy enough to buy the car from. They special-ordered the car they wanted from this salesman.

It was mid-September and I had already started high school when the car came in. It was a 1969 Chevelle Malibu, an absolutely beautiful car. It had a medium-blue vinyl roof with a silver-blue paint job and a medium-blue interior. I had hopes of someday of driving it back and forth to school. Soon after it was purchased, I could see that such was not going to be the case, as Dad laid full claim to the car.

I joined the workforce, having landed a job at the nearby car wash located at Michigan and Oakman. I was paid practically slave wages. The car wash paid cash and took 30 percent of my wages for taxes. They only reported collecting 10 percent to the IRS, thus beating us workers out of 20 percent.

Nonetheless, part-time jobs for kids were hard to come by. Some ad agency came up with an ad campaign to promote the hiring of teens. The lyrics of the jingle accompany the ad went, "Give a kid a job, and give a kid a job."

The car wash was a short walk to Eastern Dearborn High School. Eastern was steeped in tradition. The building looked like an old Ivy League campus building. A lot of the upperclassmen pulled a prank on the sophomores by selling elevator tickets, promising that the buyers would be able to make out with their girlfriends in the elevator. The elevator would save the buyer a lot of time, as he would not have to go up and down the stairs. The only problem was that there was no elevator at Eastern.

There was a water fountain that only the seniors could drink out of. If someone who was not a senior was caught drinking from it, he or she would be punished by being forced to kiss the seal that was on the floor in the main hallway, with all the dust and dirt from the foot traffic as a topping. These traditions were the seniors' way of having fun with the underclassmen.

Many times I had gone to the Henry Ford Museum and had seen Edison's workshop there. Always fascinated by his accomplishments, I wanted to learn more about electricity. With this in mind, I signed up for electrical engineering classes. I also signed up for math classes, which were needed for engineering degrees. Electricity was going to be my major, while auto shop would be one of my minors. Every student at Eastern had to have six semesters of English, one of the mandatory majors needed to graduate. The other major that also consisted of six semesters was an elective, which in my case was electricity.

The one class I will always remember is my creative writing class. Since I wanted to write a book, I thought that would be the class I needed. I would learn how to be creative and write stories and such. I knew I was going to be in trouble when, after the first few assignments, the teacher, to whom I gave the name of "Mr. Skinnyprick" because he was really skinny and a real prick. One day in class he called me up to his desk and said to me, "We have a lot of talented students in this class. You are definitely not one of them."

My reply was, "As a teacher, aren't you supposed to teach us how to write?"

"This class is not for you, Mr. Lawson. You should try to transfer to another class. I will help you do that."

"Well, I think I am going to tough it out."

I left school that particular afternoon feeling like a real dumb shit. But when the general called me once again, he lifted my spirits by making me feel useful. I was surprised to hear him say, "Brett, we want you to go to Vietnam."

"General, sir, I don't think you want me to tell you my feelings on Vietnam."

"Why is that, Brett?"

"Well, sir, one thing that I do know is that we can't win that war because we cannot use armor in the jungle. It is useless there. Second thing is that we are fighting a guerilla war, and that can go on for who knows how long. Next, we have to shut their supply lines down, and we are not doing that. So, the first thing I would do is to get Congress to okay troops and bombing into Cambodia. If they do not want to give us permission to go into Cambodia, then it is time to end the war in Vietnam. We are just wasting men and material trying to win a war when the legislature is handcuffing us. Plus, we are using fuel that we are already short on. Those bombing runs are costing us a fortune. I think we should force the North Vietnamese to the negotiating table and end the war. If they violate the peace terms by invading the South, we will never trust the Communists again. The United States could then pivot our forces. Since the Commies won't let us in the front door, we try the back door, which is the Middle East. Who do you think the Arabs want in the Middle East, us or the Communists, General, sir?"

"I am sure they don't want the Communists, Brett," he said. With that he told me goodbye and hung up the phone.

A few days later, since Maria was the liaison between me and the Defense Department, she came by the house and told me, "Brett, there are two generals who want to talk to you."

Since it was easier to find their way on Franklin Street, Maria had the generals meet us at the Franklin Restaurant. She led the way from my house to Franklin Street, where the generals were waiting. Maria introduced me as Brett. The officers were General Panateras and General Schwartzberg.

General Panateras seemed very excited. He asked, "Brett, how did you come up with such a plan for pulling out of Vietnam and concentrating on the Middle East?"

"General Panateras, sir, I am a history buff. I do well in the subject. I also like to watch war movies, not because of the blood and guts, but for learning strategies. I just figured we need oil, and oil is in the Middle East. And there is nothing in Vietnam but jungle. To win the war, it would take the South Vietnamese wanting to fight the Communists badly enough that they are willing to die to get their freedom and keep it. Until then, we are going to keep fighting. We cannot continue fighting the Communists in every country across the globe. I figured that the Middle East is the place to be, as it is much easier to win in the desert than in the jungle because you can use armor. It seems to me we are spreading ourselves much too thin. We have troops in Europe, the Panama Canal, Korea, and other places. The way I see the situation is that every time an invading force attacked North Africa, it was the beginning of the aggressor's undoing. When the Romans invaded Africa, it was their eventual undoing. The same with Hitler; he went to North Africa and was pushed back into Europe."

"Why do you think that is, Brett?" General Panateras asked.

"Well, sir, it is kind of simple. As with every battle, it is about supplies. Somehow the Allies broke the German codes. When the Germans tried resupplying their troops, the Allies sunk their ships to keep the supplies out of the enemy's possession. It just seems that when an army gets farther away from its motherland, supplying the troops becomes more difficult."

"Brett, your country needs men like you. General Schwartzberg and I would like you to go to West Point Academy. Would you like to go, Brett?"

It had always been a dream of mine to go to West Point, but to do so you needed a sponsor like a congressman. Now I had two generals willing to sponsor me. I was totally elated.

"Well, sir isn't the academy like a college—and you have to finish high school first?"

"Brett, did you say high school? You mean you haven't even finished high school yet? What is your age?"

"I am fifteen, General, sir. I would really like to go to the academy, but I promised my mother and father I would finish high school. If I went to West Point, sir, I would have to move my family near to the academy."

"Why would you need to move them near there, Brett?"

"Sir, it is long story. There is a group of what I believe to be a team of CIA and Secret Service trying to kill my whole family."

"Brett, I will check to see if it is a CIA team working in the area. I can assure you, I will find out."

General Schwartzberg then said, "Brett, I want you to show me where you live, so I can to talk to your mother and father." As we walked into the house and upstairs, we were met by my father and mother. He told them, "Your son is one of the most brilliant military minds of our time. You should take good care of him." General Schwartzberg proceeded to tell my parents about the good things I had done.

As General Schwartzberg was leaving with General Panateras, the latter turned to my father and said, "You get your family out of this dump, and that's an order, Mr. Lawson. Brett, I will get back to you, but before I do, give me a little time to see if I can work something out for you."

After the generals left, I told my father, "Dad, they want me to go to the academy. What do you think?"

"My father smiled a broad smile, gave me hug while patting me on the back, and said, "Well, if you go to West Point and you graduate, you come out a lieutenant." For the first time, I truly felt my dad was proud of me. He wanted me to attend West Point. He seemed excited about me going

It was almost a week later when General Schwartzberg called me on the phone. The news he gave me was a major letdown. "Brett, there is a CIA team working in the area. They said that you are a junkie, so I will be unable to help you any further. You are on your own, Brett. Good luck." Then he said goodbye.

When I finished talking to General Schwartzberg, I felt like someone had placed a slab of concrete on my back and told me, "See if you can get someone to help you now." Exactly who had told Schwartzberg that I was a junkie I don't know, but I had a feeling it was Maria, since she was communicating with the general about the tanks. Since she had called him and invited me to talk to him, it seemed reasonable that she was the one who'd told him I was a junkie. I had helped with plans to get a new tank developed, developed a plan to leave Vietnam, and come up with a plan to guard the Middle East, all for free. Taking away the respect I had earned was Maria's style. Team Garcia was making me do all the work and then not paying me for it. It was the same situation as the raid on Burton. I did something nice down in the Corridor and never got a penny for my work. I'd now had enough of all Maria's lies and her fixing things so I couldn't even earn a living. The members of Team Garcia were making me risk my life, but what they did not know was that I was secretly keeping track of all the murders, or at least the ones I knew they'd committed. I had the locations of who was murdered and when they were murdered. I now had physical evidence of these crimes, but I was going to have to stay alive. If Rico Garcia made a mistake, I was going to see him put in jail or killed.

My first semester of high school ended. I did not fare well. For the first time in my life, I flunked not only one class but two. One of those was chemistry, which I usually aced. Mr. Paxley had wanted us to memorize the periodic table. I'd had a hard time with all the difficult classes I had elected to take, like algebra. The other class I flunked was creative writing, with the teacher who had warned me I was not talented enough for his class. The problem with that class was partly the teacher. There were some assignments that I felt were just downright goofy and off the wall. One of those assignments was when Mr. Skinnyprick had us doodle for twenty minutes. He then had us write a poem about what we had just doodled. I think that was my breaking point, when I knew I was going to flunk the class. It was just not my cup of tea. As I looked back on that class, I discovered that I had more of a technical skill at writing. So Mr. Skinnyprick had been right for the most part. One of the other classes I'd found difficult was electricity; I'd found all those formulas hard to learn. My counselor had warned me, "Brett, those are all very difficult classes to take all at once. Maybe you should take some of those classes in the second semester."

With guidance from Mr. McCrea, I decided to back off in the second semester. This involved changing tracks. At Eastern, classes were rated

A-track, B-track, or C-track, with C-track being the lowest of the three. I asked to be put onto B-track for all my English classes.

After I changed the degree of difficulty of some of the classes on my schedule, things began to get much easier. My grades improved to slightly above average. Still, I would have to go to summer school to make up for the English and chemistry classes I'd flunked.

Chapter 61

HONEY ASKS FOR A FAVOR

It was spring 1969. I had suffered setback after setback and disappointment after disappointment. I could not get my mind off the Corridor girls, and thus I was becoming extremely depressed. I was hoping to get my teeth fixed, and imagining going on a real date, not just for purposes of sex, but also to make real love to one girl, or even more than one. I had seen other young ladies and young men of my age from around my neighborhood who were beginning to pair up and become couples. That is what I wanted. I wanted to be part of a couple and have a steady girlfriend. I just wanted to be able to go on a regular date. After a nice dinner and a little wine, I would take the girl home, somewhere clean and well-kept. While mom did her best to clean, it was still just a shit hole we were living in. It was no place for mad, passionate lovemaking.

Alas, those were only dreams of what could be. I had hoped that I would meet up with some of the girls before we all turned eighteen. It would not be long before the girls would be getting married and, soon after that, having kids.

I was pleasantly surprised when one afternoon the girl I had nicknamed Honey showed up at my door with five other girls for a sex party. I had been nice to her in the Corridor, and thought I might have gotten to her. They wanted a couple more of my guy friends, so we were walking back to her car when she asked, "Brett, do you think I am too fat?"

I was determined to be kind to her no matter what. "Honey, you are what I call a big girl, but not fat," I replied, trying to compliment her.

"Do you think I am bigger than when we saw you in the Corridor?"

"Well, you are little bigger," I said, continuing to be nice.

"What looks bigger?" Honey asked.

"Well, for one thing, your thighs are bigger."

"Does that bother you?" she asked.

"No. Not at all," I replied.

We both climbed into her car, which did not have enough room for seven people. One of the girls who was of lighter weight sat on my lap. I was really looking forward to this outing.

After driving a bit but before we picked up my friends, Honey suddenly stopped her car and said, "I have changed my mind." She asked me to get out of her car. I did as she wished and got out, not saying anything to her. I walked the short distance back to my house, where I sat down on the porch.

It was a couple of hours later when Honey came back. She wanted to have sex. I asked where the rest of the girls were. She said, "I took them all back home because I wanted you all to myself, Brett."

"Honey, you should have realized, one woman can't satisfy me."

"Brett, please, you told us all that if we needed sex, we should see our boyfriends, but if we needed a good lay, we should come and see you. Brett, I need to get a good lay badly!" she said.

Thinking she was being honest, I felt I should reward her for that.

"You are right, Honey, I did say that. And I look at what I said like a promise. Let us go inside."

After we were finished, Honey was about to leave. She said to me, "Brett, you are a good-looking man, but you really need to do something about your breath." One of the most faithful of the Corridor girls, so I figured she was being honest about my breath. Based on her statement, I knew it was time to do something about my breath.

Having just been humiliated, I felt like I was just a dumb hillbilly. I went upstairs, where my dad was. I said to him, "I want enough money to fix my teeth and to buy another house for Mom."

"There isn't any money. You gave it all away."

"I never gave it away. You stole it and then gave it to your son Russell. Don't try telling me you don't have it, because Grandpa Holbrook told me Maria has the money. He is no liar. You are the liar. You remember telling me that you were going to leave but that you had to steal my money first?"

"Brett, how in the hell do you remember that?"

"Dad, you are acting like a real retard. You gave Maria control of seven and a half million dollars. You really think your son is going to end up with the money? You don't care if you die or not because you have made him rich. Well, I got news for you about what is going to happen. If you die, then they will kill Maria. Then your son will be all alone with the money, and at the Mexican cops' mercy. They have already been trying to kill us because they think we've got the money. If I can't have my own money, I will kill the three of you before I will let those crooked Mexican cops have the money. That is why I have been keeping you alive, Dad, even though you have been helping them try to kill me."

"I got more news for you, Dad. Maria doesn't give a shit if your son gets the money or not. She just wants the money for herself. With her college education, she thinks she is much smarter than you, and that you are a stupid hillbilly. She thinks she has a seven-million-dollar pussy. For that kind of money, Dad, you could have screwed Marilyn Monroe, but she might have given you blond babies, which I know you hate. Not only that, but also Maria says that women, whatever their nationality, like fucking niggers because they have bigger dicks, which really turns women on. While I was working in the Cass Corridor, she brought a black with a twelve-inch dick into the room where I was staying. She couldn't get her pants off fast enough. I left when I saw that. How does that dick taste, Dad? Because you know she blew him. I can't believe you are screwing that skanky-ass whore."

While my philosophy was that a person can have sex with whomever he or she wants, it is different when you are in a relationship. Everything I told my father was true. Maria wanted to play psychological games. I was now going to play them with her. I knew that my dad would not stand for her having sex with black men, with a penis either small or large, as he had a son with her.

Only a couple of days had gone by when Maria came by the house. She was fuming. She asked me, "Brett, what did you say to your father?"

"I just did what I do for you, and answered his questions honestly."

"Did you say anything bad about me?"

"Yeah, I said you got a really big ass." I did not really say that during my conversation with my dad, but I had thought it. Now it was my turn to play games with Maria's mind and destroy her ego.

"Brett, when my son gets old enough, he is going to be the one to kill you."

I knew she was bluffing. She was not going to wait that long before she tried to kill me again. I called her bluff.

You know, Maria, I am the only reason you and you son are alive. So far, I have done nothing but try to help you. I don't think you want a war with the man who has seen to it that you've remained alive. Now you have now pissed me off, so bring it on, bitch."

There was yet another tragedy for the Kennedy family, this one occurring on July 19, 1969. It would become known as the Chappaquiddick incident. Ted Kennedy was driving home from an engagement with a woman named Mary Jo Kopechne. He drove off the bridge and ended up in the water. His companion ended up dead. Ted arrived at home with no memory of what had happened. Where was Team Garcia when this incident happened? Officer O'Connell experienced loss of memory after accidentally shooting his daughter. Biddleman had no memory of shooting Officer Gatewood. Vernoil was blamed for a phony accident and could not have been driving the car. The only crime Vernoil had committed was driving while dead with a gunshot to the head. Now Ted was involved in an accident. All these incidents involved Team Garcia in one way or another.

Chapter 62

GOING STEADY

It was shortly after I'd told Maria off, in my junior year, spring 1970, that I decided to join the cross-country team. I was running through the school halls in the morning before classes, when, late from my exercise and close to the start of classes, I was approached by a beautiful brunette. She told me her name was Laura DaRetzo, and asked for my name.

"Brett. Brett Lawson," I said.

"Brett, how would you like to go out sometime? My parents are old-fashioned Italians who won't let me date until I am eighteen, but I can sneak out during school."

How could anyone say no to this beautiful young woman? I replied, "I would like to do more than just go out, but let's get together anyway."

"Brett, would you like to walk me home? My parents won't mind that."

"That would be great. It will give me the opportunity to get to know you a little better."

"Then meet me at the east entrance after sixth hour. It will be our first date, okay?"

"Sure."

It would be the first of many walks. During each walk, I would learn a little more about Laura. And each day I would say to her, "You are more beautiful today than you were yesterday." Among the things that she told me about herself was that her father hated hillbillies and her mother wanted her to marry an Italian Catholic boy. I could see that I was not going to be a big hit with this family. I had made up my mind that this was the girl I wanted to see more of after I was done with high school.

One of the guys who were selling jewelry for side money had a pretty ring that I thought would be perfect for Laura. It was a nice ring, one that would say I wanted more out of the relationship, but not enough to say we are engaged. It featured a black-and-white split pearl set into pure silver. The price was thirty-five dollars, which was almost two weeks' pay at the car wash. I bought it. Meeting Laura at the east entrance one day soon thereafter, I was excited to give her the ring. I grabbed her hand, placed the ring on her finger, and said, "Laura, will you be my girl?"

"Yes, Brett, I am so excited! This is first time someone ever gave me a ring. Brett, I have been waiting for a man like you."

It was then that I noticed the dress she had on, with red and blue polka dots against a white background. I had seen that pattern before. I asked her, "Did you make that dress, Laura?"

"Yes, Brett. Do you remember the little girl you used to walk to St. Bonaventure School in the South End?"

"Yes, Laura, I do. What has that got to do with this dress?"

"Brett, you told me it was your favorite dress, saying that it seemed patriotic because it has red, white, and blue colors, the colors of the flag. You weren't fibbing to me, were you?"

"No, Laura. That is one thing you should know about me: I don't tell too many fibs. This must mean that you are Vinny's niece."

"Brett, I don't like to talk about Uncle Vinny. He got my brother killed. I also don't like the business he is in."

I wanted to tell her that Vinny had not gotten her brother killed, that it was a crooked cop who had gotten him killed. I decided not to get involved in a family dispute, though. Still, I hoped she would not hold Vinny responsible for her brother's death up until the end of Vinny's days. This was another case of someone passing judgment without knowing all the facts.

One afternoon Maria came up to me in the hallway of Eastern. She said to me, "Brett, the narcs need your help. There are an awful lot of drugs flowing through this school. Will you help them stop the flow of drugs?"

I think she knew that I would not help her, but I would help the narcs. Maybe they would be led to Carlos. I definitely wanted Rico's ass in jail. When I returned to school the next day, Maria asked me again, "Will you help to bust the junkies carrying narcotics?"

I resented the fact that I had revealed the drug dogs to law enforcement. Now I was doubly angered that I had to show the cops the technique on how to use the dogs. Not only did I have to show them how to train the dogs but, since they were so inept at using the dogs, I had to instruct them on that too. Maria never once offered to pay me anything.

I told her, "Get me a dog. I will help them." I was not about to buy the dog for her. Let her buy a dog.

The day after Maria had asked me to help the narcs who were working under cover. Maria got one of their drug-sniffing dogs. Maria came and got me out of class during last period, which started at 2:30 in the afternoon. I soon realized I could not search every room in the school in less than an hour, so I told her, "This is not going to work. I am going to have to come up with a new plan." I turned the dog back over to Maria her.

"What are you going to do, Brett?"

"Give me a couple of days. I will come up with something."

It had been three days before I had figured out how to pull a raid on the junkies. First, I had only one hour to do it, so I told Maria, "I am going to need two patrolmen at each exit, and two dogs, one at the east and one at the west exit."

"What have you got planned, Brett?" Maria asked.

"If you want my help, do like I told you to do. Call me to the office when you are ready. Make sure it is 2:30 at the latest."

Three days passed. The narcs called me to the office. I asked, "Is everybody in place?"

"We are ready to go, Brett," Maria said.

I walked to the east hallway, checked things out, and walked back to the principal's office. I got on the public address system without the principal questioning it, as all the cops that were there knew what I was doing,

I then announced, "This is a drug raid. If you are carrying narcotics, step out into the hall and put the drugs on the floor in front of your feet. If you surrender your drugs voluntarily, you will not be charged. If you don't, and if the dogs find your drugs, you will definitely go to jail."

I walked out of the principal's office and down the hall where thirty to forty kids who had exited their classrooms and stood in the hall with drugs at their feet. The drugs ranged from marijuana to cocaine. There was even a syringe full of heroin, which junkies called pee. The narcs had a janitor standing by who was sweeping the drugs up and putting them in a big box.

We told the students who had surrendered the drugs, "You all are free to go, but first you have to tell us your name, and where you got your drugs."

I figured they were probably going to give us a line of shit, but if they did not, their confessions could produce some good leads on dealers, which is really who the narcs should have been concentrating on. Besides, I had another plan in case the students decided to lie to us. The next step was to march everybody past the dogs through only two exits.

Sure enough, there were a few of the students who did not believe they would be caught. They were arrested.

Maria walked up to me and said, "Brett, the narcs are impressed. You got more drugs out of the school than a whole team of narcs did in a nine-month investigation. What's next on the agenda?"

"It is real important to keep this hush-hush, but we are going to do it again tomorrow. Meet me in front of the office at 2:30 tomorrow. And have everything set up the same way we did it today." I left to meet Laura and walk her home.

The next day around 2:15, I met Maria. After the last bell rang, I gave the students time to settle down. Then I went on the public address system and announced another raid. It was a repeat of the day before. We collected just as many drugs. One difference was that no one was arrested unless they had lied to us the day before. Carlos arrested one of the kids in my electronics class. I told all the students who had surrendered their drugs to "Leave the drugs on the floor and go back to class! *Hurry!* They are going to arrest you! Forget the dope! The cops are going to bust you to make me look like a jackass."

Maria then asked me, "Brett, how did you know that that the students would bring in drugs on the second day?"

"Well, it is like anything else that gives you pleasure. For instance, if someone takes your candy away, then you either fight over it or you go get another candy bar. The druggies can't take their dope back, so they would have to buy more—and that's what they did."

She called Carlos over and told him what I had told her. He began laughing heartily. Maria then said, "Brett, I don't know how you do it, but you are an absolute genius."

"You know, Maria, when it comes to outsmarting the drug dealers, I would have to agree with you."

Chapter 63

MARRIAGE SUGGESTION

Things were going hot and heavy, heating up between Laura and me. We had found all the spots inside the school to have make-out sessions. We also spent our lunch periods making out. In fact, we were spending all our spare time together. It was March when Laura brought up the *m* word. She said to me, "Brett, the school year is coming to an end soon. I won't be able to see you again till the fall, when school begins. Why don't we get married? I want to marry you so I can spend all my time with you. I want to be with you every waking minute. I know you feel the same way. What do think?"

"Laura, I love you, but I am not ready for marriage now. Maybe when you turn eighteen you could move out and are on your own."

"That won't work. I have to get married, Brett, to get my dowry. Brett, I have to get out of that house."

"Laura, we are going to need permission from your parents to get married because we are underage. Let me think about it for a couple of days."

I loved Laura very much, but I had some reservations about marrying her. The first negative was her father who hated hillbillies. I would have to ask him for his daughter's hand in marriage. The other thing was her mother, who wanted her to marry an Italian Catholic. Something that Vinny taught me when I was a little boy kept ringing in my head. He told me, "Someday, Brett, you will meet a girl you care a great deal about. You must remember this: you should always, always respect her mother's wishes." I just could not disrespect Laura's mother. Nor was I going to ignore what Vinny had taught me.

The next day, the rumors started to fly that Laura and I were getting married. I was met at the main stairwell by Giles Fairfax, an old friend from the South End. He asked, "Brett, are you and Laura getting married?"

"I am contemplating it, Giles."

"Brett, I am going to warn you of this: she wants out of her parents' house so bad, she will marry anyone to make that happen."

"How do you know this, Giles?"

"I use to date her, Brett. She wanted me to marry her."

"Are you are just saying that to get her back?" I asked.

"Brett, I could have her back anytime I wanted. I just thought I would warn you not to get stuck in a bad marriage."

With that last statement, I knew he was being truthful. Giles had been a straight shooter ever since I'd first met him. He and I were friends.

Soon I found myself having a hard time giving up on Laura. Deep down, I wanted to stay with her. I had been looking for a girl who wanted me and would accept me for who I was, even with my bad teeth. The girl I wanted would also have to be sharp enough to know my teeth could be fixed. I needed a girl who saw the good in me and who realized that my teeth were only a temporary setback. I thought I had found that in Laura.

The day after I had talked to Giles, I met Laura in the special entryway where we always met. I told her, "Laura, I think you are one of the most beautiful women on the planet. Your body is perfect. I have been proud to walk the halls with you. You are the type of woman who comes along once in a man's life and whom he wants to hang onto for the rest of his life, but I just cannot get married right now."

With that, she handed me my ring back and walked out of my life.

A few days later, Maria came up to me and said, "I want to take you to meet someone."

"No thanks! I am not going anywhere with you."

I did not weigh very much. She dragged me into her car after putting me in a posthypnotic trance. When a therapist uses a posthypnotic suggestion, it puts the subject in a hypnotic state without the therapist having to put the subject under every time he wants to use hypnosis. It also renders the subject powerless to do anything about it. One's vision becomes blurry until one is almost blind. The subject has no power in his or her muscles, which go limp. I could not resist her efforts to get me in her car. I didn't know where she was taking me, but I saw that we crossed the Ambassador Bridge.

I asked her, "Where are we going?"

"We are going to New York, Brett."

I knew at this point, once we were in Windsor, that she had committed the crime of kidnapping and had crossed an international border. Kidnapping is a felony and an FBI case. I knew we were driving through Windsor because my father and I had gone to Windsor to attend the Standard-bred sulky races at Windsor Raceway. While under hypnosis, I fell asleep. I did not awake until we were somewhere in New York. Inside a New York precinct, Maria took me into an office and introduced me to a cop named Todd Kirby, evidently one of the best narcotics officers in New York City. The tactics he used in making arrests were featured in the movie *The French Connection*.

Maria said, "Brett, this is Todd Kirby. He used the same technique to get the junkies to throw down their drugs on the floor as you did."

"Hey, kid, who do you think thought of that technique first, you or me?" Kirby asked.

"Kirby, I think we both are a couple of geniuses who happen to be on the planet at the same time. One thing is for sure, though: I thought of drug dogs first."

"I think you are right on all counts, kid," Kirby said.

What happened next I could not believe! Having been knocked out again with the hypnosis, I found myself on the rooftop of some building. All of a sudden I heard a voice say, "Are talking to the cops Brett?"

I turned to see who'd said that. It was Vinny. The cop was in front of me, Maria was to my left, and Vinny was to my right. I asked the cop, "What the hell is going on?"

The cop said, "Die for me, Brett."

The cop apparently wanted me to die so he could kill Vinny. I was not going to give that bitch Maria the pleasure of watching Vinny and me die. I'd never believed in that pagan ritual of dying in someone's place. I said, "Nobody here has to die. Vinny is my friend! I want to know why I was brought here against my will. And why do you want my friend dead? I am not going to die on a rooftop twelve hundred miles from home."

The cop said, "It's too late, Brett."

I couldn't figure out what Vinny was doing in New York, or what crime he had committed.

During this whole time, Maria had said nothing. She now opened the door to the rooftop entrance, walked me down the stairs, and led me back to her car. I climbed in the car, worried she might just pull out a gun and shoot me. But I got back to Detroit safely. I was extremely pissed. She did not shoot me because I would have to die voluntarily—and I was not about to give her permission to kill me. Team Garcia was now pulling out all stops to either put me in jail or have me killed.

I waited until my father came home from work that night. Then I explained what Maria had done, saying that we would need to find a new house to get away from Team Garcia.

I returned to school with Laura constantly on my mind. I had skipped school two days—the Thursday and Friday of that week, heading into the weekend—and had worked 7:00 a.m. to 7:00 p.m. for four days straight, for a total of forty-eight hours, in addition to what I had worked earlier in the week. I had done the same thing the following week, so I now had over one hundred dollars to spend on the junior prom. I already had tickets, and I had already set up the tux rental. With the breakup, I was stuck with both of the tickets to the prom. And since the tuxedo rental was paid for, I was stuck there too. Now I needed a date and somewhere to go for dinner.

One evening after I'd gotten home from work, some girl knocked on the screen door, peeked in, and called my name. She said, "Brett, its Talk Dirty to Me."

I ran to her, picked her up, and swung her around as she wrapped her legs tightly around my waist. We kissed a passionate kiss. I carried her to my room. We fell on the bed. Man, was she a sight for sore eyes! I had been down and out about my breakup with Laura. I thought Talk Dirty to Me would give me some happiness, at least for a short while. I now had found my date to the prom. We would have a nice dinner and get laid to boot. Things all of sudden were looking good. We started undressing. I was aroused, ready to go. Her body had gotten even better, more filled out. She could not have looked any better. *She is even prettier than I remember,* I thought to myself. *I am going to bang her brains out.*

When we were half undressed, she said to me, "Brett, I thought I would never see you again. I had no idea how to look you up, until one of the girls told me how to find you. She had come by your house. I really want to have sex with you. I need you badly. But if I have sex with you, the cops are going to make me cry rape."

"Which cops?" I asked.

"Maria and a male cop named Carlos, whom I had never seen before."

There went my every hope of developing a steady romance with Talk Dirty to Me, or any chance we had of going to the prom together.

"I need for you to tell me your real first name."

"It's Maddie, which is short for Madelyn. Why do you ask, Brett?"

"Every time I see you, I seem to get closer to you, Maddie. I don't want you to think I like you just for sex. Now, put your clothes back on."

"I feel the same way, but sexually we are great together. Are you sure you want me to get dressed, Brett?"

"Maddie, if they make you tell a lie and say that I raped you, then that will be how they will be able to control you. And if you don't do as they ask, they will possibly hurt you or your family. The other option is that you can tell them to piss off and take whatever punishment they dish out. The best solution is not to have sex at all. That way, they can't hurt you. I will do anything I have to do to protect you because I care an awful lot about you. While I like all the Corridor girls, you are extra special. I don't want that band of crooks to use you to hurt me."

"Oh, Brett, are you sure we can't have sex? I am willing to lie."

"That's how the cops screw you up. They get you to start telling lies. Then they make you tell more lies until you get caught, and then you are the one that will get in trouble for lying."

Just then Carlos and Maria walked in.

"Did you have sex with her?" Maria asked.

I replied, "No, we did not have sex, Maria."

"Why didn't you have sex with her, Brett?"

"I am not in the mood. I have a sudden pain in my ass," I replied.

I walked out of the house so I could get far away from those two assholes. They'd just ruined the best time I could have ever had, and that was with Maddie. They had ruined any chance of that at all! The only chance of a good time I had left was to find another date, but the prom would not be as much fun without Maddie. I was fuming. It was getting to the point where I was going to have to do something about Maria. She had shown up in my house with Carlos, hoping to hit me with a phony rape charge, which meant they were working together, trying to set me up. One way I could stop her was by talking to my dad.

So that is what I did.

Once I got back home, I approached my father. "Dad, you are going to have to do something about Maria. She kidnapped me and took me to New York by way of Canada, which makes it an international crime. Now she had tried to get one of my friends to cry rape so she could bring me up on a phony rape charge. She is harassing me at school, and my grades are falling. She is doing everything she can to see I don't graduate. Dad, I keep telling you, if I kill her, your son will have to die also. Now, Dad, I don't want to hurt anybody, so I am counting on you to tell her to knock it off. Otherwise, I will have to kill her."

He never responded to what I had said.

Chapter 64

SCRAMBLE FOR A PROM DATE

Having no prospect of taking either Maddie or Laura to the prom, I began scouting the hall for someone else to take. Most everyone gathered in the main hall, where the school seal was located. That's where I first spotted her, a girl with dark brown silky hair that draped over her breasts, a meticulously cared for face, and not a blemish anywhere. She had an almost unbelievable body. Man, was she beautiful, from the front, the back, and even the sides. Every which way you looked at her, she was beautiful. I had not seen her before. I had not paid much attention to other girls since I was seeing Laura. I did not know this girl's name, so I began asking around, trying to find out what her name was. I learned she was Katelyn Coughlin. I immediately began a quest to find out as much as I could so I could look up her phone number in the phone book.

One day, I had worked up enough nerve to call her. When I did finally call, she and I had a pleasant conversation. We talked about what our plans were after graduating school. I had abandoned my hopes of being an engineer and was willing to settle for being an electrician if my father would come through for me. GM usually was hiring apprentices. I was now hoping to get an apprenticeship with my dad's help.

I called Katelyn two to three times a week. During one of our phone conversations, I asked her to the prom. She promptly told me, "Brett, I don't get into those types of functions. I would not go with you or anyone else. Some of the people who go to those dances are really hung up on themselves."

"I have tickets. And I have reservations at a restaurant, so we could have a nice dinner."

"Not interested, Brett."

"Okay, then we could make it some other date, like a concert."

"That is a possibility."

I hung up thinking I might be stuck with the prom tickets, but then I thought of one more girl. She was nice, was friendly toward me, and was always smiling and wishing me a good morning or afternoon, whatever the case was. Her name was Jane Vanover. She was high on my list of possible dates. I decided she would be the one I would ask.

We were sitting next to each other in English class when I asked her, "Jane, would you like to go to the junior prom with me?"

"I thought you were going with Laura?"

"We broke up. You won't need a thing. I have reservations at Tokyo Gardens. We will be riding with Jake Barnett and his date."

"Fine, let me see if I can get a dress."

A week later, Jane had still not given me a definite answer about going to the prom with me, so I called up a girl I had known since third grade, Alyssa Kashani. She was very pretty and had been part of the senior homecoming court. She had recently broken up with her boyfriend Kerwyn Beamon. I called her up and asked her, "Alyssa, how would you like to go to the prom with me?"

Elatedly, she said, "I did not think anyone was going to ask me to go. Yes, Brett, I'd love to go with you."

"Then it's a date!"

"Oh yes definitely yes!"

I made the date with Alyssa because Jane had not given me an answer. I had made arrangements to ride with Jake Barnett and his date given that my license had been recently been suspended for sixty days. The Tokyo Gardens, where we were to have dinner, was a restaurant popular for its atmosphere, although its food did not have a reputation for being very good.

The night of the prom arrived. I had everything prepared. I had gotten Alyssa's corsage, and Jake Barnett picked me up at my house. He and I headed to Alyssa's house. I went inside and introduced myself to her parents. Then I pinned her corsage on her shoulder. She looked absolutely beautiful. She had her hair in the back done in a French twist. As far as I was concerned, I was taking the belle of the ball. Alyssa's oldest brother had set the curfew at 2:30 a.m. She and I headed to Jake's car, a '68 white Camaro. Next we had to pick up his date. She was a couple of years older than Jake and she already had a baby. Not wanting to pry into his business, I kept the questions to a minimum.

Not knowing how to dance, I'd figured the girls would dance with each other, but such was not the case. At the prom, Alyssa almost begged me to dance with her.

She said, "Brett, you have to dance a little bit with me. Even if you don't know how, you can try, *please?*"

I tried dancing some old dance steps I had been taught back at Franklin, but it seemed awkward and was not working out. I was content on being a wallflower and talking to the some of the guys I knew. The time seemed to drag on. I now understood why Katelyn and other students avoided these types of functions. At around nine thirty, Alyssa, Jake, his date, and I climbed into the car and headed to the restaurant, where we were going to meet two other couples, including Douglas Turner, who was also a Franklin grad. The other couple was friends of Jake Barnett's date. We promptly introduced ourselves and then sat down. Now I was more in my element, eating. The restaurant had a stream and a small waterfall running through it with live koi in a pond. Overall, the atmosphere was very nice. The surroundings were romantic. Now if only the food was as good it would be an improvement on how the night had gone so far. When the waitress arrived, we all ordered New York strip steaks, figuring, *How can you mess up a steak except by overcooking it?*

Our salads arrived promptly. Our steaks arrived soon afterward. I bit into my steak. It was so tough that I thought I was chewing on a rubber steak. I was extremely hungry, so I struggled to get the first bite down. I tried a second bite, which was full of gristle—totally inedible. I gave up on this steak, deciding not to risk choking. Unable to eat any more of the steak, I concentrated on the baked potato.

We all finished dinner. I surveyed everyone's plate. No one had eaten even half of his or her steak. I thought to myself, *This will be a restaurant I will never come back to. Good atmosphere, lousy food.*

The people in our group all headed back to our cars. I had no idea what Jake had planned. He drove us all over the city of Detroit as if we were sightseeing. After about two hours, I sensed that Alyssa was getting bored. So was I. It was now around one o'clock in the morning, much earlier than Alyssa's brother had recommended I bring her home. I told Barnett to take us home, first dropping off Alyssa and then swinging me by my house. When we got to her house, I walked her to the door, gave her a friendly kiss goodnight, and ended the worst date I'd ever had.

I saw Alyssa a few days later. I walked up to her and told her, "Alyssa, I am sorry the prom date did not work out as well as I would have liked. I would like to take you out again to make up for it. I promise it will be a nicer time. And I will learn how to dance."

"Brett, I am sorry, but Kerwyn and I still have feelings for each other. Right now, I don't know what is going to happen between us."

"Okay, Alyssa, I just thought I'd offer."

What a strange relationship the two of them had. He'd let someone else take his girlfriend to the prom. I shook it off and started back to class, when I was stopped by Jake, who had been showing the pictures from the prom to one of our classmates named Devin Thompson. Devin asked how our dates went. Pissed that mine had not gone well, I figured I would feed him a line of bullshit, so I told him that Jake and I both had gotten blow jobs—and gotten laid too. Next thing I knew, Thompson had spread that line of bull all over the school. It was in between classes when Kerwyn stopped me in the main hall and said, "So, you got yourself a blow job and got laid by my girlfriend, eh?"

"Kerwyn, it was a joke. Thompson did not go to the prom. He was asking me and Jake all kinds of questions, so I led him to believe that we had gotten blown and laid. It was just a date to the prom, nothing else."

"We will see about that."

During our next change of class, Kerwyn came up to me and said, "Brett, I deeply apologize. Alyssa said the same thing you said. She told me that you were a perfect gentleman all night long. I believe her."

"Thanks, Kerwyn. It means a lot to me that my word is good to you. Plus, it takes a hell of a man to say he was wrong."

"Brett, I don't know what it is, but there is something special about you that make people like me like you."

Chapter 65

VALLEY D'AZZOLES

I was in my last hour of electronics, the last class of the day, when Theo Poulos asked me if wanted to check out his new car. He told me it had a 426 Hemi and said it was very fast. He had just gotten it the week before. I said, "Yes, let me check it out." It was green in color with a black interior, and had an automatic transmission. He showed me the engine. I was impressed.

We got into the car and drove around to the other side of the school, where he yelled for a guy named Ali to come over to the car. Ali said, "You stinking hillbilly," and then proceeded to spit in my face.

I reached for the door handle so I could get out and stomp Ali's ass, but Theo grabbed hold of me and would not let me out of the car. He started to pull away, to get me away from Ali.

That's when he said, "I told him to do that, Brett."

"Why would you tell him to spit in my face, Theo?"

He refused to answer me. I jumped out of the car. Ali was gone. I had no idea where he had gone to. This was a matter of pride. To save face, I had to retaliate. Ordinarily, I would call the police and let them handle it. One thing the common Arab was weak at but that I was strong in was a willingness to go to jail. The Dearborn police would probably just take the report, and take no action. Then, if I decided to take action against Ali, I would be the number one suspect if I had reported the incident. I decided this was a conspiracy between Ali and Theo against me. The sad part was that I knew Ali's family and they lived in the South End and were nice people. Now I might hurt him to save face. His father was Imah Azzole. His mother, the poor thing, was Stuckwiddan Azzole, and his brother was Wattan Azzole. I even knew his grandfather because he lived with his son and the rest of the family. His name was Heeza Azzole. The one shining spot in the whole family was Ali's sister. She was going to college and was pretty enough and smart enough. And man, what a body. Often with Arab families, the women are married off in a prearranged marriage, sometimes to their own cousins, but I could tell you that Nada Azzole, Ali's sister, was certainly not going to marry her cousin, Anudda Azzole. His family had originated from a place somewhere in Arabia called Valley of the Azzoles. Where, it is not exactly known. It is a kept secret. You have to be an Azzole to get in to the valley. It is similar to the Valley of the Kings, but instead of being a king, you have to be an Azzole to get in there.

The one place you will never see an Azzole is in Israel. Israel doesn't allow Azzoles to enter. If Arabs wish to get into Israel, they have to sneak in. As far as I am concerned, Jewish women are very beautiful, but I wondered how friendly they were to men who were not circumcised.

Not all Arabs are like the Azzoles. Not all want war. The true Muslim is peace loving with strong convictions, wanting only to raise his or her family like everyone everywhere else does. The sexiest women I have ever met were Muslim women with an education. They are taught that the men are kings of the homestead. They seem to have an instinct and a deep desire to see that their man is satisfied. Couple that with an education, and you have a recipe for success.

There are Azzoles in almost every country. Spain has some Azzoles, left over from the Moor invasion sometime around the eighth century. It took almost nine hundred years, but the Spanish at one point had finally had enough of the Azzoles and rounded them up. Then they put them on ships and sent them to Central America, along with the Spanish troops. Many people think the Spanish took the Aztecs' gold, but such is not the case. The Aztecs were so glad to have the Arabic women that they gave the gold to the Spanish for the expenses they had incurred. The Spanish, seeing that this was easy money, kept traveling back and forth to Spain, providing the Aztecs with Arab women until the Aztecs had no more gold. The Spanish got rid of most of the Azzoles and got rich in the meantime.

As I said, there are Azzoles all over the world, except in two places: Israel and China. Next door to China, though, is North Korea, where there is a large number of Azzoles. The reason they have Azzoles there is all you have to do is give the North Koreans some food which is rare there. If you travel to North Korea, however, whatever you do, don't take your dog.

After thinking about all this, I decided I would retaliate against Ali by getting one of my Arab friends to back me up in the dispute. I hunted down Mitch Imahboub. This plan of mine would prevent any other Arabs from backing up Ali, thereby keeping them out of the fray. Mitch, Ryan Tierney, and I had made a pact that if one of the three of us got into a hassle, the other two would back him up. I went to Mitch and told him what had happened.

His response was, "Ali is a senior, Brett. Leave it alone."

"Mitch, being a senior has nothing to do with anything. I have been your friend since fourth grade and you are not going to back me up?" I said.

"Nothing I can do, Brett."

"That's fine, Mitch, but do not count on me to back you up either."

I walked away, thinking, *He must be part Azzole, probably on his mother's side!*

I went to Ryan, who gave me the same answer. I could not believe neither of them would back me up in this dispute.

I now was left with three choices: to fight Ali and half the male Arab student body; to shoot Ali; or humiliate his family and show all white students what assholes the male Arabs were. I think you know what decision I made.

Chapter 66

THE LOAN ARRANGER

I was heading to my electronics class down the main hall when I saw a man approach one of the students I worked with at the car wash named Brad Sheenman. Both Sheenman and the man came down the hall toward me. Once they were close enough, Sheenman introduced me to the man he was with.

"Brett, this is Steven Spielberg. He makes good movies."

My immediate thought was, *Wow! I hit the jackpot! God has got to be Italian. He is rewarding me for not blowing Ali Azzole away.*

"Brett, I am a relatively new director. I make full-length feature films, and I am looking for investors to invest in my film."

Curious, I could not figure out who had told Spielberg to come and see me about money. I decided to find out how much he wanted, and discover where this conversation was going to take us. I asked, "How much money are you looking for?"

"Brett, I think I can make the film for somewhere between two and three million dollars." He then started telling me some things about the film, saying that it was about a small alien from outer space. He mentioned another movie about a man who had saved a lot of Jewish people's lives. It was to be called *Schindler's List*. All the while he was speaking to me he seemed to be staring off down the hall.

I knew right then that he was not staring at something. He was seeing the future, as I did. I remembered what the general had asked me to tell him, about how I was able to know what would take place in the future. I had told him, "I don't know. I just do it."

I asked Steven, "You were picturing how the scenes in your films were going to look just now, weren't you?"

"Brett, how did you know that?"

I knew at this point that this man had a very rare talent, and also that he was going to make film history. I wanted to be on board to help him accomplish his goals.

"Mr. Spielberg, there are people in this world who can picture in their mind exactly how things will appear in the future. I believe many people have the basic ability to do this, but not to the degree that people like you and I do. And that is the difference between success and greatness. You now know two men who can do that, you and I. Most of us have a niche in life. Yours is film; mine is war. As far as getting you some cash goes, I am working for twenty dollars a week at a local car wash. I promise you this, though: I will do everything I can to get the money for you. So meet me at my house tomorrow evening at six. Here is my address and phone if you need to call."

Steven came by promptly at six, which impressed me. Grandpa Holbrook had drilled into me the idea that when a man shows up on time, he is trustworthy, and if he is late, he usually ain't worth a hoot. I introduced Steven to my father. Then I told my guest, "Steven, I have three possibilities for getting you an investor. One is my dad. Next there is Vinny, Then there is the man who, or so I say, has all the money in the world. He is a general in the US Army. Let's get the first one out of the way. Dad, Steven is a movie director. He is looking for people to invest in his films. Do you have any money you could invest? We are looking at two million, with one million returned plus your initial two-million-dollar investment."

"No, I don't have that kind of money to invest in a movie."

I knew that my father had my seven million. I was willing to put up the money, but with Dad controlling the money, I had no chance. It was now on to the next option I was off to see Vinny. After having Dad dig out my gun and holster, I began strapping my holster on.

Steven began to seem a little nervous. He asked, "What is the gun for, Brett?"

"It's for a show of strength, Steven. It is just so the people we are going to talk with know that we are no pushovers and that we are serious. Don't worry, there won't be any gunplay, I promise."

"Who is it we are going to see?"

"Vinny, an Italian businessman," I replied.

"You mean the Mafia, Brett?" Steven asked.

I scolded him fiercely and said, "Don't ever say that again! Take that word out of your vocabulary. There is no such thing as the Mafia; there are only Italian businessmen! When you call them the Mafia, you are insulting them, the Italian people, and their heritage. If you refrain from referring to them as Mafiosi, it will mean you are their friend and not a threat to them. It could someday save your life, or save you from an ass-whooping. Let's go see if we can get you your money."

We walked down Lasher Street to Roulo, where Vinny lived. Along the way, Steven asked me to explain what we were going to do.

"Well, we are going to ask my friend to lend you two million dollars. In return, you'll pay him a set amount of return."

"You mean interest, don't you, Brett?"

"*No interest!* We give a set amount of return. Otherwise, the interest might change and be more than you expected."

"What do we have to do for the money?"

"That's the simple part. We just put up collateral."

"What do you have for collateral, Brett?"

"Well, you put up your life and I put up my life. If we don't come through, they kill us both."

"Wait a minute, Brett, there is no way I am going to do that! Come on, let's get out of here."

"What, are you afraid now? Are you losing your confidence in yourself? I believe in you enough to put my life up so you can make your movie. Steven, you've got to have faith in me. I am really good."

When we got to Vinny's, two of his men were sitting on the porch. I asked to see Vinny.

"Brett, people in this neighborhood have lots of money?" Steven asked.

"Most people are poor around here, Steven, but Vinny has more money than God."

One of Vinny's men replied, "Vinny is not around. What do you need him for?"

"I want to discuss some business with him. I've got a million-dollar offer for him," I said. The man scampered into the house and then reemerged with Vinny.

"What's up, kid?" Vinny asked.

"Vinny, this is Steven. He is an up-and-coming director who makes good movies, but he needs investors. He wants to make you an offer for you to invest in his movie. You put up two million, and we give you back your two million, plus one million as a loan fee paid to you. How about it, Vinny? Do you think you want to invest?"

"I want more money, Brett."

"Okay, Vinny, how about this? We make a second movie, you put up two million, and you get one million back as a fee for the loan. Now you make two million dollars total."

I could tell Vinny was considering my offer. Then he gave me his answer. "No, Brett, I can't invest in a movie. Movies are just too risky."

"Vinny, we got collateral. Steven will put up his life and I will put up mine."

"No offense, Brett, but your life isn't worth two million dollars to me. And if you were dead, it would mean nothing to me. You would be worth more to me alive, so I would rather keep you alive."

"Vinny, I just know his movie is going to make money. I thought you would want to make some money also. I would tell you I would do you a favor in return, but I don't think I could do a two-million-dollar favor. I have been an advisor to you for a while now. I'm telling you that you are making a bad business decision." I could see I was wasting my time, and that I would have to find another investor. I was simply not willing to beg for the money. I didn't think Steven was either.

Steven and I headed back to my house. He made a comment about something to which I had never really paid much attention before. He said, "Brett, I am beginning to realize you have an awful lot of friends. I mean a lot. Brett, I know you are disappointed, but I don't think I would have taken Vinny's money anyhow."

I said to him, "You know, Steven, I have always felt that for every friend you make, that's one less enemy you have. So I try to have a lot of friends and a whole lot less enemies. That seems to work for me. Maybe the Jews ought to try that philosophy as well, because Israel has an awful lot of enemies."

"Where would you start, Brett?"

"Well, first I would establish common ground. What do you think are some things that Arabs and Jews have in common, Steven?"

"Offhand, I couldn't say, Brett."

"See, that is exactly my point, Steven. No one really ever gives it a second thought. What makes men fight? They fight because they are upset with their leaders and the type of freedom they have. The most basic reason they fight is that they do not have enough to eat or enough to drink, and not enough sex. That is the whole philosophy of the Arab soldier. His life is miserable. He would rather fight than sustain his meager existence."

"Not enough sex, Brett?"

"Yeah why do you think the sheiks who own everything have harems? If the soldiers don't have enough to eat, then tell them you will get them food. Not enough to drink? Help get them enough to drink. Try that with the Arabs. Try convincing the Arabs that there is a much better choice than to try to blow each other away. If you ask me, sex is the best alternative to offer them. If you can convince your enemy that he will have more sex in his life, then he will be more peaceful toward you. Having sex takes the edge off and makes people less mean."

Steven began to chuckle. He said, "Brett, you are certainly unique. That is a very interesting philosophy."

"I believe that Pancho Villa had the best answer to the question of why men fight. He said, 'I would rather die on my feet than continue living on my knees.'"

"Who said that, Brett?"

"Pancho Villa is credited with saying that, as far as I know. He was one of the revolutionary generals during the Mexican uprising circa 1910.

"Steven, I have not given up yet. I want to try one more possible source, but I will have to wait until tomorrow afternoon. I need you to be here around 2:00 p.m."

"Okay, Brett, I will be at your house promptly at 2:00 p.m."

The next day, Steven arrived at my house with three minutes to spare. I greeted him and promptly said to my father, "Dad, I need you to call the general." I'd decided to keep the general's name a secret. "I need to ask him for a favor."

My father dialed the phone and handed it to me.

"Hello, sir. I need a favor."

"Brett, what can I do for you?"

"Sir, I have a friend who is a director in Hollywood. He is looking for investors to finance one of his films. I am not looking for a donation, but I need a little help."

Suddenly, Steven, grabbed the phone and tried to talk to the general, but the general was having no part of it. Steven handed the phone back to me.

"Brett, *never, ever, ever, ever hand the phone to anyone else while I am talking to you! Does your friend know who I am?*" He had given me a type of ass-reaming I had not had in a really long time.

"No, sir, I did not give him your name."

"Brett, what exactly do you want me to do?"

"Well, sir, I am not looking for a handout. I've never taken any money for my services. I was wondering if you could help us secure a loan, maybe by way of some bank connection the government has."

"Brett, that is very noble of you. All I can tell you is that the decision to make a loan is entirely up to a bank. I will ask around and see what I can do."

Somehow, I knew my words had been of no avail. Two days after I had called the general, he called back and said there was nothing he could do to help. With that, I had no other way of obtaining the money for Steven. About four days later, Steven looked me up. I was waiting for class to begin when he came up to me and said, "Brett, I got the money."

Elated, I asked, "Where did you get it, Steven?"

"Never mind the money, Brett. I am going to do something for you, but first I need to ask you a question. Did you say that having an Arab state in the heart of Israel would be like putting a dagger inside the state of Israel?"

"Yes, I said that. I don't understand why you think badly of me for saying what the Israelis say. Isn't it true?"

"Brett, what year was the state of Israel formed?"

"I am not too good with dates, Steven, but I think it was 1948 or 1949."

"That's right, Brett. Who was the first prime minister of Israel?"

"David Ben-Gurion was the first prime minister of Israel."

"Most people can't even get one of those questions right, but you got all three right. Brett, I want you to go to Hollywood with me."

I was stunned. It had been my dream to be an actor ever since I had to give up my ambitions of being a pilot. Now I would be giving up my potential career as an engineer. I was totally elated. Still, I had a few questions before I would go to Hollywood to act. There was some information I needed in order to make the decision.

"Steven, I don't want to go to Hollywood and trying acting and appear on camera with a mouth full of rotten teeth. Plus, people say I can't act."

"I will get your teeth fixed. Plus, I will direct you. That way, you can learn to act. It will be easy because I will be doing the teaching. Brett, you have what it takes. You have star qualities. I can tell by the way the girls look at you. I can tell by how many friends you have. They all like you. You are the type of person to whom people gravitate to. You will be my star, Brett."

I thought about how I would have to get Mom a decent house in a city other than Dearborn. I had talked to her previously about moving far away, telling her that if I went to the West Coast and ultimately made enough money, I wanted to have her and the kids follow me.

She said she would never move that far away from her mother and father. Five hundred miles was already too far, she had told me.

There was the matter of Steven's safety to worry about. I knew Team Garcia hated hillbillies, but did they hate Jews also? I had already lost a number of friends and was not willing to lose anymore. I asked Steven, "When will we go to Hollywood?"

"Today, Brett. We have to go now—in a few hours."

"Can I at least finish high school? I've got a little more than a year left to go. Steven, my father only got as far as tenth grade. I promised my mom and dad I would finish high school. It is really important to my dad. People always look down on him because he did not finish high school. He will be very proud to see me graduate."

"Brett, I can't wait that long. We have to go today."

I had known Steven a short while, but I could tell that, just like me, when he said he would do something, he would do it, and he would not let anything stand in the way of his goal. I had pinned the situation down. If I went to Hollywood, I would be taking a risk and possibly putting my mom in danger. She could end up dead. I just could not do that, especially after reliving her rape over and over in my head. Being in Hollywood could also put

541

me at risk. I could end up dead. If Team Garcia decided to pay me a visit in Hollywood, then both Steven and I could end up dead. I felt like an NCAA sports star whose mom wanted him to graduate rather than go to the NFL.

After weighing all these possibilities, I wished that Mrs. Spielberg were there to coach me and provide me with some of her female intuition. My decision had boiled down to "boy sacrifices movie career to watch over mother." There was no one to help.

I said, "Steven, I trust you. And I just know that you will make it big time. I would like nothing more than to drop what I am doing and go with you, but I can't leave my mom in Dearborn."

"Okay, Brett. Before I go, tell me, what is your favorite movie of all time?"

"It would have to be *The Ten Commandments*, Steven."

"What makes you like it so much, Brett?"

"Well, one thing is that the movie is about the Bible. And it makes me think of my grandfather. Second is the way they did the special effects."

"Which one did you like most?" Steven asked.

"No matter what anyone else says, the best scene is when Moses parts the Red Sea. You hear everybody trying to figure out how they did that scene. You hear all kinds of theories, like it was done with gelatin or the film was run backwards but nobody who wasn't in on the film knows how that scene was really done."

"Brett, what studio produced that film?" Steven asked.

"I am not sure, Steven, but I think it was MGM."

"What does *MGM* stand for, Brett?"

"It stands for 'Metro Goldwyn Mayer.'"

"What nationality were those men, Brett?"

"People don't go to a movie because of the nationality of the producers. They go there to have a good time and to be entertained."

"Brett, please, you have to come with me. Hollywood is going to love you."

Steven was stroking my ego. I thought that I was just an average-looking guy, but he thought I was more than that. The thought of hobnobbing with Hollywood's elite, and then banging some of the most beautiful women on the planet in an all-night sex session like I had experienced down in the Corridor, was making me salivate. He had pushed my buttons. I got tongue-tied trying to get the words out, but I said to Steven, "My mom loves me. She needs me to help protect her. The only way I can do that is to move her to a safer city. All I need is less than a year to settle her in, and then we can both make a boatload of money."

"Brett, I can't wait. You have to come with me now. There are no second chances."

"Okay, Steven. It is just not possible for me to go at this time."

"Well, I wish you luck, Brett. I have to leave. Goodbye."

"Hopefully I will see you soon, Steven," I said. I watched as he walked down the hall to the west exit. As I watched him leave, it felt more like I was walking out on him, and that I was losing the best friend I had ever had. I would have had a lot more friends and a whole lot fewer enemies had I gone with him. He was leaving me behind. Even with all those questions about Israel and its short history, he would never know how I had come up with a plan to protect Israel. I would have to keep that knowledge a secret for many years to come. If only he had known, I think he would have told me, "Well done," being proud to know me. As I left school that day, I thought that this was just one more episode I would chalk up to Team Garcia. They had made it impossible for me to leave and go to Hollywood. The only thing to do now was to work feverishly from that point on to get my family out of Dearborn. Maybe then I could go to Hollywood. Maybe Steven could find some work for me.

With Steven gone, I had no choice but to continue classes and lift myself out of a depressive mood by spending time with the friends I had left. Of all the classes I had, my electronics class was the most fun. One guy I enjoyed

544

conversing with was Hal Hartman. He and I had a lot of fun together. Hal was just an all-around nice guy. One day, when we had slow day, he said, "Brett, I need some help writing a speech for my English class, but I have no idea what to write about."

"Whose class is it?"

"Mr. Overberg." Overberg was the toughest of all the teachers.

"Hal, they say you should write about things that you know or like. What are some of those things?"

"Well, Brett, the thing I like most is riding on the dunes in my dune buggy."

"Then dune buggies it is."

The electronics class was two hours long. Hal and I had his speech written in well under an hour.

I was disappointed when later he told me he had gotten a C on the speech. With the two of us having worked on it, I thought it deserved better than a C. But that was Mr. Overberg, who was a very tough grader.

Time was flying by. My junior year soon came to a close. I stayed in touch with Katelyn from time to time, by phone only. Anytime I had asked her out, she came up with some silly excuse, such as that she had to wash her hair. I would always try a comeback, like, "Wash it early." Then I would ask her out the following night, hoping she would eventually say yes, but that day never came. Still, I refused to quit. She was just too pretty and well-built.

Finally, the school year ended. I had done very well in my classes, but not with Katelyn. I made up my mind that I would call her only sparingly throughout the summer. I felt there were other girls I could date until Katelyn was receptive to having a date with me.

Chapter 67

THE LAST SUMMER IN DEARBORN

It was early afternoon when two girls came through the space between the buildings on Franklin Street. "Brett, we're two of the girls from the Corridor. We want you to have sex with us. Do you have a room to yourself in your house?"

"Yes," I said. "I have the whole floor to myself."

"Lead the way, Brett." I led them to the lower floor of my house, where I showed them the bedroom.

"Gee, Brett, this place is a real dump."

"Well, it is not the prettiest place, but my mom keeps it clean."

The one who had been doing all the talking said, "I don't like it here, Nancy. Let's go."

"Well, honey, you don't look all that good either. I would have had sex with you, but not now."

They walked out in a huff, but I really didn't care. It would have been nice to get laid, but I was not about to beg.

With that, the summer had started off with a flop. But it would soon pick up.

My sister Veronica was a terrible student. When she got a D+ on her report card, it was the equivalent of someone else getting an A+. She did not like school, and had missed a lot of classes. She really did not care if she got an education. While she was not smart, she was pretty. She had figured she was going to screw her way to the top of the social ladder, spreading her legs to the highest bidder. She got one of the neighborhood ex-cons named Ron Trammel in trouble. I had told Ronnie to stay away from her, but he refused to listen. He had a really nice car, and he bought her nice things. He made the mistake of taking her out of state to Missouri. I believe he took her there to get married, because Missouri's age to get married was lower than Michigan's. Charged with violating the Mann Act, he ended up in jail. All Veronica was looking for was a man who had a lot of money and was willing to spend a good portion of it on her.

She was very sexually active. Often after having sex, she would cry rape and blame someone totally innocent. If she turned up pregnant, she would get an abortion. Here her stupidity showed. She was so dumb that she did not know that the doctors could determine blood type from semen. After a few times of Veronica crying rape, the Dearborn police told me that if she were found dead, there would not be an intense investigation. They were not going to waste the taxpayers' money investigating her death. Having eventually caught on to what she was doing, they knew that she was flirting with danger. They had warned her that she was going to piss the wrong person off, who would then leave her dead body in a field somewhere.

I caught a lucky break. My dad said that a twenty-two-year-old guy named Parker wanted to talk to him about Veronica.

Dad told Parker that he should talk to me. I could not believe that my dad was letting me decide Veronica's fate. I suppose he figured I would be better at deciding what to do about her.

The knock came at the door. I opened it to see a man a few years older than Veronica and I.

He introduced himself to me. "Brett, my name is Parker Byron. I want to ask you for permission to marry Veronica."

I asked, "Parker, do you know who she has been hanging around with over by Desirae's bar?"

"I know all about what she has been doing, and I don't care. I have been giving her twenty dollars a couple of times a week to keep her away from those people."

"Parker, did you serve in the armed forces?" I asked.

"Yes, Brett. I served for three years on active duty, and three years reserve duty. I am a very good shot with a rifle. The army sent me all around the world for shooting competitions. I did very well. Brett, I promise you, I will take good care of her. I just think she is the prettiest thing I ever saw. I want her to have my children."

"Parker, just for the record, I like you already. I want to talk to my mom and dad and tell them what our options are regarding Veronica. Then I want to talk to Veronica. I will give you my answer tomorrow. I like everything about you."

After Parker left, I went upstairs to talk to my mother and father. I laid out the options, which were to kick Veronica out of the house and let her go live with her buddy Josita, who was Rico's sister, or allow her to marry Parker.

My mom began to cry. She said, "Can't we let her stay just a little longer?"

I said, "Mom, if she stays here, she is going to continue what she is doing. If she gets caught, she is going to embarrass the whole family. All your brothers and sisters will be laughing at you, and even Grandpa may want her dead. Then there is Dad's side of the family. If she stays here, Mom, I will have no choice but to kill her."

"Lou, Brett is right. I am not going to let Veronica embarrass me and have my family laughing at me. I say let him marry her. What do think, Lou?"

"Is he a good man, Brett?"

"He is as good as you are going to find from this side of town."

"Then I think that will be okay," Mom said.

Parker came by the next day. I asked, "Parker, you have been hanging around Desirae's bar, right?"

"Yes. I drink there so I can see Veronica."

"Then you know Rico also?"

"Of course I know him."

"Well, he is going to be pissed that you are marrying Veronica, because he loves her too. He'll hurt not only me but also you and Veronica. I need you to cover me. And I will cover you. Is that a problem?"

"I got your back, Brett," Parker said.

"Then you have my blessing, Parker. And don't disappoint my mom. She wants you to take good care of Veronica."

"I will do that, Brett."

"When do you and Veronica plan on getting married?"

"We'll get our blood tests and the permission papers, and then get married the day after that."

Parker and Veronica were married the first week in July. They came by the house on their wedding day. Shortly after they were married, I was talking to my dad. Maria was there at the house so she could see Veronica on her wedding day. I asked my dad, "Why don't you give Veronica and Parker one hundred thousand dollars of that dog money? That way they can get off to a good start and buy a nice house. Then they can have a few kids." I was testing him to see who had the money, him or Maria.

"Oh no, that is my son's money," Maria said emphatically.

Her response told me exactly what the two of them were planning. They kill me or get me killed, and then they ride off in into the sunset with their son and my money. Maria and Dad had stolen the money that rightfully belonged to me, and she now claimed it was her son's money. I was trying to show my dad one more time that Maria was a money-grubbing bitch who was willing to kill me so her son could have money that was mine.

I said, "See what I mean, Dad? She is only worried about the money," hoping he was getting the message.

Dad had no response. He chose not to give Parker and Veronica the money, so they lived with Parker's parents for a short time until they got their own place. I had done cartwheels the day they were married. I now had my freedom back, no longer having to watch out for her. Still, I wanted to see them make a good go of their marriage.

When I came home one day after school, I saw my mom on her hands and knees washing dishes in the bathtub. I blew a gasket! As my father was coming up the back stairs, I told him, "If you can't get us a new house, I am going to steal back every penny of my money you have! We can live better than this on welfare, so we don't need you! I am tired of being embarrassed when someone comes to visit! They tell me what a dump this is! I am tired of living like a slave! I am sick of you acting like you are broke, pretending that the money does not exist so you can give it to your little bastard! He is living like a king, while you make us live in squalor with the mice and the roaches! You are pissing me off enough that I want to kill your bitch, her son, and you! If I can't have the money that rightfully belongs to me, then he can't have it either! He will never see a penny of that money, one way or another. It's my money. I would rather kill him than let those Mexican cops get it! Get us out of here! And I mean now!"

After my tirade, Mom and Dad finally began looking for a new house. Moving would mean leaving the shit hole we were living in. After years of the basement flooding, it finally knocked out the furnace. For the previous two years, with the furnace not working, we'd heated the shit hole with an oven and a twenty-four-inch stove located in the upper flat. The lower flat had no heat whatsoever. Slowly but surely, each one of the water pipes—with no heat to keep them from freezing—had burst. I thought this house should have been condemned the day the furnace went out.

I hoped that this would be the last summer I spent in Dearborn. I decided that I was going to enjoy it. I would drive my car and pick up my friend Ryan Tierney, and then we would meet his family at Camp Dearborn. When there, we could have a barbecue and go waterskiing. The best part, though, was checking out the girls on the beach. After spending the day at the beach and eating a nice hearty meal of burgers, we attended the dance at the canteen. All in all, it was a nice place to spend the day.

I would spend as many weekends there as I could.

At one point, as I had figured he would do, Rico Garcia started with his antics again. As he had done many times before, he raped a woman and had her blame me for the rape. This time it was Mrs. Goff, Barney Goff's mother. As had happened other times, Barney, along with a friend of his, Matty Dorsey, began chasing me, hoping to hurt me so as to get revenge for the rape of his mother.

Not wanting to hurt Mrs. Goff's son after she had been raped, I chose to run from Barney and Matty. I was actually laughing as I ran from them, because they could not catch me. I would have fought Barney by myself, as he was not much of a fighter, but I knew that I could not win a fight against the two of them. It had occurred to me that Barney's family was from Tennessee. Rico was a member of Team Garcia, who were having the hillbillies kill each other. I used great restraint in keeping from hurting Barney, in the hopes that the cops would eventually catch on and arrest Rico, who was the real culprit. That never happened.

Barney continued to chase me by himself, only now he was carrying a knife. I, in turn, got one of my dad's .22 semiautomatics. I was doing everything to avoid a conflict, but Barney was dead set on getting revenge. Once my patience wore thin, I was left with no other choice but to fight him. The next time he came after me, I shot him in the foot so he could not run as fast. He began swearing at me, telling me he was going to kill me. I shot him in the forehead. It was only a .22, so it only knocked him out, but he was going to have a hell of a headache when he awakened. He was taken away by ambulance to the hospital, still unconscious.

There was a weakness in all the crimes Team Garcia had committed. Somewhere in their story, they had to lie to avoid prosecution. I would continue to be truthful, knowing that sooner or later, I would catch them all in a lie that would be their downfall. I now had a plan. I went on about my business, and began to stalk Rico, but I stalked him in a different way. I would wait patiently until he thought he had me cornered, and then I would spring a trap on him.

Chapter 68

THE HUNT FOR A RED HOUSE IN OCTOBER

My parents tried to find a house in Dearborn so I could continue to attend Eastern, but the real estate market made that impossible. I did not care what city I lived in as long as it had an honest police force.

There was a housing shortage in the suburbs of Detroit. It was a sellers' market, meaning that prices were at a premium. My aunt Marilyn told my father that her husband's sister was selling her house. My parents wanted to go see the house, so Aunt Marilyn made the arrangements. When it came time to go look at the house, my parents took me with them. It was an average-sized three-bedroom brick ranch located in Taylor. It was not as large a house as I had wanted for my mother, but it was a step up from the house in the ghetto of southeast Dearborn. It did not have a garage, which was also a negative. Mom and Dad liked it, though, for the price. It was more of a house than they could buy in other cities. They thought about it as they looked at other houses, but they ended up settling on the Taylor home. They wanted to make an agreement to assume the mortgage, but they had to have the City of Dearborn buy the current house if they were to assume the mortgage on Margaret's house, Margaret being Aunt Marilyn's sister-in-law. The deal was made. The paperwork would be done by the end of October. My family would move into the house on November first.

September arrived. I started my senior year. I felt very anxious knowing that this would be my last semester in Eastern and that I would be attending Paul Revere High School for my last semester. I signed up for the co-op work program and was surprised when I not only got a job but also learned that it was one of the highest-paying jobs the school offered. I would be working in a meatpacking plant called Dearborn Packing Company. The pay was $2.50 per hour, which was a good wage considering that my father was earning only $2.85 per hour working at GM. I worked from 6:00 a.m. until 10:00 a.m. I then attended my classes from 11:00 a.m. to 3:00 p.m.

One afternoon, after returning to school from lunch at a burger joint, I met Rico who pulled his gun. He had been hiding among the other students, who were on lunch break also, so I had not noticed him. I saw that he had Salmi Easley, one of the Franklin jailbirds, with him. Rico pulled out his gun, the long-barreled .38 he always carried.

I asked him, "What the hell are you doing, Rico? I am at school!"

"I am going to shoot you, Brett."

I did not have either of my guns with me, so I had to think fast, as I was about to be shot. The only thing I could think of was to do what I always did: walk away and hope that Rico had enough honor not to shoot me in the back. So I turned my back to him and said, "Rico, I am unarmed." Then I walked into the school. Amazingly, he did not shoot me.

It seemed as though the members of Team Garcia were doing everything they could to keep me from graduating. The kidnapping by Maria and all the false accusations of rape were intended to stop me from graduating. Now Rico was harassing me at school, pursuing me come hell or high water! Having given up a movie career to do so, I was going to finish high school.

As if the incident with Rico were not enough, something else happened. I was coming back from lunch one day when I walked into the school and was met by Francesco DaHomo. Everybody called him "Frankie" for short. He was one of the officers of the class; I do not remember which office he held. I had forgotten because I did not pay attention to school politics. I had known once, but it soon slipped from my memory. Frankie was a homosexual, which did not bother me in the least. I was never belligerent with him, unlike many straight men that beat up homosexuals and stole their wallets and gold jewelry. One of my very best friends was a homosexual. I loved him more than I loved my own brothers. I would do anything for him except perform a homosexual act with him. He always was respectful of that and never asked for sex from me.

I was surprised when Frankie approached me and propositioned me. He said, "Brett, I want to do something for you. My father is a honcho at Ford Motors. If you go on a date and have sex with me, I will get him to get you a really high-paying job."

I thought, *Man! Frankie must be really hard up. Either that or he thinks I am really stupid.* To test him to see if he was serious, I said, "Frankie, have your dad get me the job first. Then we will talk about dating and sex." I was thinking, *If I can get Frankie to get me the job, I'll fix him up with my homosexual friend.*

"No, Brett, we go on a date and have sex first."

I did not say anything more and walked away, fuming. I had other things on my mind. Plus, I had to get to class.

Frankie chased me down, and once more asked me to go on a date with him.

I grew tired of being nice to him. He had pissed me off, assuming I was a homosexual. So now, I was going piss him off. If you want to piss a woman off, you use the *c* word, and if you want to piss a homosexual off, you use the *f* word. I just exploded, saying in my angriest voice, "Look, you damn faggot, get the hell away from me. What do you think I am, some sort of whore?"

I could see that I had gotten to him and pissed him off. He replied in an angry voice, "Brett, don't even think about going to any of our reunions, because I am really going to embarrass you."

At this point, with all that I had on my mind, I did not give two shits about seeing anybody ten years from now.

One positive thing had come out of that situation: even a homo found me attractive, which reaffirmed what Mr. Spielberg had told me about my having the "on screen" looks.

That same evening, seeing I had some unfinished business with Laura, I stopped by where she worked on my way home. I went up to the register she was working at and asked her, "So, are you able to date now, or are you still confined at home?"

"Oh no, Brett, I still can't date, but not because of my parents. I got married over the summer. This is my husband," she replied, pointing to the man who had been standing by her register.

I said, "Oh, I am sorry, Laura. I had no idea you got married. I will leave you alone. I won't bother you ever again."

I started to walk away. She asked, "What did you want anyway, Brett?"

I did not want her to know what I had really come there for, so I decided to leave it to her imagination. I said, "It wasn't anything important, just to say hello." I walked off thinking that Giles Fairfax had been right. Either that or Laura had gotten one over me very fast.

The weekend came. Dad called me away from the rest of the family. "Rico told Parker that he was going to kill you. Don't worry, though. Parker said he had told you before he and Veronica got married that he was going to back you up if Rico tried anything. How did you know he would come after you?"

"Dad, all those Mexican buddies of yours; including your bitch, blame me for everything that happens. And every time I do something nice for them, they threaten to kill me."

Dad said, "I want you to load this gun and use it. Make sure it has a full clip. And hand the gun to Veronica." He then handed me the .22 semiautomatic.

He also gave me a box of shells. I began to load the gun, wiping my fingerprints off each shell as I loaded it. It was later in the afternoon when Dad told me that Rico was on Franklin Street. I went over to Franklin. Rico pulled out his gun, the same .38 he always used, and led me down Franklin to Dix, all the time holding his gun on me. He kept the gun on me until he forced me between two buildings, at which point he ordered me up against the back wall. Here I was facing a gun once again. I was not shaking or even nervous. The old adage of "you will get used to it" fit the moment. I did not know if I was about to die or not. I kept wondering where Parker and was, when all of sudden he walked up behind Rico along with Veronica, holding his army carbine.

"There is no need to look. If you want me dead, then shoot me. If you do though you are going to die, too, Rico," I said.

He held his gun in his outstretched arm, as if to surrender. Not touching him, I ordered him to the ground. For some reason, he tucked his gun in his waistband. I tried to get the gun out of his waistband. He refused to relinquish it. I handed the .22 I'd been holding to Veronica and told her to do as I ordered her to do. One more time, I tried to get the gun away from Rico.

Then Rico said something that left me no choice. "Brett, when I get up from here, I am going to kill you."

At that point, I had run out of patience. It had been ten years since I first met Rico, and all that time he had been trying to kill me or drug me. I had tried to reform him by being friendly, but nothing worked. I was going to give him one last chance to die on his feet, but he would not give me the gun. I could not take a chance that Rico would hurt any one of us. I thought *why should I care if he dies on his feet or not? He has been sneaking into my house and was drugging both me and my mother! He did not fight by the rules.* When Rico refused to give up that damn gun, I ordered Veronica to shoot him once in the body. She fired one round that hit its mark. Once more, I tried to get his gun. He tightened his grip on it. I ordered Veronica to fire three rounds to his head. When she fired the third round, I saw the life go out of Rico's body. He went limp. I was supposed to feel good, but I felt bad. Maybe I had a little of my grandfather in me, but I had not been good enough to get Rico to reform. I had always felt that life is very precious and that I was put here to save as many lives as I could. I always got far more pleasure out of saving lives than taking lives. By this time in my life, I had saved millions of lives, although Team Garcia was keeping all the lives I had saved a secret. Given all the rapes Rico had committed, and who knows how many murders he'd committed, it was just time for him to go. His whole life's ambition was to become a pimp and a drug dealer. The lure of drugs was just too great for him, which fact made it that much clearer to me the importance of keeping drug users off the streets.

Chapter 69

A STRATEGIC MOVE

It was November 1, 1970, when my family began the move to Taylor. We had just finished up with the final trailer load when my father asked me a question.

"Brett, why don't you die and make me rich?"

He could not have hurt me more if he had speared me through the heart. Before I gave him any response, I was going to find out as much as I could, in case he died and left the money to my half-brother, Russell.

One thing was certain: my dad had lied to me and lied to my mom. And everything that was happening or had happened was the result of his not being able to keep his penis in his pants, which showed how stupid my father was. He believed that Team Garcia would just let him and Maria ride off into the sunset with my money without trying to steal it from them.

"How do you want me to make you rich by dying?"

"Well, you have a lot of money in your account."

"What account, and how much money is it?" I asked.

"It's five million dollars."

"You mean to tell me you had the money hidden all the time when you told my friend Steven that you didn't have any money? I could have gone to Hollywood and made another couple of million dollars with that money! Where did the money come from?" I knew where the money had come from. I just wanted to hear it from his mouth.

He refused to answer me. "Why don't you die and help your mom by making us rich?" he said again.

At this point, I was so pissed that my blood had reached the boiling point. Angrily, in my deepest voice, I said, "I made you rich, and you gave the money to Maria and your son. Now you tell me there is another five million."

"No, there is just the five million," my dad said.

"If there was five million dollars, why didn't you give Veronica some of that money?" His asking me to die so that he could have the money meant that he still had control of the money, and my name being on the account meant that he wanted me out of the way so I couldn't lay claim to the money. Maybe after all these years of my telling him what Maria really thought of him, I had finally gotten through to him. She was college-educated and looked down on my dad as a stupid hillbilly, and like he was just another pretty face. He had asked her to help him write a mob movie, but she never

565

came through, although she had written plenty of books. I could tell she cared only about the money.

Maria felt no fondness for my mom or us kids, even though she was paid by the federal government to protect my mother and her children. She was two-faced, pretending to like us to our face and, when our backs were turned, saying nothing but bad things about us. I would not approve of my father keeping the money. There was a chance I might be able to get my money back. He could do whatever he wanted with the money if I gave him permission. Given that he was at home now, he had even more reason to leave my mom again. His record of taking care of my mother and us kids was anything but stellar.

I think that my telling my dad that Team Garcia wanted the money had awakened him to the realization that his keeping the money actually put Russell in danger. If something happened to Maria and my dad, Team Garcia would not wait to kill Russell to get a hold of the money. I said to my dad, "Why did you make Mom live in this dump all those years? You made her live all this time in this dump and never gave her any part of that money."

When he didn't answer, I realized he was trying to keep me stupid and ignorant. As with all the times before when he had not answered, I would have to wait and gather the information by myself. It was 1970. There were not a lot of millionaires in the country, and even fewer multimillionaires. I had known I had a lot of money, but I never knew for sure who was watching over it. I could not trust my father. His word was not worth a shit anyway. I never found out where he was keeping the money, or if he had put it in Maria's name or Russell's name. It started out as seven and a half million dollars, and now it was down to five million. I now saw my father's true colors. He loved his son Russell so much that he was willing to kill my mother, me, and Veronica to get rich. He wanted to get back with Maria and Russell, and wanted to take the three smallest siblings with him. Everything had been kept a big secret. This was the first time I was being told the truth. To be able to catch people in a lie, you have to remember what they've said to you, or haven't said. Eventually, if you remember, you will catch them in a lie. My father was now telling me the truth, which had been a long time coming. This was the first time I had any inkling that my father had control of all that money.

All this trouble I've had – the guns and violence, the threats, the false accusations, show why I was given a hard way to go. When Maria took me to New York and tried to get me to die on the rooftop there, her sole plan was to get rid of me. I was my mom's pride and joy, and Maria had tried to have me killed hundreds of miles from home. She knew that my death would have devastated my mom. Now, my father wanted me to die, to either make his other son rich or, even worse, to make him rich. I could not believe what an egotistical ass he was. It was now apparent to me that Maria had fanned the flames of his ego, telling him that he was very handsome and that Russ looked just like him. She did this so he would love his son that much more. And Dad, being the egotistical jackass he was, just gobbled it all up.

My father always felt that black-haired males were more attractive than blond males. That was why he was so stuck on himself and why he wanted a black-haired son. However, it had been my experience that quite a large proportion of the female population would rather have a blue-eyed, blond-haired man. The reason my dad wanted me to kill Rico was so that I would end up rotting away in prison somewhere. Thinking of this, I realized that I had given my father more credit for being smart than he deserved. When it came to Maria's son, his other son, he was a real nutcase. I was only seventeen, but throughout the years of my childhood, I had learned that if someone wanted you dead, they were not going to make just one attempt and then stop. They were going to keep trying to kill you until they succeed, especially if they were cops. So if you got the opportunity to kill someone who wanted to kill you, the only reasonable option was to kill them first. I had tried everything to make my father see the light, but to no avail. The only thing left for me to do the next time I had a conflict with him was to kill him, I thought. I knew it would be a hard decision to make, but it was now necessary, for my mom's sake and for all of our sake.

Dad and I got into the car and headed back to our new home in Taylor. Residents of other cities had nicknamed it "Taylortucky" because there were so many southern residents in the city.

It was few days later when Jordan Bowman, the cop whom I'd met at my grandfather's farm, and who was a member of Taylor's police force, came by my house along with his son, John. John was a large strapping teen who looked like the sort who would do well in street fight. Jordan began asking me questions.

"Brett, what is your grandfather's name? And where does he live."

I told him, "My grandfather's name is Will Holbrook, and he lives on a small farm in Kentucky."

"Can you describe the farm to me?" Jordan asked.

"Well, it is just a small farm. To get to it, you cross a little bridge over a creek. His shooting range is in the front yard."

Jordan exclaimed, "It's him!"

I did not know it at the time, but John Bowman would become one of my very best friends. He was our paperboy. I treasured John's friendship. He took me around and introduced me to some of the people who knew who I was and what I had done in Detroit. One of the places he took me to was Burns' Gun Shop.

"Brett, you may not be famous in Dearborn, but downriver you are a real celebrity."

One of the owners reached out to shake my hand, saying, "Brett, I am really pleased to meet you."

"Brett, my dad would be honored to sign for a permit for you to carry a gun," John said.

I could not understand why I was such a celebrity in the downriver area. No one was telling me why, but I just accepted it because I did not think it was anything that should be discussed. I was not looking to be famous. If I had been looking for fame, I would have pulled out all stops to become a Hollywood star by starring in Steven's films.

"John, I can't do that. The crooked Mexican cops were stealing our guns, committing murders with those guns, and then blaming us for the murders. I wouldn't want to put your dad at risk. Everything I do has to be done without a gun. However, I would like to get a new gun. If your dad can figure a way I could get a gun without endangering him, let me know."

A few days later, Jordan and John came by and said, "Brett, we want to take you to the Taylor gun range to see how well you can do."

"I am ready to go. Let's get going."

The range was located on Racho Road behind the city dump. No slugs could penetrate the dirt mounds. I was surprised to see how technical the range was. They had a machine with a target that moved away from your shooting position as you fired. This way, they could determine the range of your gun. Jordan gave me a .22 Magnum that had a front and rear sight. I knew I was not going to do very well with it, but I tried anyway.

Jordan said, "Brett, you did not do very well with that gun."

"Jordan, I don't do real well with a gun with a sight on it. A front sight is okay, but when you have a rear sight when the gun moves, it blocks the barrel tip so I can't see the front sight. The only guns I like with a sight are a .357 with a four-inch barrel, and a 7 mm. The 7 mm has a dovetail sight. Some cop took me to Wyandotte and had me shoot with a 7 mm most of the night."

"You mean one like this?"

"Yes, Jordan, I like that gun a lot."

"Brett, that cop was me. We were at the Wyandotte pistol range together."

"It was you? One of the Mexican cops named Carlos Garcia was there too."

Jordan then said to John, "It's him. No doubt about it."

They took me home. Jordan said, "I will stay in touch."

While I was living in Taylor, I continued to attend Eastern so that I could keep my job at Dearborn Packing Company, which would enable me to save some money for Christmas and for car maintenance, as it was a good-paying job. I wanted to attend classes at Eastern long enough to make it through the end of the semester, which would be in seven weeks.

I had called Katelyn a number of times asking her to go out with me. I decided I would give her one final test by telling her that I would wait for her in the main hallway if she felt like talking to me at school, figuring she must have known what I looked like by then. When I saw her coming down the main hall, my heart began to beat really fast. No girl had that kind of effect on me. She stopped to talk to some other girls not more than five feet away from me. She didn't say a word to me all the time she was there. I was crushed. I figured I'd do that one more time the next day. If she did not say anything to me then, I would no longer waste my time chasing her. The next day came, and it was a repeat of the previous day. Katelyn had once told me during our conversations that she was looking for a man who would make her financially comfortable. I'd thought, *Gee, Kate, I am not looking to get married. I just want to go have a romantic dinner and get laid.* After two days of her not talking to me at school, I decided to call Katelyn one last time to give her the courtesy of letting her know what I'd decided. I called her up and said to her, "Kate, I am soon going to leave Eastern. I am sorry to say, I won't be able to walk down the hall and watch you with that sexy stride of yours. I will be moving to Taylor, so I won't be calling anymore. Maybe sometime after high school we can get together for a date."

She said, "Okay," kind of weakly. I got the feeling that she was going to miss our phone conversations.

When I hung up, I felt like I had been kicked in the stomach. All that I could think of was that she wanted a man who could make her financially comfortable. I would have liked to be that man. I was willing to work to become that man, but at present, I was not succeeding with that goal. Beautiful and well-built, she deserved a man who could take good care of her.

With just under seven weeks to go until the end of the semester, I got called to the main office. Mr. Barton, the school assistant principle, said, "Brett, you have to leave Eastern."

I said to him, "I don't understand why I have to leave."

"Your sister, Danessa, asked that her records be transferred to Paul Revere High School in the Taylor school district. You have to attend school there."

I had been prepared for a situation like this, so I told him, "Well, I am seventeen years old. I live with my uncle Rollie."

"That does not matter. You have to go to the school where your parents pay taxes. If you don't leave, I am going to get a court order to bar you from the school. If you fight me, I will tie you up in court so long that you will never graduate."

I wanted to fight. I knew I could win as long as my uncle Rollie said I lived with him. I also knew my cheap-ass father would not pay for a lawyer. So it was off to Revere High School, but first I had to earn some extra money. I worked two weeks at my co-op job before reporting to Revere High School. I had the job at Dearborn packing company because I had worked morning co-op at Eastern, and Revere had afternoon co-op, so with the school change, I would be losing my packing job and have to find another one.

When I finally did enroll in my classes and begin school at Revere, I discovered that the kids there were all nice and pleasant. One guy in particular in my electronics class was very nice. He had approached me to make sure I was well settled in, which made me feel welcome. He was a handsome young man and very friendly. I was sure he had no problems getting dates. His name was Rodney Shorter; his parents had also originated from Kentucky. I am sure that is why we felt comfortable with one another and why we had become friends so quickly. In a later class, he invited me to his house, saying it was relatively easy to find. I took him up on his offer to drop by. It was Rodney who had raised my interest in motorcycles. I had never had anything like a motorcycle, not a go-cart or anything else motorized. He had a bike, and so did his older brother, Steve. Rodney asked for Steve's permission so I could use his bike and we could go trail riding in the woods near his house. Steve said yes. I got a quick lesson on how to ride, and then we were off to the woods near Rodney's house. I was hooked and really enjoyed riding.

I had settled in to school quite nicely and was beginning to make some good friends. However, I was unprepared for what was about to happen. One night I awoke out of a sound sleep. I did not feel right and could not see properly, which meant that I had been drugged. My vision was all blurry. I could not figure out what was going on. I could sense that someone was in the house, but I could not see who it was. When my vision cleared, I saw it was Carlos. After handing me a .22 semiautomatic pistol, he said, "I want you to kill the paperboy. He wants to hurt your mother, Brett. When he starts to walk up to the front lawn, I want you to shoot him. Now, go kill him."

I walked down the hall from my bedroom, turning to confirm who was there and who was with him. It was my dad and Carlos. I walked outside, stuck the gun in the paperboy's face, and asked him, "Why do you want to hurt my mom?"

He kept saying over and over, "Brett, its John!"

Finally my head began to clear. I now could see that it was John.

"John, they are trying to make me kill you." Not wanting to let the same thing happen to John that had happened to Joe Pepitone when Simms shot him, I fired the .22 into the ground so as to waste the shot. Since you only get one shot, no one else could shoot John. In less than five minutes, Jordan Bowman arrived at my house.

"What was the trouble here, Brett?" Jordan asked me.

"Jordan, you had better watch out. One of those Mexican cops was here. He drugged the piss out of me while I was sleeping. No matter what they tell you, you should know that they are trying to hurt your family. They wanted me to shoot John so it would look like it's me who wants to hurt your family."

"Why do they want to hurt me?" Jordan asked.

575

"They are a bunch of real nutcases. I believe they are doing it because you are guarding my mom and me. If they drug me and get me to hurt you or your family, then I will be nothing more than a lowlife junkie to you, at which point you'll stop protecting us. Then, once we don't have any protection, they can do anything they want to us because the police don't care what happens to a junkie."

"What was the reason you fired your gun?"

"When I realized it was John, I wasted the shot so no one else could shoot him. Jordan, I would never hurt John. He is one of my very best friends. I would never hurt him."

"Okay, Brett, we will see what they pull next. And thanks for the heads-up."

Finally I was acquainted with a good honest cop who knew me and my grandfather, and what type of people we were. I had hoped that this would be Team Garcia's final attempt to kill me or to put me in jail. Unfortunately, it wasn't.

The following event is kind of sketchy in my memory on account of the technique that Team Garcia was now using. It was late in the night, and very dark, a few days after the incident with John. I was taken somewhere in my neighborhood, blinded by a Team Garcia member, and marched up to a door. Whichever team member it was opened the door, pushing me through the doorway and into the house. I heard somebody say, "It's Brett, Dad."

It sounded like Jimmy, Jordan's eldest son, whom I had a few classes with. I immediately said, "Yes, Jimmy, it's Brett. Don't shoot me, Jimmy. The cop has completely blinded me."

Neither Jordan nor Jimmy shot me. Jordan took me home. I never found out which Team Garcia member had done that to me. On the way to my home, Jordan asked, "What do you think the purpose was for them to do that to you, Brett?"

"I think that they set me up to look like I was breaking into your house. And you or someone who lives with you was supposed to shoot me, Jordan."

"Why do you think they are doing all these things to you?" Jordan asked.

"Jordan, they have murdered hundreds of people. I know how they committed those murders and how they got away with them. I am the lone witness to all those murders. They want to kill me to cover up what they did. They also may or may not be CIA, or the Secret Service. Those badges have a lot of credence to a local police force. If they say you are a junkie, then you are a junkie. If they say you are cop killer, then you are a cop killer. That means they can tell a local cop anything they want and the cop is going to believe them. If I had to shoot the whole team for each lie the team told, I would need a complete arsenal."

"How many are there, Brett?"

"I am not sure, but I know of at least six. There was Carlos's nephew

Rico, but he ended up dead. That might be another reason they are trying to kill me."

"I can see I am going to have to keep better tabs on you, Brett."

"Thanks, Jordan."

It was two days later when the Dearborn police called me. "Brett, we need help. Carlos is on a rampage."

I was absolutely fuming that they'd had the balls to call me for help.

"I love you guys, but you arranged gunfights with me and Rico, and you tried to get me to die. You kicked me out of school. The mayor himself came to my house and told us he wanted us to move, and now you want me to help you? I could give two shits about your city. If you want my help, then I will need you to give me twenty-five thousand dollars. If you do that, then I will solve your problem."

"Brett, we can't afford your fee."

"I am an adult now and I no longer can work for free so if you want me to do a job for you are going to have to pay me to work. Well, you get paid, but you don't want to pay me for risking my life." I had assumed that the person on the line was a Dearborn police officer seeking my help. He hung up abruptly when I said I wanted to get paid. I then went back to what I was doing before they'd called.

As I knew they would, the Dearborn police called me back three days later.

"Brett, we are begging you, we need your help badly. Please come and help us."

"I need the money to track what Carlos is doing and where he is going. I surely don't have any money, so the one thing you can do is take away his gun and his badge. Team Garcia can't do what they do without guns and badges. So take their guns and their badges away. The last thing Carlos and his team of maniacs want to do is to go to court and testify."

"Thanks, Brett. We owe you one."

Chapter 70

COUNTDOWN TO GRADUATION

It was December. I had been at Revere High for seven weeks. It was time for the second marking period, and soon it would be time for Christmas vacation. Unbeknownst to me, Taylor schools had an absenteeism policy that allowed twenty absences per semester. If a student was absent more than twenty times, then he or she automatically failed. I was surprised when I got my report card to see that I had failed two classes, one of which, naturally, was English. I said to my English teacher, "I don't understand why I failed your class."

"Mr. Lawson, you missed over fifteen days of classes."

"Well, that is definitely less than twenty," I said.

"Well, you may be able to miss twenty days in another teacher's class, one who is more lenient, but if you miss ten days in my class, you automatically fail."

I checked with the teacher of the other class I'd failed, Mr. Garner, and I got the same exact reply. I had not made a good of a start at Revere, although I knew I was a better student than my grades indicated. The teachers did not know that I had to battle for my life and study all at the same time.

Over Christmas vacation, the man named Reggie Tierney who had given me rides to and from Eastern in Dearborn had bought his girlfriend, Maureen, a riding horse, which he kept stabled at a place called Tripps Riding School in Novi. He invited me to go with them one day, saying that they would teach me how to ride. We traveled in my car to the farm. They saddled the horse, whose name was Misty. Maureen rode the horse for about half an hour. She wanted me to get on the horse and try to ride it. I got up on the horse, but she would not budge. The horse would only let Maureen ride her. I finally gave up. Reggie said to me, "Brett, there are a lot of girls that come here. They always have a big Christmas party every year. Would you like to go to the party and meet some of the girls?"

"Yeah, sounds like a winner."

"Well, in that case, I have to take you inside and introduce you to Roxanne. They check everyone out before they let anyone stay on the farm for any length of time."

He took me inside. Roxanne checked me out asked me a few questions, and then gave me the approval to come to the party, which was the weekend before Christmas. We walked outside. There were some girls there whom Reggie knew, so he introduced me to them. One of them was Donna Pacer, who seemed to take an instant liking to me. She appeared to be around the age of fifteen, and blonde.

She struck up a conversation with me, saying, "I like your car. It's very pretty. What model is that?"

"It's a '69 Chevelle Malibu," I answered. Since Dad had bought a new Maverick, I was fortunate enough to drive the Malibu.

One of the other girls was a Cassandra Aaron, and the third one was Sadie Sykes, who was a rotund little young woman who did not say much of anything to me. She just watched.

Donna asked, "Will you be coming to the Christmas party next weekend, Brett?"

"Yes. All three of us will be coming to the party unless something comes up."

"We will see you at the party, then."

They left us. With our riding was finished, we packed up to go. Then we headed home.

The following week was the party. After I picked up Maureen and Reggie, we headed to Novi. After arriving, we went inside and down to the basement which was very large. There were four picnic tables and coolers full of beer and soft drinks. The room was full, the girls outnumbering the guys, and there was plenty of booze and beer. I hadn't drunk a lot before this party. Maybe occasionally I'd had a beer, which, most of the time, I drank only about half. After about an hour, Maureen asked me, "Brett, do you want a mixed drink?"

Never having had a mixed drink before, I asked, "What are you drinking, Maureen, and what does it taste like?"

"It is a 7&7," she answered.

"What's in it?" I asked.

"Whiskey and 7-Up, and you don't have to drink it if you don't like it," she answered.

She brought me my drink. I tasted it. It was delicious. I went through my drink relatively fast. Maureen quickly brought me another one. It was not long before I started to feel the effects of the alcohol. I had begun making out with one of the girls, a blonde who was fairly well-built. I was making out with her in a pornographic manner, with dry-humping and the works. Suddenly, I felt someone twisting the skin on my back. I looked to see who was doing that to me. It was Roxanne, the owner of the farm. She started lowering the boom on me.

In a very loud voice, she said, "Get off her. She is fourteen years old."

I immediately did as she asked. Then I sat on top of a picnic table next to a guy drinking beer. He looked over to me and asked, "What are you drinking?"

"I am drinking 7&7," I answered. He was a fairly handsome guy. I could tell he was a friendly sort by the way he smiled as he was talking to me. He was probably a fun guy to be around, I thought.

"That explains everything. Here, do you want to have a beer?" he said, handing me a beer.

"I think I have had too much to drink, and besides, I heard you are not supposed to mix your beer and whiskey."

"No, it's that you don't mix wine and any other alcohol. My name is Garrett Mahony."

"My name is Brett, Garrett. I am very pleased to meet you. Your name sounds Irish. Are you Irish?"

"I am half Irish, half Indian, Brett."

One of the girls I had met the week before, Cassandra Aaron handed me a small bottle of champagne and wished me a merry Christmas. I seemed to be leveling off from my alcohol high when Cassandra came up to me about twenty minutes later. She asked, "Aren't you going to drink my champagne?"

"I will drink it right now. We will drink a toast to you and me." I made a toast to Garrett, and I drank the champagne straight down. There was only a cup and a half in the bottle. Cassandra hugged me and then left the party.

It was not ten minutes later when I got an awful taste in my mouth. My throat, all the down to my gut, felt like it was on fire. I ran upstairs, went outside, and began puking my guts out. I simply could not stop. I had been doing well until drinking that champagne, so that must have been what triggered the vomiting. That night I swore off whiskey because it seemed to sneak up on me. I had a nasty hangover the next day. I dedicated that I would stick with beer or another type of alcohol, like gin or vodka.

With Maureen owning a horse and paying boarding fees, she wanted to get as much riding in as she could, at least one day each weekend. It had become a regular activity to go to Tripps. On one of the visits to Tripps, I met one of Sadie's friends, Carrie Sharp. She should have been named "Slurp," because she looked delicious. Tall, at about 5'8", with long, dark, silky, wavy brown hair, she was absolutely voluptuous. The only thing that kept her from being a perfect ten was that she had a little gap between her upper two front teeth, which to me was not a deterrent. Her most alluring quality was her sense of humor. She liked having fun and telling jokes; she had an all-around bubbly personality. She was definitely the type of woman one marries and has kids with. I had set my sights on her and wanted to date her in the worst way, but I would bide my time to see where I stood with her.

In the coming weeks, I would get to know a lot of the owners who boarded horses. I would even be invited to their homes to meet their families. Garrett lived in Farmington Hills, a ritzy city. He invited me to his house for a couple of beers. His sister, Eva, happened to be home. She was absolutely gorgeous. Stunning, she had all the features of a cover girl. I thought. *I wish I had found my way out to the affluent neighborhoods, because it is becoming evident to me that the best-looking women are here, probably because their husbands have a lot of money and go for beauty, although a lot of pretty women are also intelligent.* I felt that I had spent too much time in the South End with all those brunettes. After Garrett had introduced me to his sister, in came his mother.

"Brett, this is my mother, Felicity."

"I am pleased to meet you, Mrs. Mahony. I can see where Eva gets her extraordinary good looks. I thought she was your sister."

"Brett, I can tell that with a line of bullshit like that, you are a real charmer. In this family, flattery will get you everywhere, especially with me. So from now on, just call me Felly."

"I will do as you ask, Felly." *Bullshit* seemed a harsh word coming from the mouth of a woman as pretty as Felly, but it seemed to bring her more down to earth, making her appear not at all stuffy.

I had not yet met Garrett's dad, so I said to him, "I do not see your dad, Garrett."

"He works two jobs. He works at the railroad so he can get a pension, and he owns an insurance agency."

"Wow! That must be taxing on him!"

"My mom and Eva both work at the agency to take some of the pressure off him. I work there at night, cleaning up the office in exchange for gas money. Let's go. I want to introduce you to another friend. We'll get a pizza while we are there."

Garrett lived on 9 Mile and Inkster. We headed toward 9 Mile and Telegraph Road. Across Telegraph, there was pizzeria called Papa Gino's. We got out of the car, went inside, and were greeted by a blond guy about our age. He came up to the counter. Garrett introduced me to him.

"Brett, this is Jamie Walters."

We exchanged pleasantries. Then Jamie asked Garrett, "What do you need, Garrett?"

"You got anything special, Jamie?"

"I got an extra-large pizza that was a phony address. I will let you have it for three bucks, or a six-pack of sixteen-ounce Buds.

We jumped into Garret's car and drove to the nearest party store, grabbed a six-pack, and headed back to the pizzeria. We gave Jamie the six-pack of beer, grabbed the pizza, and headed back to Garrett's.

My circle of friends was growing. Between the girls at Tripps, Garrett, and his friends, I had made quite a few new friends.

One weekend, I headed to Tripps. Donna Pacer started a conversation with me. She asked, "Brett, have you ever had a steady girlfriend?"

"Yes. Her name was Laura."

"Did you give her a ring or a pin?"

"A ring that had a black-and-white split pearl."

"Are you coming back tomorrow?"

"Yes, I will be back tomorrow."

"Why don't you bring the ring? I would like to see how pretty it is."

"Okay, I will do that." I went inside to have a few beers with the other people. I left shortly after that and headed to Farmington Hills to visit with Garrett for a while. We sat around and watched an old western starring Errol Flynn. After the movie was over, I headed for home.

The next afternoon, I grabbed Laura's ring and headed to Tripps. When I got there, Donna was waiting for me. I had just barely finished parking my car when she opened the door and sat down in the passenger seat. Anxiously she asked, "Did you bring the ring?"

"Yes, I brought it. Would you like to see it?" I pulled out the ring and held it out for her to see.

She asked, "Can I try it on?"

"No," I said.

The next event caught me totally off guard. She grabbed the ring and put it on her finger.

"Give me back the ring, Donna."

"No, you gave it to me."

She opened the door of the car and began running around the barnyard yelling, "I am going steady! He asked me to go steady. He gave me a ring. He thinks I am pretty. He picked me over all of you."

I waved to everyone, trying to let them know that Donna was lying, but it was to no avail. I walked up to her and asked politely, "Donna, please give me back the ring." I noticed that she was crying. That is when I figured out that this girl was delusional. She needed to know that she was pretty and that she was loved. I did not know what to do, but I knew I did not want to psychologically screw her up, so I decided to let her think what she wanted to think. In the meantime, I would date who I wanted without her knowledge. I knew I was not going steady. Maybe, over time, Donna would get better. There was only one problem with that plan, though: none of the other girls at the stables wanted anything more to do with me. I asked the one girl who knew most of the goings-on at the stables, the one whom I knew would have the answers I was looking for, Sadie, "How come none of the other girls will talk to me?"

"Brett, you are branded. You are Pacer's property now. No one wants anything to do with her or the man she is dating."

"I understand now." The situation I was in meant that I could no longer expect any loving from the girls at Tripps, so I would have to start looking for dates nearer to home.

Chapter 71

ESCAPE FROM ORCHARD LAKE

It was mid-January when I met Garrett and Eva at Tripps. We were to pick up Damon Pacer, Donna's brother, and Denny Morris, one of the stable hands. Both of them worked there driving the tractor and the wagons for all the hayrides. We were just cruising around and drinking beers when Denny suddenly came up with an idea to pull a B&E and steal some office equipment. I was not interested, but I did drive them to the location they intended to rob. I parked down the road, out of sight of the main highway. Garrett and Damon left to go into the building with no hesitation at all. They came back with an adding machine, which was worth about five hundred dollars.

Garrett had wanted some tools for his father's repair garage, so next we went to another one of Denny's targets, the Orchard Lake Country Club, which was located, naturally, in Orchard Lake. I pulled up to the country club maintenance building and dropped off Garrett, Denny, and Damon. Eva and I went down the road and, after a short period, started making out. Garrett came back after about half an hour. He said, "Brett, I can't get them out of the building. You want to see if you can get them out so we can leave?"

"Oh no, I am not stealing any tools for you guys. If I want tools, I will buy my own. If you can't get them out of there, I am going to leave those thieves behind. You'd better go and get them out."

"Brett, whatever you do, please don't go home without them. Please, for me? They could freeze to death, being drunk and all that," Eva said.

Garrett soon came back and said, "Brett, you are going to have to try and get them out of there. The cops are going to bust us if we don't leave."

"Brett, why don't you go down there and try to get them out? Do it for me! I want to get out of here too," Eva said.

Eva was smart and beautiful, which was a combination that really turned me on. I would have gone to hell and back if she asked. I did not want her or me getting caught stealing. I was reluctant to go to the maintenance garage, but she had asked me to, so I headed down there and tried to get those two idiots out. They were stuck on the idea of staying in the building. I decided to turn the lights on. The first thing a cop will do is illuminate the area so he can see the full scope of what is going on. I'd hope that with the lights on, Damon and Denny would leave. Damon immediately turned them off. I again turned the lights on, and Damon turned them off. About five minutes later, I saw the strobes of a police car. Denny, was running out of building with a large toolbox, said, "Cops."

How the hell he had picked up that toolbox, I didn't know. It had to weigh between two hundred and fifty and three hundred pounds. In the meantime, my instincts kicked in. Given my mistrust of police, I started running toward the woods that bordered the golf course. All of sudden, I heard a gunshot. I turned and saw the gun smoke rising. Denny had fallen down. He tried to get up two or three times. I thought that maybe he had been shot. Since shots were fired, it would now mean that this crime was now a felony. I ran up the hill and lay down in a driveway at the end of the row of beach houses that lined the shore of the lake. Soon after that, a police car came down the road and pulled into a driveway about five doors down. The officer went inside for a few minutes, came back out, got back into his car, and left. I could not believe the cop hadn't seen me. When the cop left, I got up and walked down toward the homes on the beach side. Suddenly, two cop cars and about four cops were on the opposite side of the lake, about two hundred yards away. I covered my head with both arms, with my hands clasped together behind my head. If I got shot, the coroner would know that my hands had been in a defensive position, because the cops would have to shoot through my hands. With my head buried in the sand, I heard glass breaking and footsteps coming toward me. The person who had come out of the house asked me, "What did you do, kid?"

I told him the gist of the story, and then I said, "I think they may have shot my friend. Don't back up the other cops, because we were unarmed."

He then told me, "Stay on the snow and they won't shoot you."

"Why is that?"

593

"It means your blood is as pure as the driven snow."

I did not understand his answer about the snow, but I did discern from his words that he was a cop. I decided to stay on the snow. I began working my way around the banks of the lake to avoid going through the ice. Every time a cop car came by, I hit the deck. Each time I did so, I got snow on the front of my jacket because the ice was covered with snow. I did that several times until I had reached the road that ran by the lake. My core temperature had dropped severely. I was wet from the snow. I was beginning to tremble. If I did not get warm soon, I would suffer the effects of hypothermia. I found an apartment building that had a lobby with heat coming out of ducts. I stripped down to my underwear so as to partially dry my clothes and feel the heat. I stayed there for about forty-five minutes until I had warmed up a bit. I decided, since it was approaching midnight that I would hitch a ride to Garrett's house to get my car. I would have to avoid any cop cars. If I knew one thing about cop cars, it was that all their lights always worked. I waited until I saw a car with a malfunctioning light. Finally, my luck was changing. It was a 1962 Fairlane with a burnt-out right headlamp.

I knew it was a Fairlane because my uncle Rollie had one. Plus, I had become kind of expert at recognizing cars by their front ends from working at the car wash.

It was almost Midnight and the driver asked what I was doing out this late and especially in the middle of winter. I fed him a line of bullshit in reply. Feeling sorry for me, he offered to drive me to Garrett's house. I quickly accepted. He turned the heat in his car up to full blast because he could see me shivering. We eventually reached Garrett's house, and it was now after midnight when we arrived. I rang the doorbell, hoping someone would answer so I could get my keys. Garrett answered the door and told me not to call for a few days. He could not talk because I had pissed his father off when his father was trying to get romantic with his wife.

I jumped in my car, turned the heater up as far as it would go, and headed home. Once I made it home safely, I continued as if nothing had happened.

Chapter 72

JUDGE ELIZABETH GIFFORD

It was a week later when Garrett called and asked me, "Where do you work?"

"I work at small independent body shop that specializes in working solely on Corvettes." I worked there along with Reggie Tierney. I knew why Garrett had called. He was going to turn me in to the cops in exchange for a lighter sentence for himself. It did not bother me, as all I had done was drive the car and try to get those two idiots Denny and Damon out of the building.

To my surprise, the Roseville cops came to the shop and said to the secretary, "We're Roseville police. We have a warrant for Brett Lawson."

I happened to be standing in the office. I said, "That would be me, guys. Just call me Brett."

"Brett, do we need the cuffs?" one of the cops asked.

"No. Where am I going to run to?" I responded.

They transported me to the Roseville jail, where they booked me and fingerprinted me. After that was done, it was seven in the evening. They sent out for a burger and a Coke for me. Soon afterward, a detective from Orchard Lake and his driver picked me up from Roseville. They drove me to the Oakland County Jail, where I was rebooked there. A guard took me to a cell where the toilet did not work. It was full of human waste that must have been there for a month. Then they brought Denny down to my cell. He was walking without bending his right leg. For some reason, Denny was keeping the fact that he had gotten shot a secret. I knew that he had been shot, and that this was going to be a real mess.

Denny asked me, "Brett do you have any money? I am going to be here a while. I could use all you can give me."

I reached into my pocket, pulled out all the money I had, and gave it to him—eight dollars and change.

"Brett, whatever you do, don't go upstairs voluntarily. If you go upstairs, you will have to fight all night long. And you are too small for that."

Shortly after that, the sheriffs came and took Denny back to wherever they had been keeping him. I was stuck with another inmate in the cell. It stunk like an outhouse all night.

At about 8:30 a.m., the Oakland County sheriffs took me to the courtroom of Judge Elizabeth L. Gifford. I was then allowed to talk to my parents. As I approached them, I saw that my father was extremely upset. He said, "Brett, no one in our family has ever done anything like this."

When my father said that, I thought of both of my grandfathers, and all my uncles and aunts. None of them had done anything as stupid as I had.

Tom, Garrett's father, was standing nearby. I was sure he had overheard my father.

When it was my turn for arraignment, I went in front of the judge.

She asked me, "Mr. Lawson, do have a job?"

"Yes, Your Honor, I have a job."

"So you have transportation to the job and to the court? What mode of transportation do you have?"

"I have a car, Your Honor."

"Do you have a balance on your car, Mr. Lawson?"

"No, Your Honor, my parents paid cash for my car."

"Mr. Lawson, I am going to release you with one thousand dollars' personal bond." I got my next court date. The next step was to hire an attorney.

When we got home, Dad started making the phone calls to find an attorney. He found one cheap enough to his liking. His name was Monte Ahearn. When we arrived at Monte's office, I saw that it was a bit cluttered. The man himself reminded me of the actor who played Oz in *The Wizard of Oz*. He did not appear to be a rich lawyer, but he seemed to know the law well. Dad hired him. There was plenty of time before my next court appearance.

While I was awaiting my next court appearance, Garrett asked me to come by his house. I drove out to his house. We sat around watching TV for a while. Later he asked me, "Brett, do you want to meet one of my friends I go to school with?"

"Sure. Let's go."

Garrett instructed me to drive down to Farmington Road and over to his friend's house. We got out of the car. Garrett's friend was waiting for us with a beer in his hand. Garrett said, "Brett, this is Richmond Pymentola, but everyone calls him Richie."

Richie extended his hand. I reached out to shake it. The first impression I had of Richie was that both he and Garrett were heavy beer drinkers. Garrett and I had a short conversation, and then we headed back to Garrett's house. When I pulled up in front of Garrett's house, he started going through the glove compartment and reading some of the papers.

Garrett said, "Aha! Now I got you!" He grabbed some of the paperwork and went into his house.

The time for the next court date had arrived. Garrett and I each had a lawyer, and we each had our turn with the prosecuting attorney. When it was my turn, my lawyer came back with an offer of two years in state prison. It was my first offense. I started listening to find out what deal Garrett was going to get. I heard Garrett say to one of the prosecutors, "I got him for you. He has done this before." Then he pointed to me. "He lied to the judge too."

At this point, Garrett was desperate to get his case dismissed. Apparently he would do so at my expense.

I blew up! I had heard enough from that jackass. I walked over to Garrett, who was sitting just outside the courtroom in the anteroom, and said, "That's right, Garrett, tell him everything you and your buddies did. Let Brett take all the blame. Then when it's my turn, I am going to tell everything and make *you* do two years in state prison! Do you know what they call it when you talk to the cops? They call it sucking the cops off. In return, the cons make you suck them off. You are squealer, so you'll be sucking off the convicts until you fall over in exhaustion." I walked over to where Tom and Felly were standing and began to tell them just what had happened from my point of view.

"Tom, you are a good man. You work two jobs so your family can have nice things. All this is happening because your son wanted to steal tools for your garage. All I did was drive the car. And then I went down and tried to get those assholes out of that building. Then, because Garrett would not leave *them* behind, he left *me* behind and took off with my car! I almost froze to death getting back home. I know you did not teach him this, but he committed a crime. Now he wants me to pay for it! Tom, your son is a sissy. If he doesn't stop blaming me, I'll see to it he goes to prison."

It was right after that conversation that I told the prosecutor, "I want to see the judge." He went back to her chambers. Emerging a few minutes later, he led me to the judge's chambers. She was sitting in front of her desk and did not have her robe on, which meant that the conversation would be off the record.

"Mr. Lawson, I will let you have your say, but I have some questions I'd like to ask you first. Do you mind answering my questions?"

I said, "No, I don't mind at all, Your Honor."

"The first thing I would like to know is, did one of the people who were with you run out of the building carrying a toolbox?"

"Yes Your Honor. That would be Denny."

"How big would you say that the toolbox was?"

"I would say about three feet long by thirty inches high by thirty inches deep, Your Honor."

"How much would you estimate that toolbox weighed?"

"Your Honor, that toolbox is probably a Snap-On, which are high-quality toolboxes. I would say that full of tools, it had to weigh at least two hundred pounds."

"Would you be able to carry one with one hand?"

"No. Not a toolbox the size of that one, Your Honor. This was no toolbox like you carry around your house. Mechanics make their living with their tools, so they have high-quality tools and high-quality toolboxes."

"Mr. Lawson, how do you know so much about tools?"

"Your Honor, I work in a garage. The first thing you learn when working in a garage is to respect a mechanic's tools, because that is how he feeds his family. You don't even ask to borrow his tools."

"Now I would like to hear why you don't think the court is being fair to you."

"Thank you, Your Honor, for hearing me out. First off, I wanted no part of stealing someone's tools, Your Honor. I drive thirty-five miles one way to earn thirty dollars a week. It costs me ten dollars just for gas, and that's not counting the wear and tear on my car. The other kids involved in this crime are from Farmington Hills and Novi, which are much more affluent cities than the city I live in, which is a blue-collar city named Taylor. They are trying to portray me as a habitual criminal so they get a lighter sentence. All I did was go down to that maintenance building and turn on the lights because Damon and Denny were refusing to leave the building. Damon kept turning the lights off after I turned them on. What I was trying to do was to get them to leave. I am not a thief. I work to buy the things I want."

"Why would you turn on the lights?"

"Judge when police officers are investigating a crime, the first thing they do is to illuminate the area and have the suspects show their hands."

"Mr. Lawson, are you a narcotics officer?"

"Well, sort of, in a way, Your Honor, but remember that I am still in high school. My very best friend is the son of a Taylor policeman. And I have a lot of friends who are policemen. Your Honor, is it against protocol for you to call me Brett?"

"No, I will refer to you as Brett from now on. The police said you broke into an officer's house along the beach and stole a gun while attempting to flee from the scene. Is that true?"

"Someone has told you a monstrosity of a lie, Your Honor. I am very proficient with a gun and have guns at home. If I thought I was going to need a gun, I would have brought my own gun. The one thing that angers me more than anything else is a lying cop. Your Honor, I think by telling you that lie, they are saying to you, 'She's so easy, we can tell her anything and she will believe it.' Your Honor, I don't believe that is true, or else you would not have agreed to hear my side of the story in your chambers. They have insulted you by lying to you like that. If I were a judge, I would absolutely not put up with it."

"Now I am going to ask you for advice, Brett. What would you do if you were me?"

"First, I would pin them down in the lie they told, and issue a stern warning that they not tell another lie in your courtroom. If they do, the punishment should be termination of employment. Then I would call all parties together and quiz them about the report that said I broke into the officer's house."

"Do you think you will be able to prove they lied?"

"I would say yes with about 95 percent certainty, unless they lie again, which will get me sidetracked."

"Brett, I want you to wait outside the courtroom. I am going to get everyone together in my chambers."

An hour and a half later, we were all called into the judge's chambers—everyone but Damon and Denny. This included the cops, and the cop who owned Tripps. Garrett, Eva, Tom, Felly, and my dad were present.

The judge looked at me and said, "Brett, this is Officer Stone, the police officer who filed the report indicating that his house was broken into and the intruder stole a handgun. Do you want to question him concerning that report?"

"Yes, Your Honor, I do. Officer Stone, why don't you tell us what happened that night?"

"Well, I was sleeping when I heard what sounded like breaking glass. I noticed my gun was gone. I ran to the back door and saw someone lying down on the bank of the lake, at which point I called for backup."

"Well, weren't there a couple of squad cars across the lake with rifles with night scopes trained on the suspect?" I asked.

"That's right."

"Then why would you go outside when you have a suspect with a gun lying in your yard? You heard the glass break, but you did not hear him in your house, and yet you say he stole a gun?"

"It was just a kid. I did not want to shoot him."

"Did the glass hit something hard, which allowed you to hear it break?"

"Yes, I have patio blocks. It hit them to make the breaking noise."

"So the glass fell on the outside, then?"

"Yes."

"Did you step on any of the glass?"

"I may have stepped on some." All of a sudden Stone started to cry a river. He said, "He was just a kid. I couldn't find the heart to kill him."

"Your Honor, the glass that was broken would be on the inside if I was breaking in, not on the outside. When someone is breaking into a home, the force of the blow against the glass forces the glass to the inside of the home. When someone is exiting a home, the force drives the glass outside of the home.

"Your Honor, I believe that the reason the police falsified the report and said that I stole a gun from Officer Stone was to establish that I was armed, which would make them justified in shooting me. That would therefore constitute a conspiracy to commit murder."

I then heard Eva say, "Damn, Brett, you are really good." She could not have said sweeter words to me.

The judge said to me, "Mr. Lawson, I am dismissing any and all charges against you."

"Your, Honor, there is a widespread conspiracy against my family. It might be a good idea to keep a record of what has transpired here. I did go into the building to try to get my friends out, so I think the minimum charge would be a better idea."

"Mr. Lawson, I will not only do that—I will put a flag on your file."

"Thank you, Your Honor."

I was to appear in front of the judge one last time to formalize everything. While in the courtroom, the judge said, "Mr. Lawson, in a previous appearance in the court, you stated that your vehicle was paid for, but it has been brought to the court's attention that there was a contract made at the time of purchase, which is still ongoing. You lied before the court. Can you explain that to the court?"

"Yes, Your Honor. Your Honor, my vehicle is a 1969 Chevy. In 1969, I was sixteen years of age. Under Michigan law, any person under the age of eighteen cannot sign or enter into a contract, or even be asked to enter into a contract. I have no knowledge of any contracts made by my parents. My mother told me that she and my father had paid cash for my car. I had no knowledge of anything to the contrary. When I was confronted by Mr. Mahony, it was only then that I knew that my mother had lied. When I confronted my mother, she explained that she and my father did not want anyone to know their personal business, Your Honor."

"Did you give the contract to Mr. Mahony to examine?" the judge asked.

"No, Your Honor. He rifled through the glove box, found it, and refused to give it back when I asked for it."

"Mr. Lawson, you mean he took the contract belonging to your parents without their permission?"

"Yes, Your Honor."

"Mr. Lawson, that is a crime, and that, coupled with the other crimes he has committed, means he should do jail time. By saying you lied to the court, he has opened himself up to a slander suit in the eyes of the court. Since his parents also participated in the crime, they also are subject to a slander suit. The court will approve of your suit against them if you wish to bring it to the court. Would you like to bring forth a suit against the Mahonies, Mr. Lawson?"

"Not at this time, Your Honor. The Mahonies are very good parents, Your Honor. Suing them would only bring bitterness between us. I would much rather have them as friends than as enemies."

"Would you like to press charges against Mr. Mahony?" asked the judge.

"Your Honor, I don't think that would be beneficial to the public to give Garrett a jail sentence. The best thing for him would be to accept the fact he was wrong, and to quit trying to get out of trouble by blaming someone else. I think a stern lecture from the judge, with all her wisdom, would be most beneficial to him and society, along with ninety days' house arrest."

"You are excused, Mr. Lawson. The court will take your recommendations under advisement."

"Thank you, Your Honor."

I walked out of the courtroom and was met by Tom and Felly. Felly, with watery eyes, asked, "Brett, why didn't you file a suit against us like the judge recommended?"

"There are several reasons, Felly, but the main one is because of Tom. If Tom needs something, he goes out and works for it. He is even willing to work two jobs for it. I am the same way; I work for the things I want. I have enough enemies, some of whom are trying to kill me, and I don't need any more of them. I like to have as many friends as I can, and that includes Garrett. Another reason is that I would never hurt Eva by hurting the two people she loves most. Finally, your son has hurt you. Now, not only is he a thief, but also he has branded your daughter and me as thieves."

"Who are you, Brett?" Felly asked.

"I am your friend, Felly. I am the best friend you've ever had."

I walked away from this incident having learned something, which was that Team Garcia's sphere of influence now included Oakland County. They were willing to lie to judges in the hopes of having me convicted of something I did not do. They even set me up for what I call a shoot, which is what cops do when they stage a crime scene after they shoot you. That is what the police force in Orchard Lake tried to do.

Chapter 73

GRADUATION

I put the episode at Orchard Lake behind me. I never found out how the judge punished the cops, and quite frankly, I hope she threw the book at them.

I made one last trip to Tripps to pick Donna up. One of the stable hands, Marty, said to me, "Donna is only going out with you because you have a nice car."

I already knew that was part of the reason. Not caring if word got back to Donna and pissed her off, I retorted, "That's fine by me. I am only going out with her because she gives me sex. It works for me, and she's happy too, so you could say we are using each other." Since Donna had forced me into going steady with her, I did not want to hurt her, but I was looking forward to finding a new relationship. I was not plunging into the relationship with Donna, but the sex was good. Knowing that Marty drove a piece of junk, I had smarted off to him and tried to piss him off, as if to say, "If you drove a nice car, you could get laid too."

Around this time, a major change in my life happened. As I was on my way to work at the 'Vette shop, I went to make a left turn and was hit by two cars. My car was totaled. The cop who investigated the accident gave me a ticket for not yielding the right-of-way. He made that brilliant deduction because the drivers of the two other cars agreed that the light was yellow and not red. My insurance company hired an attorney for me to dispute what the other drivers had stated. The attorney got the ticket dismissed on account of the fact that the cop had not witnessed the accident and therefore could not testify as to what happened. My dad took the money from the insurance settlement and bought me a clunker, a 1963 Chevy Impala.

Shortly after that, I was banned from the Tripps property. I don't know what happened to Donna. She visited Tripps quite frequently. I think she went there purposely because I could not meet her there or go on the property. I am sure it was like Marty had told me: she didn't want to be with me because I no longer was driving a nice car. While the Impala was old, it was reliable. I consoled myself by hanging out with Garrett and Eva more often, and also with Carrie and Sadie. I had told myself that I was not going to let Donna force me into any kind of a permanent relationship. The relationship was on the rocks and I planned to end the relationship soon because I felt she was avoiding me. I was not letting my chance to have another relationship go by, even if it was only friendship.

One of the things that I enjoyed a great deal was hanging out in Hines Park. There was a section of Hines called Horseshoe Drive, where the section of the road going through the park formed a horseshoe. This part of the park was where all the teens gathered to enjoy some booze or herbal refreshment, and to have some interesting conversations. I kept my alcohol consumption to a minimum. Sex was often part of the agenda. When couples were ready to do so, they headed up one of the hills and into the woods. The cops usually left everyone alone. Carrie went there quite frequently. She was there so often that she picked up a nickname considered by the circle of partygoers to be a small honor. How the group determined the name, I had no idea. I always looked forward to going to the park. Every time I went there, I had a good time. Plus, I had hopes of someday going up the hill with Carrie.

I was back at Revere. It was nearing the end of April 1971, fewer than two months to graduation. I headed out of the school one day and started toward my car when I saw a member of Team Garcia wearing a Dearborn uniform and holding a rifle while coming toward me. It was obvious he was with Team Garcia because was not wearing a Taylor policeman's uniform. He was most likely there to get revenge on me for taking Rico down. He was trying to set me up to be shot. I was now questioning why Jordan Bowman would allow this to happen in Taylor. I felt alone in my quest to stop Team Garcia. That cop gave me an unloaded gun and took me to a ladder that led to the rooftop of the school. He ordered me to go up the ladder. I refused. When I did that, he grabbed his gun and said, "Get up that ladder now!" There were other cops standing behind me. I did not know for sure which department they were with, so I complied with his order. When I got to the roof, the cop gave me a twenty-two rifle ordered me to start firing at the cops who had pulled up on the grass on the north side of the school. The grassy area ran all the way from the school to Northline Road. I started to fire at the tires of the police cars. Once the tires were flat, the Taylor cops would know the rounds I was firing were live. After that, I stood up; I was at the end of my rope. I wanted that police officer dead. I was ready to die to get rid of that bonehead. I did not know who the Team Garcia member was who had forced me to the rooftop.

I saw the Team Garcia cop reaching for his glasses, as they had fallen off his face. I ran over to him and knocked his hat off so I could make a 100 percent positive identification. When the hat came off, I saw that he had a full head of hair, unlike Carlos. At that point I knew it was the cop I called Skinny Ray.

Skinny Ray normally had that hat on down just above his eyes. He usually wore a pair of black sunglasses. This made it hard to identify him with just his nose and chin exposed. After knocking off his hat, I tried to throw him headfirst off the roof, but I was not quite strong enough to do this. The Taylor cops then helped me climb down the ladder. When I got to the ground, the Taylor cops explained that Skinny Ray had tried to set me up, saying that Lieutenant Bowman had gotten wind of it.

I went home. The Mellus, the downriver newspaper, reported the next day that on the prior day, Wednesday, a gunman had been on the roof of Revere High School. *Wow,* I thought, *I have made the news.* But as I read it, the story said that someone else was the gunman. I found out later that the story was about the same incident I had been involved in, but the names had been changed to protect the innocent. In the English class I had with Jim Bowman, when he was having a conversation with some other students, I heard him say to them, "My dad knocked the shooter's glasses off at 110 yards with a 9 mm."

"How could you miss at that distance, Jimmy?" I asked.

"Brett, it was a 9 mm pistol!"

"How did they know that it was 110 yards?" I wondered.

"They measured the shot."

"Jimmy, I thought you were saying that your dad used a rifle. I would not even attempt that shot with a pistol."

"By the way, Brett, someone said it was you on that rooftop."

"You mean to tell me that the story in the newspaper and the story about that crooked cop are the same incident?"

"That's right, Brett," Jim replied.

"You know, Jim, I would not even try that shot if you cut the distance in half."

I think Jordan Bowman had sent Team Garcia the message that he was not going to be a party to any illegal activity in his city. I was now convinced that the Taylor police was a fine police force, and that Jordan Bowman was an extremely fine police officer and highly intelligent. For a brief moment I had felt abandoned, but Jordan came through in the end. I was sure that no police department, other than the ones the Garcias were working for, ran around pumping the citizens full of narcotics.

Undaunted, and confident of the Taylor police force's honesty and integrity, I continued with my schooling. I had long given up on the idea of being an engineer, although I still enjoyed the electronics classes. My friendships continued to grow. A young man named Rod Shorter would become one my most loyal friends. We partied together, but I never told him all the good things I had done in life, only so I did not endanger his life as well as mine. I was determined to graduate, as that was the one thing Dad loved about me: my passion for an education. I was not going to let anyone stop me from graduating.

Graduation Day finally arrived in early June. While I did not graduate with honors, I was lucky enough to graduate at all, given the many obstacles I'd had to overcome. I felt that I had exposed Team Garcia and their tactics to Jordan, who was now aware of their actions. This left me with a feeling of security. I felt that my mom would be safe if I had to be away from her for any length of time, because Jordan would be checking on her from time to time.

I told my father, "Dad, I want to go to Los Angeles and look up my friend Steven. Maybe he can still get me in the movies."

"You want to be in the movies? You are not a movie star! Nobody is going

to want to see you, let alone pay to see you. Your best bet is to go get a job."
I think he was angry because I had no plans to go to college at that time.

Previously I had asked him for some of the dog money so I could go to
college. His response was, "I will help you get a loan."

It really pissed me off that he would not give me some of my own money
for school. I took a temporary job at the Detroit Racecourse, a local racetrack.
My job title was hot walker. I fell in love with the job immediately. It did not
pay very well, but it was a lot of fun, and fun had been a rarity in my life. I
had been going to the racetrack since I was ten years old. I just loved horses. It
gave me the idea that maybe someday I would own a thoroughbred horse farm
and breed Thoroughbred racehorses, as there was good money to be made in
breeding. The bad news was that I picked up the disgusting habit of smoking.
The job would be short-lived because the man who owned all the racehorses
that we raced turned to breeding in place of racing. I would now have to go
to LA or get another job. Without my parents supporting me while I was in
LA, it looked like I was going to have to enter the workforce as an unskilled
laborer. But I felt I was destined for greater things.

Mine and Donna's relationship had been on the rocks for a while now
and I waited till I caught her doing something that I would not feel guilty for
leaving her. Donna had taken a job at a nearby hamburger joint. It was much
like any other slider joint, with the same type of burger. I would occasionally
go there for lunch and to see Donna. I noticed one day when I was at this
restaurant that she was not wearing her ring. She had pulled it out of her

pocket. On another day when I went there to have lunch, I noticed that again she was not wearing her ring. She went into the back, soon returning to the front counter with the ring on her finger. A lot of things flashed through my mind. She obviously wanted to play games with me. Marty, the stable hand had been right about how shallow Donna was. I was now driving a 1963 Chevy, which was just an old clunker. I guess it was essential to Donna that her boyfriend has a nice car so as to elevate her social status. I was not in the mood to play mind games with an immature sixteen-year-old bitch. The sex was not that great enough to put up with the grief that came along with it. She was not that pretty, and she was whoring around. She had roped me in to this relationship right from the beginning. Plus, she had her faults. She was so flat-chested that she would be a prime candidate for a tattoo on her chest reading, This Side Up. It was now time for me to bow out of the relationship.

I had been looking for an excuse to blow her off. I said to her, "Donna, I want my ring back." It wasn't that it was valuable, but it did have sentimental value to me.

"What's the matter, Brett?"

"I am all done with you, Donna. I want my ring back. Don't make a scene. I just want to end this now." She then gave me the ring back. I walked out of the restaurant feeling free again. For the previous couple of months, Donna had made feel like a lowlife and a real dummy. Also, I felt that I did not have enough money for her. None of that had bothered me. What did bother me was that she had begged me to wear my ring and then treated me the way she did.

However, I felt my ego lift because now I was free to party with some of the girls I had eyes for, such as Carrie and Eva. We would party together at a little nightclub called Lucky's, which was on 10 Mile near Grand River. The club must have had a sign somewhere that read, "All hot babes must come here." We would go there often, Garrett, Carrie, Sadie, and I. The other watering hole we frequented was the Riverbank Lounge on Grand River, which was located in Redford Township. We passed many a night at those two places, having a lot of fun, doing a lot of dancing, and sharing a lot of laughs. I did not try to pick up any girls. I usually only danced with the girls who had come with us to the club. I did not want to offend some girl I had never seen with my bad teeth and bad breath.

It was when I thought of my teeth that my hatred for what my father had done to me became almost unbearable. It was almost as if he were saying, "You are never going to get a good woman without getting your teeth fixed, and I am not giving you the money to have them fixed." Getting my teeth fixed was now my topmost priority. But I didn't know how I was going to afford it, as my job at the racetrack had ended, and I had no chance of hooking up with Spielberg anytime soon—or even at all, since I did not have enough money for a lengthy stay in LA. I would keep a vigil and hope that I could at least talk to him one more time.

Three years later, in 1974, I got married. I found a really sharp dentist who did work that was virtually painless. I had gotten my teeth fixed. Suddenly I could smile with confidence. Having worked, I'd saved over two thousand dollars for all the dental work. I didn't ask my father for any money. I paid for all the work myself. After my divorce in 1981, I got involved in the nightclub scene again. To avoid catching any sexually transmitted diseases, I usually dated women who were friends of friends. I was doing what I wanted, I had a nice smile, I was single, and I had a pocket full of money to party with. And party I did!

Chapter 74

MOM AND DAD'S RETIREMENT

My father retired in 1987.

My grandfather had worked over forty years in the cold, wet, dark nastiness of the coal mines. When he had time, he preached the Gospel, consoled families of the bereaved, and said a few words over the deceased. One of his favorite pastimes was working in his garden so he could have fresh vegetables at dinnertime. Maria and Dad stole the money he had earned from the dogs. Isn't that pathetic, stealing from a preacher? I am not going to mention the names they deserve to be called, but I do want everyone who uses those dogs to know who perfected the technique used to train the first drug-sniffing dogs.

As for my mother, she worked in a small factory until she had put in enough time to draw a pension of $400 a month. She and my father retired and moved to Cherokee Lake in Bean Station, Tennessee. Mom was where she wanted to be. Two of her sisters had property around the lake, and her brothers would come down to the lake to fish and spend time with her. She adored and loved all of her brothers and sisters and greatly enjoyed their visits. The most enjoyment she found was in taking her grandchildren to the lake and teaching them to fish. Her biggest enthusiast was Jeremy, my sister Lynette's son. He loved going fishing. He often told her he was going to move to Tennessee and go fishing with her all the time.

My father contracted lung cancer in 1990. He died in 1993. I knew that if my father did not return the money before he died, I would probably never recover the money that was rightfully mine.

My mom continued to pay the taxes she owed, but the federal government never responded to her needs for her and her children. My mother never acknowledged the dog money. I don't know if my father had brainwashed her and convinced her that I was crazy and that no money had ever existed. He wanted Maria's son to have the money so badly that he had lied to us all. I never found out if it was a case of Mom simply not acknowledging the money. If she just had acknowledged that the money existed, it would remind her too much that my father had the affair with Maria. It would be devastating if she knew the money was real. It would crush her if she knew that her husband had forsaken her kids, yet given that much money to Maria's child. It was as if he was telling her that he did not love her or her kids, which would be too much for her to handle.

After my father's passing, Mom lived on a meager fifteen hundred dollars a month with her pension and my father's pension combined. Despite the amount of money she had to live on, she made it a point to buy a gift at

621

Christmas for each one of her children, her grandchildren, and even her great-grandchildren. The gifts were small, but they were nonetheless gifts. She would sometimes cut back on her food to buy those gifts. She loved the children very much. Giving them gifts always gave her great pleasure. She inherited that love from her father and mother.

It was Christmastime when Mom was diagnosed with ovarian cancer. My siblings and I all figured that this would probably be her last Christmas, so we made arrangements to have that one last Christmas together with her at her house by the lake. All the kids, grandchildren, and great-grandchildren were there. We had a blast, although Mom slept quite a bit. During one of her waking periods, she confided in me, "I just want to live one more year."

"Well, Mom, I think you are just too darn ornery to die, so I think you will probably get that year," I consoled her.

I had spent a week in Tennessee. The time neared for me to leave for home. My sister Lynette, who was a nurse, decided to take my mom to the hospital to get her looked at by her doctor since she was sleeping an awful lot. In the meantime, I readied myself to go home to Michigan.

It was around 10:00 p.m., eighteen hours since I had started my day, when my sister Veronica called me in Michigan and said that Mom was pretty bad off. Apparently she was calling for me. I needed to return quickly. Whenever Mom needed help, it was me she called for. Somehow, I always seemed to work things out for her. This time, though, I didn't think I could make things better. Still, I would be by her side. My second wife, Marlene, and I repacked, knowing we would be in Tennessee for at least a couple of days. I stopped by Mom's cabin to get the name of the hospital and the room number she was in. My wife and I rested for about an hour, and then headed to the hospital.

When I walked into my mom's room, Veronica was there alone. My mother had IVs in her arm and an oxygen mask on her face. I went over to her bed. I wanted to tell her something, but first I wanted to make sure she could hear me. I told her that if she was able to hear me, she should move her left thumb. She moved her thumb. I then put my arm under her head, hugged her tight, and said, "Mom, I love you very much. I will always love you, no matter what happens." I stayed by her side for over an hour. The room began to fill up with our relatives. I promised Mom that I would watch out for the rest of the kids. Mom was always looking out for her brood. If she could have, she more than likely would have asked me to watch over them for her.

I left because I desperately needed rest. At that point I had been up for thirty-five hours. I did not want to watch my mom when the moment of her death came, what with all the wires and tubes sticking out of her. I had watched men die and seen them exhale as their last breath went out of them.

Instead, I wanted to remember my mother as the kind, sweet, beautiful woman she was. I wanted to remember my earliest memories of her and my sisters, going to Clark Park and having picnics there. One year, on my third birthday, she had baked a cake in the form of a bunny rabbit with icing covered in coconut so it looked like fur. She even took plain paper and formed two ears and colored them pink so they looked like real ears. It looked like a real live bunny. For some reason, I never forgot that birthday, or the effort she extended to make that cake.

I thought about how hard Mom had worked at the foam factory. I had worked there for a short while and had seen how hard she worked. She was bending and stooping all day long using a machine called the glue machine. She was determined from the start, when she entered the workforce that her children would not want. The only way she knew how to provide for us was by working hard. I began to wonder if I had made the right decision by letting my dad live. As I watched my mother dying, I could not help but think that Burt could have made her much more comfortable on the seven million dollars. My life, and my brothers' and sisters' lives, would have been much easier if he had used that money on us. I had suspected for a long time that he no longer loved my mom or us kids, and that we were an anchor to him. The only question I had was how mom would have reacted if I had killed him. The more I thought about it, the more I believed that his meanness was intentional. I should have killed him. Being mean was his way of making sure that Russell got the dog money, my money.

EPILOGUE

In 1963, the seven and a half million dollars my father stole from me was the largest amount of money ever stolen in the United States. In today's terms, the value of that money would be in excess of one hundred million dollars. A mass murder of hundreds of people starting in the year 1961 had also occurred. The murders I describe in the previous chapters are not fiction. Only the names are fictionalized. The crimes were committed by agents of two federal government agencies. Only the FBI answered my call for help, and subsequently their agent was shot by a member of Team Garcia, which indicated that the members of Team Garcia were in fact freedom junkies. They had a strong desire not to go to jail and would do anything to stay free, which made them hypocrites in addition to freedom junkies. They destroyed hundreds of families with their tactics, using a technique called drug-induced hypnosis. They drugged innocent people, including women and children.

The men who committed these crimes have gotten away with them because of the reluctance of their fellow officers and law enforcement officials to doubt, much less convict, their law enforcement brothers, thus creating what is called the blue wall of silence. By doing this, they have unknowingly, or perhaps knowingly, aided corrupt cops in their crimes. As a result, hundreds, maybe thousands, of innocent people are dead. These murders and the use of narcotics to kill could have been carried out in only one of two ways: either with or without the CIA or Secret Service's knowledge. Did the US government secretly authorize the use of the drugs in an effort to eradicate the Ku Klux Klan and other radical factions within US borders, or were the agents acting on their own? If the latter, then Washington is oblivious to what is going on with its field agents, and does not want to expose itself to being held liable for their crimes. There were a few times when Maria told me that everything the team was doing was ultra-secret, which would mean that Washington knew everything and was keeping it a secret. This would indicate that Washington was aware, and may even have ordered the commission of these crimes.

One thing for sure is that Team Garcia used their positions as Secret Service agents to carry out their own personal agendas. They used their badges to rape, rob, murder, steal, and extort. They acted more like the Gestapo than the Secret Service. I believe this technique is now being used at the local level as well, which marks the beginning of a police state. Today there are four agents, tomorrow eight, the next day sixteen, so on and so on, growing exponentially. As long as Washington approves of these tactics and the use of narcotics as a form of torture, we, the citizens of the United States, are in danger of losing our civil liberties and our country as we know it. If these tactics are allowed to continue, all we will have left will be a network of corruption. I tried my best to stop Team Garcia, but with every law enforcement agency in the country aiding them, I couldn't do much more than gather the evidence against these killers and wait for the opportune time to expose them. I have all three components of a case needed to convict them of murder: motive, method, and opportunity. I have eyewitness testimony as well as physical evidence. If Team Garcia is ever convicted or if they are never convicted, the damage to our country is done and Washington has failed the people miserably.

As the lone witness to these crimes, I would provide the prosecutor with an eyewitness account of some of the murders that occurred. The case would be a virtual slam dunk. Once I pass away, the case will go down the toilet, and Team Garcia will make a clean getaway. I have made every attempt to bring this group of men and women to justice, but it has been to no avail. I've only succeeded in making myself and my family a target of Team Garcia's wrath. This is the federal government's last chance to compensate all the victims' families and their descendants by prosecuting these criminals and giving the families large jury awards. This will be hard to do as long as Team Garcia has their badges and continue to lie to our judges. Our judges are some of the most highly educated people in the country, but they are being duped by the lies told to them by people like Team Garcia. There should be a very severe punishment for a cop who lies to a judge. At the least, a cop who lies to a judge should lose his or her pension. Let the lying bastards work their whole lives for nothing. Until a punishment like this is put in place, the cops are going to take the chance of lying to our judges and juries.

I have done everything I can to save as many lives as I can. Thanks to my grandfather, who perfected the technique of training drug-sniffing dogs, these dogs are now used all over the world to detect narcotics. My grandfather was rewarded with seven and a half million dollars, but his daughter was gang-raped and drugged. His grandson, me, was shot in the back of the head, shot in the chest, stabbed in the chest, and shot in the chest while taking a bullet for a cop, and had his face slashed with a switchblade in a hospital room by a cop after saving that cop's life. My grandma's brother and her nephew were both murdered. I was an eyewitness to all this! This is the way the federal government has rewarded my grandfather and his family.

Lastly, I, along with General Schwartzberg, planned a strategy for the defense of Israel and our peaceful Arab allies in the Middle East should tensions escalate. The year we developed the strategy to be implemented in case of escalation of hostilities in the Middle East was 1968. I was fifteen years old. Hostilities did escalate as I had feared. I have protected my country, the Middle East, and our NATO allies, and have changed the world and made it a better, safer place. Some people have even used the term *hero* to describe me. So why was Team Garcia trying to kill me or get me killed? The money was one reason. Another reason was that they wanted to cover up the murder all of those people they murdered with narcotics. Of course, killing me would mean they could avoid prison, as the lone witness to their actions would be dead.

One thing is for sure. I spent ten years of my life trying to stop Team Garcia. I have endured multiple stab wounds and gunshot wounds trying to get information about how the drug dealers worked. When it no longer became feasible for me to stop the rest of the Dearborn police from backing up Team Garcia, I had to move out of their jurisdiction. Even after I moved, they continued to try to kill me or frame me for something I did not do, hoping to avoid prison by doing so. How long before the federal agencies catch on to these crooks? As long as they have the protection of a federal badge, they will continue to murder. As long as they have those badges, neither I nor the United States government is safe.

I never found out Johnny Doe's real name or his mother's name. Both have eluded me all my life. There are times when I cannot sleep at night because I visualize the image of Johnny's head after Carlos destroyed it with that .44 Magnum. It's a shame, but Johnny Doe's mother went to her grave never knowing what happened to her son or that he was killed in such a brutal fashion by people who had been hired to protect her family. Carlos never paid for the murder of Manuel D or Johnny Doe. He continues to serve as a police officer in the city of Allen Park, Michigan. Russell Thurston, Maria's son, was hired on as a police officer in the same city. Washington had better catch on soon because now there is a second, and possibly a third and fourth, generation using the same illegal techniques. The danger looms with the possibility that this technique could be used for generations to come, maybe even leading to a police state.

These murders have all gone uninvestigated because the victims were so-called 'junkies' unworthy of a thorough investigation. The murders these men have committed have gone undetected by the FBI. These cases will most likely remain unsolved. And many more people will die unless the FBI gets wind of the tactics Team Garcia is using. The FBI will never solve these crimes because there is no record of any crime being committed. As good as FBI agents are at their jobs, they cannot solve a crime if there is no proof a crime was ever perpetrated. That there is no record of these murders just goes to show how adept Team Garcia was at covering up their crimes. As long as the members of Team Garcia are free, the citizens of the United States will be at risk.

Just remember—if you someday run into someone who seems destitute and drugged, be not too quick to judge that person because it may be yet another victim of Team Garcia.

ABOUT THE AUTHOR

Brett D. Lawson was born in Kentucky and raised in Dearborn, Michigan. He is a retired salesman in the automotive industry. Lawson was an advisor to two of the United States' finest generals and was instrumental in helping end the Vietnam War.

Printed in the United States
By Bookmasters

Printed in the United States
By Bookmasters